HTML5
Developer's
Cookbook

HTML5
Developer's
Cookbook

Chuck Hudson

Tom Leadbetter

✦✦Addison-Wesley

Upper Saddle River, NJ • Boston • Indianapolis • San Francisco
New York • Toronto • Montreal • London • Munich • Paris • Madrid
Capetown • Sydney • Tokyo • Singapore • Mexico City

Many of the designations used by manufacturers and sellers to distinguish their products are claimed as trademarks. Where those designations appear in this book, and the publisher was aware of a trademark claim, the designations have been printed with initial capital letters or in all capitals.

The authors and publisher have taken care in the preparation of this book, but make no expressed or implied warranty of any kind and assume no responsibility for errors or omissions. No liability is assumed for incidental or consequential damages in connection with or arising out of the use of the information or programs contained herein.

The publisher offers excellent discounts on this book when ordered in quantity for bulk purchases or special sales, which may include electronic versions and/or custom covers and content particular to your business, training goals, marketing focus, and branding interests. For more information, please contact:

U.S. Corporate and Government Sales
(800) 382-3419
corpsales@pearsontechgroup.com

For sales outside the United States, please contact:

International Sales
international@pearson.com

Visit us on the Web: informit.com/aw

Library of Congress Cataloging-in-Publication Data

Hudson, Chuck, 1969–
  HTML5 developer's cookbook / Chuck Hudson, Tom Leadbetter.
      p.   cm.
  Includes index.
  ISBN 978-0-321-76938-1 (pbk. : alk. paper)
  1. HTML (Document markup language) 2. Internet programming. 3. Web site development. I. Leadbetter, Tom, 1983– II. Title.
  QA76.76.H94H836 2012
  006.7'4—dc23
                                                    2011040007

ISBN-13: 978-0-321-76938-1
ISBN-10:   0-321-76938-4
Text printed in the United States on recycled paper at RR Donnelley in Crawfordsville, Indiana.
First printing, December 2011

Editor-in-Chief
Mark Taub

Senior Acquisitions Editor
Trina MacDonald

Development Editor
Michael Thurston

Managing Editor
John Fuller

Project Editor
Anna Popick

Copy Editor
Kim Wimpsett

Indexer
Jack Lewis

Proofreader
Lori Newhouse

Technical Reviewers
Evan Burchard
Siddharth Ram
Tim Wright

Publishing Coordinator
Olivia Basegio

Cover Designer
Gary Adair

Compositor
Rob Mauhar

❖

To Alex, my grandfather, thank you for sharing your love of life and books.

—Chuck

To Lucy, thanks for being you.

—Tom

❖

Contents at a Glance

Contents

Introduction

Hypertext Markup Language (HTML) is a core language for creating and structuring web pages. For more than 20 years developers have been writing HTML, and for the first few years the language underwent radical changes, but in the late 1990s things slowed down a bit. Until now.

A Brief History of HTML

In 1991 Sir Tim Berners-Lee wrote a document called "HTML Tags," which described 20 elements that would be used for writing web documents. By mid-1993 the Internet Engineering Task Force (IETF) had published a proposal for the first HTML specification. The proposal draft expired, and it was not until November 1995 that the first specification was published: not HTML 1.0, but HTML 2.0.

HTML 3.2 was released in 1997, and this was followed up by HTML 4, published in 1998. HTML 4 had three variations: Strict, Transitional, and Frameset. During this period, browser vendors, such as Microsoft and Netscape, started implementing HTML in slightly different ways, and we had our first round of browser wars (http://en.wikipedia.org/wiki/Browser_wars).

XHTML

After the release of HTML 4, the World Wide Web Consortium (W3C) decided to stop the evolution and development of HTML and work on Extensible Hypertext Markup Language (XHTML) 1.0, an XML-based language that was considered the future of the Internet. There were no new elements in XHTML—in fact, the specification was the same as HTML 4—but developers had to conform to new syntax rules: Tags had to be closed, or self-closed, and attributes had to be quoted. This required stricter, tighter coding standards and ensured that developers would be using a single style of writing. Around this time in 2001, Cascading Style Sheets (CSS) started becoming more prominent and popular, and with the rise of blogging, the increased awareness of web standards was significant.

Beginning in 2002, the W3C released drafts of XHTML 1.1. While XHTML 1 was essentially HTML with a splash of XML, XHTML 1.1 was essentially XML. Although it was supposed to be more forward-thinking, it was not backward compatible, so if it was used in website development, the website would not work in current and older browsers.

This caused concern among the web community, with browser vendors, and even within the W3C itself. Not everyone was convinced that XML was the future markup of the web.

Web Forms, Web Apps, and the WHATWG

In 2004, individuals from Apple, Mozilla, and Opera began working on their own specification, aiming at creating backward-compatible code that could be used to create web applications. W3C rejected this proposal, and this led to a group being formed calling itself the Web Hypertext Application Technology Working Group (WHATWG).

The WHATWG began working on Web Forms 2.0 and Web Applications 1.0. The editor for the specifications is Ian "Hixie" Hickson, and issues and ideas are raised via a public mailing list. Although initially there was work on two specifications, Web Forms 2.0 and Web Applications 1.0, they have now been merged into one specification, called HTML5.

XHTML 2 versus HTML5

So, while WHATWG was developing HTML5, over at the W3C, the XHTML 2 specification was languishing. In 2006, the W3C decided that it had made the wrong decision in abandoning HTML in the previous years, and although it would still develop XHTML 2, it would once again look at the development of HTML. The W3C decided to use the work done so far by WHATWG as the starting point for a new version of HTML.

Although this was positive news, it also led to a confusing state because there were now currently three different types of markup being worked on: two by the W3C, HTML 5 and XHTML 2; and one at the WHATWG, HTML5 (notice there is no space compared to the W3C "HTML 5"). So, with HTML5/HTML 5, the specification was being developed at the same time but by two groups.

WHATWG operates in a very different manner than the W3C, and it is able to move at a much faster pace. Because of the public mailing list at WHATWG, ideas were put forward regularly, and web developers were able to question some of the decisions made. The specification team was, and still is, able to implement good ideas, reject bad ideas, and change or remove items of the specification based on community feedback quickly. HTML5 was developing much quicker at WHATWG than at the W3C.

After a couple of years of this, in 2009, the W3C announced it had stopped work on XHTML 2. HTML5 had "won."

So, where does that leave the specification? Well, it is still being developed primarily by the WHATWG, while the W3C then takes the specification and puts it through review.

The process has not exactly been perfect, but there are exciting outcomes.

Which Specification Should I Be Looking At?

There is a version of the specification at the W3C (http://dev.w3.org/html5/spec/spec. html) and one at the WHATWG (http://whatwg.org/specs/web-apps/current-work/ multipage/). Both are huge, heavy documents. In March 2011, Ben Schwarz launched the "WHATWG HTML5 specification for web developers" (http://developers. whatwg.org), which we suggest using. You can also keep up-to-date with the specification via the mailing list if you are interested in the daily discussions: http://lists. whatwg.org/htdig.cgi/whatwg-whatwg.org.

The base HTML5 specification is just that, a base. A major shift has occurred to match the speed at which the technology is growing. New add-on specifications are being worked on all the time by teams in both the WHATWG and the W3C, and they include features such as network connection information and device camera information. Browser vendors are working together to help define these features and fast track the inclusion of the functionality into their browsers. The next couple years will prove to be very exciting.

The Principles of HTML5

HTML5 has been created in a way that supports existing content or, in other words, is backward compatible. The major concern over the proposed XHTML2 specification was that it would break the majority of websites. HTML5 has been built on the foundations of HTML 4, so browsers can continue to support HTML, not just new HTML5 elements but all of the things that are in HTML 4. Sites that work now in HTML 4, or XHTML, are expected to work fine in HTML5.

Using HTML5 means you can continue to code in the style that you have used previously. We will cover this more in Chapter 1, but HTML5 has been written with developers in mind, so you can keep using HTML syntax or XHTML syntax, and browsers will know what to do.

HTML5 also tells the browsers how it should handle errors caused by incorrect markup implementation. Previously, browsers would interpret the errors themselves, and thus each browser would have its own quirks. HTML5 has been written for developers like us and for browser vendors so that in the not too distant future, we are all working to and from the same standard.

Perhaps the true power of HTML5 is how it addresses the needs for web application developers. Because browsers are so powerful, we can create websites that are very much like applications: They can provide photo sharing, drawing, file editing, and other features. Previously, these features required layers of JavaScript and a plug-in such as Java or Flash. But this meant accessibility issues and relied on the stability of third-party software. HTML5 gives us new standards for how we can create web applications, with powerful APIs for things such as canvas for drawing, drag and drop, offline storage, and native video in the browser. With specified standards, browsers will handle these things correctly and in a stable fashion over time. The web community will help develop and grow the standards, continuously pushing and improving them, and developers will not have to create hacks to get these features to work.

What Exactly Is HTML5?

HTML5 is not just one technology. It is more of an umbrella term that has been adopted for the inclusion of new and enhanced HTML elements, CSS styles, and JavaScript APIs and events. The intersection of these technologies provides for a wide range of new features to enhance the user experience, make websites more like native applications, and integrate to devices. The following are just some of the new or enhanced functions available:

- Improved semantics
- Forms
- Canvas drawing
- Drag and drop
- Local storage
- Page-to-page messaging
- Desktop notifications
- Video and audio
- Web sockets
- Geolocation
- History
- Microdata

Although not strictly part of the HTML5 specification, geolocation is a cool, new technology being developed at the same time, so it gets talked about in the same breath as HTML5. And yes, we are going to talk about geolocation in this book as well.

Not everything new in web development is HTML5. CSS3 is *not* HTML5, but because it is new and very cool, it gets put in the same category as HTML5. CSS is a completely different language and technology than HTML. CSS is presentation; HTML is structure. You can do some pretty awesome things with CSS3, but developers and the community should be aware that there is a difference.

And although we do not want to get into a debate over whether HTML5 is a Flash killer (it's not), the bottom line of HTML5 is that there is now an incredible amount of functionality built directly into the browser, and it is all standard.

Does HTML5 Have a Logo?

Yes, HTML5 sure does have a logo. In years gone by, web developers and site owners have put icons on their site showing that they adhere to various W3C guidelines, such as (X)HTML, CSS, or accessibility. This trend has cooled down a bit recently, but in early 2011 the W3C released a series of logos, which initially caused quite a stir in the web community because it grouped many web technologies, including CSS3, under the HTML5 umbrella. As mentioned, CSS3 is not HTML5, but with the W3C seemingly admitting otherwise, the web community raised its concerns.

Thankfully, the W3C changed its aim and definition of the logos, so the main logo (Figure I.1) "represents HTML5, the cornerstone for modern web applications," and the smaller logos (Figure I.2) "represent aspects of modern web applications and web sites—style, semantics, graphics, and so forth."

So, the logos are there for developers who want to show support for the key web standards. The use of the icons or logo is not required, but they are available if you would like to use them to show your adoption of the various features. The logos are available from http://w3.org/html/logo, and there is a logo builder available so you can select different icons and styles.

The Cookbook Style

This book is designed to be a show-by-example text and follows the cookbook style of providing a topic explanation and recipes that support the topic. The recipes in most cases attempt to show how the technology might be applied to real-world coding problems, rather than showing an example that has no real purpose. Like a recipe used in the kitchen, it is our hope that you will find these recipes valuable starting points for your own programming solutions.

Figure I.1   The HTML5 logo
(The HTML5 logo is attributed to the W3C, www.w3.org)

Figure I.2   Smaller icons representing different technologies: (from left to right) Device Access; 3D, Graphics & Effects; CSS3; Semantics; Multimedia; Connectivity; Performance & Integration; and Offline & Storage

In general, the book has been laid out to cover simpler topics in the beginning, building on these topics to more complex subjects later. We include HTML5 elements and CSS3 additions in early chapters and migrate to various JavaScript APIs and events in later chapters. We know that for any one of these topics a whole book could be written on all the intricacies. This is the case especially with topics such as CSS3, and there are many good books available.

For each topic covered in a chapter, we have included a table that shows the level of support for the feature across common browsers. We have included one or more recipes showing how the technology can be employed. In most cases, the recipes have a series of instructions, the code listing or listings, and then a walk-through of the recipe. Each recipe has also been posted on the book website: www.HTML5DevelopersCookbook.com.

> **Note**
>
> Various components that make up HTML5, such as JavaScript APIs, are still being defined through specifications and incorporated into the various browser platforms. We have focused on those elements that are well specified and supported by one or more of key browsers. However, it should be understood that HTML5 is constantly growing through new features and functionality. In Chapter 15, we cover some of these upcoming features and functions around device integration.

Recipes are divided into three categories: Beginner, Intermediate, and Advanced. These categories are meant to provide some sense of the difficulty of the topic covered, while trying to also provide some sense of the amount of effort and time you may need to allocate to complete the recipe. These are broad categorizations, and the time and effort required we know will vary greatly by reader.

Third-Party Libraries

If you have been involved in web development for any amount of time, one of the first things you will notice about the recipes in this cookbook is that very few recipes leverage third-party libraries of JavaScript such as jQuery and the myriad other libraries available. There are a few minor exceptions to this where we specifically address support by third-party libraries or integrations to address hurdles that the libraries may solve. In general, though, we have tried to focus on the core HTML5 technology since each reader will have their own favorite set of libraries to use and each library will have its own level of support and integration methods for HTML5 features.

We firmly believe libraries play an important role in the daily web design and development of sites and applications. We have our own favorite libraries as well. In many cases, the libraries that have already integrated many of the HTML5 features are integrating them in a similar manner to how they are defined. So, understanding how to use the component in generic JavaScript will allow you to more easily leverage the component in the library of your choice.

HTML5DevelopersCookbook.com

By nature, a cookbook of this type is full of code listings that support the recipes. Because of how fast the HTML5 technology is being expanded, it is essential that the book have a companion website to keep the material up to date. The www.HTML5DevelopersCookbook.com website has been set up for this purpose and has not only electronic versions of the recipes and supporting files available for execution and download but also additional resources.

When Will HTML5 Be Ready for Use?

There is the common concern that developers cannot or should not start using HTML5 right now, but that is not the case.

Do I Have to Wait Until 2022?

No, you do not have to wait until 2022! In a 2008 interview, HTML5 editor Ian Hickson gave a timeline that HTML5 would not be ready until 2022. This was blown out of proportion in the media and web community. What we believe Hickson meant was that the final proposed recommendation will not be released until around 2022, but that does not mean you cannot put to use all the features that have already been defined and incorporated. As you might have gathered from the discussion of the history of HTML, specifications take an incredible amount of effort and time, and a specification has many stages it needs to go through before it is finished.

A popular argument involves the status of CSS 2.1. CSS 2.1 has been in development for more than 10 years, and only in the summer of 2011 was it finalized, but in the years while it was being developed, we all still used CSS, didn't we? We are now at CSS3, and who knows when that will be "ready." This is a prime example of how the web community is pushing the technology and future of the web ahead of the specifications.

So, Can I Use HTML5 Now?

Yes, you can use HTML5 now! There will not be a time when you have to stop using HTML 4 and start using HTML5. Who knows when the W3C will announce that HTML5 is officially ready; we may all be employing HTML6 features by that point. But the browser manufacturers are embracing HTML5 features wholeheartedly and incorporating new features all the time.

Because there are so many different sections and technologies within the specification and add-on specifications, you can pick and choose the parts of HTML5 you want to incorporate; it is not a case of all or nothing. Not all browsers play nice 100 percent of the time, but in Chapter 3, Browser Handling in HTML5, we explain some methods of browser handling. The latest versions of Firefox, Safari, Opera, Chrome, and Internet Explorer all support a wide range, albeit slightly different sets, of HTML5 features. However, day by day, and even during the writing of this book, we have seen significant improvements across the browsers, and this will only continue as browsers remain competitive.

So, grab yourself a text or HTML editor, a handful of browsers, and get plugged in to some HTML5.

Acknowledgments

Acknowledgments from Chuck Hudson

Whenever a challenging project such as this is undertaken, multiple people are involved in making the project a success. I was fortunate enough to embark on this book with Tom Leadbetter, my coauthor, who is an extremely talented designer and developer. Thank you, Tom, for sharing your knowledge, testing mine, and being a great sounding board for my many crazy ideas.

Thank you to my family: Ma, for your support; Dad, for cutting an entrepreneurial path; and my grandparents, for your love. To my little one, Sierra, you always succeed in bringing a smile to my face through your unending questions of why. Never stop being inquisitive. And especially to Michele, for your endless support of my bleeding-edge technology addiction and endless "projects." Your understanding, while I agonized many times over a single line of code, means the world to me.

Tom S., thanks for the many laughs over the years. I look forward to seeing what adventures are in front of us.

Finally, thanks to all my friends and family for the time to do this project; you have all taught me that through passion and perseverance anything is possible.

Acknowledgments from Tom Leadbetter

First, let me thank my coauthor, Chuck Hudson, who has helped me throughout the writing process and provided valuable feedback when it was needed the most, not to mention him writing some fantastic bits of code!

Thank you to the HTML5 Doctors—Rich Clark, Bruce Lawson, Remy Sharp, Jack Osborne, Mike Robinson, Oli Studholme, and Brandan Lennox—for their time, skills, and dedication on the HTML5Doctor.com site, which always provides wonderful knowledge and discussion for the web community.

Finally, to my wife, Lucy: Thank you so much for your support when I was struggling and for your patience when I've disappeared for many an evening and weekend. I've done my best with the book, and you've helped me all the way.

Joint Acknowledgments

Thanks to Trina MacDonald and Pearson for taking a chance on us and your continued patience as we tried to constantly improve the text. Thanks to the editors,

Michael Thurston, Evan Burchard, Tim Wright, Siddharth Ram, and Kim Wimpsett, for providing advice and detailed, insightful feedback and spotting things we would never have spotted. Many times you were able to allow us to see the forest for the trees, and the end result is much better because of it. Thank you for all your time and effort. We know it does not come without sacrifice, and it provided a good challenge.

Lastly, we would like to thank the entire HTML5 community for sharing your knowledge and you, the reader, for being trailblazers during a truly exciting time. It is our hope that you have as much enjoyment with the technologies through this book as we had in creating it.

About the Authors

Chuck Hudson has developed for the web and mobile areas since the 1990s. A successful entrepreneur, his passion of solving business problems with technology has led to consulting companies on various web technologies and speaking at conferences. Ever a geek-in-training, Hudson is also a certified PHP programmer, PayPal developer, and teacher of web programming, mobile technology, and entrepreneurship in the Boston and Atlanta areas. In 2008, he received the eBay Star Developer award for the first iOS mobile web and native apps.

Tom Leadbetter is a web designer and developer from Liverpool, United Kingdom. He has been working in the web industry, for various organizations and clients, since 2005 and has been playing about with HTML5 since early 2009. He blogs about it at HTML5Doctor.com.

New Structural Elements
in HTML5

HTML5 is not just about interactive voodoo with JavaScript APIs and video coolness. There are more than 20 new elements you can use to author your web pages, adding semantics to deliver more accessible, reusable content.

In later chapters, you will learn about new HTML5 form controls and multimedia elements. In this chapter, you will learn about the new structural elements of header, hgroup, nav, footer, article, section, and aside, focusing on how, why, and when to use these new elements, both on their own and when combined. Essentially, you will be building a basic website template with the new elements, as shown in Figure 1.1.

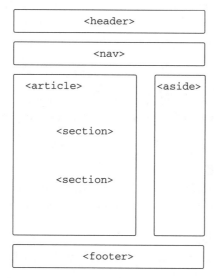

Figure 1.1   Basic page structure with new HTML5 elements

BEGINNER RECIPE:
Building an HTML5 Starter Document

You are about to go HTML5, so let's go to the top of the HTML document. Although the content in this immediate section does not contain new elements, there is a new way to write them, so it is best to be aware before we start getting into the body.

doctype

Does this look familiar?

```
<!DOCTYPE html PUBLIC "-//W3C//DTD XHTML 1.0 Strict//EN"
➥"http://www.w3.org/TR/xhtml1/DTD/xhtml1-strict.dtd">
```

The doctype should be the very first line in an HTML document. Called a Document Type Definition (DTD), the doctype is a web standards requirement, and it tells the browser how to process the document, which is why it must be the first thing in your HTML document. If you didn't use a doctype or you put *any* other code before the doctype, then the browser would be in quirks mode, and chances are the code you have written will not work properly in some browsers.

It's unlikely that you would want to memorize the previous doctype. Why would you? It's horrible and clunky. In HTML5, you now have a nice, easy-to-remember doctype:

```
<!DOCTYPE html>
```

Honestly, that's all it is. This is all you need to tell the browser you are in standards mode. If a browser does not implement HTML5, the page will still work. If you used `<!doctype html5>`, it would trigger quirks mode as well. This doctype has been chosen so it will always work in browsers, no matter what the latest version of the language is.

> **Note**
>
> If you refer to http://infomesh.net/html/history/early/, you can see the earliest HTML document, from November 13, 1990. The markup is really simple, and its simplicity reminds us of the HTML5 doctype. In fact, if you added the new doctype to that page, it would validate!

Character Encoding

The first line you need inside the head is the charset declaration, which tells the browser how the file should be interpreted; in this case, you want to send it an HTML document.

In HTML 4, it looks like this:

```
<meta http-equiv="Content-Type" content="text/html; charset=utf-8">
```

But like the `doctype`, in HTML5 it is now much simpler:

```
<meta charset="utf-8" />
```

Easy! Remember, you need this and the `doctype` on your page.

JavaScript and CSS Links

We can breeze through this little section as well. HTML5 helps you reduce lots of markup from your page, and you can simplify the calls to JavaScript (and other client-side scripting file) and CSS. In HTML4, the script and link elements needed a `type` attribute, as follows:

```
<script type="text/javascript" src="my-javascript-file.js"></script>
<link rel="stylesheet" type="text/css" href="my-css-file.css" />
```

But in HTML5, those lines now look like this:

```
<script src="my-javascript-file.js"></script>
<link rel="stylesheet" href="my-css-file.css" />
```

You may be wondering why you can now get away with doing this. Well, one of the intentions of HTML5 is to make things more sensible when you are coding. So, if you are linking to a script, the browser assumes it is a JavaScript file, and if you are using `rel=stylesheet`, it can only mean you are linking to a CSS file. And don't worry, not using the `type` attribute causes no issues in older browsers.

Syntax Writing Style

In HTML5, using the previous code examples, you can code the page in slightly various ways.

You can code in uppercase:

```
<SCRIPT SRC="MY-JAVASCRIPT-FILE"></SCRIPT>
```

You can code with no quotation marks:

```
<script src=my-javascript-file></script>
```

You can skip a closing slash:

```
<link rel="stylesheet" type=text/css href=my-css-file.css >
```

Or you can use a combination!

```
<LiNK rel="stylesheet" tYPe="text/css" href=my-css-file.css />
```

All these are fine to use; however, it is strongly encouraged that you pick a style and stay with it. This is useful not only to yourself but for other developers who may at some point have to use your code. The syntax style will be consistent. We come from XHTML backgrounds, so we will close all tags, use lowercase, and use quotation marks around attributes.

Bringing all the previous together gives you the HTML5 starting page in Listing 1.1.

Listing 1.1   **A Simple HTML5 Starting Page**

```
<!DOCTYPE html>
<html lang="en">
<head>
<meta charset="utf-8" />
<title>page title</title>
<script src="my-javascript-file.js"></script>
<link rel="stylesheet" href="my-css-file.css" />
</head>
<body>
<!-- new HTML5 elements are going to go here :) -->
</body>
```

That is it! Save the page as an .htm (or .html) file, and now you can start filling the page with great content.

> **Tip**
>
> Validation is a very useful tool for checking why things might be broken, and it is a great step to have in your development process. However, with HTML5 still developing, there are no official validator services. The W3C validator, http://validator.w3.org, will check for HTML5 conformance but does warn that is an experimental feature. Another validator to test your pages against is http://html5.validator.nu. It is worth testing your pages in both of these validators.

Where Do All the New Elements Come From?

The new structural elements have been designed to tell the browser what structure the page has and give the content semantic meaning, but where do their names come from? In 2005, Google analyzed more than 1 billion web pages to find out what class names were being used by developers and web authors (http://code.google.com/web-stats). This enabled Ian Hickson ("Hixie"), the editor of the main HTML5 Specification, to start thinking about these new elements. Even though this was five years ago, which is fairly old in Internet time, it recognizes what content is important and reused on websites.

The following are the 20 most popular class names used at the time:

footer	menu	Title
Small	Text	Content
Header	Nav	Copyright
Button	Main	Search
Msonormal	Date	Smalltext
Body	Style1	Top
White	link	

Although several of these items are presentational (for example, `white`, `style1`, `msnormal`), others make up the elements included in the HTML5 specification (`footer`, `nav`, `header`).

So, why use these new elements? Well, HTML5 allows you to give your content semantic meaning, so, for example, if you have navigation on your page, you can use the `nav` element because that element provides meaning to its content.

BEGINNER RECIPE:
Using the `header` Element to Create a Site Header

Let's start at the top of a "typical" web page.

The `header` element is often the first thing on a web page, and it usually contains things like a logo, the website name, or the main site navigation. It can be used more than once on a page, and as will be discussed, it can be used for navigation of a particular section, not just the overall page. Things like a search form or a table of contents can be included in a `header` element. Here is a basic example:

```
<header>
  <img alt="HTML5 Cookbook logo" src="logo.png" />
  <h1><a href="#">HTML5 Cookbook</a></h1>
</header>
```

As the HTML5 specification says, the `header` element can include navigation aids, so the element in Figure 1.2 could be marked up with a `header` that includes the logo, the main navigation links, and the search form. But depending on the design of the site, it might mean you have to mark up the `nav` outside of the `header`, which is fine.

The following are the possible contents of the `header` element, several of which are shown in Figure 1.2:

- Logo
- Site name/title
- Site subtitle
- Search form
- Main navigation

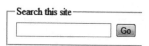

Figure 1.2   A typical header element with a site title, logo, search, and navigation area

You are not restricted to just one `header` element per page, and it does not have to be at the top of a page. As we will explain in further detail later, if you have several headings on a page, you might consider putting these in a `header` element. You can also use more than one `h1` tag per page so you may have something like Listing 1.2 (you will learn about the `article` element later in this chapter).

Listing 1.2   **Using Multiple Headers on One Page**

```
<article>
  <header>
    <h1><a href="#">Chapter 1</a></h1>
    <p>11.11.2011</p>
  </header>
  <p> Pellentesque habitant morbi tristique senectus et netus et malesuada fames
➡ac turpis egestas. Vestibulum tortor quam, feugiat vitae, ultricies eget,
➡tempor sit amet, ante...</p>
</article>
<article>
  <header>
    <h1><a href="#">Chapter 2</a></h1>
    <p>11.12.2011</p>
  </header>
  <p>Pellentesque habitant morbi tristique senectus et netus et malesuada fames
➡ac turpis egestas. Vestibulum tortor quam, feugiat vitae, ultricies eget,
➡tempor sit amet, ante.</p>
</article>
<article>
  <header>
    <h1><a href="#">Chapter 3</a></h1>
    <p>11.13.2011</p>
  </header>
  <p>Pellentesque habitant morbi tristique senectus et netus et malesuada fames ac
➡turpis egestas. Vestibulum tortor quam, feugiat vitae, ultricies eget,
➡tempor sit amet, ante.</p>
</article>
```

The code in Listing 1.2 will result in the display shown in Figure 1.3.

You could put an author and date within the `header` element as well. However, the HTML5 specification suggests that author information is more suited to the `footer` element.

If you have only a single heading (h1-6) in a `header` element, then there is no need to use `header`; the h1-6 on its own will suffice.

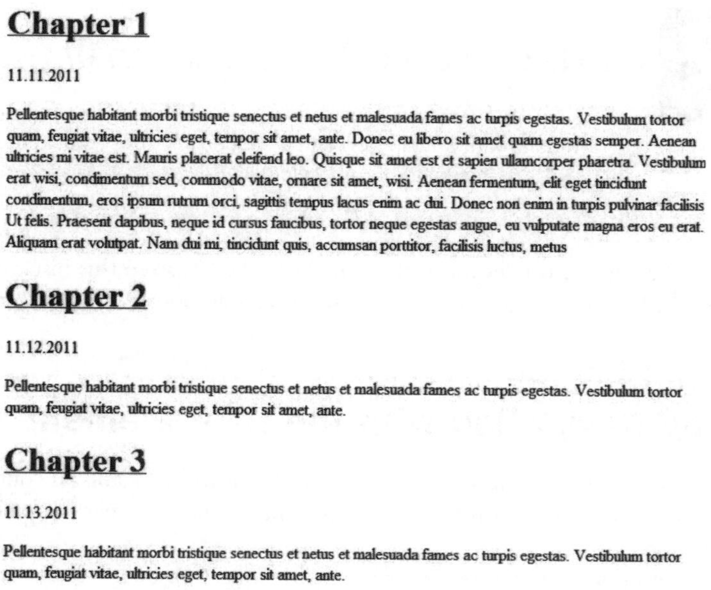

Chapter 1

11.11.2011

Pellentesque habitant morbi tristique senectus et netus et malesuada fames ac turpis egestas. Vestibulum tortor quam, feugiat vitae, ultricies eget, tempor sit amet, ante. Donec eu libero sit amet quam egestas semper. Aenean ultricies mi vitae est. Mauris placerat eleifend leo. Quisque sit amet est et sapien ullamcorper pharetra. Vestibulum erat wisi, condimentum sed, commodo vitae, ornare sit amet, wisi. Aenean fermentum, elit eget tincidunt condimentum, eros ipsum rutrum orci, sagittis tempus lacus enim ac dui. Donec non enim in turpis pulvinar facilisis Ut felis. Praesent dapibus, neque id cursus faucibus, tortor neque egestas augue, eu vulputate magna eros eu erat. Aliquam erat volutpat. Nam dui mi, tincidunt quis, accumsan porttitor, facilisis luctus, metus

Chapter 2

11.12.2011

Pellentesque habitant morbi tristique senectus et netus et malesuada fames ac turpis egestas. Vestibulum tortor quam, feugiat vitae, ultricies eget, tempor sit amet, ante.

Chapter 3

11.13.2011

Pellentesque habitant morbi tristique senectus et netus et malesuada fames ac turpis egestas. Vestibulum tortor quam, feugiat vitae, ultricies eget, tempor sit amet, ante.

Figure 1.3   Multiple header elements on one page (no styling applied)

BEGINNER RECIPE:
Using the `hgroup` Element to Group Headings

Using another new HTML5 element, the `hgroup` element, you can add further information to your `header` element.

This element is used to group more than one related `h1-6` headings. So, if your site has a subheading, you could use the element shown in Listing 1.3, which generates the layout in Figure 1.4. Although it is a useful grouping option, `hgroup` is primarily intended to tell the document outline (which we will discuss later) which of the headings is most important. In Listing 1.3, the document outline will exclude all headings except the highest one, in this case, the `h1`.

Listing 1.3   **Excluding All Headings Except** h1

```
<header>
  <hgroup>
    <h1><a href="#">HTML5 Cookbook</a></h1>
    <h2>Delicious HTML5 recipes</h2>
  </hgroup>
</header>
```

HTML5 Cookbook   *Delicious HTML5 recipes*

Figure 1.4   Website with a main logo and a subheader. These would be
inside an `hgroup` element.

In Listing 1.3, the h2 is relevant to the content of the h1, so in this instance you can
use an `hgroup`. If you have just one h1-6 heading, you do not need to use `hgroup`.

BEGINNER RECIPE:
Creating Navigation with the `nav` Element

The nav element, as you might expect from its name, is for navigational content. It is
used to link to other pages within the site or to other parts of the page (a table of contents, for example).

The most common use of a nav is for the main navigation on a website. It is common practice to use an unordered list to code navigation, as shown in Listing 1.4.

Listing 1.4   **Traditional Way of Marking Up Navigation**

```
<ul id="nav">
  <li><a href="#">Home</a></li>
  <li><a href="#">About</a></li>
  <li><a href="#">Meet the team</a></li>
  <li><a href="#">News</a></li>
  <li><a href="#">Contact</a></li>
</ul>
```

This code does not change too much when creating nav elements in HTML5. The
code for Figure 1.5 would be something like that shown in Listing 1.5.

Listing 1.5   **Navigation Markup in HTML5**

```
<nav>
  <ul>
    <li><a href="#">Home</a></li>
    <li><a href="#">About</a></li>
    <li><a href="#">Meet the team</a></li>
    <li><a href="#">News</a></li>
    <li><a href="#">Contact</a></li>
  </ul>
</nav>
```

Figure 1.5   Sitewide navigation that would be inside a `nav` element

You can put nav in the header as well, as shown in Listing 1.6, because the header allows for introductory and navigational content. However, it does not have to be in the header, and sometimes its placement might depend on styling issues. It is also quite common to see a navigation menu in the footer of a page, sometimes duplicating the main site navigation.

Listing 1.6   **The nav Element Inside a `header` Element**

```
<header>
  <h1>My super HTML5 site</h1>
  <nav>
    <ul>
      <li><a href="#">Home</a></li>
      <li><a href="#">About</a></li>
      <li><a href="#">News</a></li>
      <li><a href="#">Contact us</a></li>
    </ul>
  </nav>
</header>
```

It is not necessary to put all links on a page in a nav element. The HTML5 specification warns that only blocks of "major navigation" are considered appropriate for the nav element.

On news or blog sites, it is common to see a sidebar with links to articles and other pages. The markup in Listing 1.7 is used to produce the element shown in Figure 1.6.

Listing 1.7   **Multiple Navigation Groups in a Single nav Element**

```
<nav>
  <h2>Shared</h2>
  <ul>
    <li><a href="#">Pellentesque habitant</a></li>
    <li><a href="#">Morbi tristique senectus</a></li>
```

```
    <li><a href="#">Aenean ultricies mi vitae est</a></li>
  </ul>
  <h2>Read</h2>
  <ul>
    <li><a href="#">Pellentesque habitant</a></li>
    <li><a href="#">Morbi tristique senectus</a></li>
    <li><a href="#">Aenean ultricies mi vitae est</a></li>
  </ul>
  <h2>Watched/Listened</h2>
  <ul>
    <li><a href="#">Pellentesque habitant</a></li>
    <li><a href="#">Morbi tristique senectus</a></li>
    <li><a href="#">Aenean ultricies mi vitae est</a></li>
  </ul>
</nav>
```

Notice that there is an h2 to separate groups of links in the nav. In Figure 1.6, the h2 tags can be used as tab headings, so when a heading is selected by the user, the content switches (this effect can be achieved with JavaScript). A heading element is not always necessary but should be used to break up and structure navigation groups when possible. For styling reasons, you may need to separate the previous example into two nav structures, which is also fine.

There is a big accessibility win when using the nav element. Assistive technology, such as screen readers, will be able to search and immediately use groups of navigation rather than waiting for them to appear on-screen. Traditionally, developers have used "skip" or "jump" links as the very first things in an HTML document, and they are usually links to the main navigation or main content. However, using the nav element means you will soon be able to drop such "skip" menus. The only problem is that currently assistive technologies have limited support for HTML5 elements. However, they will soon catch up.

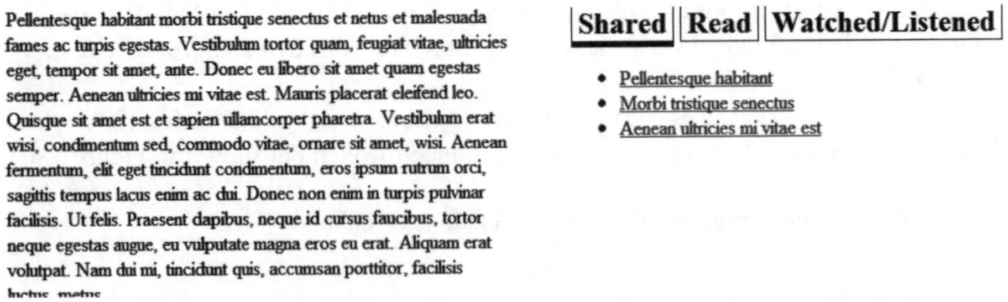

Pellentesque habitant morbi tristique senectus et netus et malesuada fames ac turpis egestas. Vestibulum tortor quam, feugiat vitae, ultricies eget, tempor sit amet, ante. Donec eu libero sit amet quam egestas semper. Aenean ultricies mi vitae est. Mauris placerat eleifend leo. Quisque sit amet est et sapien ullamcorper pharetra. Vestibulum erat wisi, condimentum sed, commodo vitae, ornare sit amet, wisi. Aenean fermentum, elit eget tincidunt condimentum, eros ipsum rutrum orci, sagittis tempus lacus enim ac dui. Donec non enim in turpis pulvinar facilisis. Ut felis. Praesent dapibus, neque id cursus faucibus, tortor neque egestas augue, eu vulputate magna eros eu erat. Aliquam erat volutpat. Nam dui mi, tincidunt quis, accumsan porttitor, facilisis luctus, metus

| Shared | Read | Watched/Listened |

- Pellentesque habitant
- Morbi tristique senectus
- Aenean ultricies mi vitae est

Figure 1.6   Example of grouped navigation in a sidebar. "Shared," "Read," and "Watched/Listened" would each be in a nav.

INTERMEDIATE RECIPE:
Using the New `article` **Element**

The `article` element and the `section` element (discussed in the next section) are arguably the two most important new HTML5 structural elements, but they are also two of the most confusing.

The `article` element is an independent block of content; it is content that could exist in its own right and content that is reusable. Consider content you see in an RSS feed; the content is nearly always individual articles. You could take them out of the feed, and they make sense on their own.

The HTML5 specification suggests some examples of how an article element can be used, such as a forum post, a magazine or newspaper article, a blog entry, or a user-submitted comment.

Listing 1.8 uses the `article` element to mark up a news item, as displayed in Figure 1.7.

Listing 1.8   Marking Up a News Item in an `article` Element

```
<article>
  <header>
    <h1>HTML5 saves millions!</h1>
    <p>32nd October 2010</p>
  </header>
  <p><strong>Pellentesque habitant morbi tristique</strong> senectus et netus et
➥malesuada fames ac turpis egestas. Vestibulum tortor quam, feugiat vitae,
➥ultricies eget…</p>
  <h2>Another heading</h2>
  <ol>
    <li>Lorem ipsum dolor sit amet, consectetuer adipiscing elit.</li>
    <li>Aliquam tincidunt mauris eu risus.</li>
  </ol>
  <blockquote><p>Lorem ipsum dolor sit amet, consectetur adipiscing elit. Vivamus
➥magna. Cras in mi at felis aliquet congue. Ut a est eget ligula molestie
➥gravida. …p></blockquote>
  <h3>And another heading</h3>
  <ul>
    <li>Lorem ipsum dolor sit amet, consectetuer adipiscing elit.</li>
    <li>Aliquam tincidunt mauris eu risus.</li>
  </ul>
  <p>This article was published in the HTML5 Times on Sunday 32nd October, 2010,
➥and was written by Tom Leadbetter</p>
</article>
```

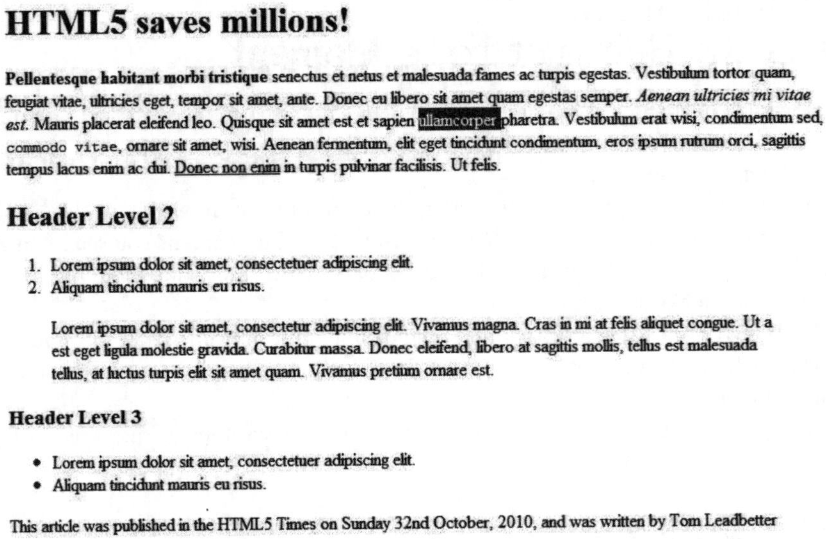

HTML5 saves millions!

Pellentesque habitant morbi tristique senectus et netus et malesuada fames ac turpis egestas. Vestibulum tortor quam, feugiat vitae, ultricies eget, tempor sit amet, ante. Donec eu libero sit amet quam egestas semper. *Aenean ultricies mi vitae est.* Mauris placerat eleifend leo. Quisque sit amet est et sapien `illamcorper` pharetra. Vestibulum erat wisi, condimentum sed, commodo `vitae`, ornare sit amet, wisi. Aenean fermentum, elit eget tincidunt condimentum, eros ipsum rutrum orci, sagittis tempus lacus enim ac dui. <u>Donec non enim</u> in turpis pulvinar facilisis. Ut felis.

Header Level 2

1. Lorem ipsum dolor sit amet, consectetuer adipiscing elit.
2. Aliquam tincidunt mauris eu risus.

   Lorem ipsum dolor sit amet, consectetur adipiscing elit. Vivamus magna. Cras in mi at felis aliquet congue. Ut a est eget ligula molestie gravida. Curabitur massa. Donec eleifend, libero at sagittis mollis, tellus est malesuada tellus, at luctus turpis elit sit amet quam. Vivamus pretium ornare est.

Header Level 3

- Lorem ipsum dolor sit amet, consectetuer adipiscing elit.
- Aliquam tincidunt mauris eu risus.

This article was published in the HTML5 Times on Sunday 32nd October, 2010, and was written by Tom Leadbetter

Figure 1.7   Basic article element with content (no styling applied)

This blog/news entry is an `article` because it is a separate piece of content. Would it appear in syndication (that is, an RSS feed)? Yes! Does it make sense on its own? Yes! It is an `article` then.

As you will discover in later chapters, you can nest a `section` within an `article`, and you can nest an `article` inside a `section`.

The HTML5 specification says an article is an "independent item of content," and it even says that blog comments can be `articles`.

INTERMEDIATE RECIPE:
Grouping Content with the `section` Element

The `section` element is an area of content or an area of a page that nearly always requires a heading. It can be used to group a whole, well, section of content, and it can be broken down into further sections if required. It is not to be used as a generic wrapper for styling purposes. A `section` can contain `article` elements, and `article` elements can have their content split into `sections`. So, as you saw with the `article` element, you need to think about when to use either `article` or `section`. Listing 1.9 is an example of when to use `section`, as shown in Figure 1.8.

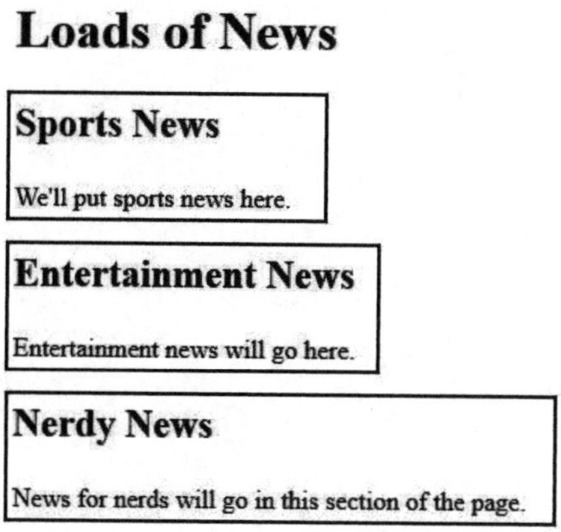

Loads of News

Sports News

We'll put sports news here.

Entertainment News

Entertainment news will go here.

Nerdy News

News for nerds will go in this section of the page.

Figure 1.8   Basic news page with sections highlighted
(no styling applied)

Listing 1.9   Creating a Basic News Page with Sections for Different Types of News

```
<h1>Loads News</h1>
  <section>
    <h1>Sports News</h1>
    <p>We'll put sports news here.</p>
  </section>
  <section>
    <h1>Entertainment News</h1>
    <p>Entertainment news will go here.</p>
  </section>
  <section>
    <h1>Nerdy News</h1>
    <p>News for nerds will go in this section of the page.</p>
  </section>
```

In Figure 1.8, each `section` has its own `header`, and each `section` is completely separate from the other. If there were other content on the page, you could wrap it all together in one `section` and give that a heading of "Types of news we do":

```
<section>
  <h1>Types of news we do</h2>
  <section>
    <h1>Entertainment News</h1>
    <p>Entertainment news will go here.</p>
  </section>
  ....
</section>
```

Additionally, you could split the "Nerdy News" section up into further sections:

```
<section>
  <h1>Types of news we do</h2>
  <section>
    <h1> Nerdy News </h1>
    <p>News for nerds will go in this section of the page.</p>
    <section>
    <h2>Gaming news</h2>
    ...
    </section>
    <section>
    <h2>Gadget news</h2>
    ...
    </section>
  </section>
  ....
</section>
```

Which Should You Use: `article` or `section`?

The `section` element is used similarly to how you use the `div` tag now. But unlike `div`, `section` has semantic meaning; it is the grouping of related content.

A `section` can have `article`s within it. Think of a news page; it might have a news section and, then within that, different news categories.

You might have a heading of "News" and then all the different types of news, like a newspaper. In HTML4, you would wrap this in a `div`, but you can wrap this all in a `section` now. Each type of news would then be in its own `section`, with its own heading.

If you think the content would make sense on its own, then it is an `article`. The HTML5 flowchart is a handy tool that will help you decide what element to use: http://html5doctor.com/happy-1st-birthday-us.

> **Tip**
>
> As you'll see later when we talk about the HTML5 outliner, it is important that you check you have used the correct markup.
>
> A common mistake in early HTML5 uptake is using a `section` to wrap entire sites, such as `<section class="container">` or `<section class="wrap">`. This is not the correct way to use `section`.
>
> As the HTML5 specification says:
>
> "Authors are strongly encouraged to view the `div` element as an element of last resort, for when no other element is suitable. Use of the `div` element instead of more appropriate elements leads to poor accessibility for readers and poor maintainability for authors."
>
> The `div` element "has no special meaning at all," so you use this to group content that does not belong in one of the new HTML5 elements. Often a `div` is needed to style something where CSS cannot target the content by any other means. If you use a

`section`, it will be added to the document outline because it is considered important to the document, whereas a `div` will not be added. So, if you are using a `section` for styling reasons, you should use a `div` instead.

BEGINNER RECIPE:
Creating a Sidebar with the `aside` Element

The `aside` element is for a group of content that is "tangentially" related to its surrounding content, such as a list of most popular posts, blog categories, or recent comments. This type of content is related to the main page content, but it is also separate from it.

In current web development, it is common for there to be a "sidebar" on the page. This does not necessarily mean it is physically on the side of the page, but it often contains things such as related links or a list of categories. The correct use of the `aside` depends on where you put it: If it is inside an `article`, the `aside` content should tangentially relate to the `article` content, such as a glossary. Or if the `aside` is outside an `article` or a `section`, its contents must be related to the page, such as related links, the site owner's Twitter feed, or ads relating to the site. Listing 1.10 shows how to create a "related links" section, as displayed in Figure 1.9.

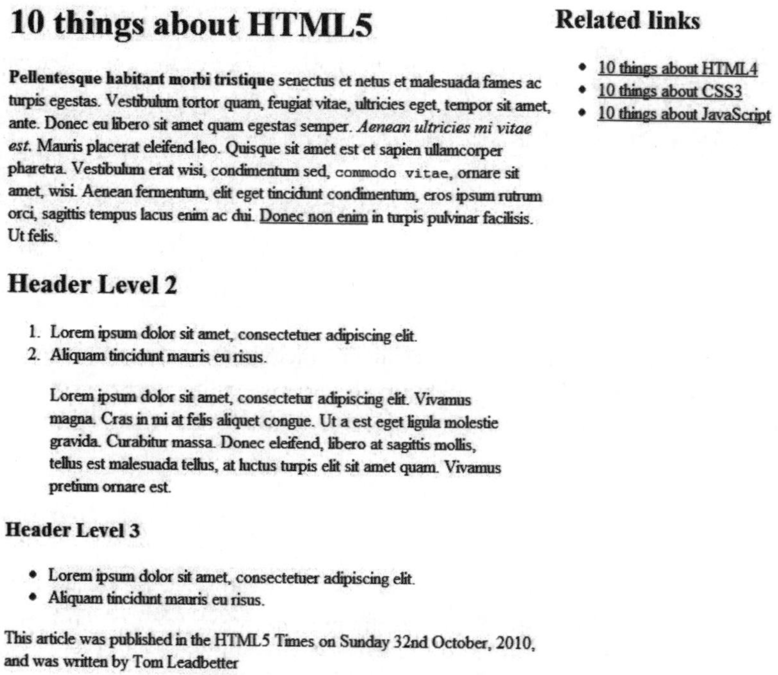

10 things about HTML5

Pellentesque habitant morbi tristique senectus et netus et malesuada fames ac turpis egestas. Vestibulum tortor quam, feugiat vitae, ultricies eget, tempor sit amet, ante. Donec eu libero sit amet quam egestas semper. *Aenean ultricies mi vitae est.* Mauris placerat eleifend leo. Quisque sit amet est et sapien ullamcorper pharetra. Vestibulum erat wisi, condimentum sed, `commodo vitae`, ornare sit amet, wisi. Aenean fermentum, elit eget tincidunt condimentum, eros ipsum rutrum orci, sagittis tempus lacus enim ac dui. Donec non enim in turpis pulvinar facilisis. Ut felis.

Header Level 2

1. Lorem ipsum dolor sit amet, consectetuer adipiscing elit.
2. Aliquam tincidunt mauris eu risus.

Lorem ipsum dolor sit amet, consectetur adipiscing elit. Vivamus magna. Cras in mi at felis aliquet congue. Ut a est eget ligula molestie gravida. Curabitur massa. Donec eleifend, libero at sagittis mollis, tellus est malesuada tellus, at luctus turpis elit sit amet quam. Vivamus pretium ornare est.

Header Level 3

- Lorem ipsum dolor sit amet, consectetuer adipiscing elit.
- Aliquam tincidunt mauris eu risus.

This article was published in the HTML5 Times on Sunday 32nd October, 2010, and was written by Tom Leadbetter

Related links

- 10 things about HTML4
- 10 things about CSS3
- 10 things about JavaScript

Figure 1.9   Basic layout of a page with a "sidebar"

Listing 1.10 **Using** aside **to Mark Up a "Related Links" Section**

```
<!DOCTYPE html>
<html lang="en">
<head>
<meta charset="utf-8">
<title>This has a nice outline</title>
<style>
article, aside, nav {display: block;}
article, aside {float: left;}
article {width: 500px;}
nav {width: 250px;}
</style>
</head>
<body>
<article>
<header>
<h1>10 things about HTML5</h1>
</header>
<p><strong>Pellentesque habitant morbi tristique</strong> …</p>
...
</article>
<aside>
  <h2>Related links</h2>
  <nav>
    <ul>
      <li><a href="#">10 things about HTML4</a></li>
      <li><a href="#">10 things about CSS3</a></li>
      <li><a href="#">10 things about JavaScript</a></li>
    </ul>
</nav>
</aside>
</body>
</html>
```

You can also nest the aside inside other elements, including the article element. Extending the previous example, you could provide the user with a glossary covering various phrases or content used in the main content that might not be known to the user:

```
<article>
  <header>
    <h1>10 things about HTML5</h1>
    <p>Pellentesque habitant morbi tristique senectus et netus et malesuada fames
➥ac turpis egestas. Vestibulum tortor quam, feugiat vitae, ultricies eget,
➥tempor sit amet, ante. Donec eu libero sit amet quam egestas semper. Aenean
➥ultricies mi vitae est. Mauris placerat eleifend leo.</p>
    ....
```

```
    </header>
    <aside>
      <h2>Glossary</ h2>
      <p>We have probably used lots of acronyms and abbreviations on this page, so
➥here is the glossary</h2>
      ....
    </aside>

</article>
```

BEGINNER RECIPE:
Using the `footer` Element

The `footer` element, as its name suggests, is typically at the bottom of the page. However, that is not always the case, although the `footer` will often be at the bottom of a section or a page. The `footer` element is intended for content about its section, including information about the author or site owner, copyright data, and site terms and conditions. If it is inside an article or section, it could contain the date the article was published, tags, categories, and other metadata.

The HTML5 specification suggests a solution to a very common web element: the copyright notice on a page:

```
<footer >
<small>&copy; Copyright HTML5 Cookbook 2011</small>
</footer>
```

The previous example would likely be just before the closing `</body>` tag. (Also notice how the copyright message is in a `small` tag. We will come to that in the next chapter.)

Like the `header` element, you can use `footer` more than once on a page. You can put a `footer` inside an article. Listing 1.11 details a page with a sitewide `footer` and also uses nested `footer` elements with an `article`, as shown in Figure 1.10.

Listing 1.11 **Page with a Sitewide** `footer` **and an** `article` > `footer` **Combination**

```
<article>

  <h1>10 things about HTML5</h1>

  <footer>
    <p>This news article was published on <time>1st April 2011</time> by <a
➥href="#">Tom Leadbetter</a></p>
  </footer>
  <p><strong>Pellentesque habitant morbi tristique</strong>...</p>
  <!-- general content -->
```

```
<footer>
   <p>This news article was published on <time>1st April 2011</time> by <a
➥href="#">Tom Leadbetter</a></p>
<a href="#">Read Tom's next article</a>
   </footer>
</article>
<footer>
   <small>&copy; Copyright HTML5 Cookbook 2011</small>
</footer>
```

This example shows two `footer` elements within an `article`. It is common to see the author or date displayed at the top and bottom of a news item or blog post, and you can use `footer` as many times as you want.

In the previous example, we introduced the `time` element, which we will be covering in the next chapter.

You can include other pieces of content in the `footer`, such as navigation (yes, using a `nav` element), partner logos, and license agreements, and you might often see text such as "This site is powered by `<cms name>`."

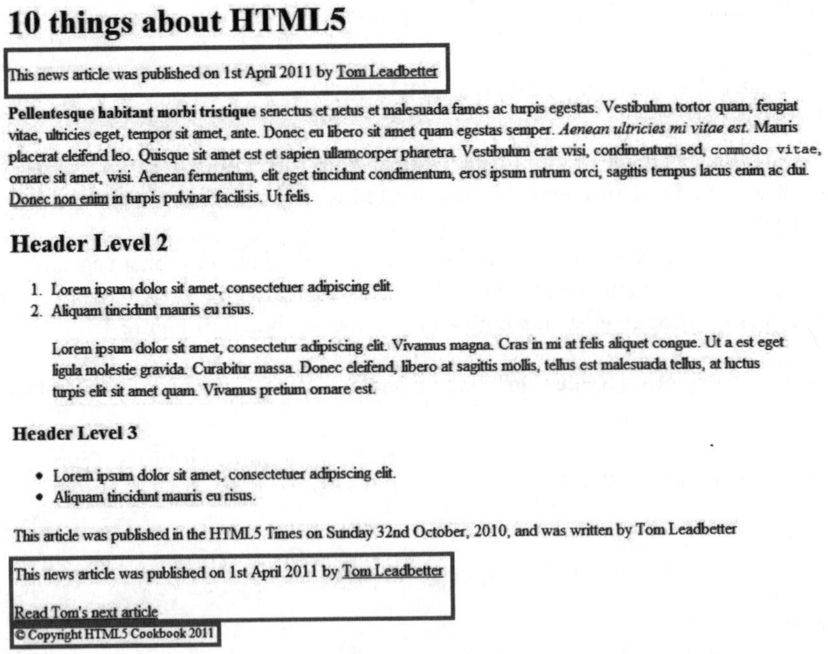

10 things about HTML5

This news article was published on 1st April 2011 by Tom Leadbetter

Pellentesque habitant morbi tristique senectus et netus et malesuada fames ac turpis egestas. Vestibulum tortor quam, feugiat vitae, ultricies eget, tempor sit amet, ante. Donec eu libero sit amet quam egestas semper. *Aenean ultricies mi vitae est.* Mauris placerat eleifend leo. Quisque sit amet est et sapien ullamcorper pharetra. Vestibulum erat wisi, condimentum sed, commodo vitae, ornare sit amet, wisi. Aenean fermentum, elit eget tincidunt condimentum, eros ipsum rutrum orci, sagittis tempus lacus enim ac dui. Donec non enim in turpis pulvinar facilisis. Ut felis.

Header Level 2

1. Lorem ipsum dolor sit amet, consectetuer adipiscing elit.
2. Aliquam tincidunt mauris eu risus.

Lorem ipsum dolor sit amet, consectetur adipiscing elit. Vivamus magna. Cras in mi at felis aliquet congue. Ut a est eget ligula molestie gravida. Curabitur massa. Donec eleifend, libero at sagittis mollis, tellus est malesuada tellus, at luctus turpis elit sit amet quam. Vivamus pretium ornare est.

Header Level 3

- Lorem ipsum dolor sit amet, consectetuer adipiscing elit.
- Aliquam tincidunt mauris eu risus.

This article was published in the HTML5 Times on Sunday 32nd October, 2010, and was written by Tom Leadbetter

This news article was published on 1st April 2011 by Tom Leadbetter

Read Tom's next article

© Copyright HTML5 Cookbook 2011

Figure 1.10   Page layout with multiple footer elements
(no styling applied)

The HTML5 specification says the footer element can include links to related documents, and although previously you used a combination of aside and nav for that, you can also use the footer element for that content, if it is inside an article. It can contain other links, such as links to previous and next articles, which would look something like this:

```
<article>
... all the content for this article...
<footer >
<a href="#">Previous article</a> | <a href="#">Next article article</a>
</footer>
</article>
```

INTERMEDIATE RECIPE:
Using the HTML5 Outliner to Ensure the Correct Structure

With these new elements, you have the opportunity to make your content flow in a logical manner and to allow people to navigate through the content using the hierarchy (using screen readers, for example), rather like a table of contents. Testing against the outline allows you to check that you are using headings and sections correctly. There are various browser extensions and websites at your disposal, but here we will be using a Google Chrome extension: http://code.google.com/p/h5o/.

Download the Chrome extension, and once it is installed, you get an icon in the address bar, as shown in Figure 1.11.

When you select this tool, you will see displayed data that looks like a table of contents, usually with the content indented.

If you have organized the content properly, you should have a structured and logical table of contents. You want to avoid "Untitled section/article." If that message is displayed, chances are that you have used the wrong markup, so you need to reexamine your markup. Note, however, that nav and aside are allowed to have "Untitled section."

Figure 1.11   Website in Google Chrome with the HTML5 Outliner
extension icon

A correct outline might look something like this:

1. Website name
    a. Blog
            i. Article title
            ii. Article title
    b. About me
            i. My name
            ii. My likes
            iii. My dislikes
    c. Contact me

Figure 1.12 shows an example document outline. The indents are correct, and there are no untitled sections (apart from the nav, but that is fine).

The outline you will create in this recipe is as follows:

1. Loads of News
    a. Bringing you all kinds of news!
    b. Untitled NAV
    c. Sports News
    d. Entertainment News!
    e. Nerdy News

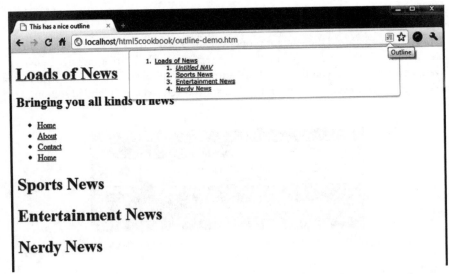

Figure 1.12   Basic HTML5 page in Google Chrome showing the results of the document outline

Listing 1.12 shows the source code for this page.

Listing 1.12 **Making a Basic Document Outline**

```
<header>
  <hgroup>
    <h1><a href="#">Loads of News</a></h1>
    <h2>Bringing you all kinds of news</h2>
  </hgroup>
</header>

<nav>
  <ul>
    <li><a href="#">Home</a></li>
    <li><a href="#">About</a></li>
    <li><a href="#">Contact</a></li>
    <li><a href="#">Home</a></li>
  </ul>
</nav>
<section>
  <h1>Sports News</h1>
</section>
<section>
  <h1>Entertainment News</h1>
</section>
<section>
  <h1>Nerdy News</h1>
</section>
```

This has a header at the top of the page, which is used as the first node in the out-line (not the page title) and then sections that also have headings. There is an hgroup element used in the header element with the text "Bringing you all kinds of news!" but you do not see the h2 in the outline because the outline reads the first heading (h1, h2, h3, h4, h5, or h6) in the element.

The section, article, nav, and aside elements begin the indents (sections) in the outline. The sections have an h1, which is displayed in the outline. You could use an h2 or h3 if you wanted; it does not matter. If you had a section with content but no heading, the outline would say "untitled section," and you want to avoid that scenario.

ADVANCED RECIPE:
Using All the New Elements to Build a News Page

Figure 1.13 and the code in Listing 1.13 show how to use all the new HTML5 elements to build a layout for a news page. It includes some basic CSS to position the

Loadsa News

Bringing you all kinds of news!

Home Sports news Entertainment news Nerdy news About Contact

Headline article

This is our most important article

10th November 2010

Pellentesque habitant morbi tristique senectus et netus et malesuada fames ac turpis egestas.

Sports news

Sports headline 1

10th November 2010

Pellentesque habitant morbi tristique senectus et netus et malesuada fames ac turpis egestas.

Sports headline 2

9th November 2010

Pellentesque habitant morbi tristique senectus et netus et malesuada fames ac turpis egestas.

Sports headline 3

8th November 2010

Pellentesque habitant morbi tristique senectus et netus et malesuada fames ac turpis egestas.

Entertainment news

Entertainment headline 1

10th November 2010

Pellentesque habitant morbi tristique senectus et netus et malesuada fames ac turpis egestas.

Entertainment headline 2

9th November 2010

Pellentesque habitant morbi tristique senectus et netus et malesuada fames ac turpis egestas.

Entertainment headline 3

8th November 2010

Pellentesque habitant morbi tristique senectus et netus et malesuada fames ac turpis egestas.

Nerdy news

Nerdy headline 1

10th November 2010

Pellentesque habitant morbi tristique senectus et netus et malesuada fames ac turpis egestas.

Nerdy headline 2

9th November 2010

Pellentesque habitant morbi tristique senectus et netus et malesuada fames ac turpis egestas.

Nerdy headline 3

8th November 2010

Pellentesque habitant morbi tristique senectus et netus et malesuada fames ac turpis egestas.

Snazzy advert	Snazzy advert	Snazzy advert	Snazzy advert

Site powered by a CMS With No Name

Site hsoted by a Host With No Name

The photos on this site are all owned by the photographer

© Copyright NoBody 2011

Figure 1.13   A news page layout using new HTML5 elements

elements, but you are not doing anything too jazzy just yet; we will save all that for a later chapter.

Listing 1.13 **Creating a News Home Page**

```
<!DOCTYPE html>
<html lang="en">
<head>
<meta charset="utf-8">
<title>Loads of News - the best news site there ever was</title>
<style>
header, nav, section, article, footer {display: block;}
header, nav {border-bottom: 1px dotted #000; clear: both; width: 100%;}
nav li {display: inline;}
section#headline {clear: both; border: 5px solid #000; padding: 1%; width: 97%;}
section#sports, section#entertainment, section#nerdy {float: left; margin: 0 5px;
padding: 1%; width: 30%;}aside, footer {clear: both;}
aside img {border: 1px solid #ccc; margin: 0 10px 0 0;}
</style>
</head>
<body>
<header>
  <hgroup>
    <h1>Loads of News</h1>
    <h2>Bringing you all kinds of news!</h2>
  </hgroup>
</header>
<nav>
  <ul>
    <li><a href="#">Home</a></li>
    <li><a href="#">Sports news</a></li>
    <li><a href="#">Entertainment news</a></li>
    <li><a href="#">Nerdy news</a></li>
    <li><a href="#">About</a></li>
    <li><a href="#">Contact</a></li>
  </ul>
</nav>
<section id="headline">
  <h1>Headline article</h1>
  <article>
    <header>
      <h2><a href="#">This is our most important article</a></h2>
      <p>10th November 2010</p>
    </header>
    <p>Pellentesque habitant morbi tristique senectus et netus et malesuada fames
➥ac turpis egestas.</p>
```

```
    </article>
</section>
<section id="sports">
  <h1>Sports news</h1>
  <article> <!-- (x3) -->
    <header>
      <h2><a href="#">Sports headline 1</a></h2>
      <p>10th November 2010</p>
    </header>
    <p>Pellentesque habitant morbi tristique senectus et netus et malesuada fames
➡ac turpis egestas.</p>
  </article>
</section>
<section id="entertainment">
  <h1>Entertainment news</h1>
  <article> <!-- (x3) -->
    <header>
      <h2><a href="#">Entertainment headline 1</a></h2>
      <p>10th November 2010</p>
    </header>
    <p>Pellentesque habitant morbi tristique senectus et netus et malesuada fames
➡ac turpis egestas.</p>
  </article>
</section>
<section id="nerdy">
<h1>Nerdy news</h1>
  <article><!-- (x3) -->
    <header>
      <h2><a href="#">Nerdy headline 1</a></h2>
      <p>10th November 2010</p>
    </header>
    <p>Pellentesque habitant morbi tristique senectus et netus et malesuada fames
➡ac turpis egestas.</p>
  </article>
</section>
<aside>
  <ul>
    <li><a href="#"><img alt="Snazzy advert" src="snazzy-advert.gif" height="128"
➡width="128" /></a></li><!-- (x4) -->
  </ul>
</aside>
<footer>
  <ul>
    <li>Site powered by a <a href="#">CMS With No Name</a></li>
    <li>Site hosted by a <a href="#">Host With No Name</a></li>
    <li>The photos on this site are all owned by the photographer</li>
  </ul>  <small>&copy; Copyright NoBody 2011</small>
```

```
</footer>
</body>
</html>
```

Now that you have the basic layout and the code sorted, you need to check the documents outline. The previous code will give you the following outline:

1. Loads of News
    a. Untitled NAV
2. Headline article
    a. This is our most important article
3. Sports news
    a. Sports headline 1
    b. Sports headline 2
    c. Sports headline 3
4. Entertainment news
    a. Entertainment headline 1
    b. Entertainment headline 2
    c. Entertainment headline 3
5. Nerdy news
    a. Nerdy headline 1
    b. Nerdy headline 2
    c. Nerdy headline 3
6. Untitled ASIDE

This looks lovely! `footer` is not sectioning content, unlike `section`, `article`, `nav`, and `aside`, so it does not show up in the outline. `nav` and `aside` are untitled, but that is fine. You could possibly give the `aside` a title if you wanted, though does an external product advertisement warrant a heading?

ADVANCED RECIPE:
Using All the New Elements to Build a Search Results Page

In Listing 1.14 you will put together several new HTML5 elements to create the structure of a search results page (Figure 1.14). Bear in mind that there is no CSS for this recipe, just HTML.

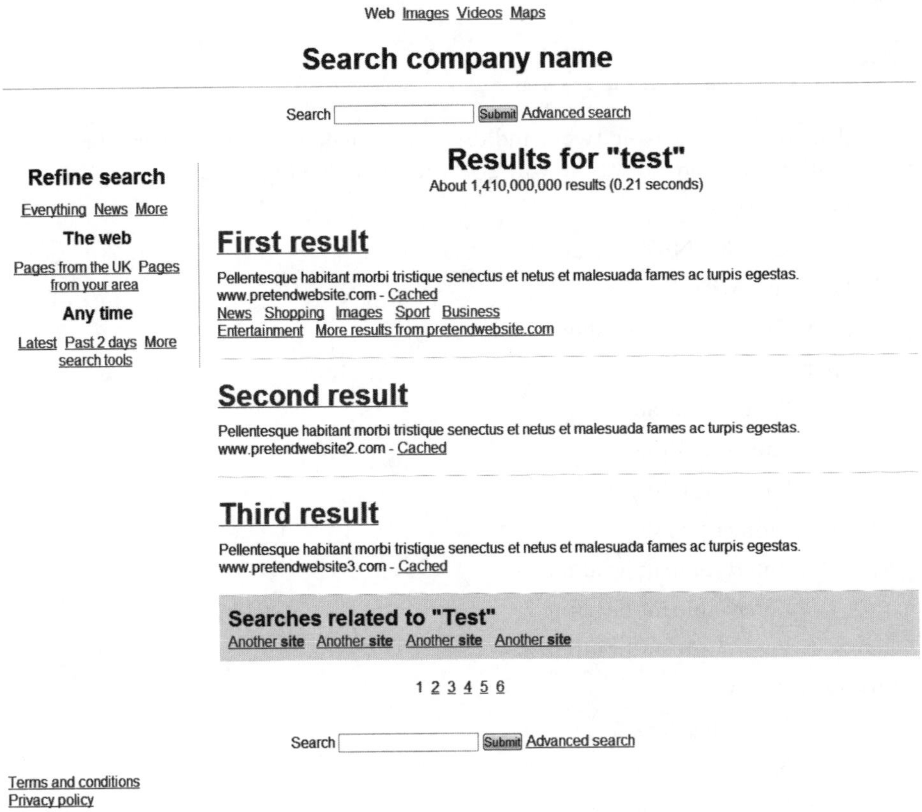

Web Images Videos Maps

Search company name

Search [   ] [Submit] Advanced search

Results for "test"

About 1,410,000,000 results (0.21 seconds)

Refine search

Everything News More

The web

Pages from the UK Pages
from your area

Any time

Latest Past 2 days More
search tools

First result

Pellentesque habitant morbi tristique senectus et netus et malesuada fames ac turpis egestas.
www.pretendwebsite.com - Cached
News Shopping Images Sport Business
Entertainment More results from pretendwebsite.com

Second result

Pellentesque habitant morbi tristique senectus et netus et malesuada fames ac turpis egestas.
www.pretendwebsite2.com - Cached

Third result

Pellentesque habitant morbi tristique senectus et netus et malesuada fames ac turpis egestas.
www.pretendwebsite3.com - Cached

Searches related to "Test"
Another **site** Another **site** Another **site** Another **site**

1 2 3 4 5 6

Search [   ] [Submit] Advanced search

Terms and conditions
Privacy policy

Figure 1.14   A search results page

Listing 1.14   **Elements Combined to Make a Search Results Page**

```
<!DOCTYPE html>
<html lang="en">
<head>
<meta charset="utf-8">
<title>Search</title>
</head>
<body>

<nav>
  <ul>
    <li>Web</li>
    <li><a href="#">Images</a></li>
    <li><a href="#">Videos</a></li>
    <li><a href="#">Maps</a></li>
    <!-- etc -->
```

```
    </ul>
  </nav>

  <header>
    <h1>Search company name</h1>
  </header>

  <form>
    <fieldset>
      <legend>Search</legend>
      <label for="searchinput">Search</label>
      <input type="search" id="searchinput" name="searchinput" />
      <input type="submit" value="Search" />
      <a href="#">Advanced search</a>
    </fieldset>
  </form>

  <nav>
    <h2>Refine search</h2>
    <ul>
      <li><a href="#">Everything</a></li>
      <li><a href="#">News</a></li>
      <li><a href="#">More</a></li>
    </ul>
    <h3>The web</h3>
    <ul>
      <li><a href="#">Pages from the UK</a></li>
      <li><a href="#">Pages from your area</a></li>
    </ul>
  <h3>Any time</h3>
    <ul>
      <li><a href="#">Latest</a></li>
      <li><a href="#">Past 2 days</a></li>
      <li><a href="#">More search tools</a></li>
    </ul>
  </nav>

  <section>
    <header>
      <h1>Results for &quot;test&quot;</h1>
      <p>About 1,410,000,000 results (0.21 seconds)</p>
    </header>

    <article>
      <header>
        <h1><a href="#">First result</a></h1>
      </header>
```

```
    <p>Pellentesque habitant morbi tristique senectus et netus et malesuada fames
➡ac turpis egestas.</p>
    <footer>
      <p>www.pretendwebsite.com - <a href="#">Cached</a></p>
      <ul>
        <li><a href="#">News</a></li>
        <li><a href="#">Shopping</a></li>
        <li><a href="#">Images</a></li>
        <li><a href="#">Sport</a></li>
        <li><a href="#">Business</a></li>
        <li><a href="#">Entertainment</a></li>
        <li><a href="#">More results from pretendwebsite.com</a></li>
      </ul>
    </footer>
  </article>

  <article>
    <header>
      <h1><a href="#">Second result</a></h1>
    </header>
    <p>Pellentesque habitant morbi tristique senectus et netus et malesuada fames
➡ac turpis egestas.</p>
    <footer>
      <p>www.pretendwebsite2.com - <a href="#">Cached</a></p>
    </footer>
  </article>
  <article>
    <header>
      <h1><a href="#">Third result</a></h1>
    </header>
    <p>Pellentesque habitant morbi tristique senectus et netus et malesuada fames
➡ac turpis egestas.</p>
    <footer>
      <p>www.pretendwebsite3.com - <a href="#">Cached</a></p>
    </footer>
  </article>    <!-- and so on... -->

  <aside>
    <nav>
      <h2>Searches related to &quot;Test&quot;</h2>
      <ul>
        <li><a href="#">Another <strong>site</strong></a></li>
        <li><a href="#">Another <strong>site</strong></a></li>
        <li><a href="#">Another <strong>site</strong></a></li>
        <li><a href="#">Another <strong>site</strong></a></li>
        <!-- etc -->
      </ul>
```

```
    </nav>
  </aside>

</section>

<nav>
  <ul>
    <li class="currentpage">1</li>
    <li><a href="#">2</a></li>
    <li><a href="#">3</a></li>
    <li><a href="#">4</a></li>
    <li><a href="#">5</a></li>
    <li><a href="#">6</a></li>
    <!-- and so on... -->
  </ul>
</nav>

<form>
  <fieldset>
    <legend>Search</legend>
    <label for="searchinput2">Search</label>
    <input type="search" id="searchinput2" name="searchinput2" />
    <input type="submit" />
    <a href="#">Advanced search</a>
  </fieldset>
</form>

<footer>
  <ul>
    <li><a href="#">Terms and conditions</a></li>
    <li><a href="#">Privacy policy</a></li>
    <!-- etc -->
  </ul>
</footer>
</body>
</html>
```

You might have other ideas about which markup to use, which is great; you should be thinking about making beautiful HTML.

The results are all within a `section` that has the heading `<h1>Results for &quot;test&quot;</h1>`. After that, each result is within its own article, each with a header and footer. The search results could go even further and be split into sections or articles again, depending on their content.

There is paging toward the bottom of the code that could be considered to be "major navigation" (remember what the HTML5 specification says), because the paging functionality is crucial to how a user navigates through their search results.

Summary

In this chapter, you learned about the new elements available in HTML5 that you can use when creating the main structure of a web page. Starting with a new `docytpe` and changes to how you call JavaScript and CSS files, you then used `header`, `hgroup`, `nav`, `footer`, `article`, `section`, and `aside` to create a page layout. Then, by examining the document outline, you checked that your structure made sense and that you used the correct elements.

Grouping, Text-Level, and Redefined Semantics

In the previous chapter, you learned about several new HTML5 elements. Those elements enable you to create the main structure of the page. In this chapter, you will learn about more new HTML5 elements (namely, `figure`, `time`, `details`, and `mark`), as well as some elements that have been redefined (`address`, `s`, `cite`, `ol`, `dl`, `small`, `b`, `strong`, `i`, `em`, `abbr`, and `hr`). You will also look at new block-level links and WAI-ARIA. These elements are known as *grouping* or *text-level* elements and deal with the content of the page.

BEGINNER RECIPE:
Marking Up Figures and Captions with the `figure` and `figcaption` Elements

The `figure` element allows you to wrap an image and give it a description. Previously, you would have had to use a `div` or something similar and then add the text to the page, and doing this meant there was no link between the image and the caption. But now with `figure`, you can associate images with a caption, using `figcaption`.

Also, `figure` does not always have to include an image; it could be sections of code, tabular data, audio, or video. Typically, however, `figure` would be used for an image; Figure 2.1 shows an example. The code used to create Figure 2.1 is provided in Listing 2.1.

Listing 2.1 **Image with Caption**

```
<figure>
  <img alt="Bar chart" src="analytics.gif" />
  <figcaption>
    Website analytics for October 2010
  </figcaption>
</figure>
```

Visitor numbers go up, then down, then back up again

November 1st 2010

Pellentesque habitant morbi tristique senectus et netus et malesuada fames ac turpis egestas. Vestibulum tortor quam, feugiat vitae, ultricies eget, tempor sit amet, ante. Donec eu libero sit amet quam egestas semper. Aenean ultricies mi vitae est. Mauris placerat eleifend leo. Ut felis. Praesent dapibus, neque id cursus faucibus, tortor neque egestas augue, eu vulputate magna eros eu erat. Aliquam erat volutpat. Nam dui mi, tincidunt quis, accumsan porttitor, facilisis luctus, metus

Pellentesque habitant morbi tristique senectus et netus et malesuada fames ac turpis egestas. Vestibulum tortor quam, feugiat vitae, ultricies eget, tempor sit amet, ante. Donec eu libero sit amet quam egestas semper. Aenean ultricies mi vitae est. Mauris placerat eleifend leo. Quisque sit amet est et sapien ullamcorper pharetra. Vestibulum erat wisi, condimentum sed, commodo vitae, ornare sit amet, wisi. Aenean fermentum, elit eget tincidunt condimentum, eros ipsum rutrum orci, sagittis tempus lacus enim ac dui. Donec non enim in turpis pulvinar facilisis. Ut felis. Praesent dapibus, neque id cursus faucibus, tortor neque egestas augue, eu vulputate magna eros eu erat. Aliquam erat volutpat. Nam dui mi, tincidunt quis, accumsan porttitor, facilisis luctus, metus

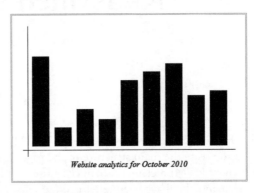

Website analytics for October 2010

Figure 2.1   `figure` element used to display a graph and a caption

There has been confusion over whether `alt` text (a text alternative for browsers that do not support graphics) is still needed in a `figure` element. Outside of `figure`, an `img` always needs an `alt`. If the image is purely presentational and it does not need to be identified by assistive technology, then an empty `alt` attribute can be applied. With `figure`, if the caption is a suitable description, then no `alt` is needed. However, because of lack of browser and assistive technology support, this currently hinders accessibility.

We suggest erring on the side of caution here and provide an `alt` anyway. In Listing 2.1, the caption is straightforward enough, but to someone using a screen reader, it is unknown how the analytics will be represented, so the `alt` text supplies this information.

Also, even though the example uses an image of a graph, there is no reason why you could not use a graph created through Canvas or SVG.

Note

Originally, the specification stated to use the (already existing) `legend` element rather than a new element (`figcaption`), but because of cross-browser styling problems, `legend` was scrapped in favor of `figcaption`.

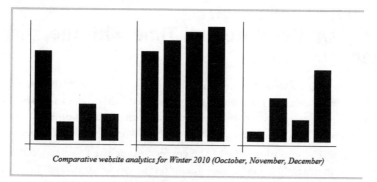

Visitor numbers for Winter 2010

January 1st 2011

Pellentesque habitant morbi tristique senectus et netus et malesuada fames ac turpis egestas. Vestibulum tortor quam, feugiat vitae, ultricies eget, tempor sit amet, ante. Donec eu libero sit amet quam egestas semper. Aenean ultricies mi vitae est. Mauris placerat eleifend leo.

Comparative website analytics for Winter 2010 (Ooctober, November, December)

Pellentesque habitant morbi tristique senectus et netus et malesuada fames ac turpis egestas. Vestibulum tortor quam, feugiat vitae, ultricies eget, tempor sit amet, ante. Donec eu libero sit amet quam egestas semper. Aenean ultricies mi vitae est. Mauris placerat eleifend leo. Quisque sit amet est et sapien ullamcorper pharetra. Vestibulum erat wisi, condimentum sed, commodo vitae, ornare sit amet, wisi.

Figure 2.2   `figure` element used to display three images, which share the one caption

As Figure 2.2 shows, you are not limited to just one image with `figure`; you can use the `figure` element to display multiple images. The code for Figure 2.2 is in Listing 2.2.

Listing 2.2   **Multiple Images Within** `figure`

```
<figure>
  <img alt="October 2010 data in bar chart format"
➥src="analytics-october.jpg" />
  <img alt="November 2010 data in bar chart format"
➥src="analytics-november.jpg" />
  <img alt="December 2010 data in bar chart format"
➥src="analytics-december.jpg" />
  <figcaption>
    Comparative website analytics for Winter 2010
    (October, November, December)
  </figcaption>
</figure>
```

Should you always use `figcaption` when displaying such content? If the image (or chart, table, and so on) is for purely presentational reasons, then just use a normal `img` tag. However, if it has additional information and is beneficial to the content, then it will likely require a description to go with it, so in this case, use `figure` and `figcaption`. Finally, `figure` can have only one `figcaption`.

BEGINNER RECIPE:
Marking Up the Date and Time with the `time` Element

The `time` element allows you to code dates and times that are readable by machines but are displayed to users in a readable fashion. So, with this you can timestamp things such as publishing dates or events that can populate other technologies (a calendar being the obvious example). The `time` element has two optional attributes:

- `datetime`: The end user will see the content inside the `time` tag, but a machine will be able to read the `datetime` value: `datetime="2011-04-01T16:00Z"`. The time part of this value (`T16:00`) is optional. You can also add a time zone offset: `T16:00+04:00`. The `Z` represents Universal Coordinated Time (UTC), which is the same as adding a time zone offset of `+00:00`.

- `pubdate`: `pubdate` is a Boolean attribute. It indicates the date, and possibly time, of the publication of its nearest parent `article` element. If there is no parent article element, then the `pubdate` refers to the whole document. Each `article` element must have only one `time` element with a `pubdate`.

The `time` element is intended to show precise dates, such "22nd January 2011," not vague dates such as "Some point in 2011." The `datetime` attribute must be in the format of the Gregorian calendar: YYYY-MM-DD, with the time coded as `T00:00`.

The following are some examples:

```
<article>....
  <footer>
    <p>This news article was published on <time pubdate datetime="2011-04-
➥01T16:00">1st April 2011 at 4pm</time> by <a href="#">Tom
➥Leadbetter</a></p>
  </footer>
</article>

<article>
  <h1>Christmas day family photo</h1>
  <p>It was lovely to have the family here for <time pubdate datetime="2010-12-
➥25">Christmas Day 2010</time></p>
  <figure>
    <img alt="" src="000001.jpg" />
```

```
    <figcaption>The Leadbetter family on Christmas morning</figcaption>
  </figure>
</article>
```

```
<p>HTML6 release date is due on <time datetime="2040-01-04">April 1<sup>st</sup>
➥2040</time></p>
```

BEGINNER RECIPE:
Making a Native Toggle Widget with the `details` Element

At the time of writing, only Chrome 13+ supports the new `details` element. We hope other browsers will support it sooner rather than later.

The `details` element creates an interactive open/close toggle effect, without the need for JavaScript and/or CSS. The `summary` element can be used within `details` to represent the summary of the content.

`details` has an optional attribute: `open`. If this is true, it will show the `details` element open by default; otherwise, the `details` element will be shut, and the `summary` will be displayed. The `summary` is the clickable part that will open/close the details.

Figure 2.3 shows what a brief author bio looks like, with the top one open by default. Listing 2.3 shows the code.

▼ Tom Leadbetter

Pellentesque habitant morbi tristique senectus et netus et malesuada fames ac turpis egestas.

Pellentesque habitant morbi tristique senectus et netus et malesuada fames ac turpis egestas.

Pellentesque habitant morbi tristique senectus et netus et malesuada fames ac turpis egestas.

Tom and Lucy Leadbetter

Pellentesque habitant morbi tristique senectus et netus et malesuada fames ac turpis egestas.

▶ Chuck Hudson

Figure 2.3 The `details` element with one section open viewed in Chrome

Listing 2.3   **Example of the** `details` **Element**

```
<details open>
  <summary>Tom Leadbetter</summary>
  <figure>
    <img alt="" src="images/tom-and-luce.jpg" />
    <figcaption>Tom and Lucy Leadbetter</figcaption>
  </figure>
  <p>Pellentesque habitant morbi tristique senectus et netus et malesuada fames
➥ac turpis egestas.</p>
  <p>Pellentesque habitant morbi tristique senectus et netus et malesuada fames
➥ac turpis egestas.</p>
  <p>Pellentesque habitant morbi tristique senectus et netus et malesuada fames
➥ac turpis egestas.</p>
  <p>Pellentesque habitant morbi tristique senectus et netus et malesuada fames
➥ac turpis egestas.</p>
</details>

<details>
  <summary>Chuck Hudson</summary>
  <figure>
    <img alt="" src="chuck.jpg" />
    <figcaption>Chuck Hudson</figcaption>
  </figure>
  <p>Pellentesque habitant morbi tristique senectus et netus et malesuada fames
➥ac turpis egestas.</p>
</details>
```

Another example is using the `details` element to show/hide a table of contents. Depending on the styling of the page and the amount of content, it could be useful to have the table of contents always in the top corner, and the user can click to expand it and navigate to a different section of the page. Listing 2.4 has the code for this, with the `details` element closed by default.

Listing 2.4   **Creating a Collapsible Table of Contents**

```
<article>
  <h1>A massive document with lots of juicy content</h1>
  <details>
    <summary>Table of contents<summary>
    <nav>
      <ul>
        <li><a href=#chapter1>Chapter 1</a></li>
        <li><a href=#chapter2>Chapter 2</a></li>
      </ul>
    </nav>
  </details>
  <section>
```

```
    <h1 id="chapter1">Chapter 1</h1>
  </section>
  <section>
    <h1 id="chapter2">Chapter 2</h1>
  </section>
....
</article>
```

BEGINNER RECIPE:
Using the `address` Element for Contact Information

The specification defines the `address` element as a "sectioning" element, like `nav` or `article`. However, we have put it in this chapter because we think it is more appropriate as a "text-level" semantic because its use concerns text content, rather than layout.

For many years, the `address` element has been used incorrectly by web developers. It is *not* supposed to be used as a generic postal address (often on a "Contact us" page). So, this code is incorrect:

```
<address>
Tom Leadbetter
1 My Street
United Kingdom
</address>
```

HTML5 attempts to clear the confusion by intending the `address` element be used for contract information for its nearest `article` or `body` element.

So, what does that mean? It means you should use the `address` element for contact information for the author of the current `article` or of the web page as a whole. Because you can use `address` inside an `article`, it means `address` can potentially be used several times on a site. The content of an `address` element can be an email address, website, phone number, postal address, or any other sort of contact information.

Because it is for contact information, it is common to use `address` within a `footer`. Listing 2.5 uses the `address` element two times: one for the author of the main page content and the other for the authors of the whole site.

Listing 2.5   **Multiple Uses of the `address` Element**

```
<article>
  <header>
    <h1><a href="#">My amazing blog entry</a></h1>
    <p>12.12.2011</p>
  </header>
  <p>Pellentesque habitant morbi tristique senectus et netus et malesuada fames
➥ac turpis egestas...</p>
```

```
<footer>
  This blog entry was written by
  <address><a href="me.htm">Tom Leadbetter</a></address>
</footer>
</article>
<footer>
  This site is owned by
  <address>
    <a href="me.htm">Tom Leadbetter</a> and
    <a href=mailto:chuck@html5developerscookbook.com>Chuck Hudson</a>.
  </address>
</footer>
```

BEGINNER RECIPE:
Highlighting Text with the `mark` Element

The mark element gives the document author a chance to highlight, or bring attention to, some text in the document.

If a user searches a site and is taken to a separate page, the term they searched for might be highlighted for their reference. We would use a mark here, rather than a strong or em because we are not giving the term any importance or emphasis, simply highlighting it for the user. Figure 2.4 shows how you can use it. Listing 2.6 shows the HTML and CSS.

Listing 2.6 **The mark Element with Additional CSS**

```
<style>
mark {background-color: #0F0; font-weight:bold;}
</style>
<article>  <header>
    <h1>Something in Latin</h1>
  </header>
 <p>Pellentesque habitant morbi tristique senectus et netus et malesuada fames ac
➡turpis egestas. <mark>Vestibulum tortor quam</mark>, feugiat vitae,
➡ultricies eget, tempor sit amet, ante. Donec eu libero sit amet quam
➡egestas semper. Aenean ultricies mi vitae est. Mauris placerat eleifend
➡leo.</p>
</article>
```

Something in Latin

Pellentesque habitant morbi tristique senectus et netus et malesuada fames ac turpis egestas. Vestibulum tortor quam, feugiat vitae, ultricies eget, tempor sit amet, ante. Donec eu libero sit amet quam egestas semper. Aenean ultricies mi vitae est. Mauris placerat eleifend leo.

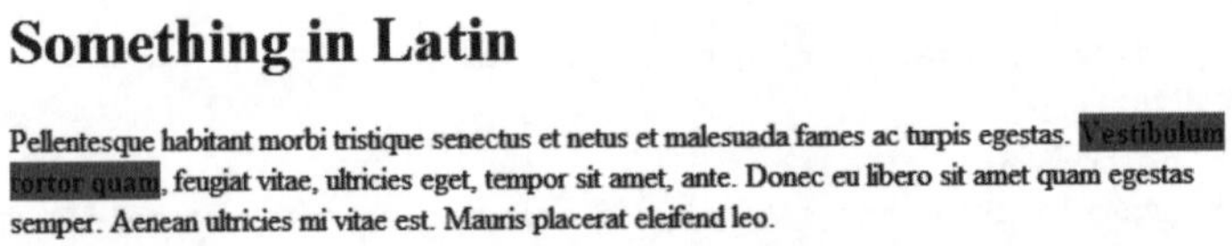

Figure 2.4 The mark element used to highlight text for a user

BEGINNER RECIPE:
Using the s Element to Show Inaccurate or Irrelevant Content

Previously the s element was specifically for strikethrough text. In HTML5, it has been redefined and is now used to represent content that is no longer correct or relevant.

What does this mean exactly? You could use the s element to represent the original retail price of a product that now has a different price, as shown in Figure 2.5. Depending on the context, it may not always be correct to display out-of-date information. However, in this case, it can come in handy to a user. Listing 2.7 shows where to use the element.

Listing 2.7   **The s Element**

```
<h1>Tom Leadbetter's Autobiography</h1>
<p><s>Recommended retail price: £45.99</s></p>
<p><strong>Now selling for just £5.99!</strong></p>
```

In HTML 4, the s element defined strikethrough text, so by default browsers will style the s element with a strikethrough.

If document text has been edited or removed, do not use the s element; use the del element instead.

Changes to Existing Elements

In the first chapter, you learned about new elements that can be used to create the layout of the page and add content. Previously in this chapter, you saw more new HTML5 elements, but they were concerned with the content itself, such as images. Just because there has been a lot of focus on new elements does not mean existing elements have been neglected. In fact, several have had their roles changed.

The cite Element

The cite element has been tweaked in HTML5. In HTML4, the cite allowed content developers to mark up the name of a speaker/author of a quote:

```
<cite>Julies Caesar</cite> once said, <q>I came, I saw, I conquered.</q>
```

Tom Leadbetter's Autobiography

~~Recommended retail price: £45.99~~

Now selling for just £5.99!

Figure 2.5   The s element used to display an old price

It was also used inside `blockquote`, which was technically incorrect in HTML 4 but nonetheless was commonly used:

```
<blockquote>
<p>Pellentesque habitant morbi tristique senectus et netus et malesuada fames ac
➥turpis egestas. Vestibulum tortor quam, feugiat vitae, ultricies eget,
➥tempor sit amet, ante.</p>
<cite>A Person who spoke Latin</cite>
</blockquote>
```

However, in HTML5, `cite` represents the title of a work, such as a book or a song. The HTML5 specification specifically says that a person's name is not the title of a work. So, you could use something like the following:

```
<p>One of my favourite books is <cite>The Day of the Jackal</cite> by <b>Frederick
➥Forsyth</b></p>
```

(The HTML5 specification suggests using the b element for author names.)

This change in HTML5 to disallow `cite` from author names has caused a bit of a stir. Well worth a read is http://24ways.org/2009/incite-a-riot by Jeremy Keith; it goes into great depth about the issue. To sum it up, the `cite` element in HTML5 is no longer backward compatible and instead the HTML5 specification suggests using the b element for names, though this tag has no semantic meaning even though the content is meaningful.

So, you have a decision to make: Do what the specification says or, as many continue to do, use `cite` for names. It is worth keeping an eye on the `cite` element to see whether its definition changes.

Note

In July 2011, there was discussion that might allow the use of `footer` in `blockquote`, which would create the perfect opportunity to add information about the quote, such as the author. So, keep an eye on this development.

The `ol` Element

The `ol` element, used to create an ordered list, has been redefined, so it now has three acceptable attributes:

- `start`
- `reversed`
- `type`

Used in Listing 2.8, the `reversed` attribute is new to HTML5 and will, when at least one browser chooses to implement it, enable you to reverse a list that counts down to one.

Listing 2.8   **Reversed Ordered List**

```
<h1>My favorite colors</h1>
<ol reversed>
  <li>Red</li>
  <li>Green</li>
  <li>Blue</li>
</ol>
```

Currently, no browser supports this, but if supported, it would render like this:

My favorite colors

3. Blue

2. Green

1. Red

The `start` attribute was deprecated in HTML 4 and so the page would fail validation if `start` was used. This proved an annoyance, but thankfully it is now back and
perfectly acceptable in HTML5. So, if you are required to start an ordered list at the
second item, use the following:

```
<ol start="2">
<li>here we go</li>
....
</ol>
```

Also back from the dead is the `type` attribute. Previously, if you wanted to change the
display of the list types, say to Roman numerals (for example, I, IV, X), you had to use
CSS. But you can do this again in HTML5. The Listing 2.9 markup shows an example.

Listing 2.9   **Nested Ordered Lists**

```
<ol>
  <li>Lorem ipsum dolor sit amet, consectetuer adipiscing elit.
    <ol>
      <li>Lorem ipsum dolor sit amet, consectetuer adipiscing elit.</li>
      <li>Aliquam tincidunt mauris eu risus.</li>
      <li>Lorem ipsum dolor sit amet, consectetuer adipiscing elit.
        <ol>
          <li>Aliquam tincidunt mauris eu risus.</li>
          <li>Vestibulum auctor dapibus neque.</li>
        </ol>
      </li>
      <li>Vestibulum auctor dapibus neque.</li>
    </ol>
  </li>
  <li>Aliquam tincidunt mauris eu risus.</li>
  <li>Vestibulum auctor dapibus neque.</li>
</ol>
```

The previous code would create this:

1. Lorem ipsum dolor sit amet, consectetuer adipiscing elit.
    1. Lorem ipsum dolor sit amet, consectetuer adipiscing elit.
    2. Aliquam tincidunt mauris eu risus.
    3. Lorem ipsum dolor sit amet, consectetuer adipiscing elit.
        1. Aliquam tincidunt mauris eu risus.
        2. Vestibulum auctor dapibus neque.
    4. Vestibulum auctor dapibus neque.
2. Aliquam tincidunt mauris eu risus.
3. Vestibulum auctor dapibus neque.

Using the `type` attribute, you can change the type of numbering you get on the lists, without the need for CSS. You can choose from five types:

type="1" = 1, 2, 3,4, 5

type="a" = a, b, c, d, e

type="A" = A, B, C, D, E

type="i" = i, ii, iii, iv, v

type="I" = I, II, III, IV, V

If you change the `ol` type to any of these, then the bullet points will render as follows:

1. Lorem ipsum dolor sit amet, consectetuer adipiscing elit.
    a. Lorem ipsum dolor sit amet, consectetuer adipiscing elit.
    b. Aliquam tincidunt mauris eu risus.
    c. Lorem ipsum dolor sit amet, consectetuer adipiscing elit.
        i. Aliquam tincidunt mauris eu risus.
        ii. Vestibulum auctor dapibus neque.
    d. Vestibulum auctor dapibus neque.
2. Aliquam tincidunt mauris eu risus.
3. Vestibulum auctor dapibus neque.

Using the different types, in the content you could refer to item 1.b.ii, rather than 1.3.2. Browsers will correctly implement the `type` attribute, but at the time of writing, it causes a validation error.

The `dl` Element

In HTML4, `dl` was a definition list, which should have contained a term and then a definition, but its own definition and use was never very clear and so was misused or ditched in favor of another element.

In HTML5, it has been repurposed as a description or association list. It is easier to get an understanding of this element by diving into some examples. Listing 2.10 uses dl to create a glossary. We have put the glossary in an aside because we can assume here that it is inside an article, likely about web development.

Listing 2.10   **Creating a Glossary**

```
<aside>
<h2>Glossary</h2>
<dl>
<dt>HTML</dt>
<dd>HTML, which stands for HyperText Markup Language, is the predominant markup
➥language for web pages.</dd>
<dt>PHP</dt>
<dd>PHP: Hypertext Preprocessor is a widely used, general-purpose scripting
➥language that was originally designed for web development to produce
➥dynamic web pages.</dd>
</dl>
</aside>
```

Listing 2.11 uses a dl to mark up movie credits.

Listing 2.11   **Adding Movie Credits**

```
<h1>The Shawshank Redemption</h1>
<dl>
<dt>Director:</dt>
<dd>Frank Darabont</dd>
<dt>Writers:</dt>
<dd>Stephen King</dd>
<dd>Frank Darabong </dd>
<dt>Cast</dt>
<dd>Tim Robbins</dd>
<dd>Morgan Freeman</dd>
<dd>Bob Gunton</dd>
...
</dl>
```

The previous code uses multiple values (dd) to the one key (dt). It might be argued that each section of credits (director, writers, and so on) could be in a section of its own, as shown here:

```
<article>
<header>
<h1>The Shawshank Redemption</h1>
<time>1994</time>
</header>
<section>
```

```
<h1>Director</h1>
<h2> Frank Darabont</h2>
<p>(bio)</p>
</section>
<section>
<h1>Writers</h1>
<h2>Stephen King</p>
<p>(bio)</p>
<h2> Frank Darabont</h2>
<p>(bio)</p>
</section>
</article>
```

It really depends on your content and how you want your content to be structured.

> **Tip**
>
> The `dl` element has been used in the past to mark up dialogue, but the spec now tells us that using a `dl` is inappropriate. Originally, in HTML5 there was a `dialog` element, but that was axed in late 2009. Instead, you should use p elements for this requirement, and if you wanted to style the name of the speaker, you should use either a `span` or a `b`. The following is an example:
>
> ```
> <p><b>John</b>: Can you use HTML5 yet?</p>
> <p><b> Jane</b>: Yes, you definitely can! </p>
> ```

The `small` Element

In HTML4, the `small` element was used to reduce the size of text. However, this was and is a presentational issue, so CSS is used for this purpose. Now, in HTML5, the small element is used for displaying small print, such as copyright information, terms and conditions, or license/legal information:

```
<p><small>This site is licensed under a <a
➥href="http://creativecommons.org/licenses/by-nc/2.0/uk/">Creative Commons
➥Attribution-Non-Commercial 2.0</a> share alike license. Feel free to
➥change, reuse modify and extend it.</small></p>
```

Because `small` is inline content, you can embed it within another element if necessary, such as `strong`, which would give importance to this small print:

```
<p><strong><small>This content belongs to me! Don't steal it, otherwise
➥there will be serious, serious trouble.</small></strong></p>
```

The `b` and `strong` Elements

In HTML 4, the `b` element was for bold, but that has changed. Now it is purely presentational; it should be used to style a section of text that does not convey any particular importance.

You will often see the first paragraph of a blog entry is styled differently, often in bold text:

```
<h2>Dark energy and flat Universe exposed by simple method</h2>
 <p><b class="lead">Researchers have developed a simple technique that adds
➥evidence to the theory that the Universe is flat.</b></p>
<p>Moreover, the method - developed by revisiting a 30-year-old idea - confirms
➥that "dark energy" makes up nearly three-quarters of the
➥Universe.</p>
```

You would not use a strong element because you do not want to add importance to the first paragraph; you are just styling it differently. However, you could also use some CSS (p:first-of-type or h2+p) to style this instead of using b. Listing 2.12 uses b to add color styles to some of the text.

Listing 2.12   **The b Element**

```
<style>
b.red {color: red;}
b.green {color: green;}
b.blue {color: blue;}
</style>
<h1>My favourite colours</h1>
<ol reversed>
  <li><b class="red">Red</b></li>
  <li><b class="green">Green</b></li>
  <li><b class="blue">Blue</b></li>
</ol>
```

The strong element shows text with strong importance, so you now normally use this to generate the bold effect, and you can nest strong to increase the importance of the content:

```
<p><strong>Do not eat my cookies</strong> and <strong><strong>do not drink
my milk</strong></strong></p>
```

The i and em Elements

The i element was, in HTML 4, for styling text in italics. Now, though, it represents text that is in an alternative voice or mood. The HTML5 specification gives some examples of its use, which include a dream, a technical term, a thought, or a ship name:

```
<p>I'm having fish tonight <i>(and then I think I'll have cookies, I haven't had
➥cookies for ages)</i>.</p>
```

In contrast, the em element represents emphasis that changes the meaning of a sentence. Depending on what word (or words) should be emphasized, wrap it in the em element, but moving the em element would cause the sentence to change its meaning:

```
<p>I thought I was meeting friends at 8pm but my wife says it's <em>9pm</em></p>
<p><em>I</em> thought I was meeting friends at 8pm but my <em>wife</em> says it's
➥9pm</p>
```

The `abbr` Element

The `abbr` element is not new in HTML5, and it has not been redefined. So, why bother mentioning it? Well, `abbr` has been merged with `acronym`. Now, the `abbr` element represents an abbreviation or an acronym. You can use the `title` attribute to expand the abbreviation, which normally means a tooltip for the user:

```
<p><abbr title="HyperText Markup Language">HTML</abbr> is the best thing since
➥sliced web</p>
```

An abbreviation is different from an acronym; NATO is an acronym, while BBC is an abbreviation. In HTML 4, both tags were available, but because of confusion by content authors over which to use, `acronym` has been scrapped, so now use `abbr` for both.

The `hr` Element

The `hr` element was used to create a horizontal line in a document. Its definition has been tweaked slightly, so it now represents a break, after a paragraph, such as a scene change in a book. Usually this will be styled to display a line or a fancy graphic between sections. It is not used very often these days because CSS can be used to add space/a graphic/a line/decoration at the bottom or top of necessary sections, such as a p, div, `article`, or `section`.

Elements That Are No More

HTML5 has gotten rid of several elements, so say bye-bye to the following elements:

- `acronym` (use `abbr`; see earlier)
- `applet` (use `object`)
- `basefont` (use CSS for presentation)
- `big` (use CSS for presentation)
- `center` (use CSS for presentation)
- `frame` (though `iframe` still exists)
- `frameset`
- `noframes`
- `font` (use CSS for presentation)
- `strike` (depending on the content, use s or `del`)
- `tt` (use CSS for presentation)
- `u` (use CSS for presentation)

That is all there is to say, really. We will not be mourning those elements, and if you are using them now, please stop straightaway!

BEGINNER RECIPE:
Wrapping Links Around Elements

A handy new feature of HTML5 is the ability to group several elements into one link. This gives you a much wider click area, something that you may have in the past used JavaScript or a combination of tags to do the job.

In HTML 4, if you were marking up a news or blog home page, with several articles to link to, you may have previously used something like the code in Listing 2.13 to make each item clickable.

Listing 2.13   **Wrapping Links in HTML 4**

```
<div class="article">
  <h2><a href="article.htm"><img alt="article thumbnail" src="thumb.jpg"
➥height="100" width="100" /> My article title</a></h2>
  <p><a href="article.htm">Pellentesque habitant morbi tristique senectus et
➥netus et malesuada fames ac turpis egestas.</a></p>
</div>
```

Listing 2.14 shows that in HTML5 you can wrap all of that in one a.

Listing 2.14   **Wrapping Links with HTML5**

```
<article>
  <a href="article.htm">
    <h2><img alt="article thumbnail" src="thumb.jpg" height="100" width="100" />
➥My article title</h2>
    <p>Pellentesque habitant morbi tristique senectus et netus et malesuada fames
➥ac turpis egestas.</p>
  </a>
</article>
```

You are able to wrap the article in an the a element as well; however, this has been known to cause a couple of browser issues, so we advise against that approach.

INTERMEDIATE RECIPE:
Adding Semantic Information with Microdata

The Microdata specification allows authors to add labels to pieces of content to make it machine-readable. Using the Microdata formatting in theory helps "machines" like Google return more accurate information about pages.

You can treat Microdata as a custom element, so you can use it to label things such as a business, a person, products, or an event. Because there is no book element, you can apply Microdata attributes to your existing elements.

Microdata has five attributes: itemid, itemprop, itemref, itemscope, and itemtype. Listing 2.15 shows a basic example, which describes a person.

Listing 2.15 **Microdata Example**

```
<article itemscope itemtype="http://data-vocabulary.org/Person">
  <h1 itemprop="name">Tom Leadbetter</h1>
  <p><span itemprop="address" itemscope itemtype="http://data-
➡vocabulary.org/Address">I live in <span item
➡prop="region">Liverpool</span>, <span itemprop="country-
➡name">UK</span>.</p>
  <p>I am a <span itemprop="title">Space Cowboy</span> at <span
➡itemprop="affiliation">Space Cowboy Inc.</span>. I also have a website:
➡<a href="http://www.tomleadbetter.co.uk"
➡itemprop="url">tomleadbetter.co.uk</a></p>
</article>
```

Listing 2.14 says that you have a person whose name is Tom Leadbetter, who lives in the United Kingdom and is a Space Cowboy working for Space Cowboy Inc.

When itemscope is used on an element, the element becomes a Microdata item. itemprop is a property of this Microdata item, and it describes what the content is. The example has two itemscope attributes: one for the overall piece of content (Person) and another for the address itemtype within.

The itemprop values in the example come from http://data-vocabulary.org, which suggests the names for various data types (events, products, and so on). You can make your own values, but for consistent results you should use standard, recognized names. Google also has examples and suggestions at http://google.com/support/webmasters/bin/answer.py?answer=99170. Using the Google webmaster Rich Snippets Testing Tool, you can check your Microdata to see how Google might render it in a search results page, as shown in Figure 2.6.

Figure 2.7 shows the other information that Google now has about the content.

This was only a small Microdata example, but there are lots of useful options. Check out the Google pages mentioned earlier for more examples of what can be created. Along with Google, there are a couple of tools that might help when you are creating Mircodata: http://foolip.org/microdatajs/live and http://microdata.freebaseapps.com.

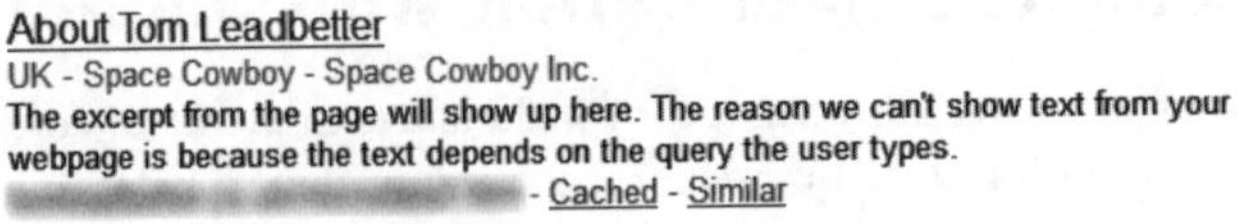

About Tom Leadbetter
UK - Space Cowboy - Space Cowboy Inc.
The excerpt from the page will show up here. The reason we can't show text from your webpage is because the text depends on the query the user types.
▬▬▬▬▬▬▬▬▬▬▬ - Cached - Similar

Figure 2.6 Google search preview

```
Item
    Type: http://data-vocabulary.org/person
    name = Tom Leadbetter
    address = Item( 1 )
    title = Space Cowboy
    affiliation = Space Cowboy Inc.
    url = http://www.tomleadbetter.co.uk/

Item 1
    Type: http://data-vocabulary.org/address
    region = Liverpool
    country-name = UK
```

Figure 2.7   Additional information Google knows

In June 2011, http://schema.org was launched, a collaboration of shared schemas from Bing, Google, and Yahoo! Schema.org has several examples and a huge selection of example data. In Listing 2.15, we are linking to http://data-vocabularly.org because this is currently supported in the Rich Snippets Testing Tool, but shortly you will be able to use http://schema.org in your Microdata, and it will likely be the destination for developers looking to learn what markup to use.

> **Note**
>
> Microformats and RDFa are two other ways of extending your HTML to describe specific infor-mation. There are a bit of politics with these options that we will not go into, but both have their strengths and weaknesses. You can actually combine Microdata with Microformats, and although Microdata is the emerging standard, Microformats is currently more popular.

INTERMEDIATE RECIPE:
Using WAI-ARIA with HTML5

Web Accessibility Initiatives Accessible Rich Internet Applications (WAI-ARIA), also known just as ARIA, is a draft specification (http://w3.org/TR/wai-aria) that improves the accessibility of web applications and web pages. ARIA enables develop-ers and content authors to develop rich Internet applications and content that can be recognized and used by assistive technology. More often than not, assistive technol-ogy does not know what a widget is and rarely are widgets accessible with a keyboard. Also consider when content is updated with an Ajax call, assistive technology does not know that the content has been updated, and so it cannot inform the user. Although we will not be talking about all the possible solutions that ARIA offers, we will be covering the Landmark Roles section of ARIA and how you can add these new roles to your HTML5 document.

Landmark Roles are regions of the page used as navigational landmarks. There are more than 50 of them listed in the specification (http://w3.org/TR/wai-aria/roles#landmark_roles), but here are the more commonly used landmark roles:

- role="article"
- role="banner"

- role="complementary"
- role="contentinfo"
- role="form"
- role="heading"
- role="main"
- role="navigation"
- role="search"

You can add these to your markup easily like this:

```
<form role="search">
....
</form>
```

This signifies that this particular form (there might be several forms on the page) is used for searching.

Looking through the previous list, you can see that some have obvious pairings with new HTML5 elements, and when you add them to the main page structure from the previous chapter, you get a layout similar to that in Figure 2.8.

Because you are using a logical structure to this markup, along with ARIA roles, one day assistive technology will be able to navigate easily to certain areas of the page

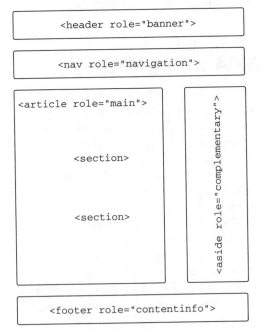

Figure 2.8   Basic website layout with ARIA roles

content. However, at the moment, there is limited screen reader support not only for HTML5 but also for ARIA elements.

You are encouraged to use skip links at the top of a document, very often hidden with CSS, which allow people navigating with a screen reader, keyboard, or another assistive technology to quickly "skip" or "jump" to important areas, usually the main navigation or the main content. The code would look similar to this:

```
<ul>
    <li><a href="#menu">Skip to navigation</a></li>
    <li><a href="#content">Skip to content</a></li>
</ul>
```

But with ARIA, the landmarks will be highlighted to a user so they can cycle through the options.

HTML5 validation accepts ARIA roles, and you can use the ARIA roles in HTML 4. They will cause a validation error.

These roles also provide you with a nifty CSS hook that adds to your arsenal of selectors. You may have several headers or footers on a page, but you want to style the main page header and footer differently, and you can target them in CSS like this:

```
/* to style all headers */
header {background: red; border: 5px dotted black;}

/* to style our main header, which likely has the site logo */
header[role=banner] {background: black; border: 5px solid red;}

/* to style all footers */
footer {background: blue; border: 5px dotted green;}

/* to style our site footer, which likely has copyright info */
footer[role=contentinfo] {background: green; border: 5px solid blue;}
```

You do not necessarily have to use CSS this way, but it is a nice option to have.

There is so much more to the WAI-ARIA spec and HTML5 accessibility, so we encourage you to do some further reading at the following sites:

- http://w3.org/TR/wai-aria
- http://html5accessibility.com
- http://paciellogroup.com/blog

ADVANCED RECIPE:
Marking Up an Article Page with Comments

Listing 2.16 has the code needed to create an article page with comments (Figure 2.9). It uses several of the new techniques covered in this chapter.

Tom's blog

Title of my article

Sunday, 12th December 2010

Pellentesque habitant morbi tristique senectus et netus et malesuada fames ac turpis egestas. Vestibulum tortor quam, feugiat vitae, ultricies eget, tempor sit amet, ante. Donec eu libero sit amet quam egestas semper. Aenean ultricies mi vitae est. Mauris placerat eleifend leo.

Pellentesque habitant morbi tristique senectus et netus et malesuada fames ac turpis egestas. Vestibulum tortor quam, feugiat vitae ultricies eget, tempor sit amet, ante. Donec eu libero sit amet quam egestas semper. Aenean ultricies mi vitae est. Mauris placerat eleifend leo.

Comments

1. **13/12/2010 11:15**

   Comment by
   Tom Leadbetter

   What a splendid article!

2. **16/12/2010 11:15**

   Comment by anonymous

   That was rubbish.

Figure 2.9   Website article with comments

Listing 2.16   **Article with Comments**

```
<!DOCTYPE html>
<html lang="en">
<head>
<meta charset="utf-8">
<title>Blog comments</title>
<style>
[role=banner] h1 {background: #333; color: #fff; padding: 5px;}
[role=main] h1 {border-bottom: 2px dotted #333; color: #333;}
b {float: left; font-family:"Palatino Linotype", Palatino, serif; font-size:
➡2.5em; font-style: italic; font-weight: bold; line-height: 1; margin: 0
➡5px 5px 0;}
</style>
</head>
<body>
<h1 role="banner">>Tom's blog</h1><article role="main">
  <header>
    <h1>Title of my article</h1>
    <time pubdate datetime="2010-12-12">Sunday, 12th December 2010</time>
```

```
    <p><b>P</b>ellentesque habitant morbi tristique senectus et netus et
➥malesuada fames ac turpis egestas. Vestibulum tortor …p>
  </header>
  <section>
    <h2>Comments</h2>
    <ol reversed>
      <li>
        <article>
          <h3><time datetime="2010-12-13T11:15Z">13/12/2010 11:15</time></h3>
          <footer>Comment by<address><a href="http://tomleadbetter.co.uk">Tom
➥Leadbetter</a></address></footer>
          <p>What a splendid article!</p>
        </article>
      </li>
      <li>
        <article>
          <h3><time datetime="2010-12-16T11:15Z">16/12/2010 11:15</time></h3>
          <footer>Comment by anonymous</footer>
          <p>That was rubbish.</p>
        </article>
      </li>
    </ol>
  </section>
</article>
</body>
</html>
```

Listing 2.15 uses some of the ARIA landmark roles, and we have used these to help style the h1 tags. We also use the b element to style the first letter of the article, to make it a bit fancier. When styling the h1 and b elements, you do not necessarily have to use the previous CSS, because there are other ways to target those elements, but it is nice to have options.

The new time element is used several times, once for the main article, with a pubdate, and then within each comment. In the previous chapter, you read that a user comment is an article, so we have used that here, and in this instance we have used the time and date as its heading. We could have used the author of the comment, but we do not want duplicate headings in the outline, and using the date and time gives it a unique identifier. This is a personal preference; there is nothing stopping you from using, for example, the comment author as the heading.

Also used is an ordered list so that each comment has a number that not only gives us an order of the comments but gives us a style option as well. We used the reversed attribute on the ol because in this case we want the latest comment to be at the top. We could potentially then have an "order by date" toggle switch and, using JavaScript, add or remove the reversed attribute. Again, you do not have to do this way, there are loads of alternatives, and the design of the comments might mean you have to consider other options.

Summary

In this chapter, you learned about a wide range of new elements and other elements that have been tweaked slightly in HTML5. New elements such as `figure` and `details` are sure to make developers' lives easier in the future, and along with new ARIA roles, you can structure your documents with greater semantics and greater accessibility. And you can add even further information to your HTML using Microdata so that search engines can provide richer, more accurate data.

3

Browser Handling in HTML5

Even though the HTML5 and accompanying specifications are not complete and the details are somewhat in flux, you can use many of the features right away. HTML5 is a developing language and incorporates a growing JavaScript API. Browser manufacturers are working hard to keep up with the growth of the new specifications. With these moving targets of new functionality and browser versions, we as developers can often run into browser support issues.

In this chapter, you will learn how to handle the differences between browsers and how you can plug the gaps using available tricks, tips, and scripts.

BEGINNER RECIPE:
Dealing with Internet Explorer

If you have been trying the code in the previous chapters in Internet Explorer (IE) 7, 8, or even 6 (we really hope you are not being forced to support IE6), then you may have noticed a slight problem—the pages you created in the recipes might not look as expected. That is because the code we have provided so far works natively only in the following major browsers: Firefox, Chrome, Safari, Opera, and Internet Explorer 9 (IE9). That is not to say that IE7 and IE8 do not support HTML5 entirely; there are various HTML5 APIs that do work in those browsers, such as drag and drop and ContentEditable.

Using JavaScript to Make HTML5 Compatible

IE6, 7, and 8, by default, do not recognize the new HTML5 elements, such as article or section, and therefore will not style these tags. If you do not do anything, the page will probably not look like you would hope. To have IE recognize the elements, you can programmatically create them through JavaScript as part of the DOM and then style them accordingly, as in this example:

```
<script>
document.createElement('article');
document.createElement('section');
//and so on
</script>
```

Of course, doing that for every single new HTML5 element would be a little tedious, and chances are that you would miss something. Luckily, you can use something called HTML5Shiv (http://code.google.com/p/html5shiv), written by Remy Sharp, which includes *all* the new elements and another bit of JavaScript called IE Print Protector (http://iecss.com/print-protector), which helps IE display HTML5 elements correctly. The "shiv" is designed to allow versions prior to IE9 to recognize the HTML5 elements and allow them to be styled using CSS.

Even though the script has conditional code within, so it runs only in IE, you might as well wrap it in a conditional comment of your own so only IE 8 and older download and run the code. This script must go in the head tag and before style sheet calls, as shown in Listing 3.1. It is up to you if you prefer to serve the html5shiv file locally or link directly to the http://googlecode.com-hosted file. Having the file locally will prevent both "resource not found" from any remote access issues and breakages due to future modifications to the JavaScript file.

Listing 3.1   **Using the HTML5 Shiv**

```
<!DOCTYPE html>
<html lang="en">
<head>
<meta charset="utf-8">
<!--[if lt IE 9]>
<script src="http://html5shiv.googlecode.com/svn/trunk/html5.js"></script>
<![endif]-->
<!-- put CSS after the shiv -->
</head>
```

Making CSS Compatible

Now that you can make IE support new HTML5 elements, you need to make it play nice with CSS. Most modern browsers know how to handle the new elements by default and without any styling; however, to make sure IE plays nice, you need to set your new elements to display: block, as shown in Listing 3.2.

Listing 3.2   **Setting Up New Elements in CSS**

```
article, aside, details, figcaption, figure, footer, header, hgroup, nav, section
{
display: block;
}
```

If you use a CSS reset, you could include the code in Listing 3.2, or there are various CSS resets currently available that include the HTML5 fixes:

- http://meyerweb.com/eric/thoughts/2011/01/03/reset-revisited
- Modernizr (which we will cover later in this chapter)
- http://html5doctor.com/html-5-reset-stylesheet

Boilerplates

Whether you are a newcomer or a veteran in the web development industry, you will have gathered various bits of best practices and code snippets that you reuse on almost every project. Depending how much time you have dedicated to organizing these components, you may already have your own *boilerplate*, which is a series of folders and files that allow you to start your project quickly. A couple of popular boilerplates are being advocated in the web community at the moment: http://html5boilerplate.com and http://html5reset.org. In addition, these boilerplates have already been extended to generate templates for your specific website or application through sites such as http://initializr.com, which uses the HTML5 Boilerplate.

These sites, HTML5 Boilerplate in particular, come with a wealth of documentation, instructions, and tips and tricks for your web project, which include markup, scripts, CSS, and optimization techniques.

The point of the boilerplates is not to just take it and start using it, but to understand what is in there and to add to or take things away that you either do not need or maybe disagree with, which is fine. The boilerplates are simply a place for you to start and gain the benefit of the work of many minds to provide HTML5 cross-browser support and performance structure. You may even end up with your own custom boilerplate based on the features you decide are important.

> **Tip**
>
> The HTML5 Boilerplate has a long list of features and benefits to leverage at the start of your project. Included in the boilerplate are browser compatibility models, older browser support options for HTML5, handling of mobile device design, and even an optimization build script. We recommend you check out the full feature set at http://html5boilerplate. com. And if you need an even more finished template to start with, check out http:// initializr.com, which uses the HTML5 Boilerplate to create templates for you.

BEGINNER RECIPE:
Testing for HTML5 Features

Earlier you learned how to make browsers recognize the new HTML5 elements and how to use CSS to get them to display properly. But not all browsers support all the new HTML5 features such as `canvas` or `geolocation`. Although you still sometimes have to do some "browser sniffing" to get a browser to behave a certain way, this is not a recommended approach, and with the scope of HTML5 and the speed at which browsers are developing, you can instead use feature detection methods. Feature detection requires JavaScript, so you need to make sure your markup is good enough so it "degrades gracefully" and that users with older browsers and JavaScript turned off can still use the site.

In general, the features of HTML5 such as `canvas` and `geolocation`, which are part of the HTML5 elements and JavaScript APIs, can be determined to exist or not exist by checking for their presence with JavaScript. In Listing 3.3, you perform a simple check on the browser to determine whether the Geolocation API is available in the browser.

Listing 3.3   Testing for Geolocation HTML5 Support

```
<!DOCTYPE html>
<html>
<head>
<meta charset="UTF-8" />
<title>3 Geolocation Check</title><script>
if (navigator.geolocation) {
  alert('Geolocation is supported.');
} else {
  alert('Geolocation is not supported.');
}
</script>
</head>
<body>
</body>
</html>
```

With JavaScript APIs, it is quite easy to check for the presence of the API, and we will show this throughout the book. However, if you are trying to check for the availability of an HTML5 element such as the `canvas` element, the process is a little bit more involved. The recognized approach for checking for an element is to create the element and then attempt to retrieve a default method or attribute of the element. If the value returned is `null` or `undefined`, then the element is not supported by the browser. Listing 3.4 shows an example of how to do this with the `canvas` element.

Listing 3.4   Checking for `canvas` **Support**

```
<!DOCTYPE html>
<html>
<head>
<meta charset="UTF-8" />
```

```
<title>3 Canvas Check</title>
<script>
if (document.createElement('canvas').getContext) {
  alert('Canvas is supported.');
} else {
  alert('Canvas is not supported.');
}
</script>
</head>
<body>
</body>
</html>
```

You first created a new element of type `canvas` and immediately after checked to see whether the element provides a `getContext` method. You will see the `canvas` methods later in the book, but it is enough to know at this point that the `getContext` method is an essential and default method of any `canvas` object. So, if the `getContext` method does not exist on this element, then the element itself does not exist and `canvas` is not supported by this browser.

INTERMEDIATE RECIPE:
Leveraging jQuery to Replace a Calendar

In Chapter 5, you will learn about all the new form features available in HTML5, but right now we will briefly introduce one of those new features, the `date` input type. The `date` input type displays a calendar widget to the user, as shown in Figure 3.1. Currently this works only in the Opera browser, and although it degrades nicely in other browsers by just showing a normal `input` element that the user can type a date into, here you want a calendar widget to appear in all browsers.

Figure 3.1 The `<input type"date" />` element displayed
in Opera 10.63

Figure 3.2   Internet Explorer with the fallback jQuery calendar

Here is the HTML code you need to get the input working in Opera:

```
<form>
  <label for="date">What date do you leave?</label>
  <input required type="date" id="date" name="date" />
  <input type="submit" value="Submit" />
</form>
```

With JavaScript, you will create an element in the DOM, add the date type attribute to it, and then test whether the browser supports it. If the browser does support it, then you celebrate by doing nothing. But if the browser does not support it, then you provide a calendar widget. Figure 3.2 shows a calendar in Internet Explorer. Listing 3.5 shows the code for creating this. In this example, we have used jQuery to provide the calendar functionality, so we have linked directly to the necessary jQuery files for ease.

Listing 3.5   **Using jQuery Calendar as a Fallback**

```
<!DOCTYPE html>
<html lang="en">
<head>
<meta charset="utf-8">
<title>Detect the date input type</title>
<script
➥src="http://ajax.googleapis.com/ajax/libs/jquery/1.4.4/jquery.min.js"></script>
<script src="http://ajax.googleapis.com/ajax/libs/jqueryui/1.8.7/jquery-
➥ui.min.js"></script>
<link rel="stylesheet" href="http://ajax.googleapis.com/ajax/libs/jqueryui/1.8.7/
themes/base/jquery-
➥ui.css" media="screen" /><script>
```

```
$(function(){
  function inputSupport() {
    var input = document.createElement("input");
    input.setAttribute("type", "date");
    var val = (input.type !== "text");
    delete input;
    return val;
  }

  if (!inputSupport() || ($.browser.webkit)) {
    //alert("the date input type is not supported");
    $('input[type=date]').datepicker({
      dateFormat: 'yy-mm-dd' // this format is the same format as in the HTML5
➡Specification
    });
  }
});
</script>
</head>
<body>
<form>
<label for="date">What date do you leave?</label> <input required type="date"
➡id="date" name="date" />
<input type="submit" value="Submit" />
</form>
</body>
</html>
```

The eagle-eyed among you will have noticed the following bit of JavaScript:
(`$.browser.webkit`). We have included this in Listing 3.5 because, frustratingly,
WebKit browsers *do* detect `<input type="date">`, but at the moment, they do not
do anything with it. The same thing happens with the input types `email`, `number`,
`tel`, and `url`. So, that little bit of JavaScript makes sure the jQuery calendar widget
works in Safari and Chrome. We hope soon these WebKit-based browsers will do
something awesome with these input types by default so we can do away with the
browser detection code.

The JavaScript code in Listing 3.5 deals only with detecting `date` type support. If
you have other types to detect, you may want to tweak the previous code so you can
test several input types. For example, see Listing 3.6.

Listing 3.6   Detecting Different Input Types

```
$(function(){
  function inputSupport(inputType) {
    var input = document.createElement("input");
    input.setAttribute("type", inputType);
```

```
    var val = (input.type !== "text");
    delete input;
    return val;
  }
  if (!inputSupport("date")) {
    alert("the date input type is not supported");
    //do something else instead
  }
 if (!inputSupport("email")) {
    alert("the email input type is not supported");
    //do something else instead
  }
});
```

If you have a small site, maybe with just a few new HTML5 elements that you want to make available in all browsers, then the previous approach may be suitable because it is a fairly quick fix. However, if you perform a lot of functional support detection, it is likely to become tedious, so you might consider using a JavaScript library such as Modernizr.

INTERMEDIATE RECIPE:
Using Modernizr to Detect Features

Modernizr is a JavaScript library (found at http://modernizr.com) that detects what HTML5 and CSS3 features the browser supports and makes it simple for developers to test and code for the browsers that do not support some of the new technologies. In the previous examples, we used standard JavaScript to test for features, but with Modernizr it is incredibly easy.

Although Modernizr does the detection part for you, it does *not*, however, fill in the gaps and add the missing functionality for you. Regardless, it is an incredibly powerful bit of script that developers should be aware of and have ready in their arsenal. Now on version 2, the Modernizr library focuses on CSS3 detection, HTML5 tag support, and JavaScript API support. For each of these areas, the Modernizr library has particular properties that can be accessed after initialization and used to dynamically change the source and thus support multiple experiences and browsers. Some of the property flags include the following:

- Geolocation API
- localStorage
- sessionStorage
- Drag and Drop
- History Management
- applicationCache

- Canvas
- Web Sockets
- Web Workers
- Web SQL Database
- Input Types
- Input Attributes

The Modernizr library, or in its terms *micro-library*, is simple to use and has been integrated into major and minor sites around the world. Until all browsers support all features uniformly of HTML5, CSS3, and the JavaScript APIs, there will be a need for tools such as Modernizr.

So, how do you use it? To generate your file, you have to select the features you want to test for. Selecting only a few features is useful because it keeps the file size down and it makes you think more specifically about the features your website will have. So first, you generate a file from the site and, as shown in Listing 3.7, include the link in the head tag and add a class of no-js to the html tag.

Listing 3.7   Setting Up with Modernizr

```
<!DOCTYPE html>
<html class="no-js" lang="en">
<head>
<meta charset="utf-8">
<title>Let's go Modernizr</title>
<script src="modernizr.js"></script>
</head>
<body>
</body>
</html>
```

The Modernizr script will run automatically when included and will replace the no-js class attribute added to the html element. The script will dynamically attach CSS classes of what functionality the browser supports and also what functionality the browser *does not* support. The following code shows the html tag after the Modernizr script has run and replaced the class attribute in Chrome version 8. As you can see, the Chrome 8 browser supports many CSS3 and HTML5 goodies but does not support, for example, WebGL, so it adds a class of no-webgl.

```
<html lang="en" class=" js flexbox canvas canvastext no-webgl no-touch geolocation
➥postmessage websqldatabase no-indexeddb hashchange history draganddrop
➥websockets rgba hsla multiplebgs backgroundsize borderimage borderradius
➥boxshadow textshadow opacity cssanimations csscolumns cssgradients
➥cssreflections csstransforms no-csstransforms3d csstransitions fontface
➥video audio localstorage sessionstorage webworkers applicationcache svg
➥inlinesvg smil svgclippaths">
```

Listing 3.8 shows a simple use of how Modernizr exposes different feature support in the CSS tags by checking for Session Storage API support. If session storage is available, then the .sessionstorage class style will be used, and if session storage is not supported, then the .no-sessionstorage class style will be used.

Listing 3.8   **CSS Options with Modernizr**

```
<!DOCTYPE html>
<html class="no-js" lang="en">
<head>
<meta charset="UTF-8" />
<title>3 Modernizr CSS</title>
<style>
  div.storageNo, div.storageYes { display: none }
  .no-sessionstorage div.storageNo { display: block }
  .sessionstorage div.storageYes { display: block }
</style>
<script src="modernizr.js" type="text/javascript"></script>
</head>
<body>
  <div class="storageNo">SessionStorage is not supported.</div>
  <div class="storageYes">SessionStorage is supported.</div>
</body>
</html>
```

So, in the previous example, the corresponding div will be displayed based on the support. But you could use this for any of the JavaScript API usage. A listing of all the properties exposed on the Modernizr object is available on the http://modernizr.com website in the documentation section.

Although this is useful for CSS development, Modernizr has a wealth of JavaScript properties that can be used for feature detection. In Listing 3.9, you programmatically alert the user whether session storage is available depending on a property of the Modernizr object.

Listing 3.9   **Feature Detection with Modernizr and JavaScript**

```
<!DOCTYPE html>
<html class="no-js">
<head>
<meta charset="UTF-8" />
<title>3 Modernizr JS</title>
<script src="modernizr.js" type="text/javascript"></script>
<script>
if (Modernizr.sessionstorage) {
  alert('SessionStorage is supported.');
} else {
  alert('SessionStorage is not supported.');
}
```

```
</script>
</head>
<body>
</body>
</html>
```

You can also use Modernizr in conjunction with jQuery and other libraries. Listing 3.5 uses a JavaScript solution to provide a calendar widget to browsers that do not support the HTML5 date input type. In Listing 3.10, we have re-created this example using Modernizr as our detection tool.

Listing 3.10   **jQuery Calendar Fallback with Modernizr**

```
<!DOCTYPE html>
<html class="no-js" lang="en">
<head>
<meta charset="utf-8">
<title>Let's go Modernizr</title>
<script src="modernizr2.js"></script>
<script
➥src="http://ajax.googleapis.com/ajax/libs/jquery/1.4.4/jquery.min.js"></script>
<script src="http://ajax.googleapis.com/ajax/libs/jqueryui/1.8.7/jquery-
➥ui.min.js"></script>
<link rel="stylesheet"
➥href="http://ajax.googleapis.com/ajax/libs/jqueryui/1.8.7/themes/base/
➥jquery-ui.css" media="screen" />
<script>
$(function(){
  //check to see browser does not support input type
  if (!Modernizr.inputtypes.date){
    $('input[type=date]').datepicker({
      dateFormat: 'yy-mm-dd' // same format as in the HTML5 specification
    });
  }
});
</script>
</head>
<body>
<form>
<label for="date">What date do you leave?</label>
<input required type="date" id="date" name="date" />
<input type="submit" value="Submit" />
</form>
</body>
</html>
```

You do not typically have to use the opening bit of the JavaScript `$(function(){})` as we did in Listing 3.10, but in this example we are using a jQuery calendar so it is needed. And that is all there is to it. It is really easy, and there are dozens of options in the Modernizr documentation at http://modernizr.com/docs, including the flexibility to extend the library with new tests.

Polyfilling

Being able to detect what HTML5 features are supported, either with your own code or using Modernizr, is only half the battle. Ultimately the goal is to be able to support the HTML5 functionality in the various browsers and versions of browsers that your users use to visit the web applications and sites you create. To allow for browsers that do not support a specific HTML5 functionality, you would need to use a third-party library that includes code for the various browsers to have the same functionality. The code or library of code that allows the feature to be supported on browsers is called a *polyfill* or *polyfiller.* An example of a polyfiller could be a library that provides `canvas` support for Internet Explorer since Internet Explorer does not support the `canvas` element directly but has its own drawing functionality such as Silverlight. You want to be able to develop with the new APIs and still offer the same experience to browsers that do not support them natively. We have seen examples of using a JavaScript library such as jQuery to plug some of the gaps, but there is no one library that will fix everything.

It is not just the older browsers that have holes in HTML5 features; new browsers do not universally cover HTML5 yet either. So, either with your own detection code or by using Modernizr, you will need to load an appropriate polyfill library to provide the same level of support for HTML5 features across multiple browsers. In fact, Modernizr provides a utility for loading scripts directly through its `Modernizr.load` method, which is based on a test for a specific feature, and the results can dynamically load a polyfill, which you provide as shown here:

```
Modernizr.load({
  test: Modernizr.canvas,
  yep: 'myCanvas.js',
  nope: 'myCanvasPolyfiller.js'
});
```

> **Tip**
>
> The `Modernizer.load` method is actually an aliased command to an included third-party JavaScript library titled yepnope.js, which you can find at http://yepnopejs.com. The library is dedicated to being a fast conditional resource loader with a small footprint. The library can be used separately or via the Modernizr load alias method. The yepnope JavaScript library is beneficial for conditionally loading either CSS or JavaScript through the testing of various types of data objects from strings to arrays.

There is a wide array of polyfills already developed for multiple components in various browsers; you can find a broad list at http://github.com/Modernizr/Modernizr/

wiki/HTML5-Cross-browser-Polyfills. This useful list is maintained by Paul Irish, lead developer of Modernizr, and has fallbacks for all kinds of things, including canvas, video, geolocation, forms, and much more.

> **Note**
>
> Having various polyfills, shims, and libraries available to support HTML5 features that may not currently be supported in one or more browsers is a powerful way to provide a uniform experience across multiple browsers for users. However, there can be a negative performance impact if you have to load multiple polyfills. The negative load time versus the functionality and support gained will need to be balanced in your development.

Useful HTML5 Verification Sites

We have been through various techniques and scripts to find out how to handle different browser behaviors, so here is a quick list of sites that will tell you which browsers support which features. As browsers update or if you are not sure about a particular feature, you can try visiting one of these sites:

- *http://findmebyIP.com*: Provides details on the browser in which you launch the page for CSS3, HTML5, Forms 2.0, CSS3 Selector Tests, script support, and IP details. In fact, it employs Modernizr to provide much of the information.
- *http://caniuse.com*: Provides tables of compatibility with various browsers for HTML5, JS API, and CSS3 and can be filtered as needed.
- *http://html5test.com*: Tests a set of various HTML5 features and scores your browser on what is supported. This can compare one browser to other browsers.
- *http://html5readiness.com*: Visualization of the state of various browsers in relation to HTML5 features.

Summary

In this chapter, you learned about some of the methods for dealing with old versions of browsers and deficiencies in versions of browsers in regard to HTML5. The case with HTML5 is that there is a wide range of support for the various CSS, HTML, and JavaScript additions that make up HTML5, but it is still maturing. You also learned about CSS resets and boilerplates, which contain modern up-to-date tools, tips, and techniques for web development.

You learned about the use of Modernizr, a powerful bit of script for feature detecting that enables you to offer fallbacks for browsers that do not yet support some of the new HTML5 features. We will not be showing how to employ Modernizr in the book since you may or may not choose to use it in your own site and because we are trying to show the base methods of performing functions. However, we recommend and fully expect that using Modernizr or one of the other tools mentioned in this chapter will provide you benefit in your HTML5 coding.

4

New Layout and Style Techniques with CSS3

CSS level 3 (CSS3) is the latest iteration of the CSS specification. Building on previous variations, CSS3 brings new features that you can implement in the latest browsers to improve the look, usability, accessibility, and performance of your web pages. CSS is *not* HTML5, we know this, and you need to know this, but we have included this chapter because they often go hand in hand and we are showing you just some of the possibilities available with CSS3 so you can make your new HTML5 websites look fantastic. In this chapter, you will learn about responsive web design with media queries, custom fonts, gradients, transitions, transformations, and, finally, animations. We are not covering all the new features of CSS3; we are simply scratching the surface of what is available.

INTERMEDIATE RECIPE:
Creating a Responsive Design with CSS3 Media Queries

Mobile browsing is ever on the rise, and some estimate it will take over desktop browsing within five years. CSS3 Media Queries gives you the ability to target specific screen widths, heights, and even orientation, so you can target smartphones like the iPhone or Android phone, as well as new tablet devices like the iPad, all with CSS. Table 4.1 shows the version of each browser that supports CSS3 Media Queries.

In the past, you may have used JavaScript to detect a mobile phone and deliver a separate style sheet or redirect the user to a specific mobile site. Or you might have used JavaScript to detect when a browser has been resized and then change some of the styles to adapt the layout. We have always had the basics of media queries, because we have always been able to target for screen or print:

Table 4.1   **CSS3 Media Queries Device
and Browser Support**

Android	**2.3+**
Chrome	**13.0+**
Firefox	**4.0+**
Internet Explorer	**9.0+**
iOS Safari	**4.0+**
Opera	**11.0+**
Safari	**5.0+**

```
<link rel="stylesheet" href="screen.css" media="screen" />
<link rel="stylesheet" href="print.css" media="print" />
```

But now you can be more sophisticated using CSS3 Media Queries. Listing 4.1 shows a quick example.

Listing 4.1   **Simple Media Query Example**

```
<link rel="stylesheet" media="screen and
(max-device-width: 480px)" href="smartphone.css" />
<link rel="stylesheet" media="screen and
(min-width: 480px)" href="screen.css" />
```

Listing 4.1 asks the device whether its horizontal resolution is 480 pixels wide or less. If so, then here you presume it is a smartphone and load `smartphone.css`. You then ask to see whether the resolution is at least 480 pixels wide; if it is, then you can use a different style sheet. Potentially, you could have several different media queries as you attempt to target all different types of devices, resolutions, and screen orientation. You might have style sheets for smartphones, smartphones with a landscape orientation, Android screen sizes, the iPad, the iPad with portrait orientation, browsers with resolutions of less than 800 pixels wide, or browsers with wide-screen resolutions. There is really no limit on how precise you can be.

So, you need a good way of organizing all your separate queries. Bear in mind you will already have all your main style sheets as well. Using the approach in Listing 4.1 would mean there are a lot of HTTP requests in the `head` tag.

Alternatively, you can include the media queries inside a CSS file, as shown in Listing 4.2, using `@media`.

Listing 4.2   **Media Queries Inside a CSS File**

```
body {background: black; color: #fff; font: normal 62.5%/1.5 tahoma, verdana,
➥sans-serif;}
h1 {font-size: 2em;}
p {font-size: 1.4em;}

/* styles for smartphones and very small screen resolution */
@media only screen and (min-width: 320px) and (max-width: 400px)
{
body {background: blue;}
}

/* styles for screen resolutions bigger than smartphones but smaller or equal to
➥1024px */
@media only screen and (min-width: 401px) and (max-width: 1024px)
{
body {background: red;}
}

/* styles for screen resolutions for a very wide resolution */
@media only screen and (min-width: 2000px)
{
body {background: green;}
}
```

In Listing 4.2 we have changed the background color depending on the screen resolution. All the media queries are part of the same CSS document, so it is important to make sure you keep the CSS document organized; it is likely you will have hundreds of line of code for your default design and then additional CSS for the media queries. Depending on your site setup, it might be easier to edit a media query type, for example adjusting `min-width: 2000px` to `min-width: 2500px`, inside a CSS file rather than inside the HTML of all your pages.

Using the `and` syntax, you can combine different queries. You can target several features: `width`, `height`, `device-width`, `device-height`, `orientation`, `aspect-ratio`, `device-aspect-ratio`, `color`, `color-index`, `monochrome`, `resolution`, `scan`, and `grid`. Along with the recognized media types of `all`, `braille`, `embossed`, `handheld`, `print`, `projection`, `screen`, and `speech`, you can combine these to target several different types of devices and sizes simultaneously. It is worth noting that `max-device-width` is the screen size of the device (like an iPhone), whereas `max-width` is the width of the viewing area only (such as a browser window); see the differences in the following code:

```
/* devices smaller than 480px; mobiles, iPhone and normal screens */
@media handheld and (max-width: 480px), screen and (max-device-width: 480px),
➥screen and (max-width: 480px) {
```

```
/* styles go here */
}

/* layout for iPad in landscape mode */
@media only screen and (min-device-width: 768px) and (max-device-width: 1024px) and
➥ (orientation: landscape) {
/* styles go here */
}
```

> **Tip**
>
> In the following code listings, we have used some different types of CSS selectors. The first is an attribute selector, used on header[role=banner], and the second is the pseudoclass selector, nth-xx(), used in several cases, such as section:nth-of-type(1). Attribute selectors are not new in CSS3, but with new ARIA-Roles, they give you more selector flexibility with CSS. There are plenty of new CSS3 selectors, including nth-child() and nth-of-type(). Using these new selectors means you can do away with using classes on many elements. For example, using nth-of-type(), you can select every other table row or list item. For more information on this, we recommend reading http://quirksmode.org/css/nthchild.html.
>
> Many of these new selectors do not work in older versions of Internet Explorer, so we recommend using Selectivizr (http://selectivizr.com), an easy-to-use JavaScript utility that makes Internet Explorer understand the new CSS selectors.

Figure 4.1 uses the example HTML markup from Chapter 2 for a news site. Listing 4.3 provides the condensed HTML. The CSS code in Listing 4.4 is for the default layout, as shown in Figure 4.1.

Listing 4.3   Condensed HTML for the News Site

```
<body>

<header role="banner">
  <hgroup></hgroup>
</header>

<nav></nav>

<section> <!-- this section is repeated three more times -->
  <article>
    <header></header>
    <img alt="thumbnail" src="box-100x100.gif" />
    <p></p>
  </article>
</section>

<aside></aside>

</body>
```

Figure 4.1   The news site with default CSS

Listing 4.4   **CSS for Default Screen Layout**

```
<style>
* {margin: 0; padding: 0;}
body {background: #fff; color: #000; font: normal 62.5%/1.5 "Palatino Linotype",
➥"Book Antiqua", Palatino, serif; margin: 0 auto; width: 1260px}
header, nav, section, article, footer, aside {display: block;}
header[role=banner] {margin: 10px 0 20px; text-align: center;}
header[role=banner] h1 {background: url(logo.gif) top center no-repeat;font-size:
➥5em; padding: 100px 0 0; text-transform: uppercase;}
header[role=banner] h2 {font-style: italic;}
header, nav {clear: both; width: 100%;}
nav {border-bottom: 1px dotted #ccc; padding-bottom: 20px; text-align: center;}
nav li {display: inline;}
nav li a {font-size: 1.4em;  padding: .5em;}
section {float: left; margin: 0 0 0 10px; padding: 10px; width: 345px;}
section h1 {margin: 0 0 10px;}
section article {margin: 0 0 10px;}
section article header p {font-size: 1em; font-weight: bold; margin: 0 0 10px;}
section article img {float: left; margin: 0 5px 5px 0;}
section:nth-of-type(1) {clear: both; margin: 0 0 10px; min-height: 200px;
➥padding: 1% 1% 1% 30%; position: relative; width: 69%;}
```

```
section:nth-of-type(1) article {margin: 0;}
section:nth-of-type(1) article img  {float: none; height: 200px; left: 0;
➥position: absolute; top: 10px; width: 360px}
section:nth-of-type(2) {margin-left: 0;}
aside {float: right; margin-left: 10px; width: 130px;}
aside img {border: 1px solid #ccc; display: block; margin: 0 auto 10px;}
footer {clear: both;}
h1 {font-size: 2em;}
p {font-size: 1.4em;}
</style>
```

Figure 4.2 shows the layout on a smaller screen size, using the media query from Listing 4.5.

Figure 4.2   The news site at a reduced screen size

Listing 4.5 **CSS for a Reduced Screen Size**

```
/* styles for screen resolutions bigger than smartphones but smaller or equal to
➥1280px */
@media only screen and (min-width: 481px) and (max-width: 1259px)
{
body {width: 800px;}
section {margin: 0 0 0 10px;}
section:nth-of-type(1), section {clear: none; float: left; padding: 10px; width:
➥375px;}
section:nth-of-type(1) article img {float: left; height: auto; position:
➥relative; width: auto;}
section:nth-of-type(2) {margin-left: 10px;}
section:nth-of-type(3) {clear: both; margin-left: 0;}
aside {clear: both; float: left; width: 100%;}
aside img {float: left; margin: 0 10px 0 0;}
}
```

Finally, Listing 4.6 has the necessary CSS media query for a display on a smartphone or if the browser has been reduced dramatically, as shown in Figure 4.3. Essentially, all we have done with just a few lines of additional CSS is to hide and resize a few elements from the screen at smaller sizes.

Figure 4.3   The news site on a smartphone

Listing 4.6 **CSS for a Smartphone**

```
/* styles for smartphones and very small screen resolution */
@media only screen and (max-width: 480px), only screen and (max-device-width:
➥480px) {
```

```
body {width: 100%;}
header[role=banner] h1 {background-image: url(logo-small.gif); font-size: 3em;
➡padding: 50px 0 0;}
section:nth-of-type(1), section {margin: 0 0 10px; min-height: inherit; padding:
➡0 1%; width: 98%;}
header[role=banner] h2, img, section article p, aside {display: none;}
section h2 a {border-bottom: 1px dotted #999; display: block; text-decoration:
➡none;}
nav, section article:last-of-type h2 a {border: none;}
}
```

Sensible Usage

Although you can create separate styles for different devices and screen sizes, the question is, should you always use media queries? They can no doubt be useful on desktop computers and laptops, but the mobile landscape has been changing for some time. More modern smartphones like the iPhone and Android devices come with browsers that are almost identical to desktop-powered browsers, so they can handle most things, and the interactivity of the device allows the user to pinch and zoom their way around a website with relative ease.

Using media queries generally means you show/hide content depending on the screen size. Many websites such as http://youtube.com, http://facebook.com, http://cnn.com, and http://nfl.com all detect that the user is using a handheld device and redirect the user to mobile-specific versions of their sites. The reason they do this is because their sites are content heavy with lots of data, pictures, videos, ads, Flash, and all sorts of things. If these sites just used media queries on smartphones, then the smartphone would still have to download all of this data even if the user could not see it. So, whether you need just new styles or a completely separate mobile site depends on your content, but if you just need to change the layout and add a few niceties, then you should probably use CSS3 Media Queries. For some excellent uses of CSS3 Media Queries, have a look at http://mediaqueri.es.

Targeting the iPhone and Android Devices

If you have used media queries to target the iPhone or Android devices, you may notice that they do not pick up the CSS changes for small screens. This is because modern smartphone browsers are powerful, and by default they display a web page the same as the page would be displayed on a desktop browser. Then the browser scales down the website to fit the small screen, which can often result in small text and images, so the user has to zoom in to read and browse. You can force the browser to use the width of the device as the width of the viewing area, also known as the *viewport*. The following code goes in the head tag:

```
<meta name="viewport" content="width=device-width; initial-scale=1.0; " />
```

BEGINNER RECIPE:
Using Custom Fonts with @font-face

Although not exactly new to CSS3, @font-face has had a resurgence under the CSS3 banner, and there are now plenty of options for the web designer and developer when it comes to choosing and implementing fonts on websites. Table 4.2 shows the version of each browser that supports @font-face.

Table 4.2   @font-face **Device and Browser Support**

Android	2.3+
Chrome	13.0+
Firefox	4.0+
Internet Explorer	6.0+
iOS Safari	4.0+
Opera	11.0+
Safari	5.0+

Note

@font-face was included in the CSS2 specification in 1998; however, it was pretty much unused because of poor browser implementation, font file type confusion, and a concern about the legalities and licensing issues of using fonts. Internet Explorer version 4 even supported custom fonts albeit only in EOT format.

Using @font-face, you can embed your own font with just a few lines of CSS. Figure 4.4 is using a font called Anagram (more on where to get fonts from later) for the h1, though it can be used for any element.

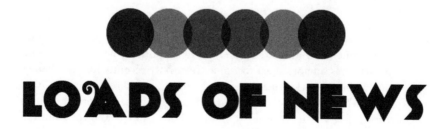

Figure 4.4   Custom font displayed using @font-face

Listing 4.7 shows the necessary code for Figure 4.4 and provides an example of @font-face in its simplest use. You name the font Anagram in `font-family`, though you can call it whatever you want, and you will be referencing it again later; see the h1 font values. In the `@font-face` declaration, the `src` for the font is in the same directory as the HTML page; you can put it in a different directory if you wanted.

Listing 4.7 `@font-face` **in Its Simplest Form**

```
<style>
@font-face {
font-family: Anagram;
src: url('anagram.ttf');
}
h1 {
font-family: Anagram, Tahoma, Verdana, sans-serif;
font-size: 9em;
}
</style>
<header role="banner">
<hgroup>
<h1>Loads of News</h1>
<h2>Bringing you all kinds of news!</h2>
</hgroup>
</header>
```

File Formats and the Cross-Browser Fix

Listing 4.7 uses only a .ttf (TrueType/OpenType) font file. Unsurprisingly, there are cross-browser implementation issues. There are several different font file formats:

- Embedded OpenType (.eot)
- OpenType PS (.otf)
- TrueType/OpenType (.ttf)
- SVG (.svg)
- WOFF (.woff)

WOFF is the new web standard for typefaces. Internet Explorer versions 8 and older need an .eot font, but Internet Explorer 9 will support the new WOFF format. And although Safari has supported .ttf for some time, only recently has the iPhone and iPad started supporting the .ttf format; previously, they needed a .svg font. So, what you need to do is deliver the same font but in different formats. To do that, you either need to convert the fonts yourself or use a tool like Font Squirrel at http://fontsquirrel. com. The @font-face Generator allows you to upload fonts and then convert them to different formats. It also generates the necessary CSS that enables the font to work across the different browsers, as shown in Listing 4.8.

Listing 4.8   **Cross-Browser** @font-face

```
@font-face {
font-family: 'AnagramRegular';
    src: url('type/Anagram-webfont.eot');
    src: url('type/Anagram-webfont.eot?#iefix') format('embedded-opentype'),
        url('type/Anagram-webfont.woff') format('woff'),
        url('type/Anagram-webfont.ttf') format('truetype'),
        url('type/Anagram-webfont.svg#webfontCiw7vqzS') format('svg');

}
```

In Listing 4.8, you reference four different formats of the same font. It might be worth organizing your fonts in a separate folder like you do for images. The previous code order is used to make Internet Explorer behave and also fixes a bug in Android. There have been several iterations of the previous code, but as browsers develop, more issues have been found. The previous code is currently supplied by Font Squirrel when you generate a fonts package, but of course it is subject to change in the future.

Type Services

Finding the right typeface can be difficult. Finding one that can be used *legally* on the web can be even more so. Font Squirrel allows you to convert fonts to the various necessary formats. To do so, you must tick a box that says "Yes, the fonts I am uploading are legally eligible for web embedding." If you tick this and are not completely sure, then you could open yourself up to some legal issues.

If you need a free font, then we suggest looking through the type library on Font Squirrel because not only does the site offer a font generator, but its main focus is providing fonts that are completely free for commercial use. Also, they do not just put any free font on there; they make sure the fonts are of high quality. Font Squirrel is not the only place to get free web fonts, but when searching elsewhere, be aware of the legalities.

Another alternative for free fonts is the Google Font Directory (http://code.google. com/webfonts). Using the API available, it is incredibly easy to use the fonts they offer. Because the fonts are hosted by Google, the loading times will be minimal. All you need to do with the Google fonts is find a font and choose "Use this font." It gives you the HTML and CSS you need, additionally offering extra font weights if the font has them. The HTML code provided to put in the head tag is similar to this:

```
<link href='http://fonts.googleapis.com/css?family=Yanone+Kaffeesatz'
➥rel='stylesheet' >
```

And Google gives you the font name to put in your CSS font stack:

```
h1 {font-family: 'Yanone Kaffeesatz', arial, serif;}
```

It is that easy.

> **Tip**
>
> You will have noticed in the previous examples that after declaring the custom font, we list some web-safe fonts such as font-family `'Yanone Kaffeesatz'`, `arial`, `serif`. We provide a fallback font in case anything goes wrong in retrieving the custom font. There could be a problem with a server, and the browser might be unable to retrieve the custom font we want, so using font stacks, we provide a fallback to a font we know is available. Font stacks should always be provided when using CSS `font-family`.

If Font Squirrel or the Google Font Directory cannot provide the font you are looking for, then other services are available. Because licensing has been an issue for years, many of the major font foundries have started to either create their own framework to allow you to legally and securely use their fonts or have partnered with a third party that helps deliver these fonts.

Services such as FontDeck and TypeKit enable you to register and choose from a range of fonts, all of which have been tweaked for improved legibility on the screen. FontDeck and TypeKit deliver the fonts in slightly different ways, but setting up, choosing, and activating fonts is a breeze on both services. Both services have free accounts with some limitations, and both offer various pricing packages.

INTERMEDIATE RECIPE:
Making Buttons with CSS Gradients and Multiple Backgrounds

You can use CSS3 gradients to make nice subtle gradients or some wacky, hideous ones. You do not have to create images, and the gradients are scalable, so once you get the hang of them, it is much less hassle than having to create, edit, and re-create images, because you can do it all with code. Table 4.3 shows the version of each browser that supports CSS3 gradients.

Table 4.3 **Gradient Device and Browser Support**

Android	2.3+
Chrome	13.0+
Firefox	4.0+
Internet Explorer	-
iOS Safari	4.0+
Opera	11.0+
Safari	5.0+

Figure 4.5   A simple CSS3 linear gradient

Listing 4.9 has the code for a basic white-to-black gradient, as shown in Figure 4.5.

Listing 4.9   **Simple CSS Linear Gradient**

```
div {
height: 200px;
width: 200px;
background: url(gradient.gif); /* for browsers that can't do gradients */
background: -moz-linear-gradient(white, black);
background: -webkit-linear-gradient(white, black);
background: -linear-gradient(white, black);
}
```

First, the gradient type (`linear` or `radial`) is set, followed by brackets that contain the start and stop colors of the gradient. You will notice that the code has four different declarations. The first is the fallback color if the browser does not support CSS3 gradients; `-moz-linear-gradient` is for Mozilla (Firefox) browsers; `-webkit-gradient` is for WebKit (Safari and Chrome) browsers; and the final background declaration is the official CSS3 gradient syntax, but no browser currently supports it.

> **Note**
>
> In 2008, WebKit was the first engine to start using gradients, and it used its own syntax style. As CSS gradients became more popular, Mozilla implemented syntax much closer to that of the official specification. However, in January 2011, it was announced that WebKit will change its gradient syntax and start using the same style as Mozilla and the official specification, which is great news for everyone, because the original WebKit syntax was more complicated and not standards-based. This book uses the new WebKit syntax.

Listing 4.10 uses input buttons with a combination of attribute selectors, box shadow, border-radius, multiple backgrounds, and CSS gradients to achieve the effects in Figure 4.6. In the `background` property, you separate multiple background styles using a comma. So, first you have the image you want to use, and then you set the gradient styles. If the gradient styles were used first, it would overlap the image.

Figure 4.6   CSS3 button gradients

Listing 4.10   **Gradient Effects for Buttons**

```
input {
border: none;
-webkit-box-shadow: 0 1px 5px rgba(0, 0, 0, .4);
box-shadow: 0 1px 5px rgba(0, 0, 0, .4);
-webkit-border-radius: 10px;
border-radius: 10px;
cursor: pointer;
color: #fff;
font: bold 1.2em Arial, Helvetica, sans-serif;
margin: 0 10px 0 0;
padding: 10px 10px 10px 30px;
text-shadow: 0 2px 2px rgba(0, 0, 0, 0.25);
}
input[type="submit"] {
background: url(accept.png) 8px 55% no-repeat #91BD09;
background: url(accept.png) 8px 55% no-repeat, -webkit-linear-gradient(#91BD09,
➡#578730);
background: url(accept.png) 8px 55% no-repeat, -moz-linear-gradient(#91BD09,
➡#578730);
background: url(accept.png) 8px 55% no-repeat, -linear-gradient(#91BD09,
➡#578730);
}


input[value="Cancel"] {
background: url(cross.png) 8px 55% no-repeat #b53109;
background: url(cross.png) 8px 55% no-repeat, -webkit-linear-gradient(#b53109,
➡#540303);
background: url(cross.png) 8px 55% no-repeat, -moz-linear-gradient(#b53109,
➡#540303);
background: url(cross.png) 8px 55% no-repeat, -linear-gradient(#b53109, #540303);
}


input[type="reset"] {
background: url(error.png) 8px 55% no-repeat #f0bb18;
background: url(error.png) 8px 55% no-repeat, -webkit-linear-gradient(#f0bb18,
➡#a46b07);
background: url(error.png) 8px 55% no-repeat, -moz-linear-gradient(#f0bb18,
➡#a46b07);
background: url(error.png) 8px 55% no-repeat, -linear-gradient(#f0bb18, #a46b07);
}
```

You can do much more than a single fade between two colors. Using a *stop*, you can add multiple colors to your gradient, as shown in Figure 4.7. Stops are added after each comma and can have a position at which they start, as shown in Listing 4.11.

Listing 4.11 shows the code used to make the left image in Figure 4.7. The gradient is becoming more complicated, but essentially each comma starts a new gradient section, and you pass it the values of a color and then a percentage at where to start it.

And you can angle the gradient by changing declarations such as left and left top, as shown in Listing 4.11, which gives the right image in Figure 4.7.

Listing 4.11 **Gradients with Multiple Stops**

```
div {
height: 200px;
width: 200px;
background-color: #000;
background: -moz-linear-gradient(45deg, #000000 0%, #FFFFFF 25%, #000000 50%,
➥#FFFFFF 75%, #000000 100%);
background: -webkit-linear-gradient(45deg, #000000 0%, #FFFFFF 25%, #000000 50%,
➥#FFFFFF 75%, #000000 100%);
background: -linear-gradient(45deg, #000000 0%, #FFFFFF 25%, #000000 50%, #FFFFFF
➥75%, #000000 100%);
}
```

There are lots of options with CSS3 gradients, including creating radial gradients, so we recommend trying some of the gradient generators to get your creative juices flowing:

- http://colorzilla.com/gradient-editor
- http://westciv.com/tools/radialgradients/index-moz.html
- http://display-inline.fr/projects/css-gradient/

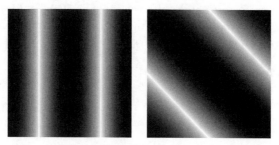

Figure 4.7   CSS3 gradients with multiple stops

INTERMEDIATE RECIPE:
Enhancing a Site with Transformations and Transitions

Previously, web developers needed to use JavaScript or a plug-in such as Flash to achieve effects and animations on a web page. But now you can do things like rotate and resize HTML elements using just CSS. Because no browser has yet to take up the official CSS syntax, you need to add CSS for each vendor. This means you will have duplicate CSS, but it needs to be done for the time being, and it is not really too much extra work. Table 4.4 shows the version of each browser that supports transformations and transitions.

Table 4.4   **CSS Transformation and Transition Device and Browser Support**

Android	2.3+
Chrome	13.0+
Firefox	4.0+
Internet Explorer	9.0+
iOS Safari	4.0+
Opera	11.0+
Safari	5.0+

Figure 4.8 shows a rotation transform applied to a `figure`.

To create the effect in Figure 4.8, you apply the `transform` property with a `rotate` value to the `figure` and the `h1`. As shown in Listing 4.12, you have to use several vendor CSS prefixes to get the effect working in WebKit, Mozilla, and Opera. There is a `-ms-` prefix, even though at the moment the IE9 beta does not support `transform` effects; we hope by the time you are reading this book, it will.

Listing 4.12   **CSS Transforms**

```
* {
margin: 0;
padding: 0;
}
body {
font: normal .9em Arial, Helvetica, sans-serif;
position: relative;
padding: 30px 10px 10px 75px;
width: 600px;
```

```
}
h1 {
left: -100px;
position: absolute;
top: 160px;
text-align: left;
-webkit-transform: rotate(270deg);
-moz-transform: rotate(270deg);
-o-transform: rotate(270deg);
-ms-transform: rotate(270deg);
transform: rotate(270deg);
}
figure {
background: #fff;
border: 1px solid #BFBFBF;
-webkit-box-shadow: 2px 2px 4px rgba(0,0, 0, 0.3);
-moz-box-shadow: 2px 2px 4px rgba(0,0, 0, 0.3);
box-shadow: 2px 2px 4px rgba(0,0, 0, 0.3);
display: block;
float: right;
margin: 20px 20px 50px 50px;
padding: 5px;
text-align: center;
-webkit-transform: rotate(10deg);
-moz-transform: rotate(10deg);
-o-transform: rotate(10deg);
-ms-transform: rotate(10deg);
transform: rotate(10deg);
}
figcaption {
clear: both;
display: block;
font-weight: bold;
padding: .5em 0;
}
p {
margin: 0 0 1em;
}

<h1>This is the page title</h1>
<p>Pellentesque habitant morbi tristique sen……</p>
<figure>
<img alt="Sandy beach" src="beach.jpg" />
<figcaption>
The view from our hotel room
</figcaption>
</figure>
<p>Pellentesque habitant morbi tristique sen……</p>
```

This is the page title

Pellentesque habitant morbi tristique senectus et netus. Vestibulum tortor quam, feugiat vitae, ultricies eget, tempor sit amet, ante. Donec eu libero sit amet quam egestas semper. Aenean ultricies mi vitae est.

Pellentesque habitant morbi tristique senectus et netus et malesuada fames ac turpis egestas. Vestibulum tortor quam, feugiat vitae, ultricies eget, tempor sit amet, ante. Donec eu libero sit amet quam egestas semper. Aenean ultricies mi vitae est. Mauris placerat eleifend leo. erat volutpat. Nam dui mi, tincidunt quis, accumsan porttitor, facilisis luctus, metus

Pellentesque habitant morbi tristique senectus et netus et malesuada fames ac turpis egestas. Vestibulum tortor quam, feugiat vitae, ultricies eget, tempor sit amet, ante. Donec eu libero sit amet quam egestas semper. Aenean ultricies mi vitae est. Mauris placerat eleifend leo.

The view from our hotel room

Quisque sit amet est et sapien ullamcorper pharetra. Vestibulum erat wisi, condimentum sed, commodo vitae, ornare sit amet, wisi. Aenean fermentum, elit eget tincidunt condimentum, eros ipsum rutrum orci, sagittis tempus lacus enim ac dui. Donec non enim in turpis pulvinar facilisis. Ut felis.

Figure 4.8   An image and text rotated using CSS

Figure 4.8 uses the `rotate` function of CSS `transform` property, but there are several others you can use: `translate`, `scale`, and `skew`. Listing 4.13 shows example code needed to implement these effects (do not forget to add the browser-specific prefixes). The code shows transform effects in use on text, but they can be applied to any element, including `body`.

Listing 4.13   **More CSS Transform Options**

```
h1 {transform: translate(100px, 200px)}
h1 {transform: skew(40deg);}
h1 {transform: scale(2);}
/* You can also chain them together in a single declaration: */
h1{transform: translate(100px, 200px) skew(40deg) skew(2) rotate(40deg);}
```

You can also do transitions and animations. There is a difference between CSS transitions and CSS animations. A transition is the transitioning between two states fired by a mouseover (`:hover`) or mouseclick (`:active`). CSS animations are timeline animations that can run on their own.

Transitions have been available for quite some time in WebKit, and Mozilla and Opera now implement CSS transitions; sadly, at the moment, IE does not. Transitions use the `transform` property shown earlier and can be applied on `:hover` or `:active`. Instead of instantly changing the values of an element when you hover on it, you can animate to those new values using the CSS `transition` property. Figure 4.9 shows a basic example of a normal text link.

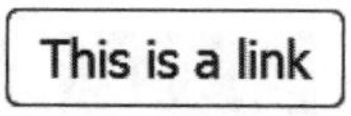

This is a link

Figure 4.9   Text link with hover effect

Figure 4.10 shows the mid-transition effect and the final effect of the link background fading to blank and the text fading to white on a mouse hover. It is hard to get this effect across in a printed black-and-white book, so we urge you to try this in a browser.

Listing 4.14 shows the code for this mouse hover effect. The color change you want to animate to is on the :hover. Without any transition, it would immediately change colors on :hover, but to get a fade effect, you use the transition property (and the vendor prefixes for WebKit, Mozilla, and Opera). Here is the key piece of CSS you need: transition: all 1s ease-in. Here you are telling the browser to animate all the properties (background and color), to use the ease-in timing function, and that the total duration of the transition is one second (1s). You can optionally include a delay value such as transition: all 1s ease-in, which delays the start of the transition and delays the element reverting to its default state.

Listing 4.14   **Animated Color Change on Mouse Hover**

```
a {
background: #fff;
border-radius: 5px;
display: block;
float: left;
padding: 5px;
text-align: center;
width: 125px;
-webkit-transition: all 1s ease-in;
-moz-transition: all 1s ease-in;
-o-transition: all 1s ease-in;
transition: all 1s ease-in;
}

a:hover {
background: #000;
color: #fff;
}
```

This is a link   This is a link

Figure 4.10   Transition effects

Figure 4.11   Photo gallery before transitions

Figure 4.12   Photo gallery image on mouse hover

So, you can achieve small, subtle effects with transitions, but you can also use them to enhance the user experience of a page. Take the thumbnail photo gallery in Figure 4.11 as an example. Using the code in Listing 4.15, with a combination of rotate and scale, you create a nice hover effect to show the image at its full size, without the need of JavaScript, as shown in Figure 4.12.

Listing 4.15   **Animated Image Zoom on Mouse Hover**

```
img {
background: #fff;
border: 1px solid #BFBFBF;
display: block;
float: left;
height: 125px;
margin: 0 10px 0 0;
padding: 5px;
width: 125px;
-webkit-box-shadow: 2px 2px 4px rgba(0,0, 0, 0.3);
-moz-box-shadow: 2px 2px 4px rgba(0,0, 0, 0.3);
box-shadow: 2px 2px 4px rgba(0,0, 0, 0.3);
-webkit-transition: all 1s ease-in-out;
-moz-transition: all 1s ease-in-out;
-o-transition: all 1s ease-in-out;
}
```

```
img:hover {
-webkit-transform: rotate(10deg) scale(2);
-moz-transform: rotate(10deg) scale(2);
-o-transform: rotate(10deg) scale(2);
-ms-transform: rotate(10deg) scale(2);
transform: rotate(10deg) scale(2);
}
```

With a bit more CSS, using the :after pseudoelement and the CSS content prop-erty, you can show the alt tag of the image when the image is zoomed in. The code is in Listing 4.16 and extends the code in Listing 4.15. This CSS shows the alt of the img on :hover, adding further information to the photo gallery. You could achieve this effect in other browsers using JavaScript, and even though we have very briefly mentioned the :after pseudoelement, we encourage you to read more about it (and the :before pseudoelement), which can be used in many creative ways in web devel-opment. Currently, this effect works only on images in Opera, so if you have Opera, give the code a whirl.

Listing 4.16   Display alt Text on Image Hover

```
img {
position: relative;
}

img:hover {
z-index: 2;
}

img:hover:after {
content: attr(alt);
display: block;
position: absolute;
bottom: -45px;
left: 0;
z-index: 2;
text-align: center;
}
```

ADVANCED RECIPE:
Creating Animations with CSS

Unlike transitions, animations do not require activation from a mouseover or mouse-click effect. Currently, animations are available only in the WebKit browser and the latest version of Firefox, but using various JavaScript techniques, you can achieve animations in other browsers. Table 4.5 shows the version of each browser that supports CSS animation.

Table 4.5   **CSS Animation Device and Browser Support**

Android	2.3+
Chrome	13.0+
Firefox	5.0+
Internet Explorer	-
iOS Safari	4.0+
Opera	-
Safari	5.0+

For a basic example, you will move an image from the left side of the screen to the right and rotate it as it is moving. It's a bit pointless showing a screenshot of this, so open Chrome, Firefox, or Safari and give the code in Listing 4.17 a go.

Listing 4.17   **CSS Animation**

```
/* CSS */

div {
float: left;
height: 100%;
position: relative;
width: 100%;
}
img {
position: absolute;
-webkit-animation-name: moveIt;
-webkit-animation-duration: 5s;
-webkit-animation-iteration-count: infinite;
-webkit-animation-timing-function: linear;
-moz-animation-name: moveIt;
-moz-animation-duration: 5s;
-moz-animation-iteration-count: infinite;
-moz-animation-timing-function: linear;
animation-name: moveIt;
animation-duration: 5s;
animation-iteration-count: infinite;
animation-timing-function: linear;
}
```

```
@-webkit-keyframes moveIt {
from {
left: 0;
-webkit-transform:rotate(0deg);
}
to {
left: 100%;
-webkit-transform:rotate(360deg);
}
}

@-moz-keyframes moveIt {
from {
left: 0;
-moz-transform:rotate(0deg);
}
to {
left: 100%;
-moz-transform:rotate(360deg);
}
}

keyframes moveIt {
from {
left: 0;
transform:rotate(0deg);
}
to {
left: 100%;
transform:rotate(360deg);
}
}/* HTML */
<div>
<img src="beach.jpg" width="250" height="188" alt="Beach">
</div>
```

On the img selector are four animation CSS properties. They are duplicated because they have to explicitly target -webkit-, -moz-. And finally, you include the non-browser-specific property names for the day that all browsers support CSS animations:

- -webkit/moz-animation-name: The name of the animation you want to use

- -webkit/moz-animation-duration: How long the animation will last

- -webkit/moz-animation-iteration-count: How many times the animation will repeat

- -webkit/moz-animation-timing-function: The type of animation; choose from ease, linear, ease-in, ease-out, ease-in-out, and a custom cubic-bezier

Figure 4.13   Background color being animated

Next, you define the animation @-webkit/moz-keyframes MoveIt. This is a simple animation so you start with a from property and end with a to value. In these properties, you are using normal CSS to move the image and also rotate it. You can change nearly any CSS property in these animations so there is a lot of potential here.

You can do more than simply using from and to properties; you can also set keyframes using percentages, which gives you greater flexibility. Figure 4.13 shows a banner that sits in the top-right corner of a page. Using the code in Listing 4.18, the background color fades smoothly between colors, with the keyframes set every 25 percent of the animation timeline.

Listing 4.18   **Animated Banner**

```
p {
background: #000;
color: #fff;
font: bold 20px Tahoma, Geneva, sans-serif;
padding: 10px;
position: absolute;
right: -65px;
text-align: center;
top: 75px;
width: 300px;
-webkit-transform: rotate(45deg);
-moz-transform: rotate(45deg);
-o-transform: rotate(45deg);
-ms-transform: rotate(45deg);
transform: rotate(45deg);
-webkit-animation-name: glow;
-webkit-animation-duration: 5s;
-webkit-animation-iteration-count: infinite;
-webkit-animation-timing-function: ease-in;
-webkit-backface-visibility: hidden;
-moz-animation-name: glow;
-moz-animation-duration: 5s;
-moz-animation-iteration-count: infinite;
```

```
-moz-animation-timing-function: ease-in;
animation-name: glow;
animation-duration: 5s;
animation-iteration-count: infinite;
animation-timing-function: ease-in;
}

@-webkit-keyframes glow {
0% {
background: #F00;
}
25% {
background: #06C;
}
50% {
background: #000;
}
75% {
background: #06C;
}
100% {
background: #F00;
}
}

@-moz-keyframes glow {
0% {
background: #F00;
}
25% {
background: #06C;
}
50% {
background: #000;
}
75% {
background: #06C;
}
100% {
background: #F00;
}
}

keyframes glow {
0% {
background: #F00;
}
```

```
25% {
background: #06C;
}
50% {
background: #000;
}
75% {
background: #06C;
}
100% {
background: #F00;
}
```

> **Tip**
>
> Transitions and animations have numerous uses. They not only add nice effects to web pages but also help designers and developers, who can create and tweak them quickly. We have shown only basic examples in this chapter to whet your appetite, so it is up to you to get creative. However, with great power comes great responsibility, so try not to go overboard with all the different effects because they can quickly turn a nice site into a tacky site. Too many transitions and animations may also affect the performance of the browser. We suggest spending time searching the Internet for examples and examining the way other designers and developers have used CSS3 to improve websites.

Summary

You have learned about a few of the new CSS features in this chapter: Media Queries, fonts, gradients, transformations, transitions, and animations. There are many more features than the features we have described; we have really only scratched the surface. There are countless possibilities for what you can achieve with these new features. If you are interested in CSS, then we suggest you do further research and study because there many other techniques and suggested practices when using some of these new features. Go exploring, and have fun playing with CSS.

5

HTML5 Web Forms

In this chapter, you will learn about HTML5 web forms and the new functionality now available to web developers. Of course, not all these new features are fully supported by all browsers, but as you will see in the recipes throughout this chapter, the new features degrade nicely. There are more than ten new input types and several new attributes to choose from, along with some new CSS tricks you can use to create forms.

Validation

Even though there are several new input types, without a doubt the biggest new feature is the built-in form validation HTML5 offers. Previously, you had to use server-side code like PHP or C# to check the contents of the submitted form and then return the page and display the errors to the user. Or you had to use some fancy JavaScript to check the contents of the data entered on the fly and tell the user whether there were any errors.

With HTML5, form validation is easy; you can provide inline validation and feedback for the users when they try to submit the form, which leads to forms being easier to complete and increases the chances of correct information being submitted. Of course, you will need some server-side code to actually process the form to its destination.

In the recipes throughout this chapter, we are adding a required attribute to most of the form elements; this is so when you test them, you can see what, if any, validation messages the browsers show. This attribute tells the browsers that the form cannot be sent without the element being completed.

HTML 4 Input Types

Very briefly we will mention the form elements that have been used for years in web development. These are still fundamental and perfectly valid form elements and are not being replaced. They will still be used widely in HTML5 and form development.

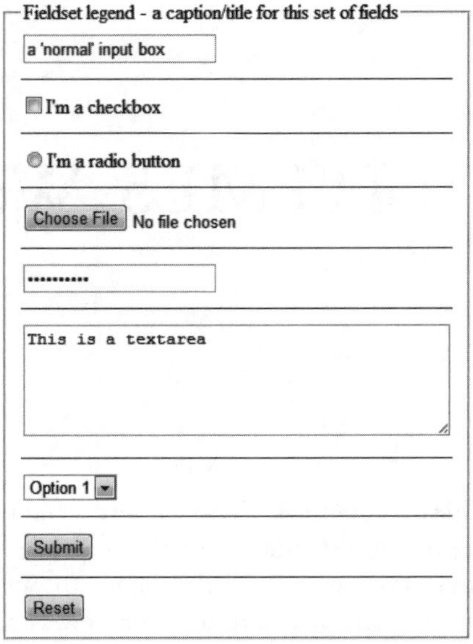

Fieldset legend - a caption/title for this set of fields

```
a 'normal' input box
```

☐ I'm a checkbox

○ I'm a radio button

Choose File | No file chosen

```
••••••••••
```

```
This is a textarea



```

Option 1 ▾

Submit

Reset

Figure 5.1   Pre–HTML5 form controls

Essentially, you have the form element, a fieldset (fieldset is an element for grouping related fields in a form), and common form elements, which give you the form controls shown in Figure 5.1.

Listing 5.1 provides the HTML for Figure 5.1. Note that an unordered list (ul) and list items (li) have been used to format this form. This is not the only way to organize a form, but it means you do not have to use the unnecessary <br/> in this code.

Listing 5.1   Page with Different form Elements

```
<form>
  <fieldset>
    <legend>Fieldset legend - a caption/title for this set of fields</legend>
    <ul>
      <li><label for="normal">Normal input box</label> <input id="normal"
➥type="text" value="a 'normal' input box" /></li>
      <li><input id="checkbox" type="checkbox" /> <label for="checkbox">I'm a
➥checkbox</label></li>
      <li><input id="radio" type="radio" /> <label for="radio">I'm a radio
➥button</label></li>
      <li><label for="file">Upload</label> <input id="file" type="file" /></li>
      <li><label for="password">Password</label> <input id="password"
➥type="password" value="mypassword" /></li>
      <li><label for="textarea">Textarea</label> <textarea id="textarea" rows="5"
➥cols="40">This is a textarea</textarea></li>
```

```
    <li><label for="select">Select</label>
      <select id="select">
        <option>Option 1</option>
        <option>Option 2</option>
        <option>Option 3</option>
        <option>Option 4</option>
      </select></li>
      <li><input type="submit" value="Submit" /></li>
      <li><input type="reset" value="Reset" /></li>
    </ul>
  </fieldset>
</form>
```

There are several new input types in HTML5 that are useful for creating forms or updating old forms. They will make your job as a developer easier but will also help the user enter correct data.

BEGINNER RECIPE:
Creating a Form to Collect Contact Information

Listing 5.2 uses three of the new input types to gather user contact information: email, tel, and url. Take a look at the code; the input types are highlighted in bold and are discussed further in the sections that follow.

Listing 5.2   **Contact Form with New HTML5** form **Elements**

```
<form>
<fieldset>
<legend>Contact information</legend>
<ul>
    <li>
        <label for="email">Email</label>
        <input required type="email" id="email" name="email" />
    </li>
    <li>
        <label for="tel">Telephone number</label>
        <input required type="tel" id="tel" name="tel" />
    </li>
    <li>
        <label for="url">Website</label>
        <input required type="url" id="url" name="url" />
    </li>
</ul>
<input type="submit" value"Submit this" />
</fieldset>
</form>
```

input type="email"

The email input type tells the browser that the content of this field should look like an email address. In Listing 5.3, we have put a required attribute on the email input. This will tell compatible browsers to examine the contents of this field before submitting the form. It does not check to see whether the email address actually exists.

Listing 5.3 email **Input Type**

```
<form>
<label for="email">Email</label>
<input required type="email" id="email" name="email" />
<input type="submit" />
</form>
```

Table 5.1 email **Input Type Device and Browser Support**

Android	**2.3+***
Chrome	**10.0+**
Firefox	**4.0+**
Internet Explorer	**9.0+***
iOS Safari	**4.0+***
Opera	**10.0+**
Safari	**5.0+***

* No validation

With browsers developing faster and faster, trying to stay ahead of the curve and of each other, there are differences in how each handles validation. The tests in Table 5.2 highlight the differences in how browsers handle forms, form validation, and feedback. Earlier, the validation messages are different from what is shown in the tests. Also notice that "test@test" is valid in Firefox but not Opera, which is the most striking difference between the two browsers.

At the time of writing, using the previous example in Chrome or Safari, there is no browser validation.

> **Note**
>
> You may be wondering whether you can style the form feedback. Well, the answer is, sort of. We will discuss CSS later in this chapter.

Table 5.2   `email` **Input Type Validation Tests**

Data Submitted	Firefox 4 Response	Firefox 4: Did the Form Submit?	Opera 11 Response	Opera 11: Did the Form Submit?
No data entered	"Please fill in this field"	No	"This is a required field"	No
test	"Please enter an e-mail address"	No	"Please enter a valid e-mail address"	No
test@test.com	No error	Yes	No error	Yes
test@test	"Please enter an e-mail address"	No	No error	Yes

input type="tel"

Like the new search input type, the `tel` input type renders as a normal text field (see Figure 5.2). It accepts any character in this field, not just numbers, because phone numbers can have non-numeric characters such as + or (. If you wanted to force the field to accept only numbers, then you can use `pattern`, which is described later in this chapter.

Table 5.3   `tel` **Input Type Device and Browser Support**

Android	2.3+*
Chrome	10.0+
Firefox	4.0+
Internet Explorer	9.0+*
iOS Safari	4.0+*
Opera	10.0+
Safari	5.0+*

* No validation

Telephone number [   ]
[Submit]

Figure 5.2   The `input type="tel"` element in Opera. It looks like a normal input text field.

input type="url"

A common requirement on a web form, such as a comments form on a blog, is to ask the user for the URL of their own website. Asking for a URL is now nice and easy in HTML5, as Listing 5.4 shows.

Listing 5.4 `url` **Input Type**

```
<label for="url">Website</label><input required  type="url" id="url" name="url"
➥/>
```

Table 5.4   `url` **Input Type Device and
Browser Support**

Android	2.3+*
Chrome	10.0+
Firefox	4.0+
Internet Explorer	9.0+*
iOS Safari	4.0+*
Opera	10.0+
Safari	5.0+*

* No validation

This input type expects the content to be a valid URL. Again, like the email type, it does not check whether it actually exists (you could do this with some additional script). A traditional URL would be a web address, such as http://mysite.com. Firefox 4.0b7 does not allow mysite.com or www.mysite.com; it requires the address to include the http://. Opera 11, however, converts mysite.com automatically into http://mysite.com, which is valid and allows the form to be submitted.

Most of the time, the content of this field will be http://mysite.com; however, it will also accept other types of URLs:

- ftp://user:password@server
- javascript:window.alert (be careful of this; you might want to write your own validation to not allow any JavaScript to be submitted)
- file://server/path
- tel:12345

Because of these additional URL types, at the moment the form would validate with hello:world. This is because most browsers have their own URL types, such as Firefox, which has about:config. So, at the moment, anything with a colon in the

URL will validate. This may change down the line as browsers refine their validation methods.

BEGINNER RECIPE:
Creating a Search Form with `input type="search"`

`input type="search"` expects a search term. It looks like a normal text field because essentially it is just a normal text field. There is nothing special about it really, but it helps browsers know it is a search field. Listing 5.5 shows how you would use it in a search control.

Listing 5.5   **The `search` Input Type**

```
<form role="search">
  <label for="search">Search term</label>
  <input  required type="search" id="search" name="search" />
  <input type="submit" value="Go" />
</form>
```

Table 5.5   `search` **Input Type Device and Browser Support**

Android	2.3+
Chrome	10.0+
Firefox	4.0+
Internet Explorer	9.0+
iOS Safari	4.0+
Opera	10.0+
Safari	5.0+

An interesting addition for WebKit browsers (such as Safari and Chrome) is that you can add the `results` attribute, which gives a little extra functionality:

```
<label for="search">Search term</label>
<input required  type="search" results="5" id="search" name="search" />
```

This code results in the search item shown in Figure 5.3. Notice the magnifying glass icon being added to the `input`, which would, if there were any, display previous search terms. Unfortunately, you cannot yet style such results using CSS or JavaScript.

Figure 5.3 The `input type="search"` element with WebKit browser-specific detail and information

Safari currently hijacks the design of the search input, but you can override that with `-webkit-appearance: none` in your CSS.

BEGINNER RECIPE:
Creating Calendar and Time Controls

A common issue web developers have to deal with is how to create calendar widgets that allow the users to pick a date from a calendar so they do not have to enter the date themselves. Creating a widget has always required JavaScript, but that is going to change. In this recipe, you will look at the various new input types that create different calendar controls, and for browsers that do not provide a calendar widget, refer to Chapter 3, where we offer a couple of fallback solutions.

Table 5.6 `datetime` **Input Type Device and Browser Support**

Android	*
Chrome	*
Firefox	*
Internet Explorer	*
iOS Safari	5.0+
Opera	10.0+
Safari	*

* No calendar widget but text input fallback provided

input type="datetime"

What will surely become a fan favorite is the new `datetime` input type. It remains to be seen what some of the major browser vendors will decide to do with this input type, but Opera natively generates a superb calendar/date picker widget, as shown in Figure 5.4.

Previously, you would have used JavaScript to provide such a complex control. Because browsers can now handle this, it could allow for integration with other services, such as connecting to your Facebook events calendar or your Outlook calendar.

Figure 5.4   The `input type="datetime"` element in Opera 11 provides the user with a calendar date picker.

Also, because the browser is handling the calendar, if your system is set up in another language, it will display that language (Novembre in Italian, for example), unlike, for instance, the jQuery datepicker (http://docs.jquery.com/UI/Datepicker).

input type="datetime-local"

Almost identical to the previous `datetime` input, `datetime-local` generates a calendar with the subtle difference that there is no "UTC" label on the right side, so there is no time zone attached to it (see Figure 5.5).

input type="date"

Figure 5.6 shows that the `date` input type is similar to the `datetime` input type shown in Figure 5.4, but here the control does not display a time option.

Figure 5.5   The `input type="time"` element displayed in Opera 11

Figure 5.6   The `input type="date"` element displayed in Opera 10.63

Figure 5.7 The input type="time" element displayed in
Opera 10.63

input type="time"

The time input type allows the user to enter a time in 24-hour format. Currently, only Opera has browser support for this element. Figure 5.7 shows how this input looks in Opera.

In this input, the user can either type in the number themselves, such as 22:11, or they can use the buttons supplied by Opera to scroll through the times.

input type="month"

The month input type displays the calendar shown in Figure 5.4 but allows only for months to be selected. The value of the input is then YYYY-MM. In Figure 5.8, the month of December is selectable. You can also select the previous or next month.

input type="week"

Very similar to the date and month input types, week allows the user to select only a week of a year. The value of the input is YYYY-W00. In Figure 5.9, the week is selectable, and it provides the week number in the left column.

Placing Restrictions on Dates and Times

There are two new attributes, min and max, which we will mention again later in this chapter; they can be used to control and restrict the dates or times of the widgets. For a date, if you wanted to make sure the user could not pick a date in the past, you could add a min attribute value in the following format: YYYY-MM-DD. It would be the same for the max attribute value to stop users selecting a date too far in the future. For the time input type, the format would be HH:MM.

Figure 5.8 The input type="month" element displayed in
Opera 10.63

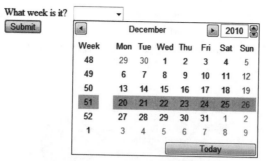

Figure 5.9   The input type="week" element displayed in
Opera 10.63

BEGINNER RECIPE:
Creating a Number Picker

The number input type is used to enter a number. It accepts only numbers; otherwise, it will return a validation error. It allows the min, max, and step attributes so you can limit the number range to suit your information needs. The step attribute allows you to specify the increment values that can be entered.

Table 5.7   **Number Picker Device and Browser Support**

Android	*
Chrome	11.0+
Firefox	*
Internet Explorer	*
iOS Safari	*
Opera	10.0+
Safari	5.1

* No number picker but text input fallback provided

Using the code in Listing 5.6, Opera creates a control that allows the user to cycle through numbers (see Figure 5.10). The number can be negative, and unless you specify a minimum or maximum, the number can be infinitely high. Using the step attribute, you can be more precise with the numbers. Figure 5.10 allows the user to step through the numbers, 0 to 10 (the min and max) in steps of 0.5. So, they can choose 0, 0.5, 1, 1.5, and so on. The user can either use the controls provided or type in a number.

Figure 5.10 The input type="number" element displayed in
Opera 11

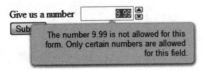

Figure 5.11 The input type="number" element with a invalid
number (only 0.5 or full numbers are allowed in this example)

Listing 5.6   number **Input Type with Steps**

```
<input min="0" max="10" step="0.5" required  type="number" id="number"
➥name="number" />
```

Because you specified the step range, anything outside of that will cause validation
errors. So, entering 9.99 in Figure 5.11 is not allowed.

BEGINNER RECIPE:
Creating a Slider (Without the Need for JavaScript)

The range input type generates a slider control. It has no text area for the user to type
into, and like the number input type, it can use the min, max, and step attributes.

Table 5.8 **Slider Device and Browser Support**

Android	*
Chrome	**10+**
Firefox	*
Internet Explorer	*
iOS Safari	**5.0+**
Opera	**10.0+**
Safari	**5.0+**

* No slider but text input fallback provided

Some possible uses of the range input type could be a "rate my *whatever*" section of
a page or a form, or it could be used to control volume on a video or audio player.

Figure 5.12   The `input type="range"` in Opera 11 (left) and
Chrome 7 (right)

In Listing 5.7, you will just look at the HTML needed to produce a basic `range` input, though in a later chapter you will learn how to make it a functioning volume control.

Listing 5.7   **The `range` Input Type**

```
<label for="range">Volume</label>
<input min="0" max="10" step="0.5" required  type="range" id="range" name="range"
➥/>
```

We have limited control over how this slider looks because at the moment the controls are browser-specific. However, you can apply a height and width to the range control. If you specify a height that is larger than the width, the volume control will render vertically instead of its default horizontal layout.

At the time of writing, Opera, Chrome, and Safari support this input type, as shown in Figure 5.12. The main difference is that Opera by default shows the increments.

BEGINNER RECIPE:
Creating a Color Picker

As Figure 5.13 shows, `<input type="color">` provides the user a choice of some basic colors with the options of entering a hex value (`#12ff00`) or using a color picker, similar to what is used in many software packages. The only desktop browser that currently supports this useful input type is Opera 11 (although the new BlackBerry browsers support the color picker as well).

Table 5.9   **Color Picker Device and
Browser Support**

Android	*
Chrome	*
Firefox	*
Internet Explorer	*
iOS Safari	*
Opera	10.0+
Safari	*

* No color picker but text input fallback
provided

Figure 5.13   The input type="color" in Opera 11

BEGINNER RECIPE:
Displaying Results with the output Element

The output element uses JavaScript to display results, usually from a calculation or from a script. It could be calculator or, using the code in Listing 5.6, to add a little extra functionality to a page such as displaying the first name of the user. It can be a self-closing tag if you don't need any additional content to appear inside it, so you have the option of <output/> or <output></output>.

Table 5.10   output **Element Device and Browser Support**

Android	-
Chrome	10.0
Firefox	4.0
Internet Explorer	-
iOS Safari	4.0
Opera	10.0+
Safari	5.0

Figure 5.14 The `output` element used to display the value of the range input type in Opera 11.

An example, as shown in Figure 5.14, would be to give the value of the `range` input type as the slider is being dragged. The default value is blank, but when the user moves the slider, the `output` value is changed and displayed to the user in real time. Listing 5.8 has the code for this job.

Listing 5.8   **The `output` Element**

```
<label for="range">Volume</label><input min="0" max="10" step="0.5" value="2"
➥required type="range" id="range" name="range" />
<output onforminput="value=range.value"></output>
```

BEGINNER RECIPE:
Using Form Placeholder Text

As you saw earlier, there are lots of new input types for you to play with, but you also have plenty of new attributes you can use alongside the new input types to improve your forms.

Placeholder text is the text displayed inside a text field when the form loads. When a user clicks or tabs into the field, it disappears. Usually, it provides a hint about what to type in the field, or it suggests the type of format that should be entered. An example would be a search form that says "Search this site" or, as you saw with the `url` input type, a hint that suggests the user start their URL with http://. Figure 5.15 shows an example.

Previously, this required JavaScript to achieve this effect, but now you can sit back and let the browser do it for you.

There are accessibility issues with `placeholder` text because currently the color of the text is by default a light gray, which is not of sufficient contrast with the default background color. You can override the text color in Mozilla and WebKit browsers by using the following CSS:

```
input::-webkit-input-placeholder {color: red;}
input:-moz-placeholder {color: red;}
```

Figure 5.15 The `placeholder` attribute in Chrome, before and after the field is activated

Table 5.11   `placeholder` **Attribute Device and Browser Support**

Android	2.2
Chrome	9.0+
Firefox	4.0+
Internet Explorer	-
iOS Safari	4.0+
Opera	10.0+
Safari	4.0+

BEGINNER RECIPE:
Creating an Autocomplete Feature with `list` and `datalist`

`datalist` is a new element in HTML5. Combined with the `list` attribute, it is used to provide a predefined list of options (see Figure 5.16), making the process of creating a list seem like an autocomplete form. Users don't necessarily have to choose from the predefined options; they can type their own answer if they wanted.

Table 5.12   `datalist` **Element Device and Browser Support**

Android	*
Chrome	*
Firefox	4.0+
Internet Explorer	*
iOS Safari	*
Opera	10.0+
Safari	*

* No drop-down list but text input fallback provided

The code for a `datalist` (displayed in Listing 5.9) is similar to a `select` element. However, with a `select` element, the user cannot type their own option if they need to do so. There is no such issue with `datalist`. Using the `list` attribute, you associate a normal input (it could be a `url`, `email`, `search`, or `tel` type as well).

Figure 5.16   The `datalist` element used to provide autocomplete options in Firefox 4

Listing 5.9   `datalist` **Example**

```
<label for="sport">What's your favourite sport?</label>
<input list="sportlist" type="text" id="sport" name="sport" />
<datalist id="sportlist">
  <option label="Baseball" value="Baseball" />
  <option label="Football (Soccer)" value="Soccer" />
  <option label="Football" value="Football" />
  <option label="Ice Hockey" value="Ice Hockey" />
</datalist>
```

In the previous example are four autocomplete options. Only Firefox and Opera currently show the autocomplete options, and they do it slightly differently: Firefox shows only options that are similar to what has been typed, while Opera shows the whole list when the field is active.

The `datalist` could be generated from a database or an Ajax call (similar to Google search engine autocomplete feature), providing the user with, say, the top 10 common answers to the question. The beauty of this new element and attribute is that if the user is using a browser that does not render this HTML5 element, doesn't have JavaScript, or there is a Ajax connection issue, the form controls render like a normal text box, and the user can type away as normal.

BEGINNER RECIPE:
Tracking the Completion of a Task with the `progress` Element

The new `progress` element is for tracking the status and completion of a task. It could be used to display the progress of a download, such as downloading a file or loading data from an Ajax call, for example.

The `progress` element has two optional attributes:

- `value`: The `value` attribute represents how much of the task (in percent) has been completed.

- `max`: The `max` attribute represents the total amount required to complete the task. Both the `value` and `max` content should be displayed inside the `progress` element so the user has feedback on the completion state.

You are downloading a very important file, please wait.

Figure 5.17   The `progress` element in Chrome

You are downloading a very important file, please wait.

45% complete

Figure 5.18   The fallback display for browsers that do not support the `progress` element

In Chrome, the following code gives you the progress element shown in Figure 5.17. The progress bar also glows, which is a nice touch.

```
<p>You are downloading a very important file, please wait.</p>
<progress value="45" max="100"><span>45</span>% complete</progress>
```

In browsers that do not support the `progress` element, you get the result shown in Figure 5.18 (screenshot from Firefox 3.6).

The idea behind this is that the green (or blue, depending on the OS and browser version) bar, or the text visual, would update live so the user knows how much time has elapsed and how much time still remains.

Table 5.13   `progress` **Element Device and Browser Support**

Android	*
Chrome	13+
Firefox	*
Internet Explorer	*
iOS Safari	*
Opera	11.0+
Safari	*

* No styled bar but provides text fallback

BEGINNER RECIPE:
Measuring with the `meter` Element

The `meter` element is used to display a measurement, such as a temperature, or to display a fractional value.

It has six possible attributes:

- min: The minimum allowed value. If there is no min attribute, then the value is given as zero. You can use negative numbers if you want.
- max: The maximum allowed value.
- value: This is the actual value and must be present when using meter.
- low: This is the low part of the value.
- high: This is the high part of the value range.
- optimum: This is the optimum value. Its value must be between the min and max. However, its value can be greater than the value of the high attribute.

The following are some basic examples:

```
<p>Your score is: <meter value="2">2 out of 10</meter></p>
<p>Your score is: <meter value="91" min="0" max="100" low="40" high="90"
➥optimum="100">A+</meter></p>
```

The meter element (shown in Figure 5.19) can be used to describe the current status of hard drive space:

```
<meter min="0" value="512" max="1024">You are using exactly 50% of your hard drive
➥space</meter>
```

Table 5.14   meter **Element Device and Browser Support**

Android	*
Chrome	13+
Firefox	*
Internet Explorer	*
iOS Safari	*
Opera	11.0+
Safari	*

* No styled bar but provides text fallback

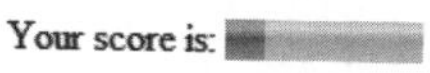

Your score is:

Figure 5.19 The meter element in Chrome

BEGINNER RECIPE:
Jumping to a `form` Element When the Page Loads

The `autofocus` attribute gives you the chance to focus a form control when the page loads. If it was focused on an `input` or a `textarea`, the user could start typing as soon as the page loads. If the field you are automatically focusing on has placeholder text, then it will be emptied because the text cursor is in the field. Previously, you would have had to use JavaScript to perform an autofocus task. The `autofocus` attribute is a Boolean attribute, so it is either on or off. Figure 5.20 shows an example.

Table 5.15 `autofocus` **Attribute Device and Browser Support**

Android	-
Chrome	9.0+
Firefox	4.0+
Internet Explorer	-
iOS Safari	-
Opera	10.0+
Safari	5.0+

The `autofocus` attribute should be used with caution. Automatically making the page jump/scroll down to content isn't the best usability practice because users with a mobile device, with a screen reader, or with low screen resolution will miss the, perhaps relevant, content above it. It is recommended that `autofocus` be used on pages where the `form` element is the main content such as a contact page or, as shown in Figure 5.17, a search site (like the form on Google.com, which does in fact have autofocus but delivered via JavaScript). Listing 5.10 shows the code used to produce Figure 5.17.

Listing 5.10 `autofocus` **on a** `search` **Input Type**

```
<label for="autofocus">Search the site</label>
<input autofocus required  type="search" id="autofocus" name="autofocus" />
```

Figure 5.20 The `autofocus` attribute used on a text field in Safari

> **Note**
>
> `autofocus` should be used only once per page. Interestingly, if you have several fields on a page, all with `autofocus`, Opera, Chrome, and Safari put the autofocus in the last field, while Firefox uses the first.

BEGINNER RECIPE:
Allowing Multiple Entries

The `multiple` attribute allows users to enter more than one value in a particular field. It can be used on any `input` type, so it could be used to create a "Send to friend" form or an email app, allowing the user to enter multiple email addresses in the To, Cc, and Bcc fields.

Table 5.16 `multiple` **Attribute Device and Browser Support**

Android	-
Chrome	**10.0+**
Firefox	**4.0+**
Internet Explorer	-
iOS Safari	-
Opera	**11.0+**
Safari	**5.0+**

Uploading multiple files is another example. Previously, this would have needed JavaScript or server-side code to detect when a file has been chosen and then display another upload option. But using the code in Listing 5.11, now you can do it in HTML5.

Listing 5.11 **Allowing Multiple File Uploads**

```
<label for="upload">Upload some files</label>
<input multiple type="file" id="upload" name="upload" />
```

Currently, only Firefox 4, Safari, and Chrome support this new attribute. Safari and Chrome display the number of files chosen. In the example shown in Figure 5.21, three files have been chosen. Firefox 4 does not automatically display how many files have been chosen; instead, it lists the full file paths inside a text box, separated by a comma, something like "C:\fileone.doc, C:\filetwo.pdf."

Figure 5.21   The `multiple` attribute used on a file input in Safari

BEGINNER RECIPE:
Basic Validation with the `required` **Attribute**

The `required` attribute has been used in many examples in this chapter. If the attribute has been used, the browser will not attempt to submit the form if the required fields are empty. In browsers that support this attribute, if required fields are empty, an error will be shown, as shown in Figure 5.22.

Table 5.17   `required` **Attribute Device and Browser Support**

Android	-
Chrome	10.0+
Firefox	4.0+
Internet Explorer	-
iOS Safari	-
Opera	11.0+
Safari	5.0+

> **Tip**
>
> Alongside the `required` attribute, you can also add `aria-required="true"`, as follows, which will improve accessibility on form elements. You may be interested to know that WordPress uses this by default for its comment form.
>
> ```
> <input aria-required="true" required type="text" id="name" name="name" />
> ```

Figure 5.22   Error message for an incomplete required field in Opera 11

INTERMEDIATE RECIPE:
Writing Your Own Validation Rule

Even though HTML5 has built-in validation, you can set your own rules using the `pattern` attribute and regular expressions.

Table 5.18   `pattern` **Attribute Device and Browser Support**

Android	-
Chrome	10.0+
Firefox	4.0+
Internet Explorer	-
iOS Safari	-
Opera	11.0+
Safari	-

As an example, you have seen that the `url` input type accepts various types of URLs. You may want to stop that and force the user to start with http://. You can do this with a custom regular expression.

The regular expression used in Listing 5.12 validates only URLs that start with either http:// or https://. It also accepts subdomains and querystrings, so http://you.site.com/search.aspx?=test is valid content, but a mailto: address is not.

Listing 5.12 `pattern` **Attribute with Regular Expression**

```
<input required pattern="(http|https)://([\w-]+\.)+[\w-]+(/[\w- ./?%&=]*)?"
➥type="text" id="url" name="url" />
```

Regular expressions can be tricky and can quickly get complicated, so depending on how confident you are, it may be best to keep them as simple as possible. And if you get stuck, there are countless answers on the Internet.

BEGINNER RECIPE:
Limiting User Input

Form entries in HTML5 can now be limited if applicable through various attributes.

step

The `step` attribute can be used on `number`, `range`, and `time` input types. It specifies the incremental steps in the numbers the `input` can take. See Listing 5.10 earlier in this chapter (with `number` input type) for an example.

Table 5.19 `step` **Attribute Device and Browser Support**

Android	-
Chrome	10.0+
Firefox	-
Internet Explorer	-
iOS Safari	-
Opera	11.0+
Safari	5.1

min, max

Seen on the `meter` element and on input types `number` and `range`, the min and max attributes set the allowed range of values on the element. These are not required attributes, and you can use either min or max, or both. These set validation rules, and the form will not submit if the min or max value is not within the range. These can be used on `date` and `time` input types to constrict the user from picking a certain value, such as on an events calendar or for searching between dates.

Table 5.20 min, max **Attributes Device and Browser Support**

Android	-
Chrome	10.0+
Firefox	-
Internet Explorer	-
iOS Safari	-
Opera	11.0+
Safari	5.1

formnovalidate, novalidate

If you have a form but you do not want to use the browser validation, then you can use the attribute formnovalidate or novalidate. Using one of these might be particularly useful if you want to save the current state of the form rather than submit, for example, if the site has a large form or if at the current stage of the process you are not concerned with validating the data because the user has other stages to complete before final submission.

Table 5.21   formnovalidate, novalidate
Attribute Device and Browser Support

Android	-
Chrome	10.0+
Firefox	5.0+
Internet Explorer	-
iOS Safari	-
Opera	11.0+
Safari	-

You can put a novalidate on the form element, and when the form is submitted, the form will ignore any incorrect formats or empty fields:

```
<form novalidate>
```

You can also put a formnovalidate attribute on any individual form element. For example, you could put it on a url input type, and the browser would ignore validation on this element (although why you would go to the effort of using a url input type and then ignoring validation is questionable).

INTERMEDIATE RECIPE:
Customizing and Styling the Form

One of the first thing designers ask is, "Can I style the new elements?" Well, sort of. Although you can't change how the date picker looks because it is generated by the browser (this *might* change in the future), you can style how the input boxes look, such as border, font, and background color, because there are CSS3 tricks you can use to style the different states of your HTML5 fields.

The code in Listing 5.13 generates what you see in Figure 5.23; notice the different field states. The fields start off orange with an asterisk image since they are required.

Figure 5.23   CSS3 used to target different states of form fields

When the field is active but is empty or contains invalid content, the box is red with an error image displayed. If the content is good, then the field changes to green with a tick image. All this without JavaScript!

Listing 5.13   New CSS3 Options for `form` Elements

```
<style>
* {margin: 0; font: 13px tahoma, verdana, sans-serif; padding: 0;}
form {padding-top: 10px; width: 310px;}
li {clear: both; list-style-type: none; margin: 0 0 10px;}
label {display: block; float: left; margin: 0 10px 0 0; padding: 5px; text-align:
➥right; width: 100px}
input {background-position: 3px 5px; background-repeat: no-repeat; border-radius:
➥5px; padding: 5px 5px 5px 25px; width: 155px;}
input:focus {outline: none;}
input:invalid:required {background-image: url(asterisk.png); box-shadow: 0px 0px
➥5px #f0bb18; border: 2px solid #f0bb18;}
input:focus:invalid {background-image: url(invalid.png); box-shadow: 0px 0px 5px
➥#b01212; border: 2px solid #b01212;}
input:valid {background-image: url(accept.png); border: 2px solid #7ab526;}
input[type=submit] {background: #7ab526; border: none; box-shadow: 0px 0px 5px
➥#7ab526; color: #fff; cursor: pointer; float: right; font-weight: bold;
➥padding-left: 5px; width: auto;}
</style>
<ol>
  <li><label for="tel">Tel:</label><input placeholder="eg: 012345" required
➥type="tel" id="tel" name="tel" /></li>
  <li><label for="website">Website:</label><input required type="url"
➥id="website" name="website" /></li>
  <li><label for="email">Email:</label><input required type="email" id="email"
➥name="email" /></li>
  <li><input type="submit" value="Send the form" /></li>
</ol>
```

We will not cover all the new CSS options, but in Figure 5.20 we have used the following psuedoclasses from the CSS3 Basic User Interface Module (www.w3.org/TR/css3-ui):

- :valid: A form element receives this class when its contents are valid according to the element type and the validation.
- :invalid: If the form element has incorrect content, then the invalid class is applied.
- :required: Any form element that has this attribute will be assigned this class.

Error Messages

We hope you have been following along with the previous examples and have noticed that error messages are displayed differently in Opera and Firefox. Opera displays a wobbly red error message, while Firefox shows a calmer yellowish error message. At the moment, you are unable to change how these errors are displayed because they are generated by the browser. This might change in the future because it is currently under discussion whether to make them editable with CSS. So, although you might bemoan that the error messages look horrible or do not meet your lovely brand guidelines, the error messages will be consistent in a browser, so it is arguably a usability win because users will come to expect these error styles when using their browser of choice.

Although you cannot yet change the style of the errors, you can change the error message text using JavaScript and the setCustomValidity() method. Listing 5.14 has an example that overrides the default error message when incorrect content has been added.

Listing 5.14   **An HTML5 Sign-Up Form**

```
<form>
<label for="email">Email</label><input oninput="check()" type="email" id="email"
➥name="email" />
<input type="submit"/>
</form>
<script>
function check() {
    var emailInput = document.getElementById("email");
    emailInput.setCustomValidity("This is not valid. Please fix it.");
}
</script>
```

ADVANCED RECIPE:
Putting It All Together to Make a Sign-Up Form

Now that you have learned about all the new HTML5 form features, let's put a few of them together, along with some CSS, to see how the new features can create a sign-up form. The HTML and CSS in Listing 5.15 provides the result in Figure 5.24.

Sign up for our amazing product. It's amazing.

Figure 5.24   A sign-up form in Opera 11 created with some HTML 4
elements, new HTML5 form elements, and CSS

So, in Figure 5.24, we have used the `tel`, `date`, `url`, `number`, `text`, `email`, `color`, and `range` input types. Also used on a couple of occasions is the `datalist` element, though we could have alternatively used `select`, but on this form we want people to type in their job titles or countries. Toward the end of the form, the `range` input type has been used and along with it the `output` element. All the elements that have data we need to capture have the `required` attribute, which will trigger built-in browser validation. And to make it look a bit nicer, we have added some new CSS3 selectors to target the required, valid, and invalid states of the elements.

Listing 5.15   A Robust Sign-Up Form

```
<!DOCTYPE html>
<html lang="en">
<head>
<meta charset="utf-8">
<title>Big signup form</title>
```

```
<style>
* {margin: 0; padding: 0;}
body {background: #fff; color: #000; font: normal 62.5%/1.5 tahoma, verdana,
➥sans-serif;}
h1 {font-size: 2.9em; font-weight: bold; margin: 1em 0 1em 10px;}
form {padding: 0 10px; width: 700px;}
legend {left: -9999px; position: absolute;}
fieldset {border: 1px solid #ccc; border-radius: 5px; float: left; padding: 10px;
➥width: 320px;}
fieldset:nth-of-type(1) {margin-right: 10px;}
li {clear: both; list-style-type: none; margin: 0 0 10px;}
label, input {font-size: 1.3em;}
label {display: block; padding: 0 0 5px; width: 200px}
input {background-position: 295px 5px; background-repeat: no-repeat; border: 2px
➥solid #ccc; border-radius: 5px;  padding: 5px 25px 5px 5px; width:
➥285px;}
input:focus {outline: none;}
input:invalid:required {background-image: url(asterisk.png); box-shadow: none;}
input:focus:invalid {background-image: url(invalid.png); box-shadow: 0px 0px 5px
➥#b01212; border: 2px solid #b01212;}
input:valid:required {background-image: url(accept.png); border: 2px solid
➥#7ab526;}
input[type=date], input[type=number] {background-position: 275px 5px; text-align:
➥left;}
input[type=color], input[type=range] {padding-right: 5px;}
input[type=range]:before{content: "1";}
input[type=range]:after{content: "10";}
div#range label {font-weight: bold;}
output {font-size: 1.3em; font-weight: bold; display: block; text-align: center;}
div {clear: both; float: left; margin: 10px 0; text-align: center; width: 100%;}
div label {width: 100%;}
input[type=submit] {background: #7ab526; border: none; box-shadow: 0px 0px 5px
➥#7ab526; color: #fff; cursor: pointer; font-size: 3em; font-weight: bold;
➥margin: 20px auto; padding: 15px; width: auto;}
input[type=submit]:hover {box-shadow: 0px 0px 25px #7ab526; }
</style>
</head>
<body>
<h1>Sign up for our amazing product. It's amazing.</h1>
<form>
  <fieldset>
    <legend>Personal info</legend>
    <ol>
      <li><label for="name">Name</label><input autofocus required type="tel"
➥id="name" name="name" /></li>
      <li><label for="birthday">Birthday</label><input required type="date"
➥id="birthday" name="birthday" /></li>
```

```
    <li><label for="website">Website</label><input
➥placeholder="http://mysite.com" pattern="(http|https)://([\w-]+\.)+[\w-
➥]+(/[\w- ./?%&=]*)?" type="url" id="website" name="website" /></li>
    <li><label for="job">Job</label><input list="joblist" required type="text"
➥id="job" name="job" />
      <datalist id="joblist">
        <option label="Space Cowboy" value="Space Cowboy">
        <option label="International Playboy" value="International Playboy">
        <option label="Web developer" value="Web developer">
        <option label="Web designer" value="Web designer">
        <option label="Jack of all trades" value="Jack of all trades">
      </datalist>
    </li>
    <li><label for="salary">Approx. annual salary</label><input
➥placeholder="&#36;" required min="0" step="1000" type="number"
➥id="salary" name="salary" /></li>
  </ol>
 </fieldset>
 <fieldset>
  <legend>Contact info</legend>
  <ol>
    <li><label for="address1">Address line 1</label><input required
➥type="text" id="address1" name="address1" /></li>
    <li><label for="address2">Address line 2</label><input required type="text"
➥id="address2" name="address2" /></li>
    <li><label for="country">Country</label><input list="countrylist" required
➥type="text" id="country" name="country" />
      <datalist id="countrylist">
        <option label="Canada" value="Canada">
        <option label="United Kingdom" value="United Kingdom" >
        <option label="USA" value="USA">
      </datalist>
    </li>
    <li><label for="tel">Tel</label><input placeholder="eg: 012345" type="tel"
➥id="tel" name="tel" /></li>
    <li><label for="email">Email</label><input required type="email" id="email"
➥name="email" /></li>
  </ol>
 </fieldset>
 <div id="personalise">
  <h2>Personalise your profile</h2>
  <label for="color">Choose a page color</label>
  <input type="color" id="color" name="color" />
 </div>
 <div id="range">
  <label for="excited">Finally, on a scale of 1 to 10, how excited are you
➥about HTML5 forms?</label>
```

```
    <input min="1" max="10" step="0.5" type="range" id="excited" name="excited"
➥/>
    <output onforminput="value=excited.value + ' / 10'"></output>
    <input type="submit" value="Sign up" />
  </div>
</form>
</body>
</html>
```

Summary

In this chapter, you learned about all the new input types and, if they are fully sup-ported, how they work in the browsers. These new input types, along with the new built-in native validation and new CSS features in good browsers, makes creating forms and providing feedback to the user much easier. Though there is a long way to go before all the browsers catch up, one day—ideally soon—you will not have to rely on JavaScript to create useful features such as date pickers, sliders, and validation. All the new input types, such as `email`, `tel`, and `date`, all "work" in browsers by, at the very least, showing a text field, so there is no excuse to not start using them.

6

Drawing with Canvas

In 2004, Apple developed a pixel-based drawing element named *canvas* for the Mac OS X dashboard that was later employed in the Safari Browser. The HTML5 specification has adopted this element and its associated set of APIs to provide basic drawing functionality. Before the `canvas` element, browsers required a third-party plug-in to render these basic drawings. Since this is a pixel-based drawing mechanism rather than a vector and layer-based system, the underlying functionality is rudimentary; however, as you will learn in this chapter, it can still provide a means to provide rich displays.

Canvas Overview

At the heart of implementing the canvas are two components: the `canvas` element in the HTML and the JavaScript to perform operations on the canvas. As with a painter, the canvas is blank until the painter uses brushes, tools, and medium to create the resulting work of art. In the same manner, you program into your JavaScript the motions using canvas shape tools, effects, and transformations. These are then drawn on the canvas, resulting in an updated view of new pixels.

The `canvas` element gives you a blank surface (thus the name *canvas*), which you can use to render graphics, images, and text dynamically. The canvas functionality is massive, so we will cover some basics such as drawing shapes and then cover some more complex effects and transformations. However, if you like this type of thing, then we encourage to do further research because we are really only scratching the surface here. We will quickly run through the basics before getting into heavy canvas usage.

Table 6.1 shows the version of each browser that supports the `canvas` element.

> **Note**
>
> For Internet Explorer 8 and older, you will need some third-party help, and that is where explorercanvas (http://code.google.com/p/explorercanvas) comes in. Because you need it for IE8 only, you can put it in conditional statements:
>
> ```
> <!--[if lte IE 8]><script src="excanvas.js"></script><![endif]-->
> ```

Table 6.1 **Canvas Browser Availability**

Android	2.1+
Chrome	10.0+
Firefox	3.6+
Internet Explorer	9.0+
iOS Safari	3.2+
Opera	10.6+
Safari	3.2+

Getting Started

Listing 6.1 has the code needed to get started with the canvas element. If you try this code in a browser, you will not see anything since no JavaScript has been added to actually draw on the canvas. A quick way to verify that the canvas has been rendered by the browser is to add a border to the element using CSS.

Listing 6.1 **Setting Up the** canvas **Element**

```
<!DOCTYPE html>
<html>
<head>
<style>
canvas {
  border: 1px solid #000;
}
</style>
</head>
<body>
<canvas id="myCanvas" width="640" height="480"></canvas>
</body>
</html>
```

The canvas element has the standard attributes of an HTML element. Minimally, you will need the id, width, and height attributes to be able to reference the canvas from your JavaScript and set the size of the canvas. In addition, the canvas element can be styled like any other element through CSS. In Listing 6.1, a border was applied to allow you to quickly verify that the canvas has been placed on the page and is sized correctly. You could also add a background color or other styles. These styles will appear by default in the canvas because by default the canvas is transparent and will render whatever is below the canvas element. This can be beneficial for overlaying the canvas on other HTML elements so that you can then draw on them.

You will notice in Listing 6.1 that we have included the end tag </canvas> in the HTML. The reason for including the end tag is to provide a fallback container and to be fully compliant with Mozilla because that browser expects fallback content. By having a fallback container, it can then display content between the tags should the canvas element not be supported by the browser. Like with other elements, you could provide an alt attribute to display text content, but if the canvas tag is not supported, then any content held within the opening and closing element tags will be displayed. This can be convenient to display anything from text to images since the canvas drawing will not be displayed.

To draw on the canvas from JavaScript, you first must grab the context of the canvas id you want to draw on. To do this, your script will get the canvas element by id and then use getContext to grab a reference to the canvas element's two-dimensional context. This context reference provides the link for then changing pixels in the canvas, as shown here:

```
<canvas id="mycanvas" width="640" height="480"></canvas>
<script>
  var canvas = document.getElementById('mycanvas').getContext('2d');
</script>
```

The getContext method can also be used to verify your JavaScript and determine whether the current browser supports the canvas drawing. A simple check using the canvas element will provide a true value if supported or a false value if not:

```
var canvas = document.getElementById('mycanvas');
if (mycanvas.getContext) {
   // canvas is supported
   ...
```

The JavaScript could then take an appropriate path of programming based on whether the browser supports the canvas functionality.

X and Y Coordinates

The last area we need to discuss before jumping into the basic canvas drawing tools is the coordinate system used for drawing on a canvas. Since the canvas is pixel based, an (X,Y) coordinate system is used to determine the particular location or pixel that is being updated. These coordinates are also used with the various tools to reference starting points, end points, and other locations. If you have used tools such as Adobe Photoshop, then using a coordinate-based drawing system will not be anything new to you. The key to the coordinate system is that the (0,0) point is located in the top-left corner of the canvas by default, with the X value increasing as you move left and the Y value increasing as you move down. As an introduction to some of the drawing tools and the canvas grid system, the first recipe in this chapter will lay this grid out for you to see on a canvas.

BEGINNER RECIPE:
Laying a Grid on the Canvas

The basis of all drawing using the canvas element is the grid system. However, for all intents and purposes, this grid system is invisible. The canvas element uses the grid system for the basic shape-drawing tools, effects, and transformations. In this recipe, you will use two of the basic shape methods, line and arc, to create a grid on the canvas with small points at the intersection of the vertical and horizontal lines. You will see how important the grid system is in using these basic drawing tools.

The canvas will be defined as being 600 pixels wide and 400 pixels high. At every 100 pixels, a vertical and horizontal line will be drawn creating the grid. To show the coordinates of the intersections, the recipe will use a canvas effect, fillText, that allows the JavaScript to apply text to the canvas element. In the end, you should have the result shown in Figure 6.1.

Let's make the grid visible now by following these steps and using Listing 6.2:

1. Create a blank HTML page with the html body tags as shown in Listing 6.2, including the canvas opening and closing tags, and fallback text in between.

2. Add the style section with the canvas id style.

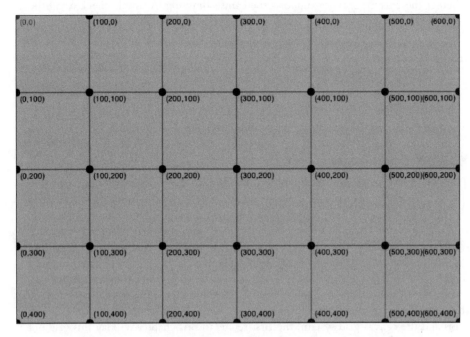

Figure 6.1   The canvas grid coordinate system drawn by using the line, arc, and fillText methods

3. Add `window.addEventListener` to launch the `showGrid` function when the page loads and the canvas and context variable declarations.

4. Add the `showGrid` function to draw the lines, points, and text on the canvas.

Listing 6.2   Drawing the Canvas Grid

```
<!DOCTYPE html>
<html>
<head>
<meta charset="UTF-8" />
<title>6.2 Canvas Grid System</title>
<style>
#canvas {
  border:1px solid #03F;
  background:#CFC;
}
</style>
<script>

// Declare our canvas and context reference variables
var canvas;
var context;

// Lay the grid on to the canvas
function showGrid() {

  // Get references to the canvas and then the drawing context
  canvas = document.getElementById('canvas');
  context = canvas.getContext('2d');

  // Set line width and color for the grid lines
  context.lineWidth = 1;
  context.strokeStyle = '#999';

  // Set the line spacing for the grid lines
  lineSpacing = 100;

  // Initialize the x and y positions
  var xPos = 0;
  var yPos = 0;

  // determine the number of horizontal and vertical lines on the grid
  var numHorizontalLines = parseInt(canvas.height/lineSpacing);
  var numVerticalLines = parseInt(canvas.width/lineSpacing);

  // Draw the horizontal lines
  for (var i=1; i<=numHorizontalLines;i++) {
```

```
    yPos = i*lineSpacing;
    context.moveTo(0,yPos);
    context.lineTo(canvas.width,yPos);
    context.stroke();
}
// Draw the vertical lines
for (var i=1; i<=numVerticalLines;i++) {
  xPos = i*lineSpacing;
  context.moveTo(xPos,0);
  context.lineTo(xPos,canvas.height);
  context.stroke();
}

// Add circles and coordinates to the grid intersections
for (var y=0; y<=numHorizontalLines; y++) {
  for (var x=0; x<=numVerticalLines; x++) {

    // calculate the x and y position
    xPos = x*lineSpacing;
    yPos = y*lineSpacing;

    // if at (0,0) then change color
    if (x==0 && y==0) {
      context.fillStyle='#f00';
    } else {
      context.fillStyle='#000';
    }

    // draw circle at point
    context.beginPath();
    // Draws a circle of radius 5 at the x and y position
    context.arc(xPos,yPos,5,0,Math.PI*2,true);
    context.closePath();
    context.fill();

    // Display the text for the coordinate
    // Check if on last vertical and place text on left
    if (x==numVerticalLines) {
      context.textAlign = 'right';
      xPos -= 5;
    } else {
      context.textAlign = 'left';
      xPos += 5;
    }
    // Check if on bottom horizontal and place text above
    if (y==numHorizontalLines) {
      yPos -= 8;
```

```
      } else {
        yPos += 12;
      }
      // Add the text to the canvas
      context.fillText('('+x*lineSpacing+','+y*lineSpacing+')',xPos,yPos);
    }
  }
}

// on page load initialize the bar chart
window.addEventListener('load',showGrid,false);

</script>
</head>
<body>
  <h1>Canvas Grid System</h1>
  <canvas id="canvas" width="600" height="400">
    The Canvas HTML5 element is not supported by your browser.
    Please run this page in a different browser.
  </canvas>
</body>
</html>
```

We will not go into too much detail here about the actual line, point, or text drawing because these shape-drawing methods and effects will be described later in the chapter. The key here is to understand the process that occurs when you want to draw on a canvas. In this recipe, you have created a canvas element in the HTML, which is 600 pixels wide by 400 pixels high. In addition, the canvas element has been styled to have a border and background color set. When the code is run in your browser, you will see this border and the background color. Since the canvas is transparent by default and the code draws lines, points, and text only on the canvas, the background style color will show through.

When the page loads, the showGrid function will be triggered. The first thing you need to do in the recipe is to get a reference to the canvas element and then get the canvas's context to be used to draw on. Once you have the context, you can set some basic settings such as the line width with context.lineWidth and the color to be used with context.strokeStyle. Then you set the spacing for your grid lines to 100, set the initial starting coordinate of 0,0, and determine the number of horizontal and vertical lines that will need to be drawn. Using this information, the code then draws all the horizontal lines by moving the position down the canvas every 100 pixels and drawing a line across the canvas. After completing the horizontal lines, the code draws the vertical lines from left to right, drawing each line from the top of the canvas to the bottom of the canvas. Remember that for the y orientation, the top is 0 and increases as you go down.

Once the lines are drawn for the grid, you then want to add the intersection points and their coordinates. To draw the points, you will draw a circle at each point with the arc tool, which you will look at in further detail later in the chapter. At each point, you also display the text of the coordinate with the `fillText` method. By default, the text will be left and top aligned, which is fine for all the points of the grid, except the right-most column and bottom-most row. If you displayed these points without changing the text alignment, then the text would not be visible because it would be drawn on the context but out of the canvas viewing area. Instead, the code will determine whether the point is in either the last column or the bottom row and modify the alignment for that position.

> **Note**
>
> Since the canvas is based on pixel manipulation, in a two-dimensional world the order in which you draw on the canvas is very important. There is no concept of layers in the Canvas API, so the order in which you build a drawing up will better determine the final product. For example, if you add the text for a signpost to the canvas prior to drawing the sign with a solid background, then your text will be covered up. Instead, you would draw your sign background and then draw your text on top.

You have just drawn your first canvas drawing and at the same time learned how the grid system works with the canvas context. Now let's look at the basic drawing shapes or methods of the canvas functionality, along with some of the effects that are available.

Canvas Tools

The canvas provides a basic set of tools, as shown next, from which you can create a wide range of simple and complex shapes on the canvas. In this recipe, you will learn briefly about each of these tools and see some quick samples of each tool.

- *Rectangle*: Draws a rectangle at a specific location with a specific width and height
- *Line*: Creates a line from point A to point B
- *Path*: Creates a path using one or more lines or curves
- *Arc*: Creates an arc given particular dimensions and employed to also create circles
- *Curve*: Creates one of two types of curves: Bezier or Quadratic

BEGINNER RECIPE:
Making Simple Shapes and Lines

In this recipe, you will draw simple shapes such as a square and triangle and learn how to draw lines and paths.

Drawing and Styling a Rectangle or Square

Using `fillRect(pos-x, pos-y, width, height)`, you can draw a rectangle or square:

```
canvas.fillRect(0, 0, 100, 100);
```

This will create a 100 pixel by 100 pixel square and place it in the top-left corner (0,0) of the canvas, as shown in Figure 6.2. By default, the square will be black in color, which is pretty boring, so let's work on adding some color.

On top of the basic toolset provided by canvas, there are a handful of effects that can be used in conjunction with the tools:

- *Fill*: Controls the fill parameters of a shape
- *Stroke*: Controls the stroke of lines used in shapes
- *Gradient*: Allows for the use of either linear or radial fill patterns in shapes
- *Transparency*: Defines the opacity level to either all shapes on the canvas or through fill RGBa values to specific shapes
- *Shadow*: Provides an easy-to-use shadow for applying to individual shapes
- *Compositing*: Masks or clips off areas of the canvas and controls the overall order of the building of shapes on the canvas

You have already briefly seen some of the methods for these effects in this chapter. The following are some of the more common effect methods that are available for shapes:

- `strokeStyle`: Specifies the color or style for lines around shapes
- `fillStyle`: Specifies the color or style used inside shapes
- `shadowOffsetX/shadowOffsetY`: Specifies the distance of the shadow
- `shadowBlur`: Specifies the level of the blurring effect
- `shadowColor`: Specifies the color of the shadow
- `createLinearGradient`: Creates a linear gradient inside the shape
- `createRadialGradient`: Creates a radial gradient inside the shape

Figure 6.2   A square drawn with canvas

So, if you use several of the effects available on the square you drew earlier with
fillRect, you can get a rather fetching purple square with a purple shadow (see Listing 6.3). For any of the effects that employ color, such as strokeStyle, fillStyle,
and shadowColor, you do not have to use an RGBa format for your colors but can
use hex values or HSLa as well. It is important to note, though, that all the styles and
effects must be done before using the fillRect method, since the fillRect method
is what then tells the canvas context to render the shape, and once rendered, the shape
is complete. Since the shape is displayed on the canvas through individual pixels, there
is no way to change the shape after drawing it. Instead, you would need to redraw the
shape to modify it, as you will learn later in the chapter.

Listing 6.3 **Styling the Square**

```
<canvas id="canvas" width="640" height="480"></canvas>
<script>
  var canvas = document.getElementById('canvas').getContext('2d');
  canvas.shadowOffsetX = 10;
  canvas.shadowOffsetY = 10;
  canvas.shadowBlur = 10;
  canvas.shadowColor = 'rgba(200, 0, 200, .3)';
  canvas.fillStyle = 'rgba(200, 0, 200, 1)';
  canvas.fillRect(0, 0, 100, 100);
</script>
```

With the color code choices available, colors can include the opacity setting, which
can be extremely handy for creating the looks of layered images. Listing 6.3 used a
semi-transparent shadow RGBa value to get the most desirable shadow effect.

There are two other methods for drawing rectangles: clearRect(pos-x, pos-y,
width, height) and strokeRect(pos-x, pos-y, width, height. The clearRect
method will clear the pixels in the given rectangle area. This will remove any pixel
changes in the area, setting the area back to the default transparent state. As you will
learn later in this chapter, using the clearRect method will be extremely helpful in
animation and can be used to clear the entire canvas by using the canvas dimensions
for the width and height or to clear just a particular area. strokeRect, in combination
with lineWidth, will draw a stroke at the coordinates and the width and height you
set it. Using a combination of these shapes and effects, as in Listing 6.4, will create an
even more unique image.

Listing 6.4 **More Styling Options**

```
var canvas = document.getElementById('canvas').getContext('2d');
canvas.shadowOffsetX = 10;
canvas.shadowOffsetY = 10;
canvas.shadowBlur = 10;
canvas.shadowColor = 'rgba(200, 0, 200, .3)';
```

```
canvas.fillStyle = 'rgba(200, 0, 200, 1)';
canvas.strokeStyle = '#09c';
canvas.lineWidth = 5;
canvas.fillRect(0, 0, 100, 100);
canvas.clearRect(25, 25, 50, 50);
canvas.strokeRect(25, 25, 50, 50);
```

Applying Gradients to Shapes

Another effect you can use with canvas shapes is a gradient. Gradient fills in the canvas can be created either through a linear (createLinearGradient) or radial (createRadialGradient) gradient. To add colors to the gradient, use the addColorStop property. Listing 6.5 creates two rectangles with the two gradient types.

Listing 6.5   **Creating Gradients**

```
<canvas id="canvas" width="640" height="480"></canvas>
<script>
  var canvas = document.getElementById('canvas').getContext('2d');
  var grd = canvas.createLinearGradient(0, 200, 200, 0);
  grd.addColorStop(0, '#000');
  grd.addColorStop(.5, '#ccc');
  grd.addColorStop(1, '#000');
  canvas.fillStyle = grd;
  canvas.strokeStyle = '#09c';
  canvas.lineWidth = 5;
  canvas.fillRect(0, 0, 200, 200);
  canvas.closePath();

  var grd = canvas.createRadialGradient(300, 250, 2, 200, 200, 250);
  grd.addColorStop(0, '#000'); // light blue
  grd.addColorStop(1, '#ccc'); // dark blue
  canvas.fillStyle = grd;
  canvas.fillRect(200, 200, 200, 200);
  canvas.closePath();
</script>
```

Listing 6.5 creates an upper-left rectangle with a linear gradient and a lower-right rectangle with a radial gradient. Both gradient methods employ different parameters to control the behavior of the gradient, as shown here:

```
createLinearGradient(startX, startY, endX, endY)
createRadialGradient(startX, startY, startRadius, endX, endY, endRadius)
```

The radial gradient method can get a little complicated, so it is worth playing around with this; try adding various addColorStop to see what happens.

Drawing Lines and Paths

To draw a line using canvas, three methods make up the process:

- `moveTo(x,y)`: Moves the current location on the canvas grid to the first point of the line; the line will be drawn from here.
- `lineTo(x,y)`: Tells the canvas where the end point will be on the line.
- `stroke()`: Called to have the canvas draw the line. If the stroke style has not been set with the `strokeStyle` method, then the default color of the line will be black.

In Listing 6.6, you start the line 10 pixels from the top left and, using `lineTo`, set the end of the line to 10 pixels from the bottom-right corner of the canvas, as shown in Figure 6.3.

Listing 6.6   **Drawing a Line**

```
<canvas id="canvas" width="640" height="480"></canvas>
<script>
  var canvas = document.getElementById('canvas').getContext('2d');
  canvas.moveTo(10,10);
  canvas.lineTo(630, 470);
  canvas.stroke();
</script>
```

Remember that the options for the line, such as width and color, must be set prior to calling the stroke method so that the style is rendered properly.

You can use `lineTo` as many times as you want to draw a variety of shapes by creating a "path" that the line takes. Let's look at drawing a triangle in Listing 6.7, which uses `lineTo` three times to draw the three sides of the triangle.

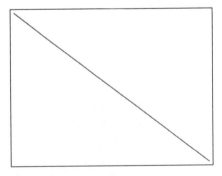

Figure 6.3   A line drawn with canvas

Listing 6.7   **Drawing a Triangle**

```
<canvas id="canvas" width="640" height="480"></canvas>
<script>
  var canvas = document.getElementById('canvas').getContext('2d');

  canvas.beginPath();
  canvas.moveTo(10,10);
  canvas.lineTo(630, 470); //diagonal line
  canvas.lineTo(10, 470); //bottom line
  canvas.lineTo(10, 10); //left line
  canvas.closePath();

  canvas.strokeStyle = '#000';
  canvas.lineWidth = 3;

  canvas.fillStyle = '#ccc';
  canvas.fill();

  canvas.stroke();
</script>
```

To have the lines create one path, you will use two new methods: `beginPath` and `closePath`. `beginPath` tells the canvas that the lines, or curves that come after, belong to one path object that is "closed" when the `closePath` method is executed. The path of lines or curves can then be treated as one object, similar to a rectangle, and then can be styled similarly.

Previewing the shape using the code in Listing 6.7, you will notice that where the line ends (top-left corner), it is a little rough, because the lines don't meet smoothly. Well, there is a method for that, `lineCap`, which accepts a value of `butt`, `round`, or `square`. This will cap the end of the line, but what about the other points of the triangle? You can use the `lineJoin` method for that, which accepts a value of `bevel`, `miter`, or `round`:

```
canvas.lineCap = 'round';
canvas.lineJoin = 'round';
```

Paths can include segments that are created not only from lines but also from curves, as you will see later.

INTERMEDIATE RECIPE:
Drawing Polygons with a Path

In this recipe, you will use the line drawing and path functionality of the Canvas API to draw a regular polygon based on a number of sides and radius provided by the user. Because the polygon is created by employing the path feature, you can then fill in the shape with color. To create the polygon, JavaScript will create a line from and to each vertex of the polygon based on mathematical formulas to determine the coordinates of the vertices. The recipe can be created by following the steps and using the code in Listing 6.8:

1. Create the page in Listing 6.8 with the `style` and `body` tags for the canvas.

2. Add the input fields for the number of sides and radius along with the button to trigger the drawing of the polygon.

3. Add the `init` function, global variables, and load event handler to set the global references to the canvas and context.

4. Add the `drawPolygon` function, which is the worker function for drawing the actual regular polygon.

Listing 6.8 **Drawing Polygons with Paths**

```
<!DOCTYPE html>
<html>
<head>
<meta charset="UTF-8" />
<title>6.8 Drawing Polygons with Paths</title>
<style>
#canvas {
  border:1px solid #03F;
}
</style>
<script>
// Global variables for the canvas and context
var canvas;
var context;

// initialization function when the page loads
function init() {

  // set the button handler
  var btnDrawPolygon = document.getElementById('drawPolygon');
  btnDrawPolygon.addEventListener('click',drawPolygon,false);

  // set references to the canvas and context
  canvas = document.getElementById('canvas');
  context = canvas.getContext('2d');
}

// function to draw the polygon on the canvas
function drawPolygon() {

  // Retrieve the user input for the polygon
  var numSides = document.getElementById('numSides').value;
  var radius = document.getElementById('radius').value;
```

```
    // Get our canvas center point to center the polygon
    var xCenter = parseInt(canvas.width/2);
    var yCenter = parseInt(canvas.height/2);

    // Clear the canvas
    context.clearRect(0,0,canvas.width,canvas.height);

    // Begin our path
    context.beginPath();

    // Map the first vertice to start with
    var xPos = xCenter + radius * Math.cos(2 * Math.PI * 0 / numSides);
    var yPos = yCenter + radius * Math.sin(2 * Math.PI * 0 / numSides);
    context.moveTo(xPos,yPos);

    // Loop through the vertices and map the lines
    for (i = 1; i <= numSides; i++) {

      // Determine the coordinates of the next vertex
      xPos = xCenter + radius * Math.cos(2 * Math.PI * i / numSides);
      yPos = yCenter + radius * Math.sin(2 * Math.PI * i / numSides);

      // Set line to the next vertex
      context.lineTo(xPos,yPos);
    }

    // Close our path of lines
    context.closePath();

    // Set the line properties and draw the lines
    context.lineWidth = 30;
    context.lineJoin = 'round';
    context.stroke();

    // Fill our new polygon
    context.fillStyle = '#00F';
    context.fill();
}

// call the init function on page load
window.addEventListener('load',init,false);

</script>
</head>
<body>
  <h1>Canvas Path Usage:</h1>
  <canvas id="canvas" width="400" height="400">
```

```
     The canvas element is not supported in your browser.
   </canvas>
   <br>
   Number of Sides: <input type="number" id="numSides" min="3" step="1" value="7"
➡ /><br>
   Radius: <input type="number" id="radius" min="10" step="1" value="150" /><br>
   <button id="drawPolygon">Draw Polygon</button>
</body>
</html>
```

Upon clicking the Create Polygon button, the `drawPolygon` function will be called. First, the function retrieves the user inputs for the number of sides and radius for the polygon. Next, the function finds the center point for the canvas to place the polygon in the center of the canvas. Then, you clear the canvas, using the `clearRect` function, so that you start with a blank canvas each time the user creates a new polygon.

Now that the canvas is set, you begin the path with the `beginPath` method. Then with some fancy algorithms, you calculate the beginning X,Y coordinate and loop through each vertex using `lineTo` to create the segments. Once all the line segments have been built, the path is closed with the `closePath` method. The `closePath` method joins all the line segments into one path, which you then use to set the line and fill of the polygon, resulting in the polygon being drawn on the canvas, as shown in Figure 6.4.

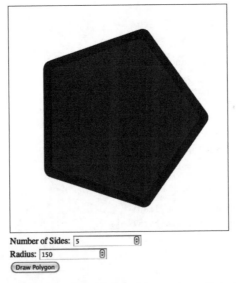

Figure 6.4 Polygon created with five sides and a radius of 150 via the path functionality

INTERMEDIATE RECIPE:
Drawing Arcs and Circles

You are not limited to just straight lines with canvas; you can add curves, too. You start with the `arc` method, which accepts the following values:

```
canvas.arc(x, y, radius, startAngle, endAngle, antiClockwise(Boolean));
```

Let's look at an example in Listing 6.9, which results in Figure 6.5.

Listing 6.9   **Drawing an Arc**

```
<canvas id="canvas" width="640" height="480"></canvas>
<script>
  var canvas = document.getElementById('canvas').getContext('2d');
  canvas.arc(100, 100, 40, 5, 1, true);
  canvas.strokeStyle = '#000';
  canvas.lineWidth = 5;
  canvas.stroke();
</script>
```

In Listing 6.9, you set the `antiClockwise` value to true. Try setting it to false and see what is drawn.

To draw a circle, use the `arc()` method, start the angle with 0, and end it with `2*Math.PI`:

```
canvas.arc(100, 150, 60, 0, 2 * Math.PI, false);
canvas.fillStyle = '#000';
canvas.fill();
canvas.strokeStyle = '#000';
canvas.lineWidth = 2;
```

Drawing Curves

Two types of curves are available in canvas: `quadraticCurveTo` and `bezierCurveTo`. The difference between the two is that `quadraticCurveTo` has one control point, whereas `bezierCurveTo` has two. The control points enable you to add curves to lines so you can create more complex shapes:

```
canvas.quadraticCurveTo(cX, cY, endX, endY);
canvas.bezierCurveTo(c1X, c1Y, c2X, c2Y, endX, endY);
```

Figure 6.5   An arc drawn with canvas

BEGINNER RECIPE:
Adding Text

The Canvas API provides two methods for adding text to the canvas: `fillText` and `strokeText`. `fillText` takes a string to display along with the X,Y coordinate to display the text at and creates the text string as filled letters, while the `strokeText` method takes the same parameters but creates an outline of the text characters:

```
fillText(text, x, y);
```

In both cases, the font type, weight, and size can be modified through the `font` property, and the fill stroke style can be controlled via the `fillStyle` and `strokeStyle` canvas properties, as shown in Listing 6.10.

Listing 6.10   Adding Text to the Canvas

```
<script>
    var canvas = document.getElementById('canvas').getContext('2d');
    canvas.font = 'bold 80px Tahoma';
    canvas.fillStyle = '#000';
    canvas.fillText('HTML5 Canvas', 10, 100);

    canvas.strokeStyle = '#000';
    canvas.lineWidth = 3;
    canvas.fillStyle = '#ccc';
    canvas.textAlign = 'center';
    canvas.fillText('HTML5 Canvas', 320, 200);
    canvas.strokeText('HTML5 Canvas', 320, 200);
</script>
```

Listing 6.10 results in Figure 6.6. Notice that in `fillText` and `strokeText`, after the string value, are the X and Y coordinates where the text will be drawn. Also, for the second example, the text is aligned to the center, and both `fillText` and `strokeText` are used, so if you just wanted a text outline, then remove `fillText`.

Figure 6.6   Text drawn on the canvas

BEGINNER RECIPE:
Drawing an Image

One of the more interesting areas of the Canvas API is the inclusion of images. With the drawImage method, you can include an image of your choosing and manipulate the image in multiple ways. The simple example shown in Listing 6.11 loads a PNG image file and results in the display in Figure 6.7.

Listing 6.11   **Drawing an Image**

```
<canvas id="canvas" width="640" height="480"></canvas>
<script>
  var canvas = document.getElementById('canvas').getContext('2d');
  var canvasImage = new Image();

  function drawCanvasImage(){
    canvas.drawImage(canvasImage, 155, 0);
  };

  canvasImage.addEventListener('load',drawCanvasImage,false);

  canvasImage.src = 'images/html5-logo.png';
</script>
```

The drawImage function has three different formats:

- drawImage(image, dx, dy): Displays an image provided in the image URL at the location x and y
- drawImage(image, dx, dy, dw, dh): Scales the image based on the display width (dw) and display height (dh)
- drawImage(image, sx, sy, sw, sh, dx, dy, dw, dh): Crops a section of the image based on the X,Y coordinate and width and height provided by (sx, sy, sw, and sh)

Figure 6.7   An image drawn onto a canvas
(the HTML5 logo is attributed to the W3C, www.w3.org)

The basic `drawImage` method takes the URL of the image and then the x and y position to display the image at. The image is not scaled or cropped in any way. In Listing 6.11, the `load` event is used to verify that the image has loaded prior to trying to display the image on the canvas. If you pass the image URL directly into the variables, then nothing will display because the image will not have loaded in to the page. So, to confirm that the image has loaded prior to asking the canvas to display the image, you listen for the load image event.

In Figure 6.4, you can see the image just barely fits inside our canvas frame; you can resize the image by using the `drawImage` method with scaling width and height options:

```
drawImage(image, x, y, width, height);
```

In this manner, the script passes in the additional width and height values, such as `canvas.drawImage(canvasImage, 50, 50, 150, 211);`, which will resize the image to 150 pixels wide by 211 pixels tall and position it 50 pixels from the top and left.

INTERMEDIATE RECIPE:
Cropping an Image

You can also crop the image, by using the third method signature, which includes cropping properties. The cropping properties are the start X and Y positions in the image and the width and height of the cropping frame. It gets a little complicated, so Listing 6.12 has comments next to each value.

Listing 6.12   **Cropping an Image**

```
function cropImage(){
  canvas.drawImage(canvasImage,
  0, // position X inside the crop
  0, // position Y inside the crop
  168, // source image width
  236, // source image height
  110, //crop position X
  110, //crop position Y
  250, //crop width
  250 //crop width
  );
);

canvasImage.addEventListener('load',cropImage,false);
```

In addition to simply drawing the image on the canvas, the API provides a means to use the image to also fill a given shape. Using the `createPattern` method, you can use an image to fill the background of a shape. First, the image is passed that you want displayed; then a `pattern` variable is created with the image. Then a shape is drawn, using coordinates and a size. The fill style of the shape is then assigned to the pattern that was created, as shown here:

```
var canvasImage = new Image();
function createImagePattern(){
  var pattern = canvas.createPattern(canvasImage, 'repeat');
  canvas.rect(0, 0, 640, 480);
  canvas.fillStyle = pattern;

  canvas.fill();
);
canvasImage.addEventListener('load',createImagePattern,false);

canvasImage.src = 'images/html5-logo.png';
```

The `repeat` parameter can have the following values:

- repeat: Repeats the pattern horizontally and vertically
- repeat-x: Repeats the pattern horizontally
- repeat-y: Repeats the pattern vertically
- no-repeat: Does not repeat the pattern

INTERMEDIATE RECIPE:
Animating a Sprite Map

Since the `drawImage` method can be used to crop a source image and draw the resulting subimage onto the canvas, you can use the same effect to animate sprite maps by cycling through the frames of the sprite image. On a set interval, the `drawImage` method is called to render a new frame of the source image each time, thus creating an animation. In this recipe, you will use a simple sprite map of three frames to animate a recycle icon. Each time the `drawImage` is called, the frame moves to the next frame. After reaching the last frame, the frame is moved back to the first frame of the source image. To create this example, use the following steps and Listing 6.13:

1. Create the page in Listing 6.13 with the `style` and `body` tags for the canvas and including the buttons to start and stop the animation.
2. Add the global variable definitions, `init` function, and `window.addEventHandler` event handler.
3. Add the `animateSprite` function, which draws the cropped image.
4. Add the `startAnimation` and `stopAnimation` functions, which are tied to the start and stop animation buttons.

Listing 6.13 **Using Image Cropping with Sprite Maps**

```
<!DOCTYPE html>
<html>
<head>
<meta charset="UTF-8" />
<title>6.13 Sprint Slice Animation</title>
<style>
#canvas {
  /* Place border on our canvas */
  border:1px solid #03F;
}
</style>
<script>
// canvas and context variables for drawing
var canvas;
var context;

// Image holder for our animation
var spriteRecycle = new Image();

// Sprite image frame variables
var sliceX = 0;
var sliceY = 0;
var sliceWidth = 100;
var sliceHeight = 100;

// animation variable
var intervalRef;

// initialize the canvas
function init() {
  // Set the button handlers
  var btnStart = document.getElementById('start');
  var btnStop = document.getElementById('stop');
  btnStart.addEventListener('click',startAnimation,false);
  btnStop.addEventListener('click',stopAnimation,false);

  // Retrieve reference to the canvas and context
  canvas = document.getElementById('canvas');
  context = canvas.getContext('2d');

  // Assign the source of our image
  spriteRecycle.src = 'recycle_sprite.png';
}

// Animate image based on slice
function animateSprite() {
```

```
  // Draw the image based on the current sprite slice
  context.drawImage(spriteRecycle, sliceX, sliceY, sliceWidth, sliceHeight, 0, 0,
➡100, 100);

  // Increment the slice of the sprite
  sliceX+=100;
  // Reset the slice to the first frame if needed
  if (sliceX>=spriteRecycle.width) {
    sliceX = 0;
  }
}


// Start the animation by setting an interval
function startAnimation() {
  intervalRef = setInterval('animateSprite()',100);
}


// Stop the animation by clearing the interval set
function stopAnimation() {
  clearInterval(intervalRef);
  // erase the canvas with clearRect
  context.clearRect(0,0,100,100);
}


// call the init function on page load
window.addEventListener('load',init,false);

</script>
</head>
<body>
  <h1>Sprite Map Animation with Canvas</h1>
  <canvas id="canvas" width="100" height="100">
    The Canvas element is not supported in this browser.
  </canvas>
  <br>
  <button id="start">Start</button>
  <button id="stop">Stop</button>
</body>
</html>
```

After the startAnimation function is called when the user clicks the start button, the function sets an interval for 100 milliseconds to launch the animateSprite
function. This is the heart of the animation timing. Each 100 milliseconds, the
animateSprite function will be called until the stopAnimation function is called
and clears the interval. Each time the animateSprite function is run, a slice of the
recycle image will be displayed. The recycle image is 300 pixels wide and contains

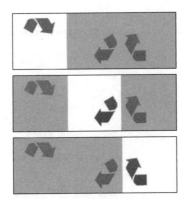

Figure 6.8   Slice frames of the sprite image as they are displayed with
each cycle

three slices that are 100 by 100 pixels. After each drawing of the slice, the slice horizontal position is moved 100 pixels to the right, as shown in Figure 6.8. If the slice is
already on the last 100 pixels, then the slice is moved back to 0.

Note that you do not have to clear the canvas before each `drawImage` because the
sprite image has an opaque background and you are drawing over the entire 100 by
100 pixel canvas each time.

> **Note**
>
> Even though the `canvas` element does not support layers in the canvas itself, there is
> a way you can imitate the functionality of layers. Since the canvas is an element on the
> page that can be styled and has a transparent background by default, there is nothing
> preventing developers from having multiple `canvas` elements defined that are positioned
> on top of each other. To control the layer position on the page, the `z-index` style attri-
> bute on the element would be used. It would not be too far-fetched to imagine a game
> that has a background canvas while a character sprite is loaded in a smaller canvas that
> is positioned on top of the other canvas. If you implement a multiple-canvas page, be
> cautious of performance issues since references must be kept to the individual `canvas`
> elements to use them.

Canvas Transformations

In addition to the canvas tools and effects that are available, a handful of transformation tools are available for use. The following are the three transformation tools
available:

- `rotate(angle)`: Rotates the underlying context grid of the canvas so that anything added to the rotated context appears rotated to the user. The angle is in
  radians and is measured clockwise.

- `scale(x, y)`: Allows the developer to control the scale for the x and y units. The scale method takes the x unit scale and y unit scale as parameters.
- `transform`: This transformation provides the developer with access directly into the transformation matrix.

Three methods are associated with the canvas that assist in performing a transformation. The `translate(x, y)` canvas method allows you to move the point of origin of the canvas to a new location. So, if you called `translate(100,100)`, the new origin point would be shifted 100 pixels down and 100 pixels to the right and become your new point of origin. This is extremely important with transformations such as rotation, because the point of origin is the point around which the rotation is performed. There are two ways to return the point of origin to the original location. The first is to simply use the `translate` method again to return the location in the opposite directions. The second and preferred method is to use the `save` and `restore` canvas methods.

The `save` and `restore` methods allow you to save the current context prior to any transformation and then restore the context to the saved version at a later time. We will use this pattern along with the `rotate` method in various recipes to demonstrate transformations with canvas. The `rotate` method takes a number of radians to rotate the canvas orientation. To convert angle degrees to radians, use the following formula:

Angle in Radians = angle in degrees * Pi / 180

Through the use of transformations such as the `rotate` and `scale` methods, you can use the canvas to create interesting animations, as shown in the next recipe.

> **Note**
>
> As with any base set of API calls that lend themselves to enlarged and repetitive functionality, such as drawing squares, circles, and so on, from the base components, extended libraries of calls have been created by various developers. In turn, many of these libraries have been productized and can provide a basis for enveloping the canvas functionality in simpler calls. In addition, the libraries have typically extended the functionality, making more complex features easier to employ. Some libraries that you may want to check out include netron, canvas toolkit, EaselJS, jCanvaScript, and gury. As the HTML5 canvas gains in popularity, we are sure that the number and breadth of libraries will continue to increase.

ADVANCED RECIPE:
Animating an Image

In this recipe, you will use two steps to "roll" a gear across the canvas from left to right. The first step will be to move the image by redrawing the image on a given interval to the right. The second step will be to rotate the image a certain number of degrees each time you move the image. As shown earlier, the rotate effect is used to rotate the context of the drawing. In this example, you will save the default canvas context and then rotate the context, draw the image, and finally restore the context. In this manner and with the combination of these methods, the code in Listing 6.14 will create the illusion that the gear image is rolling across the screen.

1. Create the page in Listing 6.14 with the `style` and `body` tags for the canvas.

2. Add the global variable definitions, `init` function, and `window.addEventListener` event handler.

3. Add the `moveGear` function, which rotates, moves, and draws the gear image.

Listing 6.14   Moving and Rotating an Image

```
<!DOCTYPE html>
<html>
<head>
<meta charset="UTF-8" />
<title>6.14 Moving Gear</title>
<style>
#canvas {
  /* apply a simple border to the canvas */
  border:1px solid #03F;
}
</style>
<script>

// canvas and context reference variables for drawing
var canvas;
var context;

// the gear image reference
var gear = new Image();

// the current x position of the image
var xpos;

// The animation variables
var stepCounter;  // counter for the current step
var stepDegrees;  // how much to rotate each step
var stepDistance; // how far to move image each step
var stepSpeed;    // how fast to rotate and move the image
var stepsFullRevolution;  // how many steps in a full rotation

// initialize the board width and height
function init() {
  canvas = document.getElementById('canvas');
  context = canvas.getContext('2d');
```

```
  // Initialize our step counter for the rotation
  stepCounter = 0;
  stepDegrees = 2;
  stepDistance = 2;
  stepSpeed = 5;
  stepsFullRevolution = parseInt(360 / stepDegrees);

  // Add the image load event listener
  gear.addEventListener('load',initGear,false);

  // Set the gear source image
  gear.src = 'gear.png';
}

// When the image is loaded then start the animation
function initGear(){
  // set the initial X position to just off left of canvas
  xpos = -(gear.width/2);
  // call the animation function
  moveGear();
};

// Function to remove old cog image and draw new image
function moveGear() {

  // Clear the old cog off the canvas
  context.clearRect(0, 0, canvas.width, canvas.height);

  // Save the present canvas context so we can return
  context.save();

  // Increment the position
  xpos += stepDistance;

  // Move our 0,0 point to the new position of the cog
  context.translate(xpos,canvas.height-(gear.width/2));

  // Rotate the context and thus our cog
  context.rotate(Math.PI * stepDegrees * stepCounter / 180);

  // Draw the newly rotated image
  context.drawImage(gear, -(gear.width/2), -(gear.height/2), gear.width,
➥gear.height);

  // Restore the context to the original orientation
  context.restore();
```

```
   // Check if the cog has left the canvas on the right
   if ((xpos-(gear.width/2)) < canvas.width) {

      // Increment the stepCounter and check if completed full revolution
      stepCounter++;
      if (stepCounter>=(stepsFullRevolution-1)) {
         stepCounter=0;
      }

      // cog is still showing - keep moving
      setTimeout('moveGear()',stepSpeed);
   }
}

// call the init function on page load
window.addEventListener('load',init,false);

</script>
</head>
<body>
  <h1>The Rolling Cog</h1>
  <canvas id="canvas" width="600" height="100">
    The Canvas element is not supported in this browser.
  </canvas>
</body>
</html>
```

When the moveGear function is called after the image is loaded, the first action performed by the code is to clear the canvas by calling clearRect. You need to do this or else "remnants" of the prior image drawn will remain on the canvas. Next, the script saves the current context, increments the horizontal position, and then positions the origin to the new position with the translate function. Then the script rotates the image based on the new origin by the stepDegrees set previously with the rotate method. Next the image is drawn, and you restore the context orientation thereafter for the next drawing function.

After drawing the gear image at the new position and angle, you check to see whether the image has moved past the right edge of the canvas by comparing the horizontal position and the canvas width. If it has moved past the edge, then you stop the animation. However, if the image is still in view on the canvas, then the script increments the step counter and sets the next timeout to kick off the moveGear function again.

Any of the animation settings can be adjusted by changing the animation variables in the top of the script. Figure 6.9 shows different stages of the image in the canvas.

Figure 6.9   Slice frames of the sprite image as they are displayed with
each cycle

> **Note**
>
> You can interact with the canvas, whether to play a game or move a shape, by catching mouse events such as mouseover and click. The coordinates provided by the event can be mapped through the offset X and Y coordinates to the location of the canvas on the page. For example, if the X,Y from the mouse click event is 150,200 and the canvas offset is 100 for the x and 100 for the y, then the coordinate for the mouse click in the canvas is 50,100. Knowing this coordinate in the canvas grid, you can then determine whether it occurred on a particular shape that was drawn on the canvas.

ADVANCED RECIPE:
Animating a Vertical Bar Chart

In this last recipe of the chapter, you will take the tools of canvas along with some effects and transformations to create a vertical bar chart from a set of sample JSON data. When the chart loads, the vertical bars will grow to their defined values based on some animation settings that have been defined such as the speed and distance to grow each column. Figure 6.10 shows the output with sample data after the animation of the bars has completed. To create this recipe, follow these steps and the code in Listing 6.15:

1. Create the page in Listing 6.15 with the style and body tags for the canvas, which has the id of graph.

2. Add the global variable definitions including the chartData JSON object, initGraph function, and window.addEventListener event handler.

3. Add the initSettings function, which sets all the properties of the graph including the number of bars and size of the bars.

4. Add the drawAxis function, which will add the x- and y-axis lines, the data marks on the axis, and the titles.

5. Add the growBars function, which is the function to animate the growth of the vertical bars to their proper height.

6. Add the drawBar helper function, which performs the actual drawing of the bar on the canvas.

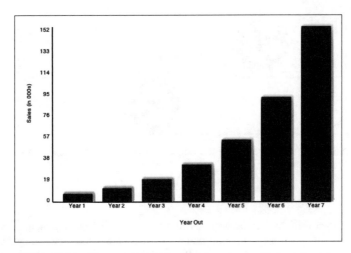

Figure 6.10   The completed vertical bar chart with sample data

Listing 6.16   **Creating an Animated Vertical Bar Chart**

```
<!DOCTYPE html>
<html>
<head>
<meta charset="UTF-8" />
<title>6.16 Growing Bar Chart</title>
<style>
#graph {
  /* outline our canvas */
  border:1px solid #03F;
}
</style>
<script>

// Canvas and drawing context variables
var canvas;
var context;

// Chart settings
var chartMargin;
var chartAxisSpace;
var chartWidth;
var chartHeight;

// bar variables
var numBars = 0;        // total number of bars
var barMargin = 20;     // margin between bars
```

```
var barWidth = 0;      // bar width
var maxValue = 0;      // maximum data value for the bars

// number of y-axis labels
var numYLabels;

// bar animation variables
var idxStep;
var numSteps;
var growSpeed;

// Chart JSON sample data
var chartData = {'bars':[
  {'title':'Year 1','value':'7'},
  {'title':'Year 2','value':'12'},
  {'title':'Year 3','value':'20'},
  {'title':'Year 4','value':'33'},
  {'title':'Year 5','value':'55'},
  {'title':'Year 6','value':'93'},
  {'title':'Year 7','value':'156'}
]}

// initialize the board width and height
function initGraph() {

  // get reference to canvas and drawing context
  canvas = document.getElementById('graph');
  context = canvas.getContext('2d');

  initSettings(); // initialize the chart settings
  drawAxis(); // draw the chart axis and labels
  growBars(); // animate the bars into the chart
}

function initSettings() {

  // set our chart settings
  chartMargin = 20; // margin around entire canvas
  chartAxisSpace = 50; // area for the x- and y-axes
  // set the chart drawing area
  chartHeight = canvas.height-chartAxisSpace-2*chartMargin;
  chartWidth = canvas.width-chartAxisSpace-2*chartMargin;

  // set the number of labels to use for the y-axis
  numYLabels = 8;

  // set the number of bars based on the chartData
  numBars = chartData.bars.length;
```

```
    // find our max data value to scale the graph
    for (var i=0; i < numBars; i++) {
      if (chartData.bars[i].value > maxValue) {
        maxValue = parseInt(chartData.bars[i].value);
      }
    }

    // determine the width of each bar
    barWidth = (chartWidth / numBars)-barMargin;

    // initialize animation variables
    idxStep = 0;
    numSteps = 100;
    growSpeed = 6;
}

function drawAxis() {
  // Set line width for the axis lines
  context.lineWidth = 2;

  // draw y-axis - from lower left to upper left
  context.moveTo(chartMargin+chartAxisSpace,chartHeight+chartMargin);
  context.lineTo(chartMargin+chartAxisSpace, chartMargin);
  context.stroke();

  // draw X axis - from lower left to lower right
  context.moveTo(chartMargin+chartAxisSpace, chartMargin+chartHeight);
  context.lineTo(chartMargin+chartAxisSpace+chartWidth, chartMargin+chartHeight);
  context.stroke();

  // Set the line width back to 1 pixel
  context.lineWidth = 1;

  // Add data marks to the y-axis
  var markerAmount = parseInt(maxValue / numYLabels);
  context.textAlign = 'right';
  context.fillStyle = '#000';
  // Loop through and add the markers to the y-axis
  for (var i=0; i <= numYLabels; i++) {
    // Determine the label and X and Y points
    markerLabel = i*markerAmount;
    markerXPos = chartMargin + chartAxisSpace - 5;
    markerYPos = chartMargin + (chartHeight -
➡ ((i*markerAmount*chartHeight)/maxValue));

    // Add the text marker at the positions determined
    context.fillText(markerLabel, markerXPos, markerYPos, chartAxisSpace);
  }
```

```
    // Add labels for each bar based on the chart data
    context.textAlign = 'center';
    // loop through each bar and add the title
    for (var i=0; i<numBars; i++) {
      // determine the X and Y positions for the marker
      markerXPos = chartMargin+chartAxisSpace + barMargin + (i *
➥  (barWidth+barMargin)) + (.5*barWidth);
      markerYPos = chartMargin+chartHeight + 10;

        // Add the text under the bottom of the bar
        context.fillText(chartData.bars[i].title, markerXPos, markerYPos, barWidth);
    }

    // Add y-axis title
    // Save the present context
    context.save();
    // Move the 0,0 point to the y-axis title point
    context.translate(chartMargin+10,chartHeight/2);
    // Rotate the current drawing context counter-clockwise 90 degrees
    context.rotate(Math.PI*-90 / 180);
    // Add our text title
    context.fillText('Sales (in 000s)',0,0);
    // Restore the context drawing orientation
    context.restore();

    // Add X Axis Title
    context.fillText('Year
➥Out',chartMargin+chartAxisSpace+(chartWidth/2),chartMargin+chartHeight
➥+40);
}

// Animation function to grow the bars vertically
// Called on a timeout based on number of steps
function growBars() {

  // Declare our bar x,y, and h
  // barWidth is predetermined above
  var barStartX = 0;
  var barStartY = 0;
  var barHeight = 0;

  // bar value variable from the data set
  var barValue = 0;

  // Loop through the bars and draw each based on step
  for (var i=0; i < numBars; i++) {
```

```
     // get the bar value
     barValue = parseInt(chartData.bars[i].value);

     // calculate the bar height, starting x and y points
     barHeight = (barValue * chartHeight / maxValue) / numSteps * idxStep;
     barStartX = chartMargin + chartAxisSpace + (i * (barWidth + barMargin)) +
➡barMargin;
     barStartY = chartMargin + (chartHeight-barHeight);

     // call the helper function to draw the bar
     drawBar(barStartX, barStartY, barWidth, barHeight);
   }

   // Grow the bars more if they have not finished growing
   if (idxStep<numSteps) {
     idxStep++;
     setTimeout('growBars()',growSpeed);
   }
}

// helper function to draw a bar based on dimensions passed
//could pass in context along with other params to customize
function drawBar(barX, barY, barW, barH) {
   // Create rectangle with fill
   context.fillStyle = '#00c';
   context.fillRect(barX, barY, barW, barH);

   // Add shadow to bar
   context.shadowOffsetX = 3;
   context.shadowOffsetY = -3;
   context.shadowBlur = 3;
   context.shadowColor = 'rgba(200, 200, 200, .3)';

   // Add line border on the bar
   context.strokeStyle = '#000';
   context.lineWidth = 1;
   context.strokeRect(barX, barY, barW, barH);
}

// on page load initialize the bar chart
window.addEventListener('load',initGraph,false);

</script>
</head>
<body>
  <h1>Growing Bar Chart</h1>
  <canvas id="graph" width="600" height="400">
```

```
    This browser does not support the canvas element.
  </canvas>
</body>
</html>
```

When the page is loaded, the `initGraph` function will be called, which will in turn call the `initSettings` function, which will set all the settings of the graph. Next, the `initGraph` will call the `drawAxis` method. The `drawAxis` function will draw two lines for the x-axis and y-axis. Then the function will add the data marks to the y-axis based on the number of marking you set in the initialization. For the x-axis, you use the title property of the JSON chart data for each bar. Notice that you align the text for each bar on the center of the bar. Lastly, the function adds the y-axis title, which is rotated 90 degrees counterclockwise, and the x-axis.

Next, the `initGraph` function calls the `growBars` function. The `growBars` function is the heart of the simple animation and increments the animation step to determine on a percentage level how much to grow each bar based on the end bar value from the `chartData`. In this manner, the function grows each bar proportionally each time the `growBars` function executes. After calculating the new dimensions for each bar, the `growBars` function will call the helper function `drawBar` with the bar dimensions to actually draw the bar on the canvas. Once the `growBars` function has looped through all the bars of the graph, the function then checks to see whether this step was the last step in the animation. If there are more steps, then the function sets a timeout to call the `growBars` function again after incrementing the step index. Figure 6.11 shows how the bar chart grows through this animation.

To change the speed or growth rate of the bars, all you need to do is change the `numSteps` and `growSpeed` variables in the `initSettings` function.

> **Tip**
>
> Creating animated and even interactive charts with the HTML5 canvas is quite simple, as you saw in this last recipe. If you want to see the endless possibilities of using the HTML5 canvas for creating charts ranging from basic line graphs to complicated rose charts, you will want to check out the RGraph JavaScript and HTML5 canvas chart library at www. rgraph.net. The developers of the library have performed the heavy lifting, and as long as you follow the license agreement, you can incorporate it into your own projects if desired. In either case, the library demonstrates the potential of using the canvas with JavaScript.

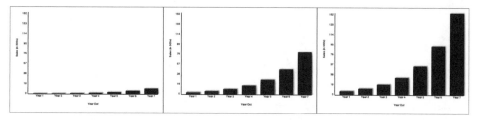

Figure 6.11   Growth of the bar chart columns

Summary

In this chapter, you learned about the Canvas API. The Canvas API has a tremendous amount to offer for drawing capabilities above and beyond what has been described. However, with these basics, you now have the tools to explore more advanced methods and topics of the Canvas API. We encourage you to push its limits and let your artistic creativity flow.

7

Embedding Video with HTML5

Unless you have been living under a rock for the past five years or so, we are sure you have used sites like YouTube and Vimeo, in other words, sites with video embedded on the page. Although those sites are the primary ones for video sharing, we have been putting videos online in some way or another for the best part of ten years. The problem has been that there is no standard for video presentation, so we have had to use plug-ins such as Flash or use the `object` element to play QuickTime files.

You may think there is no problem because these work most of the time. The issue is that you should not have to rely on third-party plug-ins to deliver video. In HTML5, you now have a new and standard way to natively render video in a web page. You can use the `video` element.

In this chapter, you will learn about the basics of the `video` element, before looking at some codecs and, as usual, some cross-browser issues. You will also learn about how you can improve video accessibility with subtitles and captions, and finally you will use the new HTML5 media API to create your own video player and controls.

BEGINNER RECIPE:
Including Video with the `video` Element

For a very basic example of how to put a video on a page using the new `video` element, take a look at the code in Listing 7.1.

Listing 7.1 **Basic Use of the** `video` **Element**

```
<!DOCTYPE html>
<html lang="en">
<head>
<meta charset="utf-8">
```

```
<title>7_1 Basic Use of the Video Element</title>
</head>
<body>
  <video src="mymovie.mp4"></video>
  <!--
    video is a self-closing element so can also be used as:
    <video src="mymovie.mp4" />
  -->
</body>
</html>
```

Easy, isn't it? At its basic level, that is all you need to get the video element work-ing with HTML5. Sadly, though, in reality it is not quite as straightforward as that. But now that we have whetted your appetite, there are a few issues you need to know about before you start using video.

Browser and Device Support

Table 7.1 lists browser compatibility with the video element. It assumes the latest ver-sion of the browser at the time of writing and every release of the browser since then.

Table 7.1   **Support for the** video **Element**

Android	2.1+
Chrome	10.0+
Firefox	3.6+
Internet Explorer	9.0+
iOS Safari	3.2+
Opera	10.6+
Safari	4.0+

So, on one hand, there is very good support for the video element across current browsers, but on the other hand, Internet Explorer versions 6, 7, and 8 do not support the video element natively, and they have a massive market share between them. Later in the chapter, we will show how to provide fallback content for browsers and devices that do not support the video element yet. But before we get to that, you need get your head around the different video types and codecs.

HTML5 and Video Codecs

HTML5 video has met with great success, particularly with big video sites such as YouTube and Vimeo, in beginning to create HTML5 video content. However, HTML5 video has a big challenge to overcome: the issue of codecs.

If you have ever uploaded videos to YouTube, you might not have taken notice what file format you uploaded because YouTube accepts pretty much any video file format and converts the video for you. But in HTML5, you have, at the moment, three main codecs and video formats to consider (see Table 7.2).

In the early days of the HTML5 specification, it was intended that all browsers should support the Ogg Theora codec (Ogg Theora is the video codec; Ogg Vorbis is the audio codec). However, Apple and Nokia had issues with this, and so the codecs were removed from the specification, never to return and with no other codec suggestion in place.

Currently, Chrome and Firefox support Ogg Theora natively in the browser. Safari has native support for the H.264 codec only at the moment. The H.264 codec is also supported in Chrome and on the iPhone, the iPad, and Android (2.3) devices.

In May 2010, Google announced the development of another multimedia format, the webM (also known as VP8) project. This is an open source codec and was quickly supported by the Chrome, Firefox, and Opera browsers.

Internet Explorer 9 supports the H.264 codec natively and will support webM only via a separately installed codec, which is not ideal.

Why Should You Care About Codecs?

The codec issues are going to be hanging around for some time to come. The biggest issue is with the H.264 codec. H.264, also known as MPEG-4, requires that vendors and users of the product, which is you if you host it on your site, are required to pay patent licensing royalties. In August 2010, it was announced that users would *not* be charged for using H.264 videos, but this has been disputed, and it is fair to say that things are not crystal clear when it comes to the licensing of this codec.

Ogg and webM, however, are both royalty-free, open sourced codecs and are considered to be the formats of the "open web." Prior to January 2011, Chrome did have support for H.264, but in January 2011 Google turned the `video` battle up a notch and

Table 7.2   **Codecs and Browser Support**

Codec	Android	Chrome	Firefox	Internet Explorer	iOS Safari	Opera	Safari
H.264	2.3	13+	-	9+	4+	-	5+
Ogg Theora	-	13+	5+	-	-	11+	-
WebM	-	13+	5+	*	-	11+	-

* Via a plug-in: http://webmproject.org/ie/

announced that support for the H.264 codec would be dropped and instead Google would support the webM video codec. This book will not get into all the details of this decision, but there are various theories about why Google made this decision. It is worth mentioning that YouTube (owned by Google) will continue to convert videos to H.264 format, but it might convert all videos to webM, and at this stage there is no word what Android (also owned by Google) devices will do regarding the H.264 format. Mobile video is large and is only going to get bigger, so we strongly suggest keeping an eye on this topic.

As you can tell, with so many browsers and devices and with such politics going on, codecs are a big challenge. The effects of Google's decision could be far-reaching, but we do not really know how far yet. And we do not know how Internet Explorer 9 is going to handle all this, so there is a lot for you to think about and keep up-to-date with.

Do not let these codec issues put you off, though, because there is still plenty you can do with HTML5 video.

> **Tip**
>
> OK, so you have heard about the different formats, but how do you create them? Well, the popular video software packages currently do not export to either Ogg or webM but will export a H.264 file. The iPhone exports a .mov file, and most digital cameras will export to .mov or .avi files. There is various software available to convert your videos, including Firefogg, a Firefox extension that encodes Ogg video, or Handbrake for encoding H.264 video. But we suggest using MiroVideoConverter (http://mirovideoconverter.com), an easy-to-use, and *free*, bit of software that converts to several different video types.

INTERMEDIATE RECIPE:
Enabling Video for All Browsers

As we mentioned in the first recipe of this chapter, the simplest use of the video element is with the following markup:

```
<video src="mymovie.mp4"></video>
```

Because of browser and codec issues, you have to provide different formats of video within the one video element, which is done using multiple source elements.

To get your video working in the latest versions of the key browsers, you need to specify a file in .mp4 format and in .webm or .ogv format, which is what you are doing in Listing 7.2.

Listing 7.2   Using the Source Element to Display Different Video Formats

```
<video width="640" height="480" controls>
  <source src="video.mp4" type="video/mp4" />
  <source src="video.webm" type="video/webm" />
  <source src="video.ogv" type="video/ogg" />
</video>
```

> **Note**
>
> In an ideal world, browsers and devices would just pick the first file they could play. While this typically works on the main desktop and laptop browsers, there is a bug on the iPad browser that stops the browser from loading anything but the first source video. Therefore, the .mp4 file must be first, as in Listing 7.2.

The `video` element has a `height` and `width` value, though you can use CSS to set a height and width. The element also has a `controls` attribute that displays the default video controls. In Listing 7.2, inside the `video` element are three `source` elements, and each `source` element links to a single video. There is a `type` attribute for each `source` because this attribute tells the browser what type of file is being provided. If the browser does not recognize the type, then it will not download the file, which is important because it will save bandwidth, and the page will load faster. The browser will pick the first file it is able to play.

Listing 7.2 provides video in Chrome, Firefox, Internet Explorer 9, and Safari and on an iPad, an iPhone, and the latest Android (2.3) devices, all without the need for a third-party component, which is awesome. But what can you give to users using Internet Explorer 6, 7, and 8, which do not support at this time the `video` tag?

Adding Fallback Content for Older Browsers

After the source elements, you can put in content that alerts users when their browsers cannot handle the `video` element. You put that content inside the `video` element, and you have various options as to what message you provide. You could offer some plain message, as shown here:

```
<p>Sorry, your browser is really old. Please upgrade.</p>
```

Or you could be more helpful and offer a direct download of the video:

```
<a href="video.mp4">Download our movie in MP4 format</a>
<a href="video.webm">Download our movie in WebM format</a>
<a href="video.ogv">Download our movie in Ogg format</a>
```

Providing a direct download option is a good idea anyway and something you should probably offer to all users, regardless of their devices, so we will put that code in our final code solution.

Mainly, we are aiming this fallback content at users who are surfing with old versions of Internet Explorer. Because Flash has a massive market share and is installed on a very high percentage of machines, you can relatively safely offer Flash content as a fallback. There are a couple of possible options for this: You can upload the video to YouTube, or you can use your own Flash Player. Going with the YouTube option makes things very easy while it sorts out the hosting issues. YouTube also provides you with the HTML code you need to embed the movie in your page, as shown in Listing 7.3.

Listing 7.3   **YouTube Video Embed Code**

```
<object width="480" height="385">
  <param name="movie" value="http://www.youtube.com/v/VIDEO_ID"></param>
  <param name="allowFullScreen" value="true"></param>
  <param name="allowscriptaccess" value="always"></param>
  <embed src="http://www.youtube.com/v/VIDEO_ID" type="application/x-shockwave-
➥flash" allowscriptaccess="always" allowfullscreen="true" width="480"
➥height="385">
  </embed>
</object>
```

So, putting all this together gives you the code in Listing 7.4, which provides video in all current main browsers, either via the native `video` element or using a Flash fallback.

Listing 7.4   **Cross-Browser Video Including Fallback**

```
<!DOCTYPE html>
<html lang="en">
<head>
<meta charset="utf-8">
<title>7_4 Cross-Browser Video Including Fallback</title>
</head>
<body>
<video width="640" height="480" controls>

  <!-- video for Safari and IE9. MP4 must be first for iPad -->
  <source src="cablecar.mp4" type='video/mp4; codecs="avc1.42E01E, mp4a.40.2"' />
  <!-- video for Chrome, Firefox and Opera -->
  <source src="cablecar.webm" type="video/webm" />
  <source src="cablecar.ogv" type='video/ogg; codecs="theora, vorbis"' />

<!-- fallback for older, less-capable browsers -->
  <object width="480" height="385">
    <param name="movie" value="http://www.youtube.com/v/ZR-H-FQDenw"></param>
    <param name="allowFullScreen" value="true"></param>
    <param name="allowscriptaccess" value="always"></param>
    <embed src="http://www.youtube.com/v/ZR-H-FQDenw" type="application/x-
➥shockwave-flash" allowscriptaccess="always" allowfullscreen="true"
➥width="480" height="385">
    </embed>
  </object>
</video>
</body>
</html>
```

You do not have to choose YouTube as a video host; you can host the file yourself and use your own Flash movie to play the video. You could make one yourself or use one of the many available on the Internet, such as the popular and customizable JW Player, as shown in Listing 7.5.

Listing 7.5 **Non-YouTube Fallback Video**

```
<video width="640" height="480" controls>  <!-- video for Safari and IE9. MP4
➥must be first for iPad -->
  <source src="video.mp4" type="video/mp4" />

  <!-- video for Chrome, Firefox and Opera -->
  <source src="video.webm" type="video/webm" />
  <source src="video.ogv" type="video/ogg" />

  <!-- JW Player fallback for older, less-capable browsers -->
  <script type='text/javascript' src='swfobject.js'></script>
  <div id='mediaplayer'></div>
  <script type="text/javascript">
    var so = new SWFObject('player.swf','playerID','480','270','9');
    so.addParam('allowfullscreen','true');
    so.addParam('allowscriptaccess','always');
    so.addVariable('file', 'video.mp4');
    so.write('mediaplayer');
  </script>
</video>
```

> **Tip**
>
> One issue that may crop up in your HTML5 video development is the issue of MIME types. When developing examples for this book, we ran into an issue getting the .ogv and .webm files to play in Firefox when uploaded to a web server. These videos played fine on our local machine, and when put on a web server (Apache), they ran fine in Opera and Chrome; however, the .ogv and .webm files did not play in Firefox. This is because Firefox needs to know the server supports the specific MIME type. Not all servers support these new video types yet, and to support them, you must make the appropriate configuration changes such as adding the following lines to your .htaccess or httpd.conf file, depending on your server platform:
>
> ```
> AddType video/mp4 .mp4
> AddType video/ogg .ogv
> AddType video/webm .webm
> ```

So, now you have the full code for offering video to all the main browsers and devices, but several additional new attributes are available.

New Video Attributes

Several new attributes are available for the `video` element. In the earlier examples, you used the `width` and `height` attributes, which are not required, but we recommend setting these values because it helps with loading time. Setting these will stretch or skew your video because the `video` element puts the video in the middle of the box, so if you set the height and width to be 200 by 1000, then the browser will shrink down the video accordingly but keep it in proportion.

The `src` Attribute

Listing 7.1 at the start of the chapter shows a very basic example of the `video` element, and it contains a `src` attribute. But using `src` means you are limited to one video file, and because of the codec and browser issues, this makes it pretty useless for the time being. Instead of using `src`, consider choosing the `source` element within `video`, as used in Listing 7.4, so you can then make the video work across the browsers.

The `poster` Attribute

The `poster` attribute is used to display a single image in place of the video while the video is downloading or just waiting to be started. The `poster` image is intended to give the viewer an idea of what the video is like or what it is about. The image can be a .gif, .jpg, or .png file (although transparent PNGs will not overlay the video).

If there is no `poster`, then the browser just shows the first frame of the video, which may be suitable for your needs. If not, here is how to set the `poster` image, and Figure 7.1 shows you how it looks on page load:

```
<video width="640" height="480" poster="poster.gif">
```

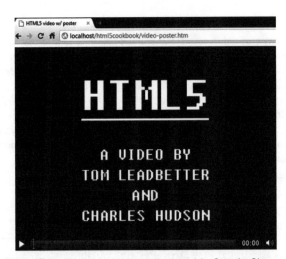

Figure 7.1   A `poster` image displayed in Google Chrome

A possible development to keep an eye on is whether you should provide alt text for the poster image. Nothing is set in stone yet, but there are some accessibility concerns, so there may be changes ahead for the poster attribute.

The preload Attribute

If you have a relatively large video on the page or you are confident the user is going to want to watch the video you have embedded (such as a YouTube page), then you can get the browser to start downloading the video when the page loads. There are three possible values for the preload attribute:

```
preload="auto"
```

auto, or you can just put preload, tells the browser to download the video when the page loads.

```
preload="none"
```

preload="none" tells the browsers not to download the video. Only when the user starts the video will it start to download. At the moment, though, only Firefox 4 seems to support this.

```
preload="metadata"
```

The metadata attribute retrieves information (metadata) about the video, including video duration, first frame, video dimensions, and track list. The browser should not download the video itself until the user starts it.

The audio Attribute (Not Currently Supported)

Although browsers do not currently support it, the audio attribute exists so you can control the default volume of the video. Currently, it has only one specified value: muted. When used, it looks like this:

```
<video height="300" width="300" audio="muted">
...
</video>
```

The idea is that if this attribute was used, then the video would be muted by default, and the user would have to turn the volume up. There is a possibility in the future that you will be able to put other values there, such as audio="2" or audio="low", to control the default audio volume. In a later recipe, you will see how you can change the volume through JavaScript.

The `loop` **Attribute**

If the `video` has a `loop` attribute, then when the video finishes playing, it will loop back to the start and play again. It is a Boolean attribute, so it is either on or off. All the main browsers support this, except, strangely, the current beta versions of Firefox 4.

The `autoplay` **Attribute**

A Boolean attribute, `autoplay` will force the browser to start downloading and playing the video when the page loads. For example, YouTube does this, and video advertisements often start playing automatically. There are accessibility and usability concerns about videos playing automatically, not to mention how annoying it can be, but the reason this is in the specification is because you now have a standard way of doing it if you *really* needed. You do not have to resort to various JavaScript hacks to achieve the effect. Note that there are already various browser extensions available to download that disable `autoplay`.

> **Note**
>
> The `autoplay` and `preload` attributes have been deliberately disabled in the iOS. This is because of potential costs and loading speed issues to the user. No data is downloaded until the user manually chooses to start the video. There are some techniques, well, hacks, to get around this. But because they are unofficial methods, they should not be used and are not covered in this book.

The `controls` **Attribute**

The `controls` attribute adds default browser-specific controls to your video, which include a Play/Pause button, seek bar, duration/time-played information, and volume controls.

The attribute is a Boolean attribute, so you either include the attribute or not. The following is an example:

```
<video height="300" width="300" controls>
...
</video>
```

If it is not included, then the first frame of the video or the `poster` will display. The user will have to right-click the video and choose from the list of options. So, it is better to provide controls with the `controls` attribute. You can use your own controls if you want, and we will talk about that later in this chapter. Figure 7.2 shows the default controls in the major browsers.

> **Note**
>
> Strangely, in Firefox, if you do not have JavaScript enabled, then the controls do not appear. Other browsers, correctly, have the controls without JavaScript.

Figure 7.2   Default controls in Chrome (top), Firefox, Internet Explorer 9, Opera, and Safari

INTERMEDIATE RECIPE:
Creating a Video with Subtitles and Captions

You can do some things to increase the accessibility of the video. For example, you can enable subtitles, captions, and descriptions to help those who are deaf or hard of hearing.

There is a `track` element available with which you can use different types of files. Here it is in its basic use:

```
<track src="subtitles.vtt" kind="subtitles" srclang="en" label="English">
```

There are different values you can use with the `kind` attribute:

- `subtitles`: The transcription or translation of the dialogue
- `captions`: Similar to subtitles, but also include sound effects and other audio information
- `descriptions`: Intended to be a separate audio file that describes the video
- `chapters`: Intended to help the user navigate through the video
- `metadata`: Information and content about the video, which isn't intended to be displayed to the viewer

The `track` element is a very recent addition to the HTML5 specification, and the standard for the subtitles/captions was originally WebSRT but is now Web Video Text Track (WebVTT). Because this technology is new and it is such a massive field of work, there are no working examples or browser implementations of this yet. However, you can display subtitles with JavaScript and using a WebVTT (.vtt) file. Listing 7.6 is a basic example with some sample data from a WebVTT file (based on the current specification). You can create and edit .vtt files with a basic text editor such as Notepad. The .vtt file contains a step, then a time period for it to be displayed, and then the content that should be displayed.

Listing 7.6   Sample .vtt File Contents

```
0
00:00:0,000 --> 00:00:2,000
This is the first bit of the subtitles
```

```
1
00:00:3,000 --> 00:00:5,000
This is the second bit

2
00:00:7,000 --> 00:00:15,000
And as you might have guessed, this is the third bit of the subtitles
```

Because no browser natively supports the track element yet, you need a JavaScript plug-in to do the work for you. In Listing 7.7, you are using a jQuery plug-in called VideoSub, available from http://github.com/icelab/jquery-videosub, which is based on an original MooTools script by Thomas Sturm (http://storiesinflight.com/js_videosub). The plug-in wraps the video in a div and then adds an additional div that contains the subtitles. In this example, you hide the subtitles by default and add a link to toggle the subtitle display. Figure 7.3 shows an example of subtitles in action. The complete code is in Listing 7.7.

Figure 7.3   Subtitles displayed on a video

Listing 7.7   **Video Subtitles**

```
<!DOCTYPE html>
<html lang="en">
<head>
<meta charset="utf-8">
<title>7_7 Video Subtitles</title>
<script
➥src="http://ajax.googleapis.com/ajax/libs/jquery/1.4.4/jquery.min.js">
➥</script>
<script src="jquery.videosub.js"></script>
<script>
$(function(){
  $('video').videoSub({
    containerClass : 'videosub-container',
    barClass : 'videosub-bar',
```

```
      useBarDefaultStyle : false
    });

    $('.videosub-container').append('<a title="show/hide video subtitles"
➥id="subtitlestoggle" href="#">Show subtitles</a>');

    $('.videosub-bar').hide();

    $('#subtitlestoggle').click(function() {
      $(this).text($(this).text() == 'Show subtitles' ? 'Hide subtitles' : 'Show
➥subtitles');
      $('.videosub-bar').toggle();
    });
});
</script>
<style>
body {
  font-family: arial, Arial, Helvetica, sans-serif;
}
.videosub-container {
  width: 640px;
}
.videosub-bar {
  background: black;
  bottom: 40px;
  color: yellow;
  font-size: 1.3em;
  font-weight: bold;
  padding: 10px 20px;
  position: absolute;
  text-align: center;
  width: 560px;
}
a#subtitlestoggle {
  background: black;
  color: yellow;
  display: block;
  font-weight: bold;
  padding: 10px;
  position: absolute;
  right: 0;
  text-decoration: none;
  top: 0;
}
a#subtitlestoggle:hover {
  text-decoration: underline;
}
</style>
```

```
</head>
<body>
<video width="640" height="480" controls>
  <!-- video for Safari and IE9. MP4 must be first for iPad -->
  <source src="video.mp4" type="video/mp4" />

  <!-- video for Chrome, Firefox and Opera -->
  <source src="video.webm" type="video/webm" />
  <source src="video.ogv" type="video/ogg" />
  <track src="subtitles.vtt" kind="subtitles" srclang="en" label="English">

  <!-- fallback for rubbish browsers (youTube, etc -->
</video>

<p>Download the video: <a href="video.mp4">MP4 file, 3MB</a>; <a
➥href="video.webm">webM file, 3MB</a>; <a href="video.ogv">Ogg file,
➥3MB</a></p>
<p>Download the subtitles: <a href="subtitles.vtt">VTT file, 1 KB</a>; <a
➥href="subtitles.txt">plain-text file, 1 KB</a></p>

</body>
</html>
```

Other Subtitle Styling Options

Listings 7.6 and 7.7 showed a basic example of WebVTT, the jQuery plug-in, and some basic CSS to display and style the subtitles. There are some alternatives that will one day be supported in browsers. First, you can add bold, italic, or underlined styles to subtitles using inline b, i, and u tags:

```
1
00:00:0,000 --> 00:00:2,000
<b>This is</b> the <i>first bit</i> of the <u>subtitles</u>
```

You can also apply a CSS class if you wanted to do something other than bold, italic, or underline. For example, you could use a custom font. To do this, you add an inline c tag with a CSS class:

```
1
00:00:0,000 --> 00:00:2,000
<c.myclassname>This is</c> the first bit of the subtitles
```

There are more options such as text position and text size. For more information on this developing standard, check out http://delphiki.com/webvtt.

The Media API

HTML5 provides a vast and exciting API for multimedia. Using the API and JavaScript, you can manipulate the video in your web pages. The following is a list of the available API events:

abort	loadstart
canplay	pause
canplaythrough	play
canshowcurrentframe	playing
dataunavailable	progress
durationchange	ratechange
emptied	seeked
empty	seeking
ended	suspend
error	timeupdate
loadeddata	volumechange
loadedmetadata	waiting

Many media properties are also available:

audioTracks	muted
autoplay	networkState
buffered	paused
controls	preload
controller	played
currentSrc	playbackRate
currentTime	readyState
defaultMuted	seekable
defaultPlaybackRate	seeking
duration	startOffsetTime
ended	src
error	textTracks
initialTime	videoTracks
loop	volume

Not all of these events and properties are available for use yet, but most of them are, including the important ones that allow you to create your own video player controls. We will not explain all the API options, just the ones needed to create your own player, but if you are interested in learning more about the API, we recommend the API demonstration at http://w3.org/2010/05/video/mediaevents.html and the very detailed specification at http://w3.org/TR/html5/video.html#mediaevents.

ADVANCED RECIPE:
Making Your Own Custom Controls

HTML5 provides a JavaScript media API for the `video` and `audio` elements. There are lots of methods and events, as shown in the previous section, for you to plug in so you can create our own video player and custom controls.

This recipe takes the video code from Listing 7.4 and adds a Play/Pause button, a seek bar, volume controls, time display, and fast-forward and rewind buttons. As we will explain later, there are some browser quirks, so the example created in this recipe is best viewed in Opera or Chrome, as shown in Figure 7.4.

The essential features you need for your own controls are the Play button, but you can create much more than that with JavaScript and the media API, as you can do using the code from Listing 7.8.

1. Wrap a `<div id="video-wrapper">` around the `video` element, and add `<div id="controls">`, which contains the buttons, sliders, and other things you need for the controls display. We have included this HTML from the start in this recipe so it is easier to read, but really you should avoid having such controls in the main markup and create them on-the-fly with JavaScript, so only users with JavaScript get these controls.

2. Declare the `video` element as an object so it can be referenced, and then remove the default browser controls by deleting the `controls` attribute that has been specified for non-JavaScript users. The Play button is disabled until the video is ready to be played.

3. For better performance and cross-browser friendliness, you wait until the video is ready and then can collect information such as its duration. And when the video is ready to play, the Play button is enabled.

4. Add `functions` and `listeners` for the buttons, other controls, and displays.

Figure 7.4   Video with custom controls, viewed in Opera 11

Listing 7.8   Custom Video Controls

```
<!DOCTYPE html>
<html lang="en">
<head>
<meta charset="utf-8">
<title>7_8 Custom Video Controls</title>
<style>
body {
  font: bold .8em Arial, Helvetica, sans-serif;
}
video {
  display: block;
}
#video-wrapper {
  -moz-box-shadow: 0 0 20px rgba(0, 0, 0, .8);
  -webkit-box-shadow: 0 0 20px rgba(0, 0, 0, .8);
  box-shadow: 0 0 20px rgba(0, 0, 0, .8);
  display: block;
  margin: 20px auto;
  overflow: hidden;
  position: relative;
  width: 568px;
}
#controls {
  background: rgba(0, 0, 0, .3);
  bottom: 0;
  height: 30px;
  left: 0;
  padding: 35px 10px 10px;
  position: absolute;
  width: 548px;
  z-index: 1;
}
button {
  background: rgba(255, 255, 255, .7);
  border: none; -moz-border-radius: 15px;
  -webkit-border-radius: 15px;
  border-radius: 15px;
  cursor: pointer;
  padding: 5px
}
#play {
  width: 70px;
}
#time, #duration {
  color: #fff;
  position: absolute;
```

```
    top: 0;
}
#time {
  left: 10px;
}
#duration {
  right: 10px;
  text-align: right
}
input[type="range"] {
  position: absolute;
}
#seekbar {
  top: 8px;
  width: 465px;
  left: 50px;
}
#volume {
  width: 50px;
}
#mute {
  float: right;
  width: 60px;
}
label[for="volume"] {
  color: #fff;
  float: right;
  margin: 5px 55px 0 15px;
}
button.speed {
  font-size: .8em
}
</style>
<script>
var video  = null;
var seekbar = null;
var playBtn = null;

// initialize the page
function init() {

  // get video container
  video  = document.getElementsByTagName('video')[0];

  // reference the range inputs
  seekbar = document.getElementById('seekbar');
  volume = document.getElementById('volume');
```

```
// set bar range change handlers
seekbar.addEventListener('change',seek,false);
volume.addEventListener('change',changeVolume,false);

// reference the buttons
playBtn = document.getElementById('play');
muteBtn = document.getElementById('mute');
rewindBtn = document.getElementById('rewind');
ffBtn = document.getElementById('ff');
fullscreenBtn = document.getElementById('fullscreen');

// set button click handlers
playBtn.addEventListener('click',playPause,false);
muteBtn.addEventListener('click',mute,false);
rewindBtn.addEventListener('click',rewind,false);
ffBtn.addEventListener('click',fastforward,false);
fullscreenBtn.addEventListener('click',fullscreen,false);

// remove default browser controls
video.removeAttribute('controls');

// initialize the video player information
if (video.readyState > 0) {
  var durationText = document.getElementById('duration');
  durationText.innerHTML = (formatTime(video.duration));

  var durationRounded = Math.round(video.duration);
  seekbar.setAttribute('max', durationRounded);

  playBtn.disabled = false;
  seekbar.value = 0;
}

// listener event while the video is playing
video.addEventListener('timeupdate', function() {
  var currentTime = document.getElementById('time');
  currentTime.innerHTML = formatTime(video.currentTime);
  seekbar.value = video.currentTime;
}, false);

video.addEventListener('ratechange', function() {
  //you could alternatively display the current playback speed
  //console.log(video.playbackRate);
}, false);

video.addEventListener('play', function() {
  playBtn.innerHTML = 'Pause';
}, false);
```

```
    video.addEventListener('pause', function() {
      playBtn.innerHTML = 'Play';
    }, false);

    //detects when the video has finished
    video.addEventListener('ended', function(){
      playBtn.innerHTML = 'Play again';
    }, false);

}

function playPause() {
  if (ifPlaying()) {
    video.pause();
      playBtn.innerHTML = 'Play';
  } else {
    video.play();
    playBtn.innerHTML = 'Pause';
  }
};

//toggle the mute status of the video
function mute(){
  var muteBtn = document.getElementById('mute');
  if (!video.muted){
    video.muted = true;
    muteBtn.innerHTML = 'Un-mute';
  }
  else {
    video.muted = false;
    muteBtn.innerHTML = 'Mute';
  }
}

//change the volume
function changeVolume() {
  video.volume = volume.value;
}

//seekbar controls
function seek(){
  video.currentTime = seekbar.value;
}

//fast-forward the video
function fastforward() {
  video.playbackRate = video.playbackRate + 2;
}
```

```
//rewind the video
function rewind() {
video.playbackRate = video.playbackRate - 2;
}

//go fullscreen (webkit only)
function fullscreen() {
  video.webkitEnterFullscreen()
}

//check if video is playing or not
function ifPlaying() {
  if(video.paused || video.ended) {
    return false;
  } else {
    return true;
  }
};

//format the time to something nice and readable
function formatTime(seconds) {
  seconds = Math.round(seconds);
  minutes = Math.floor(seconds / 60);
  minutes = (minutes >= 10) ? minutes : '0' + minutes;
  seconds = Math.floor(seconds % 60);
  seconds = (seconds >= 10) ? seconds : '0' + seconds;
  return minutes + ':' + seconds;
}

// initialize the page when loaded
window.addEventListener('load',init,false);

</script>
</head>
<body>
<div id="video-wrapper">
  <div id="controls">
    <button id="play">Play</button>
    <p id="time">0:00</p>
    <p id="duration">0:00</p>
    <label for="volume"> Vol:<input id="volume" name="volume" type="range"
➡min="0" max="1" step="0.1" required /></label>
    <button id="mute">Mute</button>
    <input id="seekbar" name="seekbar" type="range" min="0" max="1" step="0.1"
➡required />
    <button id="rewind" class="speed">Rewind</button>
    <button id="ff" class="speed">Fast-forward</button>
```

```
    <button id="fullscreen">Fullscreen</button>
  </div>

  <video width="568" height="320" controls>

    <!-- video for Safari and IE9. MP4 must be first for iPad -->
    <source src="cablecar.mp4" type="video/mp4" />

    <!-- video for Chrome, Firefox and Opera -->
    <source src="cablecar.webm" type="video/webm" />
    <source src="cablecar.ogv" type="video/ogg" />

  </video>
</div>
</body>
</html>
```

First in the code is some CSS for some basic styles and the positioning of the buttons. We haven't gone overboard with CSS here, but with CSS and the JavaScript API you could create pretty much any video player layout you want.

Now, on to the JavaScript. First you need to associate variables to some of the elements: the video itself, the seek bar, and the Play button. For non-JavaScript users, we have included the controls attribute on the video, so you remove that with your JavaScript because you do not want the default controls to show.

After that comes an important detection. You need to wait for the browser to get enough information about the video before you can start playing it. If you try to get the video duration, some browsers will fail because they are still downloading parts of the video. So, if you have a large video file, then you could be waiting a while before the browser is ready to play it. In this recipe, you are detecting the readyState value. readyState has five possible values:

- have_nothing (0)
- have_metadata (1)
- have_current_data (2)
- have_future_data (3)
- have_enough_data (4)

The value have_nothing means that the browser has no information about the video, and the other values mean that the browser has various information about the video including the duration, height and width, current position, and next frame. So, in this recipe, you are looking for when the value of readyState is greater than 0, and when it is, you then detect the duration and update the duration value on the screen. You also enable the Play button so the user can start the video. In this recipe, you are only doing a couple of things when the video is ready, but this could be the point at which you create the controls on the video or show/hide a loading graphic or maybe even show the video at all.

Alternatively, you could use the `loadeddata` event listener, which will fire when the browser has enough information about the video to allow playback to start:

```
video.addEventListener("loadeddata", function(){//do stuff}, false);
```

Now you know the duration, so using `video.duration`, you get the total length of the video clip, which you can then assign to the `input[type="range"]` seek bar, so it has an endpoint. Then you put the start point of the slider to the start (zero seconds).

You use some `addEventListener` events to detect when the play time of the video has updated (`timeupdate`), and when it has, you update the playback display and the seek bar.

Even though you have removed the default video controls and you have your own control buttons including Play and Mute, if the user right-clicks the video, depending on the browser, they may have options there to play/pause, show controls, mute, save the video, and more. You can't remove or change these browser defaults, but you can hook into these events as well. In this recipe, you have code that listens for a play or pause, and when these happen, the button text is changed.

You also want to know when the video has ended so you can change the text of the Play button. This event is useful because you could do several things when a video has finished, such as start another video from a playlist. You detect the video has ended by detecting the ended event using an event listener:

```
video.addEventListener("ended", function(){//do stuff}, false);
```

After the `addEventListeners`, you have various functions that you use for other video functions, such as checking whether the video is playing; setting the volume (`video.`**`volume`** `= volume.value`); making the video play in full-screen mode (`video.`**`webkitEnterFullscreen`**`()`), which works only in a WebKit browser); and checking the playback rate (**`playbackRate`**). You also add playback functionality so the user can control the position and direction of the video: There is a seek bar so the user can jump to a place on the timeline (`video.`**`currentTime`** `= seekbar.value`), as well as fast-forward and rewind buttons.

As you will have discovered, browsers have various quirks when dealing with custom controls:

- Currently, the only way to make the video full-screen is to use the `webkitEnterFullscreen` function, and this currently works only in Safari. As you can tell from the name, this is not yet a standard way of making videos full-screen; in fact, there may not ever be one in the specification. However, browser vendors know that this is something users want, so it is likely that there will be nonstandard, browser-specific ways of doing this in the future. There are other ways of making a video full-screen with a combination of JavaScript and CSS. However, several browsers have a full-screen mode when you right-click the video itself anyway.

Figure 7.5   Video with custom jQuery controls, viewed in Firefox 4

- Only Safari, Chrome, and Opera currently support `<input type="range">`, and only Opera allows this element to have a transparent background, so it looks a little ugly in Chrome, and in Safari it just is not visible. Firefox and IE9 default to a text box, which shows the time updating within it.

- The fast-forward button does not work in Firefox, and it is very jerky in IE9. The rewind button doesn't work in any browser yet.

Because of such browser inconsistencies both in the display of controls and in how they work with the API, you might want to consider using other controls. For example, in Figure 7.5, the video controls are created with a jQuery slider. Several other video players are available to download, such as those available from http://sublime-video.net and http://videojs.com.

Summary

In this chapter, you learned about the various issues of the `video` elements such as browser support, but the biggest issue is that of codec support, so it worth keeping an eye on the development of the codec wars.

But aside from the codecs, you learned about ways to get videos natively playing in all the current major browsers, without the need for a third-party plug-in such as Flash. For older browsers that do not support the `video` element, you can fall back to a link or to an embedded Flash file. You also created a video player with subtitles using the latest standard of WebVTT files, though this is an emerging standard, so be sure to keep abreast of any changes and practices.

Finally, we covered several components of the media API available for creating custom controls, which you can style with CSS.

8

Embedding Audio with HTML5

Like the new `video` element, the new `audio` element allows you to embed an audio file into the page without the need for an additional plug-in like Flash. No longer having to rely on these third-party plug-ins, audio plays natively in modern web browsers, including browsers on many mobile devices.

In this chapter, you will learn the basics of the `audio` element and then look at ways to solve cross-browser issues. Then you will learn about the API available to see how you can create your own audio player.

BEGINNER RECIPE:
Including Audio with the `audio` Element

For a basic example of how to put audio on a page using the new `audio` element, take a look at the code in Listing 8.1. The `controls` attribute has been added; otherwise, nothing would display on the user interface.

Listing 8.1 **Basic Example of the** `audio` **Element**

```
<!DOCTYPE html>
<html lang="en">
<head>
<meta charset="utf-8">
<title>8_1 Basic Audio Example</title>
</head>
<body>
  <audio src="music.mp3" controls />
</body>
</html>
```

Table 8.1   **File Type and Browser Support**

Codec	Android	Chrome	Firefox	Internet Explorer	iPhone	Opera	Safari
Ogg Vorbis	-	13+	4+	-	-	11+	-
MP3	2.3	13+	-	9+	4+	-	5+
WAV	-	-	-	-	-	-	-

The code is pretty straightforward, but like the video element, there are some issues with the audio element. If you are trying the code in Listing 8.1 with an .mp3 file and the audio is not playing, this might be because you have ran into some codec issues.

We covered the codec woes in more detail in Chapter 7, and while the information there relates specifically to video file types, it is a similar situation with audio file types.

There are two main audio codecs: Ogg Vorbis (.ogg) and MP3 (.mp3). You can also consider WAV (.wav), but we will be concentrating mostly on Ogg Vorbis and MP3 because WAV files are usually large and so not suitable for loading on the web; WAV files also do not support metadata such as artist and title. Although the MP3 format can be considered almost a standard file type, MP3 is part of the MPEG4/H.2.64 group and, therefore, a closed, royalty-pending file type. Ogg, on the other hand, is considered "free" and "open." There are doubtless many arguments to be had over which file type delivers better-quality audio, but the main issue is that browser support is split. In short, Table 8.1 shows the current browser playback compatibility.

INTERMEDIATE RECIPE:
Enabling Audio for All Browsers

As you did for video in Chapter 7, you want to achieve audio playback and support in all modern browsers. You can use the source element nested in the audio element to stack different audio files, and the browser will choose which one it can play. Listing 8.2 has the code needed to provide modern browsers with an audio file they can play.

Listing 8.2   **Audio Files Stack**

```
<audio controls>
  <source src="music.mp3" type="audio/mp3" />
  <source src="music.ogg" type="audio/ogg" />
</audio>
```

The audio element does not need height or width attributes, because by default each browser has its own audio player, but you can apply a height and width using CSS:

```
audio {display: block; width: 90px; height: 28px;}
```

Adding Fallback Content for Older Browsers

After the `source` elements, you can write additional code for browsers that cannot play audio natively; primarily, we are talking about Internet Explorer 6, 7, and 8. Like `video`, there are a couple of options. You can host the audio file on a site such as http://soundcloud.com and use its embed code to serve the audio, or you can use Flash Player to deliver the audio content to less capable browsers. In Listing 8.3, we are using JW Player, a very popular and customizable multimedia player, but there are many more available to choose from, or you could make one yourself.

Listing 8.3   **Using JW Player**

```
<script type="text/javascript" src="swfobject.js"></script>
<div id="mediaplayer"></div>
<script>
  var so = new SWFObject('player.swf','playerID','480','24','9');
  so.addParam('allowfullscreen','true');
  so.addParam('allowscriptaccess','always');
  so.addVariable('file', 'music.mp3');
  so.write('mediaplayer');
</script>
```

Only older browsers download the swfobject.swf and player.swf files and play the audio file in Flash Player.

Listing 8.4 puts it all together. This code provides audio in all the main browsers, either using the native audio element or, when necessary, using a Flash Player fallback.

Listing 8.4   **Cross-Browser Audio**

```
<!DOCTYPE html>
<html lang="en">
<head>
<meta charset="utf-8">
<title>8_4 Cross-Browser Audio</title>
</head>
<body>
<audio controls>
  <source src="music.mp3" type="audio/mp3" />
  <source src="music.ogg" type="audio/ogg" />
  <script type="text/javascript" src="swfobject.js"></script>
  <div id="mediaplayer"></div>
  <script>
    var so = new SWFObject('player.swf','playerID','480','24','9');
    so.addParam('allowfullscreen','true');
    so.addParam('allowscriptaccess','always');
    so.addVariable('file', 'music.mp3');
    so.write('mediaplayer');
  </script>
```

```
</audio>
<p>Download the audio file: <a href="music.mp3">MP3 file, 3MB</a>; <a
➡href="music.ogg">Ogg file, 3MB</a></p>
</body>
</html>
```

New Audio Attributes

Several new attributes are available for the `audio` element, which you will learn about now.

The `src` Attribute

Listing 8.1 earlier in the start of the chapter shows a basic example of the `audio` element, and it contains a `src` attribute. But using `src` means you are limited to one audio file, and because of the codec and browser issues, it makes it pretty useless for the time being. But ideally one day it will be all you need. Instead of using `src`, consider choosing the `source` element within `audio`, as used in Listing 8.4, so you can then make the audio work across the browsers.

The `preload` Attribute

If you have a relatively large audio file on the page or you are confident the user is going to want to listen to the audio you have embedded, then you can get the browser to start downloading the file when the page loads. The `preload` attribute has three possible values:

`preload="auto"`

   `auto`, or you can just put `preload`, tells the browser to download the audio file when the page loads.

`preload="none"`

   `preload="none"` tells the browsers not to download the audio. Only when the user starts the audio will it start to download. At the moment, though, only Firefox 4 seems to support this.

`preload="metadata"`

   The `metadata` attribute retrieves information (metadata) about the audio track, including audio duration, the first frame, and the track list. It should not download the audio itself until the user starts it.

The `loop` Attribute

If `audio` has a `loop` attribute, then when the audio finishes playing, it will loop back to the start and play again. It is a boolean attribute, so it is either on or off. All the main browsers support this, except, strangely, Firefox 4.

The `autoplay` **Attribute**

A Boolean attribute, `autoplay` will force the browser to start downloading and playing the audio when the page loads. Advertisements often start playing automatically. There are accessibility and usability concerns about audio playing automatically, not to mention how annoying it can be, but the reason this is in the specification is because you now have a standard way of doing it if you *really* needed to, and you do not have to resort to various JavaScript hacks to achieve the effect. There are already various browser extensions available to download that disable `autoplay`.

> **Note**
>
> The `autoplay` and `preload` attributes have been deliberately disabled on the iOS. This is because of potential costs and loading speed issues to the user. No data is downloaded until the user starts the audio. There are some techniques, well, hacks, to get around this. But because it's a hack, we do not really want to tell you such bad habits in this book.

The `controls` **Attribute**

The `controls` attribute adds browser-specific controls to your audio file, which include a Play/Pause button, a seek bar, duration/time-played information, and volume controls. The following is an example:

```
<audio controls>
...
</audio>
```

It is a Boolean attribute, so either you include it or you do not. However, if you do not include `controls`, then nothing is displayed and so obviously the user cannot control the audio. So, we cannot tell you how important it is that you do not use `autoplay` without also using `controls`.

You can use your own controls if you wanted to by using the API to create stop and start controls, which we will come to later in this chapter. Figure 8.1 shows the default controls in the major browsers.

> **Note**
>
> Strangely, in Firefox, if you do not have JavaScript enabled, then the controls do not appear. Other browsers, correctly, have the controls without JavaScript.

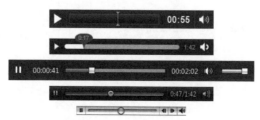

Figure 8.1   Default controls in Chrome (top), Firefox, Internet Explorer 9, Opera, and Safari

Free Audio Files for Testing

For testing purposes, you will probably want some free audio files. There are dozens of options, but we have used some from sites including http://beatstorm.com, http://free-soundtrackmusic.com, http://vocaldownloads.com, and http://freesound.org.

They come in various formats, and as you have read, you will need to convert them to play in different browsers. We suggest trying the following tools: http://media.io or Free MP3/WMA/OGG Converter, available from http://download.cnet.com/Free-MP3-WMA-OGG-Converter/3000-2140_4-10793572.html.

The Media API

HTML5 provides a vast and exiting API for multimedia. Using the API and JavaScript, you can manipulate audio files in your web pages. The following are the available API events:

abort	loadstart
canplay	pause
canplaythrough	play
canshowcurrentframe	playing
dataunavailable	progress
durationchange	ratechange
emptied	seeked
empty	seeking
ended	suspend
error	timeupdate
loadeddata	volumechange
loadedmetadata	waiting

The following are the media properties available:

audioTracks	muted
autoplay	networkState
buffered	paused
controls	preload
controller	played
currentSrc	playbackRate
currentTime	readyState
defaultMuted	seekable
defaultPlaybackRate	seeking
duration	startOffsetTime
ended	src
error	textTracks
initialTime	videoTracks
loop	volume
mediaGroup	

Not all of these events and properties are available to use yet, but most of them are, including the important ones that allow you to create your own audio player controls. We will not explain all the API options, just the ones needed to create the following recipes. If you are interested in learning more about the API, we recommend the API demonstration at http://w3.org/2010/05/video/mediaevents.html; although it is a video demonstration, the API is applicable to audio as well. There is also the very detailed API specification at http://w3.org/TR/html5/video.html#mediaevents.

INTERMEDIATE RECIPE:
Creating a Beat Mixer

So far, you know how to get audio to play natively in the modern browsers. In this recipe, you will create a beat mixer so you can test how the browser handles multiple audio elements playing at the same time. There are some browser quirks, so we suggest using Chrome and Opera for this recipe.

This recipe uses .mp3 files for Safari and Internet Explorer and .ogg files for Chrome, Firefox, and Opera. We are not concerned with older versions of Internet Explorer in this recipe. This is a simple recipe to get started with audio and the API.

You will start with six audio elements in a list, though potentially you could load audio files in on the fly. There is minor CSS used for basic layout and styling, and there is a class for when the audio is not playing. For each audio element, there is an onclick event for toggling the play state of the file. You can see the page in Figure 8.2, and the code is in Listing 8.5.

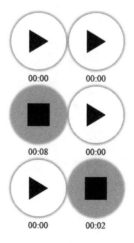

Figure 8.2   The beat mixer in action, viewed in Firefox

Listing 8.5   **Creating a Beat Mixer**

```
<!DOCTYPE html>
<html lang="en">
<head>
<meta charset="utf-8">
<title>8_5 Beat Mixer</title>
<script
➥src="http://ajax.googleapis.com/ajax/libs/jquery/1.6.1/jquery.min.js">
➥</script>
<script>
  $(function(){
    $('audio').each(function(index){
      $(this).removeAttr("controls");
      $(this).addClass('stopped');
      var currentTime = $(this).next('div');
      currentTime.html("")
      $(this).click(function() {
        if (this.paused == false) {
          this.pause();
          $(this).addClass('stopped');
          this.currentTime = 0;
        } else {
          this.play();
          $(this).removeClass('stopped');
        }
      });

      this.addEventListener('timeupdate', function() {
        currentTime.html(formatTime(this.currentTime));
      }, false);
    });
  });

  function formatTime(seconds) {
    seconds = Math.round(seconds);
    minutes = Math.floor(seconds / 60);
    minutes = (minutes >= 10) ? minutes : '0' + minutes;
    seconds = Math.floor(seconds % 60);
    seconds = (seconds >= 10) ? seconds : '0' + seconds;
    return minutes + ':' + seconds;
  }
</script>
<style>
* {
  padding: 0;
  margin: 0;
}
```

```css
ul {
  list-style-type: none;
  margin: 50px auto;
  width: 205px;
}

li {
  float: left;
  margin: 0 0 5px 5px;
}

li:nth-child(odd) {
  clear: both;
  margin-left: 0;
}

p {
  clear: both;
}

audio {
  background: url(images/stop.png) center center no-repeat #ccc;
  -webkit-border-radius: 50px;
  -moz-border-radius: 50px;
  border-radius: 50px;
  -moz-box-shadow: 0px 0px 5px rgba(0, 0, 0, 0.5);
  -webkit-box-shadow: 0px 0px 5px rgba(0, 0, 0, 0.5);
  box-shadow: 0px 0px 5px rgba(0, 0, 0, 0.5);
  cursor: pointer;
  display: block;
  height: 100px;
  margin: 0 0 5px;
  width: 100px;
}

audio.stopped {
  background: url(images/play.png) center center no-repeat #fff;
}

li div {
  clear: both;
  text-align: center;
}

</style>

</head>
<body>
```

```
<ul>
  <li>
    <audio controls loop>
      <source src="guitar.mp3" type="audio/mp3" />
      <source src="guitar.ogg" type="audio/ogg" />
    </audio>
    <div></div>
  </li>

  <li>
    <audio controls loop>
      <source src="beat.mp3" type="audio/mp3" />
      <source src="beat.ogg" type="audio/ogg" />
    </audio>
    <div></div>
  </li>

  <li>
    <audio controls loop>
      <source src="turntable.mp3" type="audio/mp3" />
      <source src="turntable.ogg" type="audio/ogg" />
    </audio>
    <div></div>
  </li>

  <li>
    <audio controls loop>
      <source src="clap.mp3" type="audio/mp3" />
      <source src="clap.ogg" type="audio/ogg" />
    </audio>
    <div></div>
  </li>

  <li>
    <audio controls loop>
      <source src="boxingball.mp3" type="audio/mp3" />
      <source src="boxingball.ogg" type="audio/ogg" />
    </audio>
    <div></div>
  </li>

  <li>
    <audio controls loop>
      <source src="synth6.mp3" type="audio/mp3" />
      <source src="synth6.ogg" type="audio/ogg" />
    </audio>
    <div></div>
  </li>
```

```
</ul>
<p>Audio from <a href="http://beatstorm.com">beatstorm.com</a>; <a
➥href="http://www.vocaldownloads.com">vocaldownloads.com</a>; <a
➥href="http://www.freesound.org">freesound.org</a></p>
</body>
</html>
```

First, you hide the default controls and use CSS to show a Play button. When a user clicks an `audio` element, you check to see whether the file is paused. If it is not paused, then you use the `play` method to start the audio. If the file is playing, then you pause the file using the `pause` method. When playing or pausing, you toggle a class to show different button actions. When you pause the audio, you actually stop it as you set its `currentTime` back to 0. And while the tracks are playing, you are using the `timeupdate` listener event to show how long a track has been playing.

Browser Quirks with the Beat Mixer

This recipe has some browser quirks. First, Firefox 4 does not support the `loop` attribute, so the audio track will not automatically repeat itself, though you could do this yourself with JavaScript by detecting when the track has `ended` and then `play` it again. And second, though the JavaScript will work in IE9 and Safari, this recipe will not work in those browsers because those browsers do not, yet, support the styling of the `audio` element. If you remove the line of code that hides the `controls` attribute, then it works OK in those browsers. Alternatively, you style the `li` to hold the play/stop icons.

ADVANCED RECIPE:
Adding Streaming Radio

In this chapter so far, you have looked at playing "physical" files (.mp3 and .ogg), but what about streaming content? Traditionally we have always needed Flash to stream audio, but now you can do it natively. In this recipe, you will use a JSON list of publicly available radio streams. Using API events, including `onerror`, `play`, and `volume`, a user can select a stream from a drop-down list, and it will begin playing. How cool is that? It is Internet radio in the browser, without any plug-ins. You can see a preview of the player in Figure 8.3, and the code for this recipe is in Listing 8.6.

The streams are in either OGG or MP3 format, and the OGG streams will work in Firefox, Opera, and Chrome. The MP3 streams will work in Chrome, IE9, and Safari. If the format is not supported in that browser, then an error message will display.

1. Use HTML and CSS to create the layout and controls for the player.

2. Create a JSON-based list of radio stations and their URLs.

3. If there is an error, then use the API to detect what type of error.

4. Add each station as an `option` to the station list.

5. When a station is chosen, fire the function `setStation`, which changes the `src` of the `audio` element and plays straightaway.

Figure 8.3   HTML5 Audio Stream Player, viewed in Chrome

Listing 8.6   **Streaming Radio Player**

```
<!DOCTYPE html>
<html>
<head>
<meta charset="UTF-8" />
<title>8.6 Streaming Radio Player</title>
<script>
// local variables for elements
var radioPlayer;
var radioStatus;
var radioControls;
var volumeControl;
var buttonPlayPause;

// Define our JSON list of stations
var stations = { "entries":[
    {"name":"Absolute Radio Classic Rock",
➥"url":"http://ogg2.as34763.net/vc160.ogg",
➥"type":"ogg"},
    {"name":"Absolute Radio DAB",
➥"url":"http://ogg2.as34763.net/vr160.ogg",
➥"type":"ogg"},
    {"name":"Absolute Radio 80s",
➥"url":"http://ogg2.as34763.net/a8160.ogg",
➥"type":"ogg"},
```

```
    {"name":"Absolute Radio 90s",
➥"url":"http://ogg2.as34763.net/a9160.ogg",
➥"type":"ogg"},
    {"name":"BBC World Service",
➥"url":"http://vprbbc.streamguys.net:80/vprbbc24.mp3",
➥"type":"mp3"},
    {"name":"Classic FM London",
➥"url":"http://media-ice.musicradio.com:80/ClassicFMMP3",
➥"type":"mp3"},
    {"name":"Rainwave",
➥"url":"http://stream.gameowls.com:8000/rainwave.ogg",
➥"type":"ogg"},
    {"name":"SomaFM",
➥"url":"http://streamer-ntc-aa06.somafm.com:80/stream/1018",
➥"type":"mp3"},
    {"name":"VoxNoctem",
➥"url":"http://voxnoctem.de:9113/high.ogg",
➥"type":"ogg"},
    {"name":"WBUR-Boston",
➥"url":"http://wbur-ogg.streamguys.com:80/wburlive.ogg",
➥"type":"ogg"},
    {"name":"WCLV",
➥"url":"http://auggie.wclv.com:80/hi.ogg",
➥"type":"ogg"},
    {"name":"WCPE-Classical",
➥"url":"http://audio-ogg.ibiblio.org:8000/wcpe.ogg",
➥"type":"ogg"}
]}

// Initialization function
function init() {

  // set reference to the audio element
  radioPlayer = document.getElementById('audioPlayer');

  // set error handler
  radioPlayer.onerror = function(evt) {
    switch (radioPlayer.error.code) {
      case radioPlayer.error.MEDIA_ERR_ABORTED:
        alert('Play has been aborted.');
        break;
      case radioPlayer.error.MEDIA_ERR_NETWORK:
        alert('Network error occurred.');
        break;
      case radioPlayer.error.MEDIA_ERR_DECODE:
        alert('Error occurred while decoding stream.');
        break;
```

```
      case radioPlayer.error.MEDIA_ERR_SRC_NOT_SUPPORTED:
        alert('Media resource provided is not suitable.');
        break;
      default:
        alert('Unknown error occurred: '+radioPlayer.error.code+'.');
        break;
    }
  }


  // set listener for durationchange event
  radioPlayer.addEventListener('durationchange', streamPlaying, false);

  // set references to elements
  radioStatus = document.getElementById('radioStatus');
  radioControls = document.getElementById('radioControls');
  volumeControl = document.getElementById('volumeControl');
  buttonPlayPause = document.getElementById('buttonPlayPause');

  // set the default volume
  setVolume(0.7);

  // load the station list
  loadStations();

}


// Load the stations from JSON variable
function loadStations() {

  // reference the station list select element
  var stationList = document.getElementById('stationList');

  // loop through JSON stations and create list
  for(i=0;i<stations.entries.length;i++) {
    // create option with text and value
    var newOption = document.createElement('option');
    newOption.text = stations.entries[i].name + '
➥ ('+stations.entries[i].type+')';
    newOption.value = i;

    // add the new option to the list
    try {
      stationList.add(newOption, null);
    } catch(ex) {
      // IE only
      stationList.add(newOption);
    }
  }
}
```

```
// Set the station selected
function setStation() {

  // update status
  radioStatus.innerHTML = 'Buffering...';

  // set the source and type for the audio element
  var selStationList = document.getElementById('stationList');
  radioPlayer.src = stations.entries[selStationList.selectedIndex].url;
  radioPlayer.type =   'audio/'
➥+stations.entries[selStationList.selectedIndex].type;

  // display selected to user
  var currentStation = document.getElementById('currentStation');
  currentStation.innerHTML = stations.entries[selStationList.selectedIndex].name;

  // tell audio element to play
  radioPlayer.play();
}

// Stream now playing
function streamPlaying() {

  // update display and show player controls
  radioStatus.innerHTML = 'Now playing...';
  buttonPlayPause.innerHTML = 'Pause';
  radioControls.style.visibility = 'visible';
}

// play / pause functions
// play / pause button click handler
function playPauseClicked() {
  // check if playing or paused
  if (radioPlayer.ended || radioPlayer.paused) {
    // player is paused, now play
    playerPlay();
  } else {
    // player is playing, now pause
    playerPause();
  }
}

// restart play of player
function playerPlay() {

  // update status
  buttonPlayPause.innerHTML = 'Pause';
  radioStatus.innerHTML = 'Now playing...';
```

```
  // restart play of player
  radioPlayer.play();
}

// pause player
function playerPause() {

  // update status
  buttonPlayPause.innerHTML = 'Play';
  radioStatus.innerHTML = 'Paused';

  // pause player
  radioPlayer.pause();
}

// volume control functions
// set the volume
function setVolume(newVolume)
{
  // set the volume
  radioPlayer.volume = newVolume;

  // update volume bar size
  wrapper = document.getElementById('volume_background');
  wrapper_width = wrapper.offsetWidth;
  newWidth = wrapper_width*newVolume;

  volume_bar = document.getElementById('volume_bar');
  volume_bar.innerHTML = parseInt(newVolume*100) + '%';
  volume_bar.style.width=newWidth+'px';
}

// handler for clicking of volume bar
function volumeChangeClicked(event)
{
  //get the position of the event
  var clientX = event.clientX;
  var offset = clientX - event.currentTarget.offsetLeft;
  var newVolume = offset/event.currentTarget.offsetWidth;
  setVolume(newVolume);
}

// initialize on load
window.addEventListener('load',init,false);

</script>
<style>
```

```css
* {
  color: #000;
  font-family: "Lucida Sans Unicode", "Lucida Grande", sans-serif;
  margin: 0;
  padding: 0;
}
#radioContainer {
  background-color: #ccc;
  border: 15px solid rgba(0,0,0,.5);
  -moz-border-radius: 25px;
  -webkit-border-radius: 25px;
  border-radius: 25px;
  -moz-box-shadow: 0px 0px 4px #000;
  -webkit-box-shadow: 0px 0px 4px #000;
  box-shadow: 0px 0 35px rgba(1, 1, 1, 0.7), inset 0px 0 35px rgba(1, 1, 1, 0.7);
  padding: 20px;
  margin: 40px auto;
  overflow: hidden;
  width: 420px;
}

h1 {
  font-size: 1.8em;
  margin: 0 0 10px;
  text-align: center;
    }

h2 {
  margin: 10px 0 5px;
}

label {
  left: -9999px;
  position: absolute;
}

#stationList {
  background-color:#fff;
  border: 1px solid #000;
  -moz-border-radius: 5px;
  -webkit-border-radius: 5px;
  border-radius: 5px;
  color:#333;
  cursor: pointer;
  padding: 5px;
  text-align: center;
  width: 100%;
}
```

```css
#radioPlayer {
  float: left;
  width: 100%;
}

#currentStation {
  color:#333;
  text-shadow:#999;
}

#radioControls {
  text-align:left;
  visibility:hidden;
  margin-top:10px;
}

#radioControls * {
  float: left;
}

#volumeControl {
  border: 1px solid #fff;
  cursor: pointer;
  float:left;
  height: 25px;
  margin: 0 5px;
  position:relative;
  width:60px;
}

#volume_background {
  background-color:#ccc;
  height:25px;
  width:60px;
}

#volume_bar {
  background:#fff;
  color:#333;
  height:25px;
  position:absolute;
  text-align:center;
  width:0px;
}

button {
  background: #fff;
  border: none;
```

```
    -moz-border-radius: 12px;
    -webkit-border-radius: 12px;
    border-radius: 12px;
    cursor: pointer;
    height: 27px;
    padding: 0 5px;
  }
  </style>
  </head>
  <body>
  <div id="radioContainer">
    <h1>HTML5 Audio Stream Player</h1>
    <audio id="audioPlayer">
      <p>Your browser does not support the HTML5 audio element. </p>
    </audio>
    <div id="stations">
      <label for="stationList">Stations</label>
      <select id="stationList" size="5" onChange="setStation();"></select>
    </div>
    <div id="radioPlayer">
      <h2 id="radioStatus"></h2>
      <p id="currentStation"></p>
      <div id="radioControls">

        <div id="volumeTitle">Volume</div>
        <div id="volumeControl" onClick="volumeChangeClicked(event);">
          <div id="volume_background">
            <div id="volume_bar"></div>
          </div>
        </div>
        <button id="buttonPlayPause" onClick="playPauseClicked();"></button>
      </div>
    </div>
  </div>
  </body>
  </html>
```

When the page loads, the function init is ran. This starts the process by setting up the audio player so you can reference and manipulate it, and it also sets up other controls such as Play and the volume control. It then loads the stations using the loadStations function. This loops through the JSON list of radio stations and creates the list for the user to choose from. The select element has an onChange event of setStation, which takes the selected radio station and assigns that URL as the src of the audio and also changes the type attribute (to MP3 or OGG) of the audio so that it plays correctly. If the audio type cannot be played in the browser (such as BBC World Service, which cannot be played in Firefox or Opera because it is MP3 format), then it alerts an error, with the text of the error depending on the error type.

Even though you set the source of the player, it will not play unless you tell it to, which you do with `radioPlayer.play()`. While a stream is playing, you have a listener event called `durationchange`. When this event is happening, it launches a function called `streamPlaying`, which updates the text on the screen of what station is playing; changes the Play button to Pause; and also shows the rest of the controls.

The final controls are concerned with the Play/Pause button and the volume control. When the Play/Pause button is clicked, it runs a function to check the current status: If audio is paused or ended, then `.play()` fires; otherwise, `.pause()`. In the previous chapter on video, you used a new HTML5 `range input` element for a volume control. Here you create a cross-browser-friendly version that detects at what point the volume bar has been clicked and updates the volume of the audio with `.volume`.

Summary

In this chapter, you learned how to play an audio file in the browser without the need for a third-party plug-in, typically Flash. Of course, because this is a new browser feature, there are various quirks across the browser set. Like the `video` element, you have to deal with codec issues, but you can provide older browsers with fallback options.

You also learned about various elements of the new API with which you can manipulate how an audio file behaves in the browser, controlling how to play and pause, controlling the volume, and changing which file is played.

9

Changing Browser History

This chapter discusses updates to the history interface in HTML5, specifically with two new methods in the History API (`pushState` and `replaceState`), and includes several recipes for incorporating them into your session navigation. In addition, you will learn about the `state` event, using the History API to store more than just page navigation, and advanced topics such as security and extended libraries.

History Basics

The History API, a JavaScript API, has been used in sites since JavaScript 1.0 and has not been updated significantly until HTML5. With the advent of Ajax and pageless navigation, the use of the history object to go forward, to go backward, or to go to a specific session entry became problematic. In fact, several frameworks including YUI incorporated their own browser session management techniques.

Previously, to add a page into the history of a browser without actually changing pages, you needed to change the URL by adding a hash to the URL with the # symbol. With the `history.pushState` and `history.replaceState` methods, you can now add and modify history, respectively, and when you combine them with the window `popstate` event, you can provide improved navigation for the user. By exposing the ability to add and modify page history for a site, the History API provides better back-button support in rich applications that use Ajax technologies. You can now change the "view state" of the application by simply pushing a virtual page, or context, into the history.

You can think of the browser *session history*, or pages to which the viewer has navigated in your site, as a stack, where pages are pushed onto the top of the pile when viewed. When the user clicks or taps the browser's back button, the pages are "popped" off the stack one by one. Using just JavaScript, you can move forward, backward, or a particular number of pages forward or backward using these present commands:

- `window.history.forward`
- `window.history.back`
- `window.history.go([delta])`

These methods remain available in the History API, but in addition, you can now add to the history dynamically, catch navigation events, and even control the context of pages through the HTML5 History API.

Browser Compatibility

The History API extensions are supported currently in the browser platforms listed in Table 9.1.

Table 9.1   **History API Browser Compatibility**

Android	2.2+
Chrome	5.0+
Firefox	4.0+
Internet Explorer	-
iOS Safari	3.0+
Opera	11.0+
Safari	5.0+

BEGINNER RECIPE:
Adding to History with `pushState`

You use the `pushState` method of the History API to add a new entry into the browser session stack by the current page in the browser. The method takes two parameters, `data` and `title`, with an optional third parameter of `url`:

```
history.pushState(data, title [,url])
```

The parameters of the `pushState` method are as follows:

- `data`: A string or object passed to represent the state of the page
- `title`: A string for the page displayed in the browser heading
- `url`: (Optional) The new URL to add to the history stack

The `data` parameter represents the state of the page and is automatically associated with the new entry. This can be retrieved through a window `popstate` event, as you will see later. By *state*, we mean the current context of the display of the page. For example, this could be the recipe that the person is currently viewing from a database call made by Ajax or the like.

Some browsers impose limits on the size of the `data` parameter since a state object is stored by the browser locally on the user's disk. In Firefox, this limit is 640,000 characters of the serialized representation of the state object. If you plan on, or could have the potential of, reaching this limit, you should use `sessionStorage` or `localStorage` instead (see Chapter 11, Client-Side Storage).

> **Note**
>
> Some browsers, such as Firefox, ignore the `title` parameter and will not display the value in the history session list for the user. This is browser-specific, and we hope it will be rectified in future updates.

If the `url` parameter is provided, this will replace the URL in the address bar of the browser but will not cause the browser to request the page from the website. This allows users to bookmark the URL and return to it later. You will, of course, need logic on your server-side pages to handle bookmarked addresses that do not represent real pages. The URL passed may be a relative or absolute path; however, the path must be in the same domain as the current URL. If a relative path is used, then the path will be based on the current document location. The default path for not including a `url` parameter or supplying only a querystring (such as `"?page=5"`) is the current URL of the document.

The `pushState` method is similar to the use of a hash for controlling the context of a page, which is common in dynamic, Ajax-based applications:

```
window.location = "#foo";
```

However, the `pushState` method provides more flexibility than the hash access:

- `pushState` allows you to remain on the same page or change the URL. With the hash method, the browser remains on the same URL.

- `pushState` allows you to keep contextual information in the state of the history. This can be quite helpful, as you will see later in the chapter.

This last point is important to emphasize, because it is a major improvement over the hash addition method to URLs. With each entry in the history, `pushState` allows you to store an object of data that can hold contextual information about the state of the page. The data can be as simple as a string value or as complex as a serialized JSON object. For example, say you have a page that shows the slides of a presentation. Each slide may have particulars about how it is to be displayed, such as a subtitle, a frame, credits, and so on. The state object can hold this information, making it easy to change the style of the page based on the slide you are on. You will see a recipe later in this chapter on leveraging this state object.

Let's use the history `pushState` method to add a new entry into the history session. The page checks, upon loading, for the availability of the History API in the browser by calling `typeof` on the `history.pushState` method. If the method results in "undefined," then the browser does not support the History API. You can use this check to employ a different method to implement the history or limit functionality for the user based on their current browser:

1. Create a blank HTML page with a div to show the current exhibit (exhibit).

2. Add a button that, when clicked, launches the JavaScript function nextExhibit.

3. Insert the nextExhibit function to execute the pushState method.

4. Add the pushState method call to add the context of the meerkat exhibit into the history:

   ```
   history.pushState('Meerkat','Meerkat Exhibit','meerkats.html');
   ```

5. Update the exhibit div to show the user they are at the meerkat exhibit:

   ```
   document.getElementById("exhibit").innerHTML = "At the Meerkats.";
   ```

Listing 9.1 contains the entire page.

Listing 9.1   pushState to Add Pages to History

```html
<!DOCTYPE html>
<html>
<head>
<meta charset="UTF-8" />
<title>9_1 At the Zoo</title>
</head>
<body>
<script>
// initialize the button handler
function init() {
  // attach the click button handler
  var btnNextExhibit = document.getElementById('btnNextExhibit');
  btnNextExhibit.addEventListener('click',nextExhibit,false);
}

function nextExhibit() {
  // Check to see if the history pushState API is available

  if (typeof history.pushState !== "undefined") {
    // Execute the pushState method

    history.pushState('Meerkat','Meerkat Exhibit','meerkats.html');

    document.getElementById("exhibit").innerHTML = "At the Meerkats.";

  } else {

    // the History API is not available
    alert('The History API is not available in this browser.');

  }
}
```

```
// Add the listener to initialize the page
window.addEventListener('load',init,false);

</script>
Welcome to the zoo.
<div id="exhibit">You are at the Zoo entrance.</div>
<button id="btnNextExhibit">Visit the Meerkats</button>
</body>
</html>
```

When you load the page in your browser, you will see that you are at the zoo entrance based on the title of the page and the message displayed on the page. If you click the Visit the Meerkats button, the page will push into the history the current page and then change the title and URL of your browser window without physically navigating to a new page. The JavaScript will change the message, informing the user of the meerkat exhibit. For all purposes, it will appear to the user that a new page has been loaded from the server. However, this is simply a new context you have added to history via the pushState.

Tip

In some cases, providing a url parameter in the pushState that has a value of an invalid page will cause a security exception in specific browsers such as Firefox. To rectify this, either provide a valid URL or employ the optional state parameter, which removes the exception.

If you view your browser history list, you will see the At the Zoo page as the last page, and if you click the back button, you will be taken back to the page. The message on the page will not have changed to the "At the zoo entrance," but you will learn later how to fix that.

Remember that the URL is optional but can be extremely advantageous for returning users. You will, of course, need logic on your server to handle bookmarked entries that have no true page on the server.

BEGINNER RECIPE:
Creating an Image Viewer

In the previous recipe, which walked you through your very first pushState call, you pushed into the history session one simple entry. This recipe will take this a step further by giving the user an option of multiple choices and storing each into a growing history session.

Numerous sites are available that allow users to browse a series of photos, videos, or other content by providing thumbnail links and dynamically replacing a selection. In this recipe, you will show the user a series of image thumbnails, allow them to select an image to view, and add a new history entry to track what has been viewed and allow the user to return to those images. Listing 9.2 shows the full code of the page to create the image viewer using history entries. The images and other assets referenced in the code listings are available from the book's website for your use. Place the images in an images folder so they can be referenced in the showImage function of the code properly.

Listing 9.2   **Image Viewer: Creating Several History Entries**

```
<!DOCTYPE html>
<html>
<head>
<meta charset="UTF-8" />
<title>Image 1</title>
<style>
div.imgView { height: 300px; }
div.imgView img { height: 300px; }
div.imgRow img { height: 100px; }
a { cursor: pointer }
</style>
</head>
<body>
<script>
// variable to keep track of the current image
var currentImg = 1;

// navigate to the next slide
function showImage(imgNum) {

  // check if the History API is available
  if ( typeof history.pushState !== "undefined" ) {

    // verify the image selected is not the current one
    if (currentImg != imgNum) {

      // set the image title
      var imgTitle = 'Image ' + imgNum;

      // set next slide in history entries with state object and defaults
      history.pushState( imgNum, imgTitle, '?img=' + imgNum );
      document.getElementById('imgSlide').src = 'images/slide' + imgNum + '.jpg';
      document.getElementById('imageInfo').innerHTML = imgTitle;

      // set the current page title
      document.title = 'Image ' + imgNum;
      var stateInfo = document.getElementById('stateInfo')
      stateInfo.innerHTML = imgTitle + "<br>" + stateInfo.innerHTML;
```

```
      // set the current image to the image selected
      currentImg = imgNum;
    }
  } else {
    // History API is not available
    alert('The History API is not available in this browser.');
  }
}
</script>

<!-- image view and title - set to first image -->
<div id='imgView' class='imgView'><img id='imgSlide' src="images/slide1.jpg"
➥style='height:300px'></div>
<div id='imageInfo'>Image 1</div>

<!-- thumbnail image row -->
<div id='imgRow' class='imgRow'></div>
<script>
  // create row of img links
  var newImg;
  var imgRow = document.getElementById('imgRow');
  for (var i=1; i<=5; i++ ) {
    document.getElementById('imgRow').add
    newImg = '<a onclick="showImage('+i+');"><img class="thumbnail"
➥src="images/slide'+i+'.jpg"></a>';
    imgRow.innerHTML += newImg;

}
</script>

<!-- history state display area - set to first image (page when loaded)-->
<div id='stateInfo'>Image 1</div>
</body>
</html>
```

If you run the previous recipe and select thumbnails to view, you will see the entries pushed into the history of the browser, as if the browser were loading individual pages. In Figure 9.1, we have selected images 3, 5, 4, and 2. On the left, the figure shows the drop-down menu of the browser's back button; on the right, it shows what is displayed on the page for user-selected images after selecting the images. Notice how "Image 1" is at the bottom of the list, since that is the original title of the HTML page. After the first image, the title you create dynamically gets added to the history list. The last image selected and currently shown (Image 2) is not listed in the history because this is the current context.

Image 2
Image 4
Image 5
Image 3
Image 1

Figure 9.1   Back button's drop-down list of history matching our selections

> **Note**
>
> In the previous listing, we used inline scripting to create the thumbnail buttons upon loading of the page. Normally, this would be handled by a domReady event through a framework such as jQuery. To save space and keep the code agnostic, we have scripted inline.

When you run this recipe, you will notice that if you click the back button in your browser, the page listing in the pageInfo div remains the same. Wouldn't it be nice if you could catch an event when the user clicks the back button to update the page displayed? HTML5 provides you with the pop state event for exactly this purpose, which is covered in the next recipe.

INTERMEDIATE RECIPE:
Popping State in the Image Viewer

To work in conjunction with the new methods of the History API, HTML5 defines a new window event called popstate. This event is triggered when the browser window's active history session entry changes. The history entry could change based on the browser's back or forward button being clicked by the user or JavaScript history object methods such as back and go being called. In either case, you can perform logic based on an event handler to catch this event. The syntax for the event handler takes the following format in JavaScript:

```
window.addEventListener('popstate',funcRef,false);
```

The pop state event is triggered on the JavaScript window object through the popstate event and is associated to a handler function, referenced in the previous line as funcRef. Thus, when a user navigates their history by using the back button, you can perform any necessary logic to load the correct context in the page HTML.

You will remember from the pushState call that with each entry pushed you can store data, or *state*, for that entry. The popstate event passes the state you stored to the event handler and allows for the state object to be accessed by the script. You can use this state data by accessing the read-only attribute of the event through event.state.

In Listing 9.2, you created a simple image viewer that allows the user to select a thumbnail image. When selected, the image is loaded into the viewing area, and a new page entry is pushed into the history. However, having the page in the history is not beneficial unless you can show the correct image when the user navigates with the back button in the browser or the script calls `history.back` or `history.go`. In this recipe, you will add the pop state event handler to catch the navigation event and load the right image and detail.

Add the highlighted section of code in Listing 9.3 to Listing 9.2 between the existing script lines as shown.

Listing 9.3   Image Viewer with Pops: Catching the Pop State Event

```
...
<script>

// Set up the popstate page handler
window.addEventListener('popstate',popPage,false);

// variable to keep track of the current image
var currentImg   = 1;

// history pop state event handler function
function popPage(event) {

  // get the state from the history
  currentImg = event.state;

  // set the image and title
  var imgTitle = 'Image ' + currentImg;
  document.getElementById('imgSlide').src = 'images/slide' + currentImg +
➡'.jpg';
  document.getElementById('imageInfo').innerHTML = imgTitle;
  document.title = imgTitle;

  // show we popped a history event and the popped state
  var stateInfo = document.getElementById('stateInfo')
  stateInfo.innerHTML = 'History popped : ' + imgTitle + ' : state: ' +
➡JSON.stringify(event.state) + "<br>" + stateInfo.innerHTML;

}

// navigate to the next slide
function showImage(imgNum) {
...
```

Figure 9.2   The pushing and popping of the history state

After incorporating the event handler function in Listing 9.3, run the code. When the page is loaded, select the second thumbnail and then select the third thumbnail. This performs a `pushState` for each, adding them to the history entry list. By adding the previous `popstate` event handler, whenever the user clicks the back or forward button in the browser, you catch the event and can then load the right image for the user based on the stored state on the event.

Now click the back button in the browser. The `popstate` event handler will be called. You will first retrieve the state by assigning the event state to the current image and then use this to display the correct image and set the title. For verification, you will then update the `stateInfo` div so you can see what was popped in the history (see Figure 9.2).

Note that the event is triggered even by selecting one of the entries from the history drop-down in your browser. Play around with the code to see how the `pushState` and `popstate` events handle the history traversal.

> **Tip**
>
> A user can navigate back in the history of the browser any number of steps via the history menu or the history API commands such as `go` and `back` in scripting. It is best to tie in the data element of the history entry to a key that lets you know exactly what the context of the entry is. For example, this could be a unique number to an item, a slide number, or some other unique index. In this way, when the `popstate` event is handled, the code will know exactly which element to work with instead of just the last one visited.

BEGINNER RECIPE:
Changing History with `replaceState`

The `replaceState` method of the History API is used to replace the current entry in the browser history with a new entry. The parameters are the same as `pushState`: data, title, and an optional URL field. The `replaceState` method is beneficial for updating the state of a history entry as the context changes or setting the initial state of a page. The `replaceState` method takes the following form:

```
history.replaceState(data, title [,url])
```

When a page is loaded fresh in a browser, the title and URL are stored in the history entry. However, no context data is stored along with this information. To store data along with the title and URL, you can call the `replaceState` when the page loads with the same title, URL, and your additional state data for storage in the history entry. This will in essence overwrite the current entry with the same page information and your additional data. Once a page has been loaded, a user could refine search results as an example, and after each refinement, you could replace the settings stored with the `replaceState` method.

This recipe uses `replaceState` to demonstrate how the page does not reload but changes the state of the current history entry. After the page loads, the user is able to click a button that replaces the current state, which is the key "page" and value `idxCounter` with an updated counter. The counter simply increments each time the state is replaced. To construct the page in Listing 9.4, follow these steps:

1. Create a blank HTML page with an empty `div` for `stateInfo`. This will be used to see what you are setting each time.

2. Add a button that, when clicked, launches a JavaScript function called `nextState`.

3. Insert the `nextState` function with a `history` `replaceState`:

   ```
   history.replaceState({page: idxCounter}, "page "+idxCounter,
   "?page="+idxCounter);
   ```

4. Update the `stateInfo` div, in the `nextState` showing you that `replaceState` has been performed, and increment the `idxCounter` count.

Listing 9.4 **Replacing the Current State**

```
<!DOCTYPE html>
<html>
<head>
<meta charset="UTF-8" />
<title>Page</title>
<script>
var idxCounter = 1;    // counter to keep track of page state

// initialize the button handler
function init() {
  // attach the click button handler
  var btnNextState = document.getElementById('btnNextState');
  btnNextState.addEventListener('click',nextState,false);
}

// our replaceState wrapper function
function nextState() {

  // replace the current page with the next one
  history.replaceState({page: idxCounter}, 'page '+idxCounter, '?page=' +
    idxCounter);
```

```
  // update our page state div
  var strStateInfo = document.getElementById('stateInfo').innerHTML;
  document.getElementById('stateInfo').innerHTML = strStateInfo +
    '<br>Replaced state ' + idxCounter;

  // increment our counter
  idxCounter++;

}

// Add the listener to initialize the page
window.addEventListener('load',init,false);

</script>
</head>
<body>
<button id="btnNextState">Replace State</button>
<div id="stateInfo"></div>
</body>
</html>
```

Each time you click the Replace State button, you will notice that you can verify that the state is being replaced because the URL will show the querystring you have added: page=<idxCounter>. If you look at the history drop-down menu of the browser back button, you will also notice that each time replaceState is called, a new history entry is not added to the stack. Note that you have used a different style of data for the state in replaceState. You are using a JSON-style serialized object with the key, page, and a value of the idxCounter. You are not limited to just strings for the data element of the push or replace but can have complex objects stored.

INTERMEDIATE RECIPE:
Changing the Page History

This next recipe performs several actions on the browser history when the page loads, employing pushState, replaceState, and back and forward methods. The popstate event is used to show when the event is fired with history methods. Listing 9.5 shows the code for this recipe.

Listing 9.5   **Pushing and Popping**

```
<!DOCTYPE html>
<html>
<head>
<meta charset="UTF-8" />
<title>Page</title>
<script>
```

```
// popstate event handler function
function popPage(event) {
  var strState = 'POP - location: ' + document.location + ', state: ' +
➥JSON.stringify(event.state);
  document.getElementById('stateInfo').innerHTML += strState + '<br>';
};

function loadPages() {

  logAction('pushing page 1');
  history.pushState({page: 1}, 'page 1', '?page=1');

  logAction('pushing page 2');
  history.pushState({page: 2}, 'page 2', '?page=2');

  logAction('replacing page 2 with page 3');
  history.replaceState({page: 3}, 'page 3', '?page=3');

  logAction('taking one step back');
  history.back();

  logAction('taking one step back again');
  history.back();

  logAction('taking two steps forward');
  history.go(2);

}

function logAction(strAction) {
  document.getElementById('stateInfo').innerHTML += strAction + '<br>';
  alert(strAction);
}

// Add our window event listeners
window.addEventListener('popstate',popPage,false);
window.addEventListener('load',loadPages,false);

</script>
</head>
<body>
<div id="stateInfo"></div>
</body>
</html>
```

Upon loading, the script calls the loadPages function, which pushes two subsequent pages, performs a replaceState, executes two history back commands, and then moves forward in the history two steps. The following is the output for the recipe from a Firefox browser window:

```
pushing page 1
pushing page 2
replacing page 2 with page 3
taking one step back
POP - location: 9_4_page_flow.html?page=1, state: {"page":1}
taking one step back again
POP - location: 9_4_page_flow.html, state: null
taking two steps forward
POP - location: 9_4_page_flow.html?page=3, state: {"page":3}
```

With `replaceState` occurring after pushing page 1 and page 2, you end up with page 1 and page 3 in the browser history, with page 3 being the current state. Now that you have some entries in the history stack, you go back in history by calling `history.back`. Calling `history.back` fires the `popstate` event and puts you back to page 1. `History.back` is called once more, which takes you back to the original page with no state. Notice that the state is null since the page was loaded through the browser and not via a `pushState` or `replaceState`.

Finally, you perform a `history.go` and move forward in the browser stack by two pages. This brings you back to page 3 by jumping from the original page to page 1 and then to page 3 (since page 2 was replaced earlier with page 3). This can be confusing, and you may find it easier to draw this on a piece of paper as the alerts are popped. The easiest way we have found is to create a drawing of a tower of blocks with each being a pushed entry. Replacing an entry replaces a block, while moving through history just moves the current pointer to a block in the stack (see Figure 9.3).

It is important to note that the `popstate` event will not fire until after the window `onload` event. If methods are called prior to the window's `onload` event that normally would trigger the `popstate` event, then typically only the last `popstate` event will be triggered in the browser.

> **Tip**
>
> This recipe demonstrates how the `replaceState` method can replace the state of a page after a `pushState` has been performed. The state of the original page as you have seen is null since the original page was loaded through the browser and not a `pushState`. If you need to associate a state with the original page, perform a `replaceState` when the page loads to associate your state data.

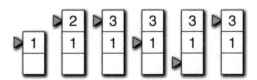

Figure 9.3   History stack entry and current pointer during recipe

ADVANCED RECIPE:
Using Advanced State Data Objects to Pass Information Across Pages

Based on the syntax of the `pushState` and `replaceState` methods, the first parameter can take either a string or an object for the data that represents the state of the page. So far, you have passed only strings or a small key and value object for the data parameter. In many cases, there is much more information about a page's context that would be nice to keep with the history entry so that when the user returns to the page, you can render the content without making calls for the information outside the browser.

Objects can be passed to the methods through JSON representation, as shown in the following example with one variable in a JSON format:

```
var stateObj = { page: 1 };
history.pushState(stateObj, 'Title 1', 'page1.html');
```

The following code shows how more complex objects can be passed:

```
var stateObj = { page: 1, title: "My Slide #1", author: "Savel"};
history.pushState(stateObj, 'Slide 1', 'slide1.html');
```

The state data object is a great way to store user selections, actions, or preferences performed on a page that is then entered into the history. Note, though, that these state data objects are lost if the user purges the browser history and can have limitations set by each browser on the length of data, but for most usages this should not be an issue.

In this recipe, you will learn how to store data with history entries in a JSON format and then pull the data back through the `window.onpopstate` event. Listing 9.6 creates a simple slide show using slide images and user preferences. The user preferences are stored with each history entry so that when the user navigates with the back button to a prior slide, the preferences are restored. The restoration of the preferences happens in the `popstate` event handler.

Listing 9.6   **Slide Presentation: Pushing Pages with Data**

```
<!DOCTYPE html>
<html>
<head>
<meta charset="UTF-8" />
<title>Slide 1</title>
</head>
<body>
<script>
// set first and last slide numbers
var minSlide    = 1;
var maxSlide    = 5;
```

```
// initialize fields used
var currentSlide   = 1;
var currentTitle   = "My Slide 1";
var borderOn       = 0;  // 0 is off, 1 is on
var slideNote      = "";

// initialize our first slide state by replacing current state
var stateObj = { slide: currentSlide, border: borderOn, note: slideNote };
history.replaceState(stateObj, currentTitle, '?slide=' + currentSlide);

// history pop state handler
window.onpopstate = function(event) {

  // show the location URL and string display of the event.state
  document.getElementById('stateInfo').innerHTML = "location: " +
➥document.location + "<br>state: " + JSON.stringify(event.state);

  // retrieve state object data
  currentSlide   = event.state.slide;
  borderOn       = event.state.border;
  slideNote      = event.state.note;

  // show the current slide
  showSlide();
}

// navigate to the next slide
function nextSlide() {

  // check if the History API is available
  if ( typeof history.pushState !== "undefined" ) {

    // validate that we are not at the end of the presentation
    if ( currentSlide < maxSlide ) {

      // retrieve any notes that have been entered
      slideNote = document.getElementById('txtNote').value;

      // set the state object with the current options
      var currentStateObj = { slide: currentSlide, border: borderOn, note:
➥slideNote };

      // replace the current slide properties in the current history entry
      history.replaceState( currentStateObj, 'Slide ' + currentSlide + ' ' +
➥slideNote, "?slide=" + currentSlide);

      // increment the current slide index
      currentSlide++;
```

```
      // set global variables to next slide and reset to defaults
      borderOn   = 0;
      slideNote  = "";
      document.getElementById('stateInfo').innerHTML = "";

      // set next slide in history entries with state object and defaults
      var nextStateObj = { slide: currentSlide, border: borderOn, note: slideNote
➥};
      history.pushState( nextStateObj, 'Slide ' + currentSlide, "?slide=" +
➥currentSlide );

      // show the now current slide
      showSlide();
    }
  } else {
    // History API is not available
    alert('The History API is not available in this browser.');
  }
}


// navigate to previous slide
function prevSlide() {

  // validate that we are not at the beginning already
  if (currentSlide>minSlide) {

    // move back one step in history
    history.back();
  }
}


// show the current slide, title, and options
function showSlide() {

  // set the current slide and title
  document.getElementById('imgSlide').src = "images/slide" + currentSlide +
➥".jpg";
  document.getElementById('slideInfo').innerHTML = "Slide " + currenSlide;

  // set the current page title
  document.title = "Slide " + currentSlide;

  // set the current slide options
  if (borderOn == 1) {
    document.getElementById('imgSlide').style.border = "5px solid #000000";
    document.getElementById('chkBorder').checked = 1;
  } else {
    document.getElementById('imgSlide').style.border = "";
```

```
      document.getElementById('chkBorder').checked = 0;
    }
    document.getElementById('txtNote').value = slideNote;
}

// handle the change of the image border option
function setImgBorder() {

  // set border based on checkbox and global property
  if (document.getElementById('chkBorder').checked == 1) {
    document.getElementById('imgSlide').style.border = "5px solid #000000";
    borderOn = 1;
  } else {
    document.getElementById('imgSlide').style.border = "";
    borderOn = 0;
  }
}
</script>

<!-- slide image and title -->
<div id='slide' style='height:100px;'><img id='imgSlide'
➥src="images/slide1.jpg"></div>
<div id='slideInfo'>Slide 1</div>

<!-- slide options -->
<input type="checkbox" id="chkBorder" onChange="setImgBorder();">Border<br>
➥Note: <input type="text" id="txtNote" value=""><br>

<!-- slide navigation buttons -->
<input type="button" onclick="prevSlide();" value="Previous Slide" />
<input type="button" onclick="nextSlide();" value="Next Slide" />

<!-- history state display area -->
<div id='stateInfo'></div>
</body>
</html>
```

This code allows the user to set an image border and a note on each slide. You could provide any number of options. A debug `div`, titled `stateInfo`, shows the context of the data as history entries are popped. You are able to display the JSON state object with the `JSON.stringify` method. To reference each stored state object value, you simply reference it by the key. To get the border state value, you would call `event.state.border`.

When the user clicks for the next slide, you create an object with the current settings and slide number. This is then passed to the `replaceState` call so that you store the state prior to pushing the next slide. You then reset the settings and push the next slide for display. Of course, this does not take into consideration previously viewed slides that appear after the current slide since each next slide gets pushed fresh into the history entries. To solve this, you can use some new client storage techniques of HTML5, which you will see in Chapter 11, Client-Side Storage.

INTERMEDIATE RECIPE:
Testing History Security

Any time you are able to modify the browser history, page title, and URL address, you need to think about security. Changing URL addresses has historically been one of the more common phishing methods, also known as *website forgery*. The new History API provides developers for the first time a method to change the content of a URL without actually loading a page. However, the HTML5 specification includes safeguards for the various browsers to follow and protect against the misuse of the History API:

- A script cannot set a domain in the URL of `pushState` and `replaceState` different from the current domain.

- The `popstate` event can reference only state objects stored in the history by pages with the same domain origin in order to maintain privacy across sites.

- A limit is placed on the number of entries a page may add to the browser history stack through the `pushState` method to prevent "flooding" the history of the user's browser.

Through these browser policies, the possible malicious use of the History API should be minimized. Let's verify one of these policies by trying to change the URL to a different domain.

> **Note**
>
> Browsers may impose limits and trim the history stack to prevent an overload from potential "flooding" attacks. The number of entries is determined by each browser, but the order of removal follows the first in, first out (FIFO) methodology.

Much has been debated about allowing JavaScript to control the URL display of the browser, without actually changing the page or causing a new page to load. The main concern is that a method such as `pushState` or `replaceState` may be used to phish for personal and confidential information by making it appear that the user is at a different location. You can imagine the havoc if you were able to change the address to anything you like. However, browsers are required by the specification of the History API to validate the address used in the `url` parameter. If an absolute path is used, then the address must be of the same origin as the original page. Let's verify that browsers protect against this possible misuse by attempting to push a different domain page into the history. Listing 9.7 provides a very simple page for pushing a new state. Try it and verify that it works in your browser by following these steps and creating a copy of Listing 9.7:

1. Create a blank HTML page that has a button that launches a pushPage function when clicked.

2. Add the pushPage function that checks for the history pushState method availability and then pushes a new context of page.html.

Listing 9.7   **A Simple Push in the Same Origin**

```
<!DOCTYPE html>
<html>
<head>
<meta charset="UTF-8" />
<title>9.7 Push across domains</title>
</head>
<body>
<script>
// initialize the button handler
function init() {
  // attach the click button handler
  var btnPushPage = document.getElementById('btnPushPage');
  btnPushPage.addEventListener('click',pushPage,false);
}

// push the new state into history
function pushPage() {

  // we check to see if the History API is available
  if (typeof history.pushState !== "undefined") {

    // push the new state
    history.pushState(null, 'Good Page', 'page.html');
  } else {

    // the History API is not available
    alert('History API not available in this browser');
  }
}

// Add the listener to initialize the page
window.addEventListener('load',init,false);

</script>
<button id="btnPushPage">Try Push</button>
</body>
</html>
```

Let's now take the previous listing and make a minor modification to see what will happen if someone tried to use the pushState to falsify a domain URL. Change the url parameter of the pushState method, as shown in Listing 9.8, to be an absolute path of a domain different from the one you are currently running in. We have chosen www.asite.com just as an example.

Listing 9.8   **Setting a Different Origin**

```
<!DOCTYPE html>
<html>
<head>
<meta charset="UTF-8" />
<title>9.8 Setting a Different Origin</title>
</head>
<body>
<script>
// initialize the button handler
function init() {
  // attach the click button handler
  var btnPushPage = document.getElementById('btnPushPage');
  btnPushPage.addEventListener('click',pushPage,false);
}


// push the new state into history
function pushPage() {

  // we check to see if the History API is available
  if (typeof history.pushState !== "undefined") {

    // push the new state
    history.pushState(null, 'Bad Page', 'http://www.asite.com/fish.html');
  } else {

    // the History API is not available
    alert('History API not available in this browser');
  }
}


// Add the listener to initialize the page
window.addEventListener('load',init,false);

</script>
<button id="btnPushPage">Try Push</button>
</body>
</html>
```

When pushing a new state into the history with the `pushState` method, the browser will verify the URL passed. If the URL is a full path and the domain is different from which it is being "pushed," the call will fail, throw an exception, or simply not do anything based on the browser. The same holds true for the `replaceState` method.

Helpful Libraries

As web developers, we need to be concerned not only about the security aspects of the History API but also the support of the API across browsers and within a browser across versions. With several of the new APIs of HTML5, the level of implementation by the various browsers differs greatly, and backward compatibility will be a problem for the foreseeable future, at least until the majority of users migrate to new versions. For the History API, this means you will need to continue to support the hash address method and `hashChange` event for backward compatibility of page states:

```
window.onhashchange = function() {
  alert("hash changed!");
};
window.location.hash = Math.random();
```

However, this does not mean you have to give up the benefits of the new HTML5 history functions. As with most browser-compatibility issues, other developers have recognized this shortcoming and created libraries to handle the differences not only between browsers but also between versions of browsers. For the History API, the leading library at this time is history.js.

You could still program your own logic, but the history.js library is available on GitHub (https://github.com/balupton/History.js) and provides an easy wrapper JavaScript library that attempts to use the HTML5 history methods if supported but falls back to the hash code method automatically if needed. Overall, the syntax is similar to the History API methods, event, and attributes you have seen in this chapter. Unfortunately, we do not have the space to play with the library here, but the library provides the following:

- Multiple browser support
- Framework support, including jQuery, MooTools, and Prototype
- Backward compatibility to older browsers with the use of hash tags

Summary

The History API available in JavaScript is extremely powerful and provides web developers with the opportunity to change the user's history at a site without changing the

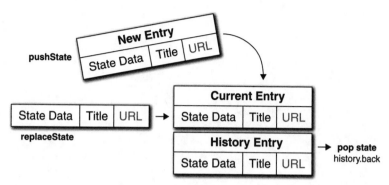

Figure 9.4   History API with `pushState` and `replaceState` methods
and `popstate` event

actual page. Sites such as GitHub and Flickr have already put the History API to great use, providing more user-friendly functionality.

In this chapter, you examined how the `pushState` and `replaceState` methods and `popstate` event work in conjunction with the history entry list (see Figure 9.4).

The following are the main technical features that HTML5 now adds to the history:

- Pushing new entries into the browser entry history
- Replacing the current history entry state data
- Managing navigation event handling and retrieving state

You should now have some ideas of how you can employ these features in your own website or application.

10

Location Awareness with the Geolocation API

For years, websites have used location information to provide enhanced user experiences, such as where the closest store is or events in your area. The location data has been gathered by using a browser's IP address and matching it in a database or just asking the user for their location. With smartphones and built-in GPS, there is a significant increase in apps that are location-aware. With HTML5 and the Geolocation API, there is an easy and fairly reliable method by which websites and web applications can access a browser's location. In this chapter, you will learn about the Geolocation API objects and methods in a series of recipes to retrieve the browser device's location information for use in your application.

Geolocation Overview

The ability to identify the location information of a browser, whether laptop- or mobile-based, provides key information that can be used for a variety of functionality, including the following:

- Displaying the browser's position on a map
- Displaying location-specific information or points of interest
- Adding location data to user contributions such as place reviews or photographs

Accessing a user's location by correlating the IP address of the browser can be problematic because the database of IP addresses and locations must be extensive and well-maintained. The location information can also be vague, providing detail only down to a general area. It is not uncommon for sites that leverage location data to ask a user for their ZIP or postal code or full address to overcome the IP address location challenges. However, this information is tied to where the user may be at the time rather than where they may be in the future. The HTML5 Geolocation API provides built-in methods that can provide quite granular information.

With the Geolocation API, the browser is now able to tell you its location in the world via latitude and longitude values with a measure of accuracy. The degree of accuracy is based on several factors, and developers can influence the degree of accuracy. Now you may be wondering, what good is latitude and longitude if you do not know the latitude and longitude coordinates of the coffeehouse around the corner? For geolocation to be beneficial, the universal means of conveying a location must be at the "lowest common denominator," and the coordinate system of latitude and longitude provides this. As you will see later in this chapter, there are several services from various providers that can consume latitude and longitude coordinates and provide additional information. And to reverse geocode (see the following sidebar), a set of coordinates is quite easy given the large geographic databases of providers such as Google.

Reverse Geocoding

Reverse geocoding, the opposite of geocoding that converts an address into a set of latitude and longitude coordinates, is the practice of converting a set of latitude and longitude coordinates into a physical address. Various services can provide this information. One of the most commonly used is the Google Maps JavaScript API V3 Services (http://code.google.com/apis/maps/documentation/javascript/services.html#ReverseGeocoding).

Browser Compatibility

The Geolocation API is still young, but given the value it holds, the API definition is being adopted rapidly by the various browsers. Table 10.1 lists the current browser support for the Geolocation API.

Table 10.1 **Geolocation API Browser Availability**

Android	2.1+
Chrome	9.0+
Firefox	3.5+
Internet Explorer	9.0+
iOS Safari	3.2+
Opera	10.6+
Safari	5.0+

Where in the World: `getCurrentPosition`

The basic function of the Geolocation API is to find the current location of the browser in the world. The `getCurrentPosition` method provides this information to you in a JavaScript asynchronous call. It is important to note that the calls that determine location in JavaScript are asynchronous in nature. Most JavaScript is performed synchronously or in the main program flow. With asynchronous method calls, JavaScript performs the call in the background and then returns the results to a function when the process is complete. By having the API call as an asynchronous call, the query can be displayed to the user without blocking the processing of the rest of the page.

The `getCurrentPosition` method retrieves the current position for the browser and takes one required parameter (a success callback function name) and two optional parameters (an error callback function and a position options object):

```
getCurrentPosition (successCallback [, errorCallback] [, positionOptions])
```

The parameters of the `getCurrentPosition` include the following:

- `successCallback`: The function to execute and pass the coordinates to
- `errorCallback`: (Optional) The function to handle any errors that occurred
- `options`: (Optional) An `options` object to handle how the position is retrieved

Since the call to `getCurrentPosition` is asynchronous, the method needs to be told which functions for success and potential failure will be executed when the method has completed. Let's jump in and find your location now with a recipe.

BEGINNER RECIPE:
Determining Your Location with a Simple `getCurrentPosition`

In this recipe, the page will use the `getCurrentPosition` method with a success callback function to determine your current location and display the properties of the position object returned. Use these steps and the code in Listing 10.1 to create this recipe:

1. Create a blank HTML page with a `div` (called `btnFindMe`) and the Find Me button, which will call the `findMe` function when clicked.

2. Add the `findMe` function in a set of script tags with the following code to check for the Geolocation API, and then call the `getCurrentPosition` method:

```
if (navigator.geolocation) {
    navigator.geolocation.getCurrentPosition(geoSuccess);
} else {
    document.getElementById('myLocation').innerHTML =
        "Geolocation API Not Supported";
}
```

3. Add the geoSuccess function that will handle the successful callback from the getCurrentPosition request.

4. Add a second div (called myLocation) to the HTML in which you will display the returned position information from the getCurrentPosition.

Listing 10.1   getCurrentPosition **to Find Browser Location**

```html
<!DOCTYPE html>
<html>
<head>
<meta charset="UTF-8" />
<title>10.1 Find Me</title>
<script>

// Initialize the page with other event listeners
function init() {
  var btnFindMe = document.getElementById('findMe');
  btnFindMe.addEventListener('click',findMe,false);
}

// success callback function for getCurrentPosition
function geoSuccess(position) {

  // grab the position DOMTimeStamp for display
  var dateDisplay = new Date(position.timestamp);

  // get reference to result div
  var myLocationDiv = document.getElementById('myLocation');

  // display the coords and timestamp object fields
  myLocationDiv.innerHTML = 'Lat: ' + position.coords.latitude + '<br>' +
    'Lng: ' + position.coords.longitude + '<br>' +
    'Accuracy: ' + position.coords.accuracy + '<br>' +
    'Altitude (opt): ' + position.coords.altitude + '<br>' +
    'Alt. Accuracy (opt): ' + position.coords.altitudeAccuracy + '<br>' +
    'Heading (opt): ' + position.coords.heading + '<br>' +
    'Speed (opt): ' + position.coords.speed + '<br>' +
    'Position DOMTimeStamp: ' + position.timestamp + '<br>' +
    'Time Date Stamp: ' + dateDisplay.toLocaleString();
}

// function called from button click to find position
function findMe() {
  var myLocationDiv = document.getElementById('myLocation');
```

```
  // check for geolocation support
  if (navigator.geolocation) {
    // make asynchronous getCurrentPosition call
    navigator.geolocation.getCurrentPosition(geoSuccess);
    myLocationDiv.innerHTML = 'Retrieving your location.';
  } else {
    // geolocation not supported
    myLocationDiv.innerHTML = 'Geolocation API Not Supported';
  }
}

// Initialize the page on load
window.addEventListener('load',init,false);

</script>
</head>
<body>
<div id='btnFindMe'>
  <button id="findMe">Find Me</button>
</div>
<div id="myLocation"></div>
</body>
</html>
```

When you click the Find Me button, the `findMe()` function will be called. The first step in this function is to check whether the browser you are using supports the Geolocation API. This check is done by using the following code:

```
if (navigator.geolocation) {
```

If the navigator geolocation object is available, then you can perform the `getCurrentPosition`; otherwise, you can handle the lack of support of the API by displaying an appropriate message that the API is not supported. Upon successfully verifying the availability of the API, the `getCurrentPosition` method is called with the callback function name of `geoSuccess`. This will be the function performed when the `getCurrentPosition` completes.

When the `getCurrentPosition` method is called, the very first action that the browser will perform is to verify that the user has authorized the browser to provide this information to the page or prompt the user to do so. Depending on the browser being used, the message and options may be slightly different. For example, in Firefox, an authorization panel drops down from the top of the browser, allowing the user to share their location or not share and remember the selection for the site. In Safari, a dialog will appear that will confirm with the user to allow, disallow, and allow for the next 24 hours.

When the browser is authorized to retrieve your location, the browser will leverage WiFi and cellular network information if available to determine the location. This

Table 10.2   **The Position Return Object**

Object	Property	Type	Purpose
coords	latitude	double	Latitude coordinate of the position
	longitude	double	Longitude coordinate of the position
	accuracy	double	Accuracy of the latitude and longitude values in meters
	altitude	double	(Optional) Altitude value if available
	altitudeAccuracy	double	(Optional) Accuracy of the altitude value
	heading	double	(Optional) Heading direction from north in degrees if available
	speed	double	(Optional) Speed if available
timestamp		DOMTimeStamp	The current local time and date

information will be passed to the success callback function as a position object. The position object holds properties of the location including the latitude and longitude (see Table 10.2).

The position object data is divided into the coords object and a timestamp, in DOMTimeStamp format. Inside the geoSuccess function you can now display the various properties of the coords object, referencing each through the position root object. For example, to retrieve the latitude of the position, you use position.coords.latitude. Each browser will handle the optional fields differently; Figure 10.1 shows the output from Chrome 14.

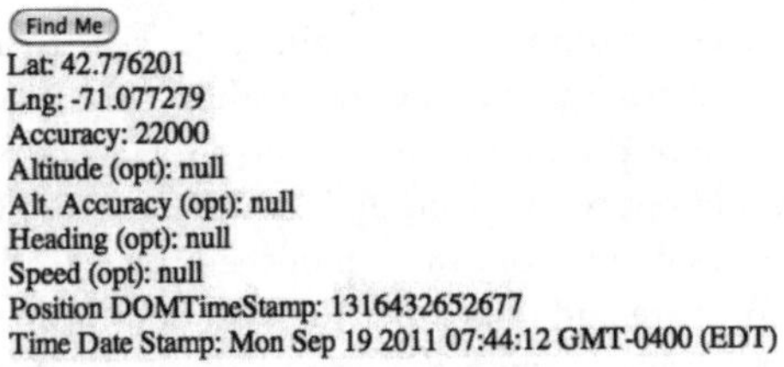

(Find Me)
Lat: 42.776201
Lng: -71.077279
Accuracy: 22000
Altitude (opt): null
Alt. Accuracy (opt): null
Heading (opt): null
Speed (opt): null
Position DOMTimeStamp: 1316432652677
Time Date Stamp: Mon Sep 19 2011 07:44:12 GMT-0400 (EDT)

Figure 10.1   Your location revealed in Chrome 14.

Location Privacy

Knowing the location of a browser, and thus the location of the person viewing the browser, can be considered to be private information. The method for allowing users to share their private location information is through an authorization action, as you saw in this first recipe. Until the user either allows or denies access to the location, the `getCurrentPosition` API call will be on hold. This is a key reason that this call is performed via an asynchronous method so that the rest of the page does not "block" waiting for the user authorization or reply.

You may be wondering at this point what happens if the user does not provide authorization for the information or the location information times out. This is where the error handler parameter of the `getCurrentPosition` comes into play and what you will look at in the next recipe.

> **Tip**
>
> As you use the Geolocation API, you may find that in some instances your page produces no result or returns a timeout error (as you will see in the next recipe). This will typically result from an error being present in your code in one of your callback functions. Since the position methods are asynchronous, these errors may or may not bubble up to your browser window based on the browser you are viewing. It can be helpful to use `console.log()` debugging in your callback functions to identify the issue.

INTERMEDIATE RECIPE:
Mapping a Location with `getCurrentPosition`

In this recipe, you will use the `getCurrentPosition` method to retrieve the location of the browser and map it on a Google map on the page. You will include in the recipe an error handler in case an error is returned from the `getCurrentPosition` method (which you will cause to happen as soon as you have the page working correctly).

Similar to the prior recipe, when the page loads, the user can click the Map Me button that will trigger the `getCurrentPosition` method. Once you receive the call, you will then use the latitude and longitude coordinates to create an instance of a Google map with a marker and an info window for the coordinates and city and state. The city and state comes from the Mozilla address object and will not be available in other browsers. If you want to show the corresponding physical address in other browsers, then you will need to use reverse geocoding, which you will see in another recipe in this chapter.

1. Leverage the previous recipe, and change the button to Map Me and the function called to `mapMe`.

2. Include the Google Maps JavaScript API V3 Overlay script tag (note that with V3 of the Google Maps kit, you no longer need a developer key):

```
<script src="http://maps.google.com/maps/api/js?sensor=false">
```

3. Modify the `getCurrentPosition` request to add the error handler function:

   `navigator.geolocation.getCurrentPosition(geoSuccess, `**`geoErrorHandler`**`);`

4. Add the `geoErrorHandler` function `geoErrorHandler(error)`, which will handle any errors that are returned by the `getCurrentPosition` request.

5. Update the HTML body `div` sections to mirror those in Listing 10.2 to have a container including a `mapCanvas`, the `mapMe` button, and `myLocation`.

Listing 10.2 Using `getCurrentPosition` to Map a Location

```
<!DOCTYPE html>
<html>
<head>
<meta charset="UTF-8" />
<title>10.2 Map Me With Error Handling</title>
<style>
  #container {
    width:500px;
  }

  #mapCanvas {
    width:500px;
    height:300px;
    border-style:solid;
    border-width:2px;
    margin: 22px 0;
  }

  #btnMapMe {
    float:left;
  }

  #myLocation {
    float:right;
  }
</style>
<script src="http://maps.google.com/maps/api/js?sensor=false"></script>
<script>

// Initialize the page
function init() {
  // Add the button click listener
  var btnMapMe = document.getElementById('mapMe');
  btnMapMe.addEventListener('click',mapMe,false);
}
```

```
// success callback function for getCurrentPosition
function geoSuccess(position) {

  // get reference to result div
  var myLocationDiv = document.getElementById('myLocation');

  // retrieve our lat and long coordinates
  var posLat = position.coords.latitude;
  var posLng = position.coords.longitude;
  var posAccuracy = position.coords.accuracy;

  // display the coords and timestamp object fields
  myLocationDiv.innerHTML = 'Lat: ' + posLat + ', Lng: ' + posLng +
➡ '<br>Accuracy: ' + posAccuracy;

  // create a google map latlng out of our coordinates
  var myLatLng = new google.maps.LatLng(posLat, posLng);

  // set our options for our map using our latlng as the center
  var myOptions = {
    zoom: 14,
    center: myLatlng,
    mapTypeId: google.maps.MapTypeId.ROADMAP
  }

  // create our google map instance
  var map = new google.maps.Map(document.getElementById('mapCanvas'), myOptions);

  // add our marker for our location
  var marker = new google.maps.Marker({
    position: myLatlng,
    map: map
  });

  // create our info window text
  var infoText = '';
  infoText = posLat + ', ' + posLng + '<br>Accuracy: ' + posAccuracy;
  if (position.address) {
    infoText += '<br>' + position.address.city + ', ' + position.address.region;
  }

  // create the info window and set the text
  var infowindow = new google.maps.InfoWindow();
  infowindow.setContent(infoText);
  infowindow.open(map, marker);
}
```

```javascript
// error handler for getCurrentPosition
function geoErrorHandler(error) {

  // initialize our error message
  var errMessage = 'ERROR: ';

  // based on the error code parameter set the message
  switch(error.code)
{
    case error.PERMISSION_DENIED:
      errMessage += 'User did not share geolocation data.';
      break;
    case error.POSITION_UNAVAILABLE:
      errMessage += 'Could not detect current position.';
      break;
    case error.TIMEOUT:
      errMessage += 'Retrieving position timed out.';
      break;
    default:
      errMessage += 'Unknown error.';
      break;
  }

  // display the error to the user
  document.getElementById('myLocation').innerHTML = errMessage;
}

// function called from button click to find position
function mapMe() {
  var myLocationDiv = document.getElementById('myLocation');

  // check for geolocation support
  if (navigator.geolocation) {
    // make asynchronous getCurrentPosition call
    navigator.geolocation.getCurrentPosition(geoSuccess, geoErrorHandler);
    myLocationDiv.innerHTML = 'Retrieving your location...';
  } else {
    // geolocation not supported
    myLocationDiv.innerHTML = 'Geolocation API Not Supported';
  }
}

// Initialize the page
window.addEventListener('load',init,false);

</script>
</head>
```

```
<body>
<div id="container">
  <div id="mapCanvas"></div>
  <div id="btnMapMe">
    <button id="mapMe">Map Me</button>
  </div>
  <div id="myLocation"></div>
</div>
</body>
</html>
```

When you click the Map Me button, the `mapMe` function will be called. As before, you check whether the Geolocation API is available and, if so, perform the `getCurrentPosition` method. If the `getCurrentPosition` succeeds, then the `geoSuccess` function is called, and the coordinates are retrieved, displayed in the `myLocation` div, and then used to create a Google map instance with the marker and info window. The result will look similar to Figure 10.2 but with your location.

In the `getCurrentPosition` method call, you add the second parameter, which is the error handler, named `geoErrorHandler`. The following are the errors that can be returned by the position methods:

- `PERMISSION_DENIED` (1): The request failed because the user did not authorize use of the location information.

- `POSITION_UNAVAILABLE` (2): The position of the device could not be determined by the browser.

- `TIMEOUT` (3): This is returned if a timeout property has been supplied and the timeout length has passed.

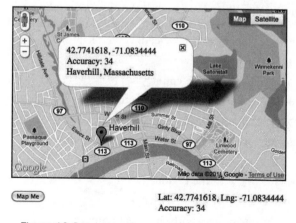

Figure 10.2 Your location mapped in a Google map

The error handler allows you to catch an error returned and take the appropriate action. A common error, PERMISSION_DENIED, results from the user not granting access to the information required by the Geolocation API call on the page. To view this error, reload your page, and when the browser asks for you to allow access to the location information, choose to not share or disallow access to your location. The error handler geoErrorHandler will be called with a position error object passed to it. The position error object, titled error in our code, will include two attributes: code and message. The code shown previously is a numerical constant that defines the type of error, while the message may contain an optional string message for you as the developer to gain more understanding as to why the error occurred. In this case, since the user has denied access to the location information, the PERMISSION_DENIED error code will be provided, and you can display your own message.

> **Note**
>
> Mozilla adds a fourth value for possible error codes: UNKNOWN_ERROR (0). This error is provided when the location retrieval fails for an unknown reason and is one that is not covered by the other errors. In Listing 10.2, the switch default case will catch any unknown error, including the UNKNOWN_ERROR provided by Mozilla. In this case, the message attribute of the error object can be more beneficial for determining the reason for the error.

In the recipe, you leverage the Google Maps JavaScript API V3 Overlay to display to the user their location with a marker. Tied to this marker, you also open an info window with their latitude and longitude coordinates. Mozilla provides an additional position attribute titled address, which is not in the W3C specification. It provides the physical location of the coordinates. This physical address location may of course not be exact since the accuracy of the position may be too large, but when available, it saves having to use another service to reverse geocode the coordinates. In this recipe, if the address object is available, you can pull the city and region attributes from it and append the values to the info window. The following are the address object attributes that are available when the object is provided:

- city: DOMString with the city
- country: DOMString with the country
- countryCode: DOMString with the country code
- county: DOMString with the county
- postalCode: DOMString with the postal or ZIP code
- premises: DOMString with the premises
- region: DOMString with the region
- street: DOMString with the street name
- streetNumber: DOMString with the street number

If the `address` object is not available, then you can use a reverse geocoding service provided by Google, as you will see in the next recipe. In the next recipe, you will look at the three options provided with the `getCurrentPosition` interface and how they can be beneficial depending on your specific needs.

INTERMEDIATE RECIPE:
Determining **Distance with** `PositionOptions`

This recipe will use `getCurrentPosition` to first locate your browser's location and then calculate the distance to a set of points, reverse geocode your position, and display this information to the viewer. To better control the location information provided, you will use the third parameter of the `getCurrentPosition` method, `PositionOptions`.

`PositionOptions` is an object passed to the `getCurrentPosition` method as a parameter and allows you to have some control over the behavior of the method. This can be beneficial given the type of application you are working with. As an example, if you are working on a location-based restaurant application for the mobile space, then the normal accuracy of the returned location may be too broad for your needs. You can set three options in the `PositionOptions` of `getCurrentPosition`, as shown in Table 10.3.

> **Note**
>
> For the `timeout` option of the `PositionOptions` parameter, the time that the user takes to authorize the access to the location information while the request panel or dialog is up is not calculated in this amount. The timeout milliseconds is calculated only for the time that the actual call is being performed.

Table 10.3   `PositionOptions` **Parameters**

Option	Default	Description
`enableHighAccuracy`	False, not enabled	(Optional) A boolean value that tells the browser that if true, you desire the most accurate location the device may be able to provide. This may be the same location depending on the device being used.
`maximumAge`	0, any age allowed	(Optional) The maximum age of the location position returned in milliseconds since a browser may cache the last location to conserve battery power.
`timeout`	0, no timeout	(Optional) The maximum time, in milliseconds, to allow for a location position to be returned by the browser.

When the page loads, the setLocation function will be called, which will trigger the getCurrentPosition method using a set of options. Once you receive the call, you will then use the latitude and longitude coordinates to create an instance of a Google map, reverse geocode the coordinates, and calculate the distance to various cities.

1. Add the setLocation method call to the body onload attribute, and add the setLocation function, making sure to include the position options object.

2. Update the Google Maps JavaScript API V3 Overlay script tag to load the geometry library that will be used for the distance calculation:

   <script src="http://maps.google.com/maps/api/js?sensor=false**&libraries=geome
   try**">

3. Add the reverseGeoCode function that takes your latitude and longitude point and retrieves the address information from a Google geocoder.

4. Add the calculateDistance function that uses computeDistanceBetween to calculate the distance to London, New York, and San Francisco.

5. Update the HTML body div sections to mirror those in Listing 10.3 to have a container, including a mapCanvas, location information, and city distance divs.

Listing 10.3   getCurrentPosition with Position Options

```
<!DOCTYPE html>
<html>

<!DOCTYPE html>
<html>
<head>
<meta charset="UTF-8" />
<title>10.3 Points To</title>
<style>
  #container {
    width:500px;
  }

  #mapCanvas {
    width:500px;
    height:300px;
    border-style:solid;
    border-width:2px;
    margin: 22px 0;
  }

  #location {
    float:right;
    text-align:right;
  }
```

```css
  #cityDistance tr:nth-child(odd) { background-color:#eee; }
  #cityDistance tr:nth-child(even) { background-color:#fff; }

  .numDistance {
    text-align:right;
  }
</style>
```
```html
<script
➥src="http://maps.google.com/maps/api/js?sensor=false&libraries=geometry">
➥</script>
<script>
```
```javascript
// global reference variable
var map;

// success callback function for getCurrentPosition
function geoSuccess(position) {

  // get our lat and lng coordinates
  var myPosLat = position.coords.latitude;
  var myPosLng = position.coords.longitude;

  // display the coords and timestamp object fields
  document.getElementById('myPosLat').innerHTML = myPosLat;
  document.getElementById('myPosLng').innerHTML = myPosLng;

  // create our latlng object
  var myLatLng = new google.maps.LatLng(myPosLat, myPosLng);

  // set our options for the map and create the map
  var myOptions = {
    zoom: 14,
    center: myLatLng,
    mapTypeId: google.maps.MapTypeId.ROADMAP
  }
  map = new google.maps.Map(document.getElementById('mapCanvas'), myOptions);

  // reverse geocode the lat and lng
  reverseGeoCode(myLatLng);

  // calculate the distance to points of interest
  calculateDistance(myLatLng);

  // update our status
  document.getElementById('geoStatus').innerHTML = 'Location Retrieved';
}

// function to reverse geocode given a lat / lng
function reverseGeoCode(geoLatLng) {
```

```
// create our object instances
var geocoder          = new google.maps.Geocoder();
var infowindow        = new google.maps.InfoWindow();

// perform our geocoding
geocoder.geocode({'latLng': geoLatLng}, function(results, status) {
  if (status == google.maps.GeocoderStatus.OK) {
    // check if we received an address
    if (results[0]) {
      // create marker on map
      var marker = new google.maps.Marker({
        position: geoLatLng,
          map: map
      });
      // set the content to the address and open the window
      infowindow.setContent(results[0].formatted_address);
      infowindow.open(map, marker);
    }
  } else {
    alert('Geocoder failed due to: ' + status);
  }
});
}


// calculate distance function
function calculateDistance(disLatLng) {

  // set up variables and objects for distance
  var conEarth = 3963.19;  // ave. miles circumference
  var gmapsSpherLib = google.maps.geometry.spherical;

  // points of interest
  var NYCLatLng = new google.maps.LatLng(40.7141667,-74.0063889);
  var LDNLatLng = new google.maps.LatLng(51.5001524,-0.1262362);
  var SFOLatLng = new google.maps.LatLng(37.615223,-122.389979);

  // distance calculations
  var distFromLDN =
➥gmapsSpherLib.computeDistanceBetween(disLatLng,LDNLatLng,conEarth).
➥toFixed(2);
  var distFromNYC =
➥gmapsSpherLib.computeDistanceBetween(disLatLng,NYCLatLng,conEarth).
➥toFixed(2);
  var distFromSFO = ➥gmapsSpherLib.computeDistanceBetween(disLatLng,SFOLatLng,con
Earth).
➥toFixed(2);
```

```
  // set display with values
  document.getElementById('divDistFromLDN').innerHTML = distFromLDN + ' mi.';
  document.getElementById('divDistFromNYC').innerHTML = distFromNYC + ' mi.';
  document.getElementById('divDistFromSFO').innerHTML = distFromSFO + ' mi.';
}


// error handler for getCurrentPosition
function geoErrorHandler(error) {

  // initialize our error message
  var errMessage = 'ERROR: ';

  // based on the error code parameter set the message
  switch(error.code)
  {
    case error.PERMISSION_DENIED:
      errMessage += 'User did not share geolocation data.';
      break;
    case error.POSITION_UNAVAILABLE:
      errMessage += 'Could not detect current position.';
      break;
    case error.TIMEOUT:
      errMessage += 'Retrieving position timed out.';
      break;
    default:
      errMessage += 'Unknown error.';
      break;
  }


  // display the error to the user
  document.getElementById('geoStatus').innerHTML = errMessage;
}

// function to initialize call for position
function setLocation() {

  var divStatus = document.getElementById('geoStatus');

  // check for geolocation support
  if (navigator.geolocation) {

    // oldest allowed is 1 minute and timeout as 30 sec.
    var posOptions = {maximumAge:60000,
      timeout:30000};

    // make asynchronous getCurrentPosition call
    navigator.geolocation.getCurrentPosition(geoSuccess, geoErrorHandler,
➥posOptions);
```

```
          divStatus.innerHTML = 'Retrieving your location.';

      } else {
        // geolocation not supported
        divStatus.innerHTML = 'Geolocation API Not Supported';
      }
    }

    // Launch the location retrieval
    window.addEventListener('load',setLocation,false);

    </script>
    </head>
    <body>
    <div id="container">
      <div id="mapCanvas"></div>
      <div id="location">
        <table id="status">
          <tr>
            <td colspan="2"><div id="geoStatus"></div></td>
          </tr>
          <tr>
            <td>Latitude:</td>
            <td class="numDistance"><div id="myPosLat"></div></td>
          </tr>
            <tr>
            <td>Longitude:</td>
            <td class="numDistance"><div id="myPosLng"></div></td>
            </tr>
        </table>
      </div>
      <div id="distance">
        <table id="cityDistance">
          <tr>
            <td>London:</td>
            <td class="numDistance"><div id="divDistFromLDN"></div></td>
          </tr>
            <tr>
            <td>New York:</td>
            <td class="numDistance"><div id="divDistFromNYC"></div></td>
          </tr>
          <tr>
            <td>San Francisco:</td>
            <td class="numDistance"><div id="divDistFromSFO"></div></td>
          </tr>
        </table>
      </div>
    </div>
```

```
</body>
</html>
```

When the page loads, you use the `getCurrentPosition` method to retrieve the latitude and longitude coordinates but with some key options passed. An object titled `posOptions` is created and then passed to the `getCurrentPosition`. In the `posOptions`, you set the maximum age option to 60000, equal to one minute, and the timeout to 30 seconds (30000). This tells the `getCurrentPosition` to pull only from a previously cached location if the age of the location information is less than one minute old. The timeout limits the length of time allowed for the `getCurrentPosition` to retrieve the position:

```
var posOptions = {maximumAge:60000, timeout:30000};
```

Once you have the position information, you then reverse geocode to get the full address using a handy `geocoder` object from the Google script and then calculate the distance to three cities. The result will look similar to Figure 10.3.

As you have seen in this recipe, you can control the behavior of the location position acquisition by setting the `PositionOptions` object in the `getCurrentPosition` call. The options allow you to change accuracy and performance, tuning your application to the experience that is needed by the user. The recipes to this point have included maps, reverse geocoding, and even distance calculations. The thought has probably crossed your mind about the mobile space and how to change the information presented to the user as their location changes. Well, the Geolocation API has just the thing, as you will see in the next recipe.

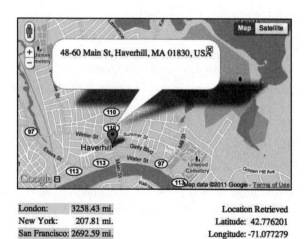

London:	3258.43 mi.	Location Retrieved
New York:	207.81 mi.	Latitude: 42.776201
San Francisco:	2692.59 mi.	Longitude: -71.077279

Figure 10.3   Calculated distance from three cities

ADVANCED RECIPE:
Following a Moving Location with
`watchPosition`

The browser that your visitor is using in many cases will be mobile-based. It is not uncommon to see people walking down the street, riding the subway, or otherwise moving about while getting information about their surroundings or their locations. The `getCurrentPosition` method provides a position object once when called. However, as a person moves around, it would be nice to "follow" the location. This is where two new methods, `watchPosition` and `clearWatch`, of the GeoLocation API are useful.

The `watchPosition` method is very similar to the `getCurrentPosition` and takes the same parameters. When the `watchPosition` method is called, the browser will create a background task and provide a reference ID to a watch process as a return. The background task will retrieve the current position, send the location to the success callback, and then set a timer to watch the position. Each time the timer is triggered and a new location is retrieved, the location is then compared to see whether it is "significantly" different. If the new location is significantly different from the last, then the success callback function is called with the new location information. The process will continue to run until the `clearWatch` method is called with the watch ID as a parameter or the browser tab or window is closed (in mobile platforms such as the iPhone, this could be when the browser is also sent to the background). The following are the interfaces of the `watchPosition` and `clearWatch` methods, respectively:

```
long watchPosition (successCallback [, errorCallback] [, positionOptions])
```

The parameters of the `watchPosition` method are as follows:

- `successCallback`: The function to execute and pass the location object to when a new location is identified by the browser
- `errorCallback`: (Optional) The function to handle any errors that occurred
- `options`: (Optional) An options object to handle how the position is retrieved

```
clearWatch (watchId)
```

The parameter of the `clearWatch` method is as follows:

- `watchId`: The long ID reference to the watch process to end

In this recipe, you will use the `watchPosition` method to retrieve the location of the browser and map a new marker on a Google map whenever the location differs from the last marker by more than a quarter of a mile. The viewport for this recipe is set in the `meta` tag for an iPhone width along with the CSS styles so that the recipe can be easily run on an iPhone to show the movement on the map. A line will be connected between the points to show a trail of the past points, and the map will be centered on the last point shown. When the user clicks the Clear Watch button, the watch process will end.

By checking the distance from the last point, this allows you to keep the map fairly clean as a person moves with their mobile device. If, however, you were working on a smaller scale such as directions in a city, a quarter-mile difference may be too large; if you were working with a fast means of transportation, a quarter mile may not be large enough. This difference check will be based on your own needs, but this recipe shows how you can filter location points using some quick distance calculations as the location changes.

1. Create the HTML page with the Start Watch and Clear Watch buttons, as shown in Listing 10.4.

2. Include the script for the Google Maps JavaScript API V3 Overlay with the geometry library and the global variables that will hold the watch ID, map, polyline, and last latitude and longitude coordinates.

3. Add the `initMap` function in the script, and set the `load` event to launch the `initMap` function.

4. Add the `startWatch` and `clearWatch` functions.

5. Add the `successCallback` and `errorCallback` functions.

Listing 10.4   **Using** `watchPosition` **to Track Your Path**

```
<!DOCTYPE html>
<html>
<head>
<meta charset="UTF-8" />
<meta name="viewport" content="width=device-width; initial-scale=1.0; maximum-
➥scale=1.0; user-scalable=0;" />
<title>10.4 Leaving My Mark</title>
<style>
  #container {
    width:300px;
  }

  #mapCanvas {
    width:300px;
    height:200px;
    border-style:solid;
    border-width:2px;
    margin: 22px 0;
  }

  #btnMap {
    float:left;
  }
```

```css
#location {
  float:right;
}

.numDistance {
  text-align:right;
}
</style>
```

```html
<script type="text/javascript"
➥src="http://maps.google.com/maps/api/js?sensor=false&libraries=geometry">
➥</script>
<script>
```

```javascript
// declare our variables
var watchId;  // our watchposition process id
var map;      // our map
var poly;     // our polyline for marking our path
var lastLatLng;  // the last lat and lng coordinate

// set constant for miles for computeDistanceBetween method
var conEarthMi  = 3963.19;

// initialize our map
function initMap() {

  // add the button listeners
  var btnStartWatch = document.getElementById('startWatch');
  var btnStopWatch = document.getElementById('stopWatch');
  btnStartWatch.addEventListener('click',startWatch,false);
  btnStopWatch.addEventListener('click',stopWatch,false);

  // set initial position to new york and create map
  lastLatLng = new google.maps.LatLng(40.7141667,-74.0063889); // new york
  var myOptions = {
    zoom: 14,
    center: lastLatLng,
    mapTypeId: google.maps.MapTypeId.ROADMAP
  }
  map = new google.maps.Map(document.getElementById('mapCanvas'), myOptions);

  // set our polyline for showing the path
  var polyOptions = {
    strokeColor: '#00FF00',
    strokeOpacity: 1.0,
    strokeWeight: 3
  }
```

```
  poly = new google.maps.Polyline(polyOptions);
  poly.setMap(map);
}

// success handler for geolocation watch position
function successCallback(position) {

  // get our latitude and longitude
  var posLat = position.coords.latitude;
  var posLng = position.coords.longitude;

  // create a new google maps latlng object
  var newLatLng = new google.maps.LatLng(posLat,posLng);

  // calculate distance from last point
  var distFromLast =
➡google.maps.geometry.spherical.computeDistanceBetween(newLatLng,
➡lastLatLng, conEarthMi);

  // verify distance greater than a quarter of a mile
  if (distFromLast > 0.25) {

    // get the polyline path array
    var path = poly.getPath();

    // Add the new coordinate to our path array
    path.push(newLatLng);

    // Add a new marker at the new coordinate
    var marker = new google.maps.Marker({
      position: newLatLng,
      title: '#' + path.getLength(),
      map: map
    });

    // recenter the map on the new coordinate
    map.setCenter(newLatLng);

    // update our display
    document.getElementById('myPosLat').innerHTML = posLat.toFixed(8);
    document.getElementById('myPosLng').innerHTML = posLng.toFixed(8);
    document.getElementById('watchStatus').innerHTML = 'Updated Position (#' +
➡path.getLength() + ')';

    // set our last coordinate to the new coordinate
    lastLatLng = newLatLng;

  }
}
```

```javascript
// error handler for geolocation watchposition
function errorCallback(error) {

  // initialize our error message
  var errMessage = 'ERROR: ';
  var divWatchStatus = document.getElementById('watchStatus');

  // based on the error code parameter set the message
  switch(error.code)
  {
    case error.PERMISSION_DENIED:
      errMessage += 'User did not share geolocation data.';
      break;
    case error.POSITION_UNAVAILABLE:
      errMessage += 'Could not detect current position.';
      break;
    case error.TIMEOUT:
      errMessage += 'Retrieving position timed out.';
      break;
    default:
      errMessage += 'Unknown error.';
      break;
  }

  // update our status
  divWatchStatus.innerHTML = errMessage;
}

// button start watch handler
function startWatch() {

  var divWatchStatus = document.getElementById('watchStatus');

  // verify geolocation is available
  if (navigator.geolocation) {

    // make sure only one watch
    if (watchId == null) {

      // set our position options
      // maximum age 40 seconds
      // timeout of 20 seconds
      // enhanced accuracy on for mobile
      var posOptions = {maximumAge:40000,
        timeout:20000,
        enhancedAccuracy:true}
```

```
      // start our watch
      watchId = navigator.geolocation.watchPosition(successCallback,
        errorCallback,
        posOptions);

      // update our status
      divWatchStatus.innerHTML = 'Watching Location ('+watchId+')';
    }
  } else {
    // update status that geolocation is not available
    divWatchStatus.innerHTML = 'Geolocation Not Supported';
  }
}

// button stop watch handler
function stopWatch() {

  // verify that we have a watch currently on
  if (watchId != null) {
    // clear our watch
    navigator.geolocation.clearWatch(watchId);

    // set the watchId flag to null
    watchId = null;

    // update our status
    document.getElementById('watchStatus').innerHTML = 'Off';
  }
}

// Initialize the page
window.addEventListener('load',initMap,false);

</script>
</head>
<body>
<div id="container">
  <div id="mapCanvas"></div>
  <div id="btnMap">
    <button id="startWatch">Start Watch</button>
    <br>
    <button id="stopWatch">Stop Watch</button>
  </div>
  <div id="location">
    <table id="status">
      <tr>
        <td>Latitude:</td>
```

```
          <td class="numDistance"><div id="myPosLat"></div></td>
        </tr>
        <tr>
          <td>Longitude:</td>
          <td class="numDistance"><div id="myPosLng"></div></td>
        </tr>
        <tr>
          <td colspan="2"><div id="watchStatus"></div></td>
        </tr>
      </table>
    </div>
  </div>
</body>
</html>
```

Let's look at Listing 10.4 in a bit of detail. When the page loads, the `initMap` function is called and initializes the map on the page. We have chosen coordinates for New York City, but you could easily set a different starting center for the map or load the map only when the watch starts. In the `initMap`, you create a polyline layer on top of the map, which will allow you to connect the coordinates from the watch and display the "path" to the viewer. The map is now initialized, and you can begin the watch of the position.

To start, the Start Watch button is clicked or tapped. As normal, you should be asked to confirm you want to share your location information. Once clicked, the `startWatch` function will be called. In the `startWatch` function, you check that there is no watch process already running by checking the global watch ID variable. This prevents more than one watch process from being started. You then set the position options and call the `watchPosition` method. The return of `watchPosition`, the watch ID, is then stored in the `watchId` variable so that you can use it to stop the process later with the `clearWatch`.

When the `watchPosition` returns with a location object, you pull out the latitude and longitude properties, create a latitude and longitude object, and then calculate the distance with the last latitude and longitude coordinates with the Google `computeDistanceBetween` method. In this case, you pass into the method the new coordinate, the last coordinate, and a constant value, informing the function that you want the return value in miles. You then check this distance to see whether it is greater than a quarter of a mile so that you do not flood the map with markers. If the next point is more than the distance, then you push onto the poly path array of points the new coordinate and add a new marker. Pushing the coordinate onto the array updates the line on the map, so with each new point the path will grow, showing where you have been, as shown in Figure 10.4.

This recipe shows how you can access the browser's location and be notified whenever that position changes. This information can be used for a wide array of applications including integration with databases of location-based services such as the Yahoo Query Language and the beta of Google Places to show nearby places of interest.

Figure 10.4   Growing the path with coordinate points

> **Note**
>
> One thing to consider as you are working with devices, especially mobile devices, and retrieving geolocation information is that the continual retrieval of device information will accelerate the use of the device's battery. This should be taken into account when you design your application and used only when needed in order to minimize the usage.

Summary

The Geolocation API provides an easy interface for adding location-specific and position-aware functionality to websites and applications. Some of the solutions that can be designed include the following:

- Display of location specific information
- Proximity awareness
- Dynamic adjustment to a locale, such as language and currency

- Map and route integration
- Geotagging data, pictures, and other items with location information

In this chapter, you learned the `getCurrentPosition`, `watchPosition`, and `clearWatch` methods along with the success and error callbacks from these methods. The possibilities are endless, and it is exciting to have this option now in browsers.

11

Client–Side Storage

The persistence of information in the visitor's browser has historically been limited to keys and values in cookies. Cookie storage is limited in size and structure, and cookies are passed with each request to their corresponding websites, creating unnecessary overhead. Certain sets of data could improve the user experience if cookies could be stored and retrieved locally, instead of being retrieved by web servers each time they are used. In HTML5, two client-side storage facilities have been added: web storage, which includes session and local storage, and database storage. In this chapter, you will learn about these new client-side storage options and work through some recipes to get you started with storing data locally in the browser.

Client-Side Storage Overview

To start talking about the new storage APIs, let's first look at what we previously had available in browsers to store information locally. Typically, to store information that could be retrieved at a later time in a visitor's browser, you had to create a cookie. Information stored may have included user preferences, form information, user keys, or the like. However, the storage of cookies is limited to approximately 4KB, contains only simple key/value pairs, and increases overhead by sending the cookie with each request to the server.

The session and local web storage options provided in HTML5 are similar to cookies in that the structure is in key/value format, in which string values can be assigned to string-based keys. A value can be accessed in the session or local storage by asking for the appropriate key in the storage object. The difference between the session and local options is simply the scope of the object in the visitor's session. In session storage, the data is stored only for that particular session with the website. Once the session has ended, through closing the window or tab in the browser, the storage will be removed. When the user returns, the session storage will be empty. If, instead, you want the data to be available across sessions, whether at the same time in another window or a new session at a later date, then you can use the local storage, which is persisted even after closing the current session.

Key/value pairs limit storing more complex information (or at least make it difficult). Thus, a third type of storage has been added to provide data storage like you would normally use on the server side: database storage. Database storage leverages a SQLite database or IndexedDB and allows you to store more complex data objects, as you will see later in the chapter. Like local storage, database storage persists across sessions. Which storage mechanism you use in your website or application depends on the type of information you need to store, the scope of the data, and how long you need the data to be persisted. Table 11.1 provides a quick way to determine the appropriate storage type.

Data Security

When we discuss data storage, we must also discuss security. Like storing information in a server database of a web application, similar security guidelines should be applied to database storage on the client side. This is especially true since unlike a server where you may have control over the firewalls, users, passwords, and other security features, a visitor's browser is outside the immediate network. This makes it that much more important to be vigilant about what is stored in the client browser and how it is stored. Encryption may be a consideration depending on the data you are storing, but if you are considering encryption of the data, you may want to reconsider storing it in the first place.

The storage options in HTML5 employ "origin-based" security by limiting access to session, local, and database client-side storage to pages that originate from the same domain from which the storage was created. In this manner, pages from other sites or applications cannot access the data. However, the "origin" security implementation uses the page's origin as the determining factor for access to the session and local storage lists of key/value pairs. Because of this, there is the potential for storage to be exposed to embedded scripts. This makes knowing the actions that the external files you use in your pages that much more important.

> **Note**
>
> Data you store using the local, session, or database objects is limited to the specific browser that is being used by the visitor at the time. If the user returns to your site or application using a different browser or a different computer, then the storage will not be accessible. Data that you would like accessible anywhere will still need to be stored on your database server or in the cloud.

Table 11.1   Client Storage Types and Properties

Storage	Format	Scope	Persistence
Session	Key/value	Session only	Session only
Local	Key/value	Across sessions	Across sessions
Database	Structured	Across sessions	Across sessions

Client-side storage is being adopted rapidly by the different browser platforms, and Chrome is the leader in this support. There is still debate about the implementation of the best database storage mechanism by the different browsers, but Table 11.2 lists the current support of the client-side storage objects by various browsers.

Table 11.2   **Client-Side Storage Browser Availability**

Android	**2.1+**
Chrome	**10.0+**
Firefox	**10.6+**
Internet Explorer	**8.0+**
iOS Safari	**3.2+**
Opera	**10.6+**
Safari	**4.0+**

Keys and Values: `sessionStorage` and `localStorage`

The session storage and local storage objects are similar in their implementations and differ only in the scope and persistence of the data that is written, as shown in Table 11.1. The browser provides a built-in storage interface for each storage type, `sessionStorage` and `localStorage`, and each uses a list of key/value pairs to store the data. You can set a value to a key and then retrieve the value by asking for the key. Both storage objects provide methods to set values, get values, remove a key, retrieve a key for a position in the list, and clear all the key/value pairs in the storage object. The methods and properties of each storage object type are the same, because they are inherited from the same `Storage` interface defined in the Web Storage specification:

- `setItem(key,value)`: Sets the key/value pair passed as parameters. If the key exists, then the value is updated with the value passed.
- `getItem(key)`: Returns the value for the key passed as a parameter.
- `removeItem(key)`: Removes the key/value pair as defined by the key passed.
- `key(n)`: Returns the name of the key for the index provided.
- `clear`: Removes all key/value pairs.
- `length`: Provides the number of key/value pairs in the storage list.

To set an item, you call `setItem` and provide a key and a value to be set:

```
setItem(key, value)
```

Here are the parameters:

- `key`: The key to file the string value under
- `value`: The value to be stored with the file

The value is a string, so if you are storing a number, it will be treated as a string in the storage and will need to be converted back to the proper data type when retrieved. The key and value will then be stored in no particular order in the list of key/value pairs in the browser storage for the domain that the page has been loaded from.

If you set the item with a key that already exists, then the value of that key will be updated with the new value provided. Thus, the `setItem` method acts as both a create method and an update method. To store the value "book" under the key "source" in the session storage, you would make the following call in JavaScript:

```
sessionStorage.setItem('source', 'book');
```

The `setItem` method does not have a return value, so to protect against possible storage errors, you can enclose the call in a try-catch block.

To retrieve the value of a key from either the session storage or the local storage, you call `getItem` with the key that you are interested in. The return will be a string value, which you can then use in your script:

```
string getItem(key)
```

Here `key` is the string key to retrieve the corresponding value.

To retrieve the value stored in the previous example, you would ask for the "source" key from the session storage by performing the following call:

```
textSource = sessionStorage.getItem('source');
```

Since the session and local storage are based around storage objects, you can also use object dot notation to access stored values of keys by using the key as the property name, as shown here:

```
textSource = sessionStorage.source;
```

Now that we have briefly discussed the `get` and `set` methods of the session and local storage, we'll show a basic recipe in action. We will start the recipes with the session object and then move to local storage.

> **Tip**
>
> In browsers such as Firefox, the user can disable storage. To validate that storage is available, your code should attempt to write and then retrieve a value. If the value cannot be retrieved, then storage may be disabled in the browser.

BEGINNER RECIPE:
Getting and Setting Session Storage

In this recipe, the HTML page will use the getItem and setItem methods of the sessionStorage object to store and retrieve the number of times that a visitor views a page in the session. This number is incremented with each refresh of the page and displayed to the visitor. Perform the following steps to create the page in Listing 11.1:

1. Create a blank HTML page with a div titled divVisits.

2. Add the init function in a set of script tags with the code from Listing 11.1.

3. Add the window.addEventListener event handler to launch the init function after the page loads.

Listing 11.1   **Displaying Page Visits Using Session Storage**

```
<!DOCTYPE html>
<html>
<head>
<meta charset="UTF-8" />
<title>11.1 Session Storage Page Visits</title>
<script>
function init() {

  // reference the div for display
  var divVisits = document.getElementById('divVisits');

  // check if our browser supports sessionStorage
  if (window.sessionStorage) {

    var visits; // number of visits to this page

    // check to see if our variable exists using dot notation
    if (sessionStorage.visits) {

      // retrieve key and convert to int
      visits = parseInt(sessionStorage.getItem('visits'));

      // increment the visits
      visits++;

    } else {
      // default to first visit
      visits = 1;
    }
```

```
        // update our visits variable
        sessionStorage.setItem('visits',visits);

        // display the number of session visits
        divVisits.innerHTML = 'Session page visits: ' + visits;

    } else {
      // sessionStorage not available
      divVisits = 'Window sessionStorage is not available';
    }
}

// onload launch our init function
window.addEventListener('load',init,false);

</script>
</head>
<body>
  <div id="divVisits"></div>
</body>
</html>
```

When you load the page created in Listing 11.1 in your browser, the init function will be launched. The init function will first check to see whether the sessionStorage object is available in the window by checking for window.sessionStorage. If the sessionStorage object is not available, then you will display a message in your div on the page.

Assuming that the session Storage object is available, the JavaScript code then checks to see whether the key "visits" exists by asking for the value through the dot notation: sessionStorage.visits. If the key "visits" exists, then the value will be returned, and the check will pass. Otherwise, you know that this is the first time for this session and will start the "visits" count at 1. If the key is in session storage, then to demonstrate the get method of retrieving values, you will retrieve the value of the key via the getItem method. When the value is retrieved, you convert the "visits" string value to an integer data type with parseInt. This conversion must be done because all values in web storage are stored as basic strings. If your script is storing and then retrieving other data types, you will want to convert these strings to their proper types.

After you have either retrieved the number of visits and incremented it by 1 or set the initial value to 1, the script will then update the "visits" key in the session storage with the setItem method. If the key was not in session storage previously, then setItem will add the key/value pair, but if the "visits" key was already in session storage, then the value will be updated with the new number of visits.

Chrome Developer Tools for Viewing Storage

You may wonder after loading the page created in Listing 11.1 in your browser how you can validate what is happening behind the scenes in the local session storage as the script runs. The Google Chrome browser has a set of tools titled Developer Tools that you may already be familiar with. If you open these tools in your browser window and refresh your page, you will be able to see the session storage key/value pairs under the Resources section, as shown in Figure 11.1.

In Figure 11.1, the domain that has stored keys is shown on the left under Session Storage, and on the right are the key/value pairs that are currently stored. In this case, the current value of visits is 2, and the JavaScript has displayed this to the user. The Developer Tools of Chrome are useful for working with the session and local storage because you can confirm not only that your script is working correctly but also add, update, and remove key/value pairs through the user interface. In the current version of the Developer Tools, you will need to refresh the storage key/value view pane with the Refresh button at the bottom if you change a key/value pair.

> **Tip**
>
> Any object that has a `toString` built-in method can be stored in the value field of the key/value pairs of session and local storage. Even more complex JSON structured objects can be stored by using the `JSON.stringify(yourObject)` and `JSON.parse(itemRetrieved)` methods to convert the JSON object to a string and then convert the string retrieved back to your object.

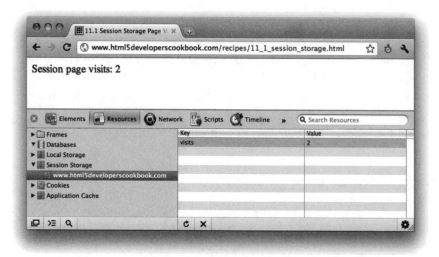

Figure 11.1   Viewing the session storage key/value pairs in Chrome's Developer Tools

This recipe performed a very simple setting and getting of a key/value pair in session storage. The next recipe will include error handling and show the availability of session storage across pages.

BEGINNER RECIPE:
Styling from Session Storage

In this recipe, you will provide the visitor to your page with the opportunity to select a theme color for the background of the pages. The visitor's selection will be stored in the session storage and retrieved on a second page to control the background color. A theme reset option is provided, which will remove the stored background key/value pair from the session storage. The following is the `removeItem` method that will be used in this recipe:

```
removeItem(key)
```

Here `key` is the key string to be removed.

Like any data storage mechanism, session and local storage have size limitations in place to protect the browser and the client's machine. Each browser sets its own size limitation, but unlike cookies, which are limited to a rather small 4KB, the sizes allocated for session and local storage are much larger. At the time of writing this book, Internet Explorer 9, for example, has a 10MB limitation. If your script attempts to set or update a value for a key and hits this ceiling, an error will be thrown. To prevent your script from abruptly ending because of this error, you should wrap your `setItem` method calls in a try-catch block. In this recipe, we will show you how to catch this error if it were to happen. The following steps and Listing 11.2 will allow you to create page 1 of the recipe:

1. Create the page in Listing 11.2 with the `style`, `script`, and `body` tags.

2. Add the `themeContent` and `themeSettings` divs, as shown in Listing 11.2 with the corresponding HTML.

3. Add the `initTheme`, `setTheme`, `resetTheme`, and `applyTheme` functions to your script.

4. Add the `window.addEventListener` statement to trigger the `initTheme` function.

Listing 11.2   **Setting a Theme in Session Storage**

```
<!DOCTYPE html>
<html>
<head>
<meta charset="UTF-8" />
<title>11.2 Theme Selector - Page 1</title>
<style>
#themeContent {
```

```
    background-color:#FFF;
    border-style:solid;
    border-width:2px;
}
#themeSettings {
  margin:10px;
}
</style>
<script>

var themeDiv; // output display div

// function to initialize the theme
function initTheme() {

  // set our div reference for output
  themeDiv = document.getElementById('theme');

  // check if our browser supports sessionStorage
  if (window.sessionStorage) {

    // set the button handler
    var btnResetTheme = document.getElementById('resetTheme');
    btnResetTheme.addEventListener('click',resetTheme,false);

    // set the select list change handler
    var selThemeColor = document.getElementById('themeColor');
    selThemeColor.addEventListener('change',setTheme,false);

    // check if we have previously set the theme color
    if (sessionStorage.themeColor) {

      // set the initial theme color
      var themeColor = sessionStorage.getItem('themeColor');
      document.getElementById(themeColor).selected = true;

      applyTheme(themeColor);
    }
  } else {
    themeDiv.innerHTML = 'sessionStorage is not supported.';
  }
}

// set the chosen theme
function setTheme() {

  // retrieve the theme color selected
  var themeColor = document.getElementById('themeColor').value;
```

```
    // use our try catch and set the theme color
    try {
      sessionStorage.setItem('themeColor',themeColor);
      applyTheme(themeColor);
    }
    catch(err){
      // error code 22 QUOTA_EXCEEDED_ERR says we ran out of space
      if(err.code == QUOTA_EXCEEDED_ERR){
        themeDiv.innerHTML = 'sessionStorage ran out of memory.';
        // perform any other handling we want to here
      }
    }
}

// function to reset the theme color
function resetTheme() {
  // remove the item from the session storage
  sessionStorage.removeItem('themeColor');

  // reset display
  document.getElementById('default').selected = true;
  document.body.style.backgroundColor = '';
  themeDiv.innerHTML = 'Theme reset.';
}

// apply a theme to the page
function applyTheme(themeColor) {
  document.body.style.backgroundColor = themeColor;
  themeDiv.innerHTML = 'Theme ' + themeColor + ' applied. ';
}

// initialize our window
window.addEventListener('load',initTheme,false);

</script>
</head>
<body>
<div id="themeContent">
  <div id="themeSettings">
    <H1>Page 1</H1>
    Choose Theme:
    <select id="themeColor">
      <option id="default" value="">Select color...</option>
      <option id="blue" value="blue">Blue</option>
      <option id="red" value="red">Red</option>
      <option id="yellow" value="yellow">Yellow</option>
      <option id="green" value="green">Green</option>
    </select>
```

```
      <button id="resetTheme">Reset Theme</button><br><br>
      <div id="theme"></div><br><br>
      <a href="11_3_theme_page_2.html">Go To Page 2</a>
    </div>
  </div>
</body>
</html>
```

After setting the theme on page 1, which is in Listing 11.2, you can verify that the theme has been stored by loading a different page that reads the storage and uses the theme information to set the proper theme. Use the following steps and Listing 11.3 to create the second page to show the theme color previously selected:

1. Create a new page based on Listing 11.3 with the appropriate sections.

2. Modify the page's a tag in both pages to correspond to the name of your pages so that you can navigate back and forth between the pages.

Listing 11.3   **Showing the Theme Page 2**

```
<!DOCTYPE html>
<html><head>
<meta charset="UTF-8" />
<title>11.3 Showing the Theme - Page 2</title>
<style>
#themeContent {
  background-color:#FFF;
  border-style:solid;
  border-width:2px;
}
#themeSettings {
  margin:10px;
}
</style>
<script>

// initialize our page
function init() {

  // retrieve the saved theme color
  var themeColor = sessionStorage.getItem('themeColor');
  applyTheme(themeColor);
}

// apply the theme to the page
function applyTheme(themeColor) {

  document.body.style.backgroundColor = themeColor;
```

```
    var themeDiv = document.getElementById('theme');
    themeDiv.innerHTML = themeColor + ' theme.';


}

// initialize the page
window.addEventListener('load',init,false);

</script>
</head>
<body>
<div id="themeContent">
  <div id="themeSettings">
    <H1>Page 2</H1>
    <div id="theme"></div>
    <br><br>
    <a href="11_2_theme_page_1.html">Go To Page 1</a>
  </div>
</div>
</body>
</html>
```

When page 1 is loaded into your browser, the page first retrieves the currently stored theme color from the session storage. The first time the page is run, there is no theme, and the return value is empty, so the theme is set to the browser's default. On subsequent loads of the page, the color would be retrieved, set to the background color, and set as the selected value in the color select control.

Note

To run recipes involving session storage, you will need to upload the pages to a server instead of running them in "local mode." The reason is that in local mode some browsers will throw an error saying that the operation is not supported. For example, in Firefox, an "Operation is not supported" code 9 error will be thrown.

Once loaded, the visitor can change the drop-down list of options to another color, which will change the page background color and store the color in session storage under the key themeColor. In the script, this setItem call to store the setting has been wrapped in a try-catch block. If triggered because of the size constraints, the code informs the visitor that the session storage is full, but you could perform whatever actions are needed when this scenario occurs. After setting the theme color, the visitor can click Go To Page 2, which will load the second page. Since the second page is in the same session as the first page, it will also have access to the session storage key/value pair saved on page 1. The second page then retrieves this item and sets the background to the stored color.

In Listing 11.2, you also added the option for the visitor to reset the theme. In this case, the recipe removes the key/value pair from the session storage with the `removeItem` method. The recipe could have also updated the key by calling `setItem` with an empty string value.

At the beginning of this chapter, we discussed how session storage allows you to store data for that session only. If you load the page created in Listing 11.2 into two tabs or windows in the same browser and then select different colors, each tab will have its own background color since there is a different session for each tab or window. To have the values available across browser windows or tabs, and even after the browser is closed and reopened, you will need to use the local storage object. We will look at the local storage object in the next recipe.

INTERMEDIATE RECIPE:
Storing Forms with Local Storage

Session storage, as shown in the previous recipes, provides you with a method to store items for the period of the visitor's session, which can be beneficial for short-term storage. At times, though, you will want to store data in the visitor's browser for use when they return or even across currently active sessions. This is where local storage is valuable. Local storage uses the same key/value pair list to store data with the `getItem`, `setItem`, and `removeItem` web storage methods. The important factor is that the data you store in local storage persists even after the session is closed.

This recipe shows an example of remembering form data that a visitor has previously filled out. A visitor could come to your site, start a form, and then navigate away or close their browser. Typically, the visitor would have found the form empty when they returned to the site. In this recipe, as the visitor fills out the form, the JavaScript catches the changes and stores the form fields and values in the local storage. Then if the page is closed and reloaded, the page checks local storage to see whether there is stored form data and automatically populates the form with the information. A similar implementation could even handle collecting form data from a multipage form and storing it locally until the entire form has been completed.

Two new concepts with the session and local storage are employed in this recipe: `key` and `length`. The `key` method allows you to retrieve the name of the key stored by supplying an index value to the `key` method:

```
DOMString key(index)
```

Here, `index` is the index of the key/value pair to return the key string for.

The recipe also uses the `length` property of the session and local storage, which returns the number of key/value pairs in the session or local storage. To return the number of key/value pairs, you would use a call like the following:

```
var numItems = localStorage.length;
```

In this recipe, you will use both the key method and the length property to loop through the localStorage key/value pairs. Let's do the following steps to get started with Listing 11.4:

1. Create a blank HTML file and add the body HTML from Listing 11.4, which holds the form and form fields you will be using. For simplicity sake, we have used onchange inline for the form fields, but you could replace these with event listeners for each of the fields.

2. Add the script tags in the head of the HTML file with the window .addEventListener function to launch the checkStorage function when the page is loaded.

3. Add the checkStorage function in the script, as shown in Listing 11.4.

4. Add the changeField function in the script, as shown in Listing 11.4, which will handle the form field changes.

5. Load the file in your Chrome browser with the Developer Tools open to the local storage area, and enter information in the fields.

Listing 11.4   **Storing Form Changes in** localStorage

```
<!DOCTYPE html>
<html>
<head>
<meta charset="UTF-8" />
<title>11.4 Storing Form Data with Local Storage</title>
<script>

// function to read storage and init form
function checkStorage() {

  // check if local storage available
  if (window.localStorage) {

    var key, value, field;

    // loop through local storage
    for (var i = 0; i < localStorage.length; i++) {

      // retrieve the key
      key = localStorage.key(i);

      // set the field from the key
      field = document.getElementById(key);

      // check for field and assign value
      if (field) {
        // retrieve the value
        value = unescape(localStorage.getItem(key));
```

```
            // set the field value
            field.value = value;
        }
    }  // end for loop
  }  // end local storage check
}  // end function

// set the localStorage with the changed field
function changeField(formField) {

  // check if local storage available
  if (window.localStorage) {

    var key, value;

    // set key to form field id
    key = formField.id;
    // set value to form field value
    value = escape(formField.value);

    // try to set item in local storage
    try {
      localStorage.setItem(key, value);
    }
    catch (err) {
      if (err.code == QUOTA_EXCEEDED_ERR) {
        alert('localStorage ran out of memory.');
      }
    }

  } else {
      alert('localStorage is not supported.');
  }
}


// initialize our form from storage
window.addEventListener('load',checkStorage,false);

</script>
</head>
<body>
<h1>My Form</h1>
<form id='myForm'>
  <table>
    <tr>
      <td>First Name:</td>
      <td><input type="text" id="firstName" onchange="changeField(this);" /></td>
    </tr>
```

```
    <tr>
      <td>Last Name:</td>
      <td><input type="text" id="lastName" onchange="changeField(this);" /></td>
    </tr>
    <tr>
      <td>Email:</td>
      <td><input type="email" id="email" onchange="changeField(this);" /></td>
    </tr>
    <tr>
      <td>Telephone:</td>
      <td><input type="tel" id="phone" onchange="changeField(this);" /></td>
    </tr>
  </table>
</form>
</body>
</html>
```

After you enter your first name in the firstName field and tab to the next field, the onchange event will fire for the firstName field. The changeField function will then execute with the form field of firstName passed as a parameter. The changeField function will then store the field data in a key/value pair in localStorage. The function uses the ID of the form field for the key and the value as the value in the key/value pair. So, if you have Developer Tools open in Chrome when you are doing this, you should now see the key firstName with the value of the text entry you supplied.

To see the real power of localStorage, close your tab or browser window and then reopen it to this form page. When you reopen the page, the checkStorage function will execute on page load. This function is designed to check whether you have previously stored any form information in local storage and retrieve this information. The function will retrieve each key/value pair by looping through the localStorage list, check to see whether there is a form field ID that matches the key name, and if so set the field value to the value retrieved.

In this recipe, you use simple text fields to show the power of localStorage, but this could be used for other types of form inputs as well. The changeField and checkStorage functions would need to be updated to handle different logic for different field types such as a select list or a radio button, but the value could be stored like the regular text input in local storage.

After the page is finished with the stored form information and the form is ultimately submitted to the server, you would ideally want to remove the fields. Besides the removeItem method that you saw before, the storage API provides a method for clearing the entire session or local storage: clear. The clear method takes no parameters nor does it return any result and "clears" all key/value pairs for the page's domain out of the list. The following is an example of the call:

```
localStorage.clear();
```

The execution of this line will clear all key/value pairs from the local storage list no matter which page added them or when they were added. Because this is an all-or-nothing type of method, you should be absolutely positive you want to clear the contents of the session storage or the local storage.

In the recipes to this point, you learned about the basics of adding, updating, and removing stored data for a site on the client machine. This assumes the visitor is on a single page interacting with the site at the time. If the stored information was changed from another page in the browser, you have had no way to automatically handle that change on a previously open page. The client-side storage API provides an event structure for session storage and local storage updates that you can catch and handle on an open page. This next recipe combines the methods you have seen along with storage update events to refresh your page content.

ADVANCED RECIPE:
Catching Events in Local Storage

In this recipe, you will use the local storage methods and properties to implement a notes sidebar, which will allow the visitor to take notes as they browse through the site. The notes are stored in the local storage of the visitor's browser, and the order of the notes is maintained. The visitor can add a new note, update a note, remove a note, or remove all their notes. In addition, if the visitor is viewing the site in multiple tabs or browser instances, the notes will automatically update on all pages when a change happens on one page.

To automatically update the list of notes on a browser tab or window based on a change in the list of the notes by the visitor on another tab or window, you will need to employ the storage event mechanism. Like other events you have seen, a storage event is raised when the session storage or local storage is modified. The event could occur when a new key/value pair is added, updated, or removed. A handler on the page can listen for these events and perform actions based on the receipt of the event. The storageEvent contains attributes that will help determine the actions that need to be taken (Table 11.3). In this recipe, you will catch the event, verify that it is from local storage, alert the visitor of the change, and then refresh the notes list so that you are showing the current list.

Table 11.3   **The** storageEvent **Attributes**

Attribute	Type	Purpose
key	DOMString	The key on which the change occurred
oldValue	DOMString	The old value
newValue	DOMString	The new value
url	DOMString	The URL of page that made the change
storageArea	Storage	The storage area that this update occurred in

Let's get started with the following steps for Listing 11.5:

1. Create a blank HTML page with the HTML `body` and `style` tags, as shown in Listing 11.5.

2. Add the `script` tags and `keyCode` variable declaration. This variable holds a key that you will prefix each stored note with.

3. Add the `window.addEventListener` line and the `initNoteBoard` and `updateNoteBoard` functions.

4. Add the note functions: `addNote`, `changeNote`, `updateNote`, and `removeNote`. The `changeNote` function loads the note into the update form, while `updateNote` modifies the note in local storage.

5. Add the `clearAllNotes` function to allow the visitor to reset the note board.

6. Add the event handler function, `onStorageEvent`, which will catch any storage events.

Listing 11.5   **Storing Notes in Local Storage**

```
<!DOCTYPE html>
<html>
<head>
<meta charset="UTF-8" />
<title>11.5 Storing Notes in Local Storage</title>
<style>
* {margin: 0; padding: 0;}
body {padding: 20px;}
h1 {font-size: 120%; margin: 0 0 .5em;}
section {width: 300px;}
#noteBoard, textarea {
  -moz-border-radius: 10px;
  -webkit-border-radius: 10px;
  border-radius: 10px;
  -moz-box-shadow: 0px 0px 4px rgba(0,0,0,.4);
  -webkit-box-shadow: 0px 0px 4px rgba(0,0,0,.4);
  box-shadow: 0px 0px 4px rgba(0,0,0,.4);}
#noteBoard {
  background: #FCFABA;
  float: right;
  padding: 10px 20px;}
#noteBoard div {
  border-bottom: 1px dashed #CCC;
  margin: 0 0 5px;
  padding: 5px 0;
  width: 100%;}
#noteBoard div.buttons {border: none;}
#addNote, #updateNote {float: left;}
```

```
#addNote {
  border-right: 1px dashed #ccc;
  margin: 0 50px 0 0;
  padding: 0 50px 0 0;}
#updateNote { display:none;}
textarea {
  border: none;
  clear: both;
  height: 150px;
  margin: 0 0 10px;
  padding: 10px;
  width: 280px;}
input[type="text"] {margin: 0 0 10px; padding: 4px; }
button {padding: 5px;}
</style>

<script>

// note prefix for storage entries
var keyCode = 'note';

// initialize our note board
function initNoteBoard() {

  // set our listener for storage changes
  window.addEventListener('storage', onStorageEvent, false);

  // set listeners for new and update note
  var btnAddNote = document.getElementById('btnAddNote');
  var btnUpdateNote = document.getElementById('btnUpdateNote');
  btnAddNote.addEventListener('click',addNote,false);
  btnUpdateNote.addEventListener('click',updateNote,false);

  // update the display
  updateNoteBoard();
}

// our storage event handler
function onStorageEvent(eventObj) {
  if (eventObj.storageArea == localStorage) {
    // alert visitor of change
    alert(eventObj.key + ' changed from "' +
      eventObj.oldValue +
      '" to "' +
      eventObj.newValue + '".');
```

```
    // update the display
    updateNoteBoard();
  }
}

// add a note function
function addNote() {

  // retrieve the number of notes we have
  var numNotes  = parseInt(localStorage.getItem('numNotes'));
  if (isNaN(numNotes)) {
    numNotes = 0;
  }

  // set our key and value
  var noteKey = keyCode+numNotes;
  var noteValue = document.getElementById('note').value;

  // set our note
  localStorage.setItem(noteKey, noteValue);

  // update the number of notes
  numNotes++;
  localStorage.setItem('numNotes', numNotes);

  // update our note board
  updateNoteBoard();

  // reset our note entry
  document.getElementById('note').value = '';
}

// function to load the note to be updated
function changeNote(noteKey) {
  // set our key and value in the update form
  document.getElementById('oldKey').value = noteKey;
  document.getElementById('oldNote').value = localStorage.getItem(noteKey);

  // show our update note area
  document.getElementById('updateNote').style.display = 'block';
}

// function to update the note
function updateNote() {

  // retrieve our new values for the note
  var key = document.getElementById('oldKey').value;
  var note = document.getElementById('oldNote').value;
```

```
  // update the key/value pair
  localStorage.setItem(key, note);

  // clear our update area
  document.getElementById('updateNote').style.display = 'none';
  document.getElementById('oldKey').value = '';
  document.getElementById('oldNote').value = '';

  // update our display
  updateNoteBoard();
}

// function to remove a note
function removeNote(noteKey) {

  // retrieve our number of notes
  var numNotes = parseInt(localStorage.getItem('numNotes'));

  // extract our note key index from the note key
  keyIdx = parseInt(noteKey.substring(keyCode.length,noteKey.length));

  // loop through notes and move each down the list
  for (var i = keyIdx; i < numNotes; i++) {
    localStorage.setItem(keyCode+i,localStorage.getItem(keyCode+(i+1)));
  }

  // update our number of notes
  numNotes--;
  localStorage.setItem('numNotes',numNotes);

  // remove the last note that is now a duplicate
  localStorage.removeItem(keyCode + numNotes);

  // update our display
  updateNoteBoard();
}

// function to remove all notes
function clearAllNotes() {

  // retrieve the number of notes
  var numNotes = parseInt(localStorage.getItem('numNotes'));
  if (isNaN(numNotes)) {
    numNotes = 0;
  }

  // loop through note key/value pairs and remove
  for (var i = 0; i < numNotes; i++) {
```

```
    localStorage.removeItem(keyCode+i);
  }

  // update our number of notes to 0
  localStorage.setItem('numNotes','0');

  // update the display
  updateNoteBoard();
}

// display our notes
function updateNoteBoard() {
  // set our display area
  var noteBoard = document.getElementById('noteBoard');

  // retrieve our number of notes
  var numNotes = parseInt(localStorage.getItem('numNotes'));
  // set default to 0 if no notes
  if (isNaN(numNotes)) {
    numNotes = 0;
  }

  var notes = '<div>My Notes:</div>';
  var key = '';
  var value = '';

  // loop through the notes
  for (var i = 0; i < numNotes; i++) {

    // create our key with our prefix
    key = keyCode + i;

    // retrieve our key
    value = localStorage.getItem(key);

    // build our display for this note
    notes += '<div><p>'+value+'</p><div class="buttons">'+
        '<button onclick="changeNote(\''+key+'\');">Change</button>'+
        '<button onclick="removeNote(\''+key+'\');">Remove</button>'+
        '</div>'+
        '</div>';
  }

  // finish off our display
  notes += '<div style="float:right;"><button id="clearAllNotes">Remove All
➥Notes</button></div>';
```

```
    // set the list to the display
    noteBoard.innerHTML = notes;

    // set listener for clearing all notes
    var btnClearAllNotes = document.getElementById('clearAllNotes');
    btnClearAllNotes.addEventListener('click',clearAllNotes,false);

}

// initialize our note board
window.addEventListener('load',initNoteBoard,false);

</script>
</head>
<body>
<h1>Note Board</h1>
<section id="noteBoard"></section>
<section id="addNote">
<h1>Add a new note here:</h1>
  <textarea name="note" id="note"></textarea>
  <button id="btnAddNote">Add Note</button>
</section>
<section id="updateNote">
<h1>Update the note</h1>
  <input type="text" name="oldKey" id="oldKey" disabled />
  <textarea name="oldNote" id="oldNote"></textarea>
  <button id="btnUpdateNote">Update Note</button>
</section>
</body>
</html>
```

When the page loads, the initialization launches the initNoteBoard function. This function attaches the event listener to catch any events that are storage events and will launch the storageEvent handler. Next, the initNoteBoard updates the display of notes by checking local storage. In the updateNoteBoard function, the script will first retrieve the key numNotes, which is a count of the number of notes that you have stored previously. Then, using numNotes, the script will loop through and retrieve each key/value pair using the keyCode, "note" with the index starting at 0. So, to retrieve the first note, the page calls getItem with the key note0. The keyCode and numNotes keys are used for two reasons. First, using them will ensure that you do not have to cycle through any other key/value pairs that may be stored in local storage for the site, and second, this will allow you to keep your notes in order. Remember that for session and local storage there is no specific order to the key/value pairs in the list. The browser will insert them using setItem in no particular order (see Figure 11.2).

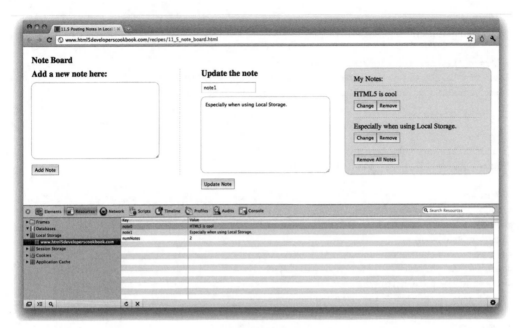

Figure 11.2   Sample output showing multiple key/value pairs in
local storage

The real power of this recipe is in the event handling. If you load the page into two browser tabs or windows and add a new note in one of the windows, the event handler will be triggered. In this case, the onStorageEvent function will be called, and the function will perform two actions. First, the function alerts the visitor that there has been a change and provides the visitor with a little information on the update. Second, the event handler calls the update display function to show the updated list of notes. If you play around with the addition, update, and removal of notes, you will see how this event handling behaves.

If you remove a note, the event handler will show you multiple changes happening in local storage. The reason for this is how the order of the notes is maintained. To maintain the order of the list, the script uses an algorithm by which entries after the one to be removed are pushed down the list and the last entry is then removed. Remember that the clear method will not only remove the key/value pairs you are interested in but will remove all key/value pairs in the storage.

Note

Storage events do not get triggered on the same page that made the session or local storage modification. Instead, storage events are propagated notices to other browser windows or tabs. To catch a change on the page that made the change, you will need to call the logic directly when the change is made.

In this recipe, you used a specific key, numNotes, to hold the number of notes that had been entered. In addition, to keep the notes ordered, you used a key prefix with an incrementing number such as note0, note1, and note2. What if the script needed to sort the list based on different criteria or needed to catalog your notes into categories? You could devise your own method using JavaScript and objects, but with HTML5 and its definition of the Web SQL Database API, this task becomes quite simple, as you will see in this chapter's final recipe.

Web SQL Database API

As you saw in the previous recipes of this chapter, the Session and Local Storage APIs allow for the storage of simple data in the client browser. If you want to store more complex objects, properties, and relationships, you will need to leverage the new Web SQL Database API or IndexedDB API. Like other APIs, these are not part of HTML5 core specification but a set of additional specifications being adopted by browsers. In general, the Web SQL Database API is currently supported by several browsers, while the IndexedDB API is still being defined and has limited support. Over time, it is expected that the IndexedDB will be more widely supported, but we will focus on the Web SQL Database API in this chapter for demonstration.

If you have had the opportunity to work on server-side pages and database access, most likely you have used a similar SQL-based database. And if not, then here is your opportunity to have a powerful data management storage system right in the browser. Table 11.4 shows the browser support for the Web SQL Database API.

Table 11.4   **Web SQL Database Browser Availability**

Android	2.1+
Chrome	9.0+
Firefox	-
Internet Explorer	-
iOS Safari	3.2+
Opera	10.6+
Safari	3.2+

The Web SQL Database API specification is based on SQLite, so if you have already used SQLite in a mobile environment such as iOS development, then it will be familiar. At the same time, if you have used a server-side database such as MySQL, the basic commands and structure will be recognizable. If you have no SQL experience, then you may want to seek some resources on SQL commands, but we will cover the basic create, read, update, and delete commands in the next recipe. Like session and local storage, the web database is available only to the pages in the same origin from which it was created for security purposes; however, unlike session and local storage, the web database can store complex data with relationship information.

> **Note**
>
> Currently, there is some debate as to the underlying database format for use with the Web SQL Database API. SQLite is listed in the W3 Web Database specification and has been implemented by several browsers. However, until there is general acceptance, the web database group of the W3C has put the specification on hold for further development. This has resulted in further pushing of the IndexedDB specification, which is gaining traction.

To interact with the web database, the API provides three core asynchronous commands. The reason these commands are typically asynchronous is so that the rendering of the browser page does not get "blocked" while waiting for a database call to return. Depending on the amount of data requested in a transaction, the page could have to wait several seconds for the set of data to be returned. The three core commands allow you to open (or create a database), create a transaction, and execute SQL statements within the transaction:

- `openDatabase`: Opens a present database or creates a database based on the parameters passed if the database is not present.
- `Transaction`: Encompasses the commands to the database so that you can perform a rollback on the entire transaction if needed. There is a read-only version available, `readTransaction`.
- `executeSql`: The method to run an actual SQL command on the open database.

The `openDatabase` method opens an established database, or if the database is not present, the method will automatically create the database described in the parameters and then open the database as follows:

```
WindowDatabase openDatabase(name, version, displayName, estimatedSize [,
➥creationCallBack])
```

The parameters of the `openDatabase` method are as follows:

- `name`: The name of the database
- `version`: A version number you assign to the database
- `displayName`: A user-friendly display name for the database
- `estimatedSize`: An estimated size for the database
- `creationCallBack`: (Optional) The function called when the database has been created for the first time

A `WindowDatabase` object is returned that will then be used to perform transactions with. The database is automatically closed when the browser window or tab is closed.

> **Tip**
>
> The version number of the `openDatabase` method is a value that you can use to track versions of your database structure and data. This can be helpful if you are using the database to provide quick, local lookups of data. When your lookup data changes and the user comes back to your website, you could check this version by having stored the value in a table in a master web database. If the lookup database was not up-to-date, then a new one could be installed. Or, you could use the error code when opening to validate that it is the wrong version.

To query the database, a transaction request must be performed. The transaction method wraps one or more `executeSql` commands to create a single transaction for the database to act on. The transaction can be used for rollback purposes if any of the SQL queries fail. The callback parameter of the transaction encompasses the inline function for the `executeSql` methods, as shown here:

```
transaction(callback [, errorCallback] [, successCallback])
```

The parameters of the `transaction` method are as follows:

- `callback`: The functionality to perform within the transaction
- `errorCallback`: (Optional) The function to handle any errors that occurred
- `successCallback`: (Optional) The success function called if all processes within the transaction were successful

The `executeSql` method takes your SQL query command as the first parameter and can include an array or optional arguments, a successful callback, and an optional error callback, as shown here:

```
executeSql(sqlStatement [, arguments] [, callback] [, errorCallback])
```

The parameters of `executeSql` method are as follows:

- `sqlStatement`: A SQL statement to be executed
- `arguments`: (Optional) An array of optional arguments
- `callback`: (Optional) The functionality to perform if the SQL statement execution is successful
- `errorCallback`: (Optional) The functionality to perform if the SQL statement execution creates an error

The error handler parameter option for the database API methods is used to catch any errors that could occur in interacting with the database. This could include instances such as an error in your SQL or an issue in accessing the database:

- UNKNOWN_ERR (0): An unknown error beyond the ones listed here occurred.
- DATABASE_ERR (1): An error occurred in the database that is not covered by an error category.
- VERSION_ERR (2): The version stated in the command does not match the version of the database.
- TOO_LARGE_ERR (3): The resulting data set from the database to your request was too large to be returned.
- QUOTA_ERR (4): There is no remaining storage space or the user declined to allocate more for your database.
- SYNTAX_ERR (5): The request failed because of a syntax error.
- CONSTRAINT_ERR (6): The request failed because it violated a constraint in the structure of the database.
- TIMEOUT_ERR (7): The transaction failed because it could not establish a database lock in a timely manner.

A common error seen is SYNTAX_ERR, which signifies there is a syntax issue in your SQL command. The message portion of the error object passed to your error handler will be critical in giving you more specifics about the particular error code.

At this point, you may be asking how this all works together to store and retrieve information in a database. The next recipe puts these core methods together to do exactly that.

ADVANCED RECIPE:
Using a Web Database for a Grocery List

This recipe will use the interfaces for the web database that we have just reviewed to create a shopping list that will be stored completely in the browser's database resource. The visitor will be able to add items to the list, including a quantity and name, and select from a drop-down the grocery department the item is found in. Whenever an item is added, the grocery list will be updated and displayed. The list will be grouped by department to make a shopping trip easier. The visitor can remove items from the list and clear the list completely. If the visitor leaves and returns to the page, the page will show the stored items.

The database that is created by this recipe will have two tables: a groceryitems table to hold the items in the list and a departments table, which will be a lookup table with a predefined list of departments. When the page first loads, the database and tables will be created, and the departments table will be populated with the department information. The groceryitems table will have four fields, as defined in Table 11.5.

The departments table will have two fields, as defined in Table 11.6.

By default when the departments table is created, the script will add four departments into the departments table.

Table 11.5   **The groceryitems Table Structure**

Field	Type	Description
itemid	INTEGER	Unique primary key for each item in the table
quantity	INTEGER	The number of this particular item to get
itemname	TEXT	The name of the item
deptid	INTEGER	The department ID that comes from the departments table

Table 11.6   **The departments Table Structure**

Field	Type	Description
deptid	INTEGER	Unique primary key for each department in the table
deptname	TEXT	The number of this particular item to get

> **Tip**
>
> Like with session storage and local storage, the Chrome Developer Tools provide a proficient way to view the SQLite database as your JavaScript executes. You can find the Database section under the Resources section in the Developer Tools window. Unlike session storage and local storage items, the database tables and data cannot be edited in Developer Tools, but this functionality may be added in the future.

For debugging purposes, a Remove Database button is also put on the page so that you can remove the database. Currently, the web database specification does not contain a method to remove a database. To work around this, and remove a database, you will have to "drop" the tables that have been created in the database, and your database will be empty. As you develop using the web database API, re-creating the database will be useful to verify your SQL database creation transactions.

To create the grocery list page, follow these steps:

1. Create the basic structure of the page with the HTML body, the shoppingdb var declaration, the window.addEventListener load event handler, and the init JavaScript function.

2. Add the JavaScript functions that are called from the init function: openShoppingDb and dbPresent.

3. To finish the initialization of the database, add the initShoppingDb, onDbError, and nullHandler functions. The initShoppingDb function creates the tables and inserts the departments. The onDbError function is a generic function to handle database errors that may occur as the script perform transactions, and the nullHandler is used to catch successful transaction events. If you load the page at this point, you should see the database being created by your script in the Chrome Developer Tools.

4. You need to display the grocery items when the page is shown by adding the initPage, getDepartments, and showDepartments functions. The "get and show" technique will be common because the transaction requests are asynchronous and will need a callback function to handle the results. In this case, the getDepartments performs the request to get the departments from the departments table and then the showDepartments function to display them. The showDepartments will create the options for our select list.

5. To finish the display on initialization, you need to show any grocery items that have been previously stored in the database, so add getGroceryItems and showGroceryItems from Listing 11.6.

6. To add an item, the addGroceryItem function is called, which will take the inputs of the input fields and insert them into the groceryitems table. If successful, the page will display the new list of grocery items. To remove an item, add the deleteItem method.

7. To complete the page, add the resetGroceryList method to clear the grocery list and the debug function of removeDatabase to drop the database tables.

Listing 11.6　Creating a Grocery List with a Client Database

```html
<!DOCTYPE html>
<html>
<head>
<meta charset="UTF-8" />
<title>11.6 Database Grocery List</title>
<style>
section {
  margin-bottom:20px;
}
</style>
<script>

var shoppingdb = null; // our database reference

// function kick off init of page
function init() {

  // check to see if database support available
  if (window.openDatabase) {

    // set the button click handlers
    var btnAddGroceryItem = document.getElementById('addGroceryItem');
    var btnResetGroceryList = document.getElementById('resetGroceryList');
    var btnRemoveDatabase = document.getElementById('removeDatabase');
    btnAddGroceryItem.addEventListener('click',addGroceryItem,false);
    btnResetGroceryList.addEventListener('click',resetGroceryList,false);
    btnRemoveDatabase.addEventListener('click',removeDatabase,false);
```

```
    // open the database
    openShoppingDb();

    // check if we have reference to database
    if (shoppingdb) {

      // check if the database initialized or not
      dbPresent();
    }
  } else {
    alert('Databases are not supported in this browser');
  }
}

// open database function
function openShoppingDb() {

  // try to open our database
  try {
    var dbSize = 5000000; // 5MB size
    shoppingdb = openDatabase('shoppingdb', '1.0', 'shopping list', dbSize);
  } catch (err) {
    // Error occurred opening database
    shoppingdb = null;
    console.log('Error opening database: ' + err.code + ' - ' + err.message);
    return;
  }
}

// function check to see if database tables present
function dbPresent() {
  // start our transaction
  shoppingdb.readTransaction(function(tx) {
    // execute sql to pull first record
    // if successful, then initialize the page
    // if not, then initialize the database
    tx.executeSql('SELECT 1 FROM departments', [],
      initPage, initShoppingDb);}
  );
}

// function initialize the page
function initPage() {
  // get the departments
  getDepartments();
```

```
    // load any grocery items present
    getGroceryItems();
}


// initialize the shopping database
function initShoppingDb() {
    // start our database transaction
    shoppingdb.transaction(function(tx) {
        // create tables for database
        tx.executeSql('CREATE TABLE IF NOT EXISTS ' +
            'groceryitems(itemid INTEGER NOT NULL PRIMARY KEY, quantity INTEGER,
➥itemname TEXT, deptid INTEGER)',
            [], nullHandler, onDbError);
        tx.executeSql('CREATE TABLE IF NOT EXISTS ' +
            'departments(deptid INTEGER NOT NULL PRIMARY KEY, deptname TEXT)',
            [], nullHandler, onDbError);

        // Fill our departments table
        tx.executeSql('INSERT INTO departments(deptname) VALUES (?)',
            ['Fresh Produce'], nullHandler, onDbError);
        tx.executeSql('INSERT INTO departments(deptname) VALUES (?)',
            ['Deli'], nullHandler, onDbError);
        tx.executeSql('INSERT INTO departments(deptname) VALUES (?)',
            ['Bakery'], nullHandler, onDbError);
        tx.executeSql('INSERT INTO departments(deptname) VALUES (?)',
            ['Grocery'], initPage, onDbError);
    });
}


// standard db error function
function onDbError(tx, err) {
    alert('Database error occurred: ' + err.code + '|' + err.message );
}


// our null handler for success
function nullHandler(tx, r) {
    return;
}


// function get the department list
function getDepartments() {
    // begin our database transaction
    shoppingdb.readTransaction(function(tx) {
        // execute our sql to retrieve the departments
        tx.executeSql('SELECT * FROM departments ORDER BY deptname ASC', [],
            showDepartments, onDbError);
    });
}
```

```
// function show the departments retrieved
function showDepartments(tx, rs) {
  // get reference to the department select
  var selectObj = document.getElementById('department');

  // loop through department recordset and add to select
  for (var i=0; i < rs.rows.length; i++) {
    row = rs.rows.item(i);
    selectObj.options[selectObj.options.length] =
      new Option(row.deptname, row.deptid, false, false);
  }
}

// function to get the grocery items
function getGroceryItems() {
  // start our database transaction
  shoppingdb.readTransaction(function(tx) {
    // retrieve the list of items
    tx.executeSql('SELECT * FROM groceryitems, departments WHERE
groceryitems.deptid=departments.deptid ORDER BY deptname ASC',
      [], showGroceryItems, onDbError);
  });
}

// function to show the grocery item list
function showGroceryItems(tx, rs) {
  var myShoppingList = document.getElementById('myShoppingList');
  var tableRow = '<table>';
  var row = null;

  // set table headings
  tableRow +=
'<tr><td>Quantity</td><td>Item</td><td>Department</td><td>Delete</td>
</tr>';

  // loop through record set returned
  for (var i=0; i < rs.rows.length; i++) {
    // retrieve our row
    row = rs.rows.item(i);

    // build our table row
    tableRow += '<tr><td>' + row.quantity + '</td>' +
      '<td>' + row.itemname + '</td>' +
      '<td>' + row.deptname + '</td>' +
      '<td><button onclick="deleteItem(' +
    row.itemid + ');">X</button></td></tr>';
  }
  tableRow += '</table>';
```

```
    // set our info in the div
    myShoppingList.innerHTML = tableRow;
}

// add a grocery item to our database groceryitems table
function addGroceryItem() {
    // open our database transaction async call
    shoppingdb.transaction(function(tx){
        // retrieve our data for the grocery item
        var itemname = document.getElementById('item').value;
        var quantity = parseInt(document.getElementById('quantity').value);
        var deptid = parseInt(document.getElementById('department').value);

        // perform our executeSql insert
        tx.executeSql('INSERT INTO groceryitems(quantity, itemname, deptid) VALUES
        (?,?,?)',
            [quantity, itemname, deptid], getGroceryItems, onDbError);
    });
}

// function remove an item from the list
function deleteItem(id) {
    // start our transaction
    shoppingdb.transaction(function(tx) {
        // execute sql to delete the item from the database
        tx.executeSql('DELETE FROM groceryitems WHERE itemid=?',
            [id], getGroceryItems, onDbError);
        }
    );
}

// function reset grocery list
function resetGroceryList() {
    // start our transaction
    shoppingdb.transaction(function(tx) {
        // execute our sql to drop the grocery item table
        tx.executeSql('DROP TABLE groceryitems', [], nullHandler, onDbError);
    });
}

// function remove database
function removeDatabase() {
    // start our transaction
    shoppingdb.transaction(function(tx) {
        // drop our tables
        tx.executeSql('DROP TABLE departments', [], nullHandler, onDbError);
```

```
      tx.executeSql('DROP TABLE groceryitems', [], nullHandler, onDbError);
  });
}

// call init on load
window.addEventListener('load',init,false);

</script>
</head>
<body>
<section>
  Quantity:<input type="number" id="quantity" />
  Item:<input type="text" id="item" placeholder="Milk" />
  Department:<select id="department"></select>
  <button id="addGroceryItem">Add Item</button>
</section>
<section id="myShoppingList"></section>
<section>
  <button id="resetGroceryList">Reset Grocery List</button>
  <button id="removeDatabase">Remove Database</button>
</section>
</body>
</html>
```

When the page is loaded in your browser, the init function will check that the Web SQL Database API is available by verifying that the window.openDatabase method is available. If available, the openDatabase method is called with the database parameters. In this case, the script sets roughly 5MB for the size because the browsers appear not to confirm with the user for database creations of this size or smaller. If your database exceeds this size at creation or later, the browser will confirm with the user to allocate more space. If this is the first time that you have run the code, then the database will be created and the handle returned; otherwise, the database will be opened.

Since the recipe uses the departments table values to load the select list of departments, you need to make sure that if this is a new database instance that you populate the departments table with your lookup information. To check whether you need to create the tables, the script checks for the presence of the database tables by doing a simple query and tries to select the first row in the department table in the dbPresent method. If the table does not exist yet, then the script creates both tables and inserts the department values into the departments table in the initShoppingDb method. After the database is loaded, the script loads the departments into the select list from the database and displays any stored grocery items by calling the getGroceryItems method. The getGroceryItems method will open another transaction to request all items from the groceryitems table and, if successful, pass the resulting data set of rows to the showGroceryItems method. The show method will then loop through the grocery items and display them in the myShoppingList section of the page.

> **Note**
>
> The `transaction` method is used for SQL commands that require write permissions in the database. By requiring write permission, the transaction puts a write lock on the database, preventing others from writing to the database at that time. If you are performing only read commands on the database, you should use the `readTransaction` method. The `readTransaction` method is called the same way as the `transaction` method.

Once the page is initialized and the database and the departments are populated, the visitor can then enter a quantity and item and select the department for the new item for their shopping list. The `addGroceryItem` will then take this information, create a database transaction, and perform a SQL insert to add the item in an inline function call. If the insert fails, you will call the error handler, `onDbError`, that will display our error. If successful, then the script will call `getGroceryItems` and subsequently `showGroceryItems` to display the resulting set of rows returned from the groceryitems table. Figure 11.3 shows the output after having entered several items.

Figure 11.3   Sample output after adding several grocery items

When the `getGroceryItems` function is called, the script will call the `readTransaction` method with an inline function call to `executeSql`. The SQL command selects from the groceryitems table all records, groups them by department, and sorts them by department alphabetically. In addition, the SQL command joins the groceryitems table and departments table on the deptid so that the return set will also include the department name to display. If the `executeSql` call is successful, the script will return the results to `showGroceryItems`, passing the transaction reference and recordset of results. To display the results from the recordset, the script loops through the recordset rows. Each row represents a record returned by the SQL query, and you can reference each field via dot notation.

To remove an item, the visitor clicks the X button, which calls the `deleteItem` method with the item ID passed. The page then uses the item ID passed to delete the item from the groceryitems table. If the call is successful, then the list is refreshed through the get and show grocery items functions. Lastly, the visitor can reset the grocery list, which will delete all items from the groceryitems table.

This recipe is a quick sample of integrating client web databases into your websites and applications. The recipe covered writing, retrieving, updating, and deleting records along with the initial creation of the database. This functionality provides the building blocks needed to implement your own database storage.

Summary

In this chapter, you learned about some of the exciting new methods to store data on the client browser. Previously, client browser technology was limited to the use of cookies. With the addition of session storage, local storage, and web databases, there is now a robust platform, albeit young, on which you have several options to store simple key/value pairs or complex data structures. With these storage options, you can create powerful offline applications, reduce round-trips to your server for data, and store robust information across browser sessions at the client.

12

Communication and Threading

The HTML5 APIs cover a wide range of improvements and areas, but two of the newest ones include the WebSocket and Web Workers APIs. These two sets fill some key gaps in website and web application development. Before these APIs, opening a bidirectional communication channel with servers was difficult. In addition, performing heavy processing in the page blocked the user interface from user interaction. The WebSocket API provides bidirectional communication between client JavaScript and a server over a socket connection, while the Web Workers API opens up basic threading options to client JavaScript. In this chapter, you will learn how to implement these APIs in some simple but effective recipes by which you can base your own solutions.

WebSocket API Overview

The WebSocket API provides a new method of communicating with servers through direct socket messages. These messages are bidirectional and can be sent from the client page to the server or from the server to the browser page at any time while the connection is open. The web socket uses a separate server-defined protocol without the HTTP request overhead, so the packets also have the benefit of being lightweight. By default, however, to enable a web socket connection, you must have a corresponding WebSocket service on the server that the messages are being sent and received from. These services can be written in a wide array of languages. Prior to HTML5, this communication functionality was available only through specialized object installations, a comet persistent connection, or frequent polling of the server from the client.

To create a web socket connection, a script creates an instance of the WebSocket interface, passing in the web service URL, as shown here:

```
var myWS = new WebSocket("ws://some.webservice.com/");
```

The WebSocket object, when instantiated, attempts to open a socket connection with the service listening at the URL provided in the constructor of the WebSocket object. If the connection is successfully opened, then the WebSocket object instance provides methods to send a message and close the connection as follows:

Table 12.1   **The WebSocket** `readyState` **Attribute Values**

Value	Constant	Description
0	CONNECTING	The socket connection is attempting to connect.
1	OPEN	The socket connection is open and ready.
2	CLOSING	The socket connection is in the process of being closed.
3	CLOSED	The socket connection is closed.

- `send(DOMString)`: Sends data in the form of a string
- `send(ArrayBuffer)`: Sends data in the form of an `ArrayBuffer`
- `send(Blob)`: Sends data in form of a blob
- `close([code][,reason])`: Closes the socket connection with an optional code as an unsigned long and a `DOMString` for a reason

To determine when the socket connection is ready for data to be sent, you can use either the connection's `readyState` attribute, which can have one of four values listed in Table 12.1, or the `onopen` event.

The following are the events available on a `WebSocket` instance:

- `onopen`: The socket connection is open and ready.
- `onclose`: The socket connection is closed.
- `onmessage`: A message has been received on the socket connection.
- `onerror`: An error has occurred with the socket connection.

Table 12.2 shows the version of each browser that supports the WebSocket API. Note, however, that the level of support varies between browsers and will be noted where applicable in the chapter's recipes.

Table 12.2   **Web Socket API Browser Availability**

Browser	Version
Android	-
Chrome	10.0+
Firefox	4.0+
Internet Explorer	-
iOS Safari	4.2+
Opera	11.0+
Safari	5.0+

BEGINNER RECIPE:
Talking Through Web Sockets

This recipe will use the WebSocket interface to open a web socket connection with a server, send a message that the user inputs, and receive an echo of the same message back from the server. In this case, we will use a free testing web socket service set up at www.websocket.org. This free online service makes it easy to test your web socket scripts by verifying that you can open a connection, send messages, and receive messages. To create this connection, perform the following steps, which result in Listing 12.1:

1. Create a blank HTML page with a message input element, the send and close buttons, and the status and message result divs.

2. Add the global variables for the web socket and URL.

3. Add the init function and event listener for the page load event.

4. Add the onOpen, onClose, onMessage, and onError functions to handle the events of the web socket connection.

5. Add the postMessage, closeWS, and updateStatus functions to handle sending messages, closing the connection, and updating the connection status.

Listing 12.1   Sending and Receiving Data Through Web Sockets

```
<!DOCTYPE html>
<html>
<head>
<meta charset="UTF-8" />
<title>12.1 Web Socket Communication</title>
<script>
// set up our global web socket reference
var directorWebSocket = null;

// assign our web socket listener address
var wsUri = 'ws://echo.websocket.org/';

// create web socket connection on page load
function init()
{
  // add the button event handlers
  var btnSend = document.getElementById('btnSend');
  var btnClose = document.getElementById('btnClose');

  btnSend.addEventListener('click',postMessage,false);
  btnClose.addEventListener('click',closeWS,false);

  updateStatus('initializing websocket connection');
```

```
    // create the web socket instance with the listener address
    directorWebSocket = new WebSocket(wsUri);

    // set up our handler functions for the web socket events
    directorWebSocket.onopen = function(evt) { onOpen(evt) };
    directorWebSocket.onclose = function(evt) { onClose(evt) };
    directorWebSocket.onmessage = function(evt) { onMessage(evt) };
    directorWebSocket.onerror = function(evt) { onError(evt) };
}

// WEB SOCKET EVENT HANDLERS

// web socket connection successfully opened
function onOpen(evt) {
  console.log('Director Connection open');
  updateStatus('Connection open');
};

// received a message through the web socket connection
function onMessage(evt) {
  console.log('Received Message: ' + evt.data);
  updateStatus('message received: ' + evt.data);
  document.getElementById('messages').innerHTML = evt.data;
};

// error received from the web socket
function onError(evt) {
  console.log('Director Connection error: ' + evt.data);
  updateStatus('error: '+ evt.data);
};

// web socket connection successfully closed
function onClose(evt) {
  console.log('Director Connection closed.');
  updateStatus('connection closed.');
};

// CLIENT FUNCTIONS

// send message through web socket connection
function postMessage() {

  // get the message from the input
  msg = document.getElementById('msg').value;

  console.log('sending ws message: ' + msg);
  updateStatus('sending message: ' + msg);
```

```
    // use send() to send the message
    directorWebSocket.send(msg);
}

// tell web socket to close
function closeWS() {

    console.log('disconnecting ws');
    updateStatus('disconnecting');

    // tell the web socket instance to close the connection
    directorWebSocket.close();
}

// helper function to change the status of the web socket
function updateStatus(msg) {
    document.getElementById('wsState').innerHTML = msg;
}

// add page load event listener to kick off init function
window.addEventListener('load', init, false);

</script>
</head>
<body>
<div id="btnTryCall">
    <input type="text" id="msg" />
    <button id="btnSend">Send Message</button>
    <button id="btnClose">Close Web Socket</button>
</div>
<div id="wsState"></div>
<div id="messages"></div>
</body>
</html>
```

When the page loads from Listing 12.1, the init function is called. In the init function, the script adds the button event listeners and then creates a web socket connection by creating an instance of the WebSocket interface, passing in the address. After creating this instance, the recipe registers for the onopen, onclose, onmessage, and onerror events, linking a function to each event. When the web socket successfully opens the connection, the onopen event is fired, and the onOpen function is called, changing the connection status displayed on the page. In this recipe, we have left in the console log statements so that in the developer log of your browser you can see the flow of the web socket connection.

The page displays an input box for the user to type a message and send through the web socket to the server. The message is sent in the postMessage function where you call the send method on the web socket with the message passed as a parameter. After being received, the web socket service repackages the text string and sends the string back to the page as a message. The onmessage event handler catches the incoming message, and the corresponding onMessage function takes the incoming message and updates the display with the data portion of the message.

If any errors occur during the opening, use, or closing of the web socket connection, the onerror event handler will catch the error and display the data portion of the error to the user. Once the conversation is complete between the page and the web socket service, you can close the web socket connection by calling the close method on the web socket.

> **Note**
>
> The service that your web socket instance sends messages to and receives messages from will typically be one of your own design and living on your web server. You can find several open source examples online in various languages for setting up a web socket server process. In the online reference list for the book, we have included links to several of these packages.

In this recipe, you opened a connection with a remote server and sent messages back and forth using the web socket connection. This can be extremely useful for bidirectional communication and especially proactive messaging from the service to a connected browser page.

Threading Through Web Workers

A prevalent issue with JavaScript running in an HTML page is that the JavaScript runs on a single thread on the page and can easily block the interface when performing heavy processing. With the HTML5 Web Workers API, a new opportunity exists for developers to separate this processing and have the functionality performed on a background thread with lower priority than the main thread of the HTML page. In this manner, the main thread can remain unblocked and allow the user to interact with the page with little to no negative effect.

The Web Workers API implementation in HTML5 provides two types of web workers: dedicated and shared web workers. A *dedicated* web worker is specific to the page that launches the web worker and is not available across pages. A *shared* worker, in contrast, can be shared across multiple pages from the same origin in the same browser instance. The shared worker has its own state, which also spans the pages, as you will see in the last recipe of this chapter.

So, what is a web worker in particular? A *web worker* is a JavaScript script separated as a file to be run on the new thread. The script to be run on the separate thread can even be passed to the web worker instead of being held in a dedicated .js file. The web worker can communicate with the launching page and the main script, and vice versa, through the use of messages that are posted between the threads.

Tip

Web workers are not able to manipulate the DOM elements of the page because the web worker runs on a separate thread than the page itself. The DOM can be modified only from the main page thread.

To create an instance of a web worker, you create a new instance of the `Worker` interface, passing in the script or file to be executed, as shown here, for creating a dedicated worker:

```
var myWorker = new Worker('worker_script.js');
```

The dedicated web worker from the previous code will execute the JavaScript when the web worker is created. A dedicated web worker will remain running and available until the thread is terminated or the page that created the dedicated web worker is closed. The following are the methods available with a dedicated web worker:

- `postMessage(Message [, MessagePort])`: Sends a message to the web worker thread. The worker thread "catches" the message with the `onmessage` event described later.

- `terminate()`: Terminates the worker thread on which the method is called.

There are two events available on a dedicated web worker: `onmessage` and `onerror`. The `onmessage` event allows the main page script to receive messages from the web worker thread or have the web worker receive messages from the main thread. Table 12.3 shows the `onmessage` and `onerror` events available on the `Worker` interface.

Note

If you have programmed in a language that supports the use of multiple threads, then you are probably aware of thread-safety issues and problems that can arise in running threads concurrently. In the HTML5 Web Workers API, messaging between threads via serialized objects protects against these issues for the most part. To prevent other concurrency issues, worker threads do not have access to the DOM page structure or non–thread-safe components. Only the main page thread can update the DOM elements of the page.

Table 12.3   The Worker Events

Event Name	Attribute	Purpose
message	onmessage	Triggered when a message is received. An event object with a data member will be provided with the message.
error	onerror	Triggered when an error occurs in the worker thread. The event provides a data member with the error information.

Table 12.4 shows the version of each browser that supports the Web Workers API.

Table 12.4   **Web Workers API Browser Availability**

Android	2.1
Chrome	10.0+
Firefox	3.6+
Internet Explorer	10.0+
iOS Safari	-
Opera	10.6+
Safari	4.0+

Note that Safari is the only browser platform that supports shared workers, which will be covered later in this chapter. After 2.1, the Android browser removed support for workers.

BEGINNER RECIPE:
Creating a Web Worker

In this recipe, you will create a simple dedicated web worker to use a rudimentary method to sum a range of numbers in the background on the web worker thread. When the HTML page loads, the web worker will be started. As the web worker progresses through the number range, the worker will provide progress percentage messages back to the main script. Once the web worker completes summing the numbers, the worker will send a message to the main script with the final result. A terminate button is provided so the user can terminate the worker at any moment.

The web worker as described will execute the commands in a thread that does not block the main page scripting and processing. To demonstrate, the page includes a timestamp button to log a date timestamp on the page. As the worker progresses, try clicking the date timestamp button to verify that the main page is not blocked by the activities of the web worker thread. The recipe will have two files: the HTML page in Listing 12.2 and the web worker JavaScript file in Listing 12.3.

1. Create the page in Listing 12.2 with the `output` tag, buttons, and log result section.

2. Add the script portion to the page, including the worker variable and `startWorkerThread` initialization function.

3. Add the `terminateWorker` function to terminate the web worker thread.

4. Add the `getTimeStamp` function and the `window.addEventListener` trigger.

Listing 12.2   **Sending the Message to the Web Worker**

```html
<!DOCTYPE html>
<html>
<head>
<meta charset="UTF-8" />
<title>12.2 Simple Web Worker Communication</title>
<script>
// global reference to our web worker
var worker = null;

// on page load start the web worker
function startWorkerThread() {

  // add button event handlers
  var btnTimeStamp = document.getElementById('btnTimeStamp');
  var btnTerminateWorker = document.getElementById('btnTerminateWorker');

  btnTimeStamp.addEventListener('click',getTimeStamp,false);
  btnTerminateWorker.addEventListener('click',terminateWorker,false);

  // create the web worker instance
  worker = new Worker('12_3_simple_worker.js');

  // assign handler for receiving messages from web worker
  worker.onmessage = function (event) {
    // display the message in our result field
    document.getElementById('result').textContent = event.data;
  };
}

// handle the button to terminate the web worker
function terminateWorker() {

  // tell the web worker to terminate
  worker.terminate();
}

// local thread to time stamp and show how main thread is
// not blocked by calculations going on
function getTimeStamp() {

  // get the current date and time and add to the time log
  var currentDateTime = new Date();
  document.getElementById('timeLog').innerHTML += currentDateTime+ '<br>';
}
```

```
// kick off the web worker on page load
window.addEventListener('load',startWorkerThread,false);

</script>
</head>
<body>
  <p>Computing <output id="result"></output></p>
  <button id="btnTimeStamp">Time Stamp</button>
  <button id="btnTerminateWorker">Terminate Worker</button>
  <section id="timeLog"></section>
</body>
</html>
```

When the page creates the web worker, you pass into the new instance the Java-Script filename to be executed on the new thread. In this case, the JavaScript file is named 12_3_simple_worker.js. Listing 12.3 provides the code for this file that loops through the range of numbers, adds them, and posts messages back to the main page script.

1. Create the JavaScript file in Listing 12.3 with the variables at the top.
2. Add the `for` loop to cycle from 1 to `maxLimit`, adding the numbers and sending back the percentage complete status.
3. Add the final `postMessage` to send the sum total to the main page script.

Listing 12.3   Performing the Task in the Web Worker

```
// The 12.3 js simple web worker file

// initialize our variables
var sum = 0;
var currentPercentageComplete = 0;
var maxLimit = 100000000;

// loop
for (var j=0; j<=maxLimit; j++) {

  // perform long way of summation
  sum+=j;

  // determine percentage complete
  newPercentageComplete = Math.round((j/maxLimit)*100);

  // minimize messages sent by only sending message
  // when percentage has changed
  if (newPercentageComplete > currentPercentageComplete) {
```

```
    // send message back to main page thread
    postMessage(newPercentageComplete + '% complete');

    // update current percentage complete
    currentPercentageComplete = newPercentageComplete;
  }
}


// finally post resulting sum value to main page thread
postMessage('Sum = ' + sum);
```

When the main page is loaded in the browser, the startWorkerThread function is called by the window load event. The function adds the button listeners; creates a new Worker instance, passing in the JavaScript filename; and assigns this reference to the worker variable. After creating this instance, the script registers for the onmessage event and defines a function when the event occurs to take the data and display the message from the worker thread in the result output. When the worker thread sends a message to the main script through a postMessage, the onmessage event handler will be triggered.

When the instance of the worker is created, the script is loaded into the thread and executes automatically. In the next recipe, you will see how you can manually tell the script when to start running after creating the thread.

As the script executes in the worker thread, a total sum is calculated (albeit in a very long and arduous way for demonstration purposes) by looping through one number at a time. As the loop progresses, the script checks to see whether the percentage progress has increased. If the completion percentage has changed, then the script posts a message to the main page through the postMessage command, including the new percentage completion amount. This posted message triggers the onmessage event handler in the main page script. The main script then takes this event and accesses the data member that contains the actual text. The main script then displays the percentage complete, as shown in Figure 12.1.

If the user did want to terminate the worker thread without closing the page, the terminate worker button can be used to tell the worker to stop immediately with the terminate method.

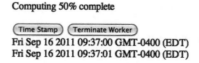

Computing 50% complete

(Time Stamp) (Terminate Worker)
Fri Sep 16 2011 09:37:00 GMT-0400 (EDT)
Fri Sep 16 2011 09:37:01 GMT-0400 (EDT)

Figure 12.1   Sample output showing multiple timestamp displays while
the worker is progressing

> **Tip**
>
> Web workers are considered heavy in their creation and execution. Web workers are best used when they are "long-lived" and will perform processing that should not block the interface main thread. You should consider carefully when to use a worker thread and how many threads are to be created. By definition, there is no limit on the number of web workers you can create, and web workers can even create instances of other workers. However, with each web worker created, there is significant overhead. It is best to keep your web workers to a minimum.

INTERMEDIATE RECIPE:
Adding Two-Way Communication

In the previous recipe, you learned how the main script can create a dedicated web worker and the worker can send messages back to the main script. The posting of messages is designed to be available between threads, which includes the main page thread that created the worker instance. This means the main script and the worker thread can send each other messages through the `postMessage` method of the `Worker` interface. In this recipe, the main script will send messages to the web worker, and the web worker will in turn send a confirmation of receipt of the message to the main script.

This recipe also looks at error handling for the worker at two levels: through the `error` event and via custom messages returned to the main script. The message that is sent through the `postMessage` method is in the format of a serialized object. This means you can send JSON-formatted strings to encapsulate multiple data members. In this recipe, you will use this method of sending complex data to inform the main script about the type of message being sent and the payload of the message. In addition, the `onerror` event handler is programmed to handle any JavaScript error as the worker script is processed. To get started with this recipe, follow these steps, which result in Listing 12.4:

1. Create a blank HTML file and add the `body` HTML from Listing 12.4, which includes the input field, button to send the message, and section to show the message returned.

2. Add the script section with the worker declaration and `onmessage` handler.

3. Add the `onerror` handler to catch any worker errors.

4. Add the `postToWorker` function to send the text input to the web worker via the `postMessage` method.

Listing 12.4 **Creating the Client Page**

```
<!DOCTYPE html>
<html>
<head>
<meta charset="UTF-8" />
<title>12.4 Worker Communication</title>
```

```
<script>
// create our web worker
var worker = new Worker('12_5_two_way_worker.js');

// create handler for messages from web worker
worker.onmessage = function (event) {

  // retrieve message portion of data
  var msgFromWorker = event.data;

  // check to see our type of message
  switch (msgFromWorker.msgType) {

    case 'MSG':
      // message sent from web worker - display
      var workerResponse = document.getElementById('workerResponse');
      workerResponse.innerHTML = 'Worker sent: ' + msgFromWorker.msg;
      break;

    case 'ERR':
      // error sent from web worker - alert user
      alert('Error from worker: ' + msgFromWorker.msg);
      break;
  }
};

// error handler for web worker
worker.onerror = function (error) {
  // simply alert user with error
  alert('Error from worker: ' + error.message);
};

// post the input to the web worker
function postToWorker() {
  worker.postMessage(document.getElementById('inputForWorker').value);
}

// initialize our handlers
function init() {
  var btnPostToWorker = document.getElementById('btnPostToWorker');
  btnPostToWorker.addEventListener('click',postToWorker,false);
}

window.addEventListener('load',init,false);

</script>
</head>
```

```
<body>
  <p>Enter a text message for the worker thread (leave blank to have worker
➥return a message type of error):</p>
  <input id='inputForWorker' />
  <button id="btnPostToWorker">Send to Worker</button>
  <section id="workerResponse"></section>
</body>
</html>
```

Like the previous recipe, you will use an external JavaScript file to hold your web worker code. Listing 12.5 contains the script for this file and can be created through the following steps. Make sure that the name of the file is the same used in the worker instantiation in your main script in Listing 12.4.

1. Create a blank file, and add the onmessage event handler from Listing 12.5.

2. Add the if condition and resulting sections to check for a valid input and send back to the main script either an error or a confirmation message.

Listing 12.5   Adding the Web Worker

```
// The 12.5 2 way Web Worker js file

// Catch messages sent to the web worker
onmessage = function(event) {

  // check for empty data and send back an error
  if (event.data === '') {
    // post message to client with error info
    postMessage({msgType:'ERR',msg:'Invalid data entry'});
  } else {
    // post message to client confirming receipt
    newMessage = 'Worker received "' + event.data + '"';
    postMessage({msgType:'MSG',msg:newMessage});
  }
}
```

When the HTML page loads, the web worker is created by loading the JavaScript worker file, but notice that the web worker does not perform any actions on creation, unlike the prior recipe. The web worker will wait until any incoming messages trigger the message handler. On the HTML page, the user is prompted to enter a text string into the input field and click the Send to Worker button. The Send to Worker button triggers a postMessage of the text string to the web worker. The web worker then checks whether this string is empty and, if so, posts a message back to the main script using a JSON string with a message type of "ERR" and an appropriate message. If the message received by the web worker is not empty, then the web worker wraps the

Enter a text message for the worker thread (leave blank to have
worker return a message type of error):

| HTML5 Rocks! | (Send to Worker)
Worker sent: Worker received "HTML5 Rocks!"

Figure 12.2   Sample output showing the message received and returned
by the web worker

string in another string to show what was received and posts this updated message back
in the same JSON format with a message type of "MSG."

After the error or message has been posted back to the main script, the `onmessage`
event handler in the main script is triggered with the message from the web worker.
The function checks to see what type of message has been sent and then either alerts
the user of an error or updates the result field with the message from the web worker,
as shown in Figure 12.2, and completes the communication loop.

To trigger the error message, leave the input field blank, and click the Send to
Worker button to send an empty string to the web worker.

This recipe and the one prior leveraged dedicated web workers, which are solely
available to the page that creates them. In some cases, though, you may have the need
to employ a web worker with a shared scope across pages. In the next recipe, we will
explain the structure of a shared web worker and how to implement the connections
to the web worker.

ADVANCED RECIPE:
Leveraging a Shared Web Worker

The scope of a dedicated web worker, as you saw in the previous recipes, is to the
page that has created the web worker. In all aspects, the web worker is sandboxed to
thread-safe operations in that environment. The HTML5 Web Workers API has a
second worker interface titled `SharedWorker`. This interface provides the same web
worker functionality but in a scope that can be shared across multiple pages in the
same browser from the same origin. Functionality in the shared web worker can be
independent to each request like a dedicated web worker or the web worker can share
its environment across the pages, as you will see in this recipe.

Since a shared web worker instance can have multiple clients communicating with
the thread, the interface is slightly different from the dedicated web worker interface.
A shared web worker uses a port assignment to identify the connection of a page to
the web worker. This identity is used by the shared web worker to identify the source
of messages and to whom messages should be posted. The following is a creation of
the `SharedWorker`:

```
var sworker = new SharedWorker('mySharedWorker.js');
```

Table 12.5   **The** `SharedWorker` **Events**

Event Name	Attribute	Purpose
`connect`	`onconnect`	Triggered when a message is received. An event object with a data member will be provided with the message.

The shared web worker has one event, `connect`, which is executed when a client thread connects to the shared web worker, as shown in Table 12.5.

As mentioned, each client connection has a port designation to uniquely identify that connection. The post message method and message events get pushed to the port so that the messaging is performed at the connection level.

In this recipe, we will explain how to use a shared web worker across multiple pages to calculate an average number from values provided from any of the connected pages. When the average is changed, the result is sent to each page for display. For ease of testing, the client pages are displayed in one container page using `iframes` rather than having to load each page individually in your browser. Thus, there are three files to be created: the main container page, which holds the `iframes` for each client page; the client page that accepts input from the user and connects to the shared web worker; and the actual shared web worker JavaScript file. Let's get started with the container file shown in Listing 12.6:

1. Create a blank HTML page with the HTML `body` and three `iframes` in `div` tags, as shown in the listing.

2. Next add the style tags and styling for the `div` and `iframe` tags to show the `iframes` in three equal columns across the page. This concludes the container file.

Listing 12.6   **Creating the Client Page Holder**

```
<!DOCTYPE html>
<html>
<head>
<meta charset="UTF-8" />
<title>12.6 SharedWorker Across Pages</title>
<!-- This is purely a container page to show
multiple pages using a shared worker. This would
perform the same if the pages were in separate
tabs or windows in the same browser. -->
<style>
  div{float:left;width:33.3%;height:500px}
  iframe{width:100%;height:100%}
</style>
</head>
```

```
<body>
  <div>Client Page 1<iframe src="12_7_sw_client.html"></iframe></div>
  <div>Client Page 2<iframe src="12_7_sw_client.html"></iframe></div>
  <div>Client Page 3<iframe src="12_7_sw_client.html"></iframe></div>
</body>
</html>
```

Next, you need to create the client page as coded in Listing 12.7, which will be loaded into each `iframe` of the container and display the input field for the user to enter a number:

1. Create a blank HTML page with the body, as shown in Listing 12.7, including the `input` tag, SEND NUMBER button, and log section.

2. Add the `script` tags and global reference for the shared worker instance called `sworker`. This will be the `SharedWorker` instance for posting and receiving messages.

3. Add the `window.addEventListener` line and the `init` function, which creates the shared worker connection and registers the `onmessage` handler for that client's port of the shared worker.

4. Add the `sendNumber` function, which takes the input value and sends the number to the shared worker for processing.

Listing 12.7   Creating the Client Pages

```
<!DOCTYPE html>
<html>
<head>
<meta charset="UTF-8" />
<title>12_7 SharedWorker Client</title>
<script>

// global SharedWorker reference
var sworker = null;

// initialize the page and SharedWorker connection
function init() {

  // reference our log output section
  var logOutput = document.getElementById('log');

  // add the button listener
  var btnSendNumber = document.getElementById('btnSendNumber');
  btnSendNumber.addEventListener('click',sendNumber,false);

  // create our SharedWorker reference
  sworker = new SharedWorker('12_8_shared_worker.js');
```

```
    // onmessage handler for messages from SharedWorker
    sworker.port.onmessage = function(msg) {

      // based on type of message display appropriately
      switch (msg.data.msgType) {
        case 'LOG':
          // received a log message, add to log
          logOutput.innerHTML += msg.data.msgText + '<br>';
          break;

        case 'AVE':
          // received a new average value, update average
          var aveOutput = document.getElementById('average');
          aveOutput.innerHTML = msg.data.aveValue;

          // add log entry
          logOutput.innerHTML += msg.data.msgText + '<br>';
          break;
      }
    }
  }
}

// send the number entered to the SharedWorker
function sendNumber() {

  // retrieve the number
  var numToSend = document.getElementById('numberToSend').value;

  // post message to the SharedWorker (notice port)
  sworker.port.postMessage(numToSend);

  // reset our value input field
  document.getElementById('numberToSend').value = '';
}

// add our event page load initialize call
window.addEventListener("load", init, false);

</script>
</head>
<body>
  Current Average: <output id="average"></output>
  <br><br>
  <input id="numberToSend" />
  <button id="btnSendNumber">Send Number to SharedWorker</button>
  <hr width="100%">
  Messages from SharedWorker:<br>
```

```
  <section id="log"></section>
</body>
</html>
```

When the client page in Listing 12.7 loads, you initialize a connection with the shared worker that is built from the file 12_4_sworker.js. The last step in this recipe is to create the shared worker JavaScript file. The shared-worker JavaScript file is provided in Listing 12.8 and created with the following steps:

1. Create a JavaScript file, named 12_4_sworker.js (or whatever name you choose as long as it matches the shared worker file parameter in your client HTML page).
2. Add the global variables at the top of the script and the `onconnect` event handler.
3. Add the `sendAllConnections` and `updateAverage` functions to the script.

Listing 12.8   Adding the Shared Worker .js File

```
// 12.8 SharedWorker js file for averaging numbers across pages

// Initialize the connections array for storing the connection ports
var count = 0;
var connections = new Array();

// Initialize our average formula variables
var average = 0;
var numValues = 0;
var sumValues = 0;

// onconnect event for SharedWorker
onconnect = function(msg) {

  // get the reference for this connection
  var port = msg.ports[0];

  // store this connection reference for future messages
  connections[count] = port;

  // increment the number of connections we have
  count += 1;

  // respond to the client and initialize their average
  port.postMessage({msgType:'LOG',msgText:'[SW] Now connected [' + count +
➥'].'});
  port.postMessage({msgType:'AVE',msgText:'[SW] Average updated: ' + average +
➥'.', aveValue:average});
```

```
    // create handler for when we receive a message from the client
    port.onmessage = function(msg) {
      // set the value passed into the SharedWorker
      var newValue = msg.data;

      // respond that we received the value
      port.postMessage({msgType:'LOG',msgText:'[SW] Received: ' + newValue + '.'});

      // update the Average with the new value
      updateAverage(newValue);
    }
}

// helper function to send a message to all clients
function sendAllConnections(msgTypeVal,msgVal) {

  // loop through the clients and postMessage
  for (var i=0; i<count; i++) {

    // post message to client with our JSON formatted message
    // with message type, text, and current average
    connections[i].postMessage({msgType:msgTypeVal,
      msgText:msgVal,
      aveValue:average});
  }
}

// our simple average update function
function updateAverage(newValue) {

  // adjust average formula variables
  numValues++;
  sumValues += parseFloat(newValue);

  // create new average
  average = Math.round((sumValues / numValues)*100)/100;

  // update all clients with new average
  sendAllConnections('AVE','[SW] Average updated: ' + average + '.');
}
```

To run this recipe, load the container HTML page into your browser. Note that at the time of writing this recipe, only Safari has support for the SharedWorker interface. When the container loads, it will load an instance of the client page into the three iframes HTML page, as shown in Figure 12.3. Each client page will create an instance of the SharedWorker interface, which creates a single shared web worker thread and connects the client page to a single shared web worker. When the client page connects, the onconnect event handler will be triggered in the shared web worker. The event handler will get the port reference that the connection is tied to so that you can send messages to this client connection later and store this port in a connections array. Next, the shared web worker in the onconnect event handler sends, to the port just connected to, a log message stating that the client has connected and what number connection the client has. In addition, the shared web worker sends to the client the current average to initialize the display on the client page. Lastly, the shared web worker registers an event handler for this port for the onmessage event so that when the client page posts a message to the shared web worker, the message can be caught.

When the shared web worker sends the log or average messages back to the client page upon initial connection, the onmessage handler in the client page will catch these messages. The client page will determine the type of message based on the fields in the JSON string passed and update the display by adding the log message and setting the average value if required.

Once all the client pages are initialized with the connection to the shared web worker, the user may enter a number into any of the client pages and click the Send Number to SharedWorker button. This will call the sendNumber function in the client JavaScript and will in turn post a message to the shared web worker with the number entered. Note that you use the port of the sworker to call the postmessage on, as shown here, which is slightly different from posting messages to dedicated web workers:

```
sworker.port.postMessage(numToSend);
```

This post message command will send the user input to the shared web worker, which will then take this number in the onmessage event that was registered and return a log message that the number was received to the client port. After sending the log message of receipt, the shared web worker will update the current average in the global variables and send this new average to all connected clients. The helper function to send to all clients loops through the connections and posts the new average in a message. Figure 12.3 shows a sample run of the recipe.

The SharedWorker interface should be considered young; it is supported in only a few browser platforms and has minimal functionality. There are also challenges with this interface that have not been worked out yet, such as handling disconnections of clients, but the interface is promising and offers a lot of functionality for developers in the future.

Tip

In developing your own web worker structure, it is beneficial to first develop the worker functionality in your main page to allow for easy debugging. Once you have the core worker functionality working, then you can encapsulate the code in a separate worker file and thread.

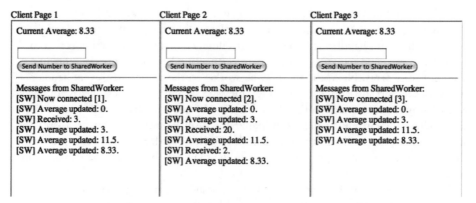

Figure 12.3   Sample output showing messages received by each client page

Summary

In this chapter, the recipes have demonstrated the use of the WebSocket API and Web Workers API for some key patterns of communication. The WebSocket API provides an easy-to-use communication method between servers and client pages, while Web Workers provides an efficient means to offload heavy processing from the main thread of your website or application. By leveraging these new APIs in your applications, you can enhance the overall user experience and functionality. The recipes in this chapter have only touched the surface of what can be done with these APIs but have given you the basis to implement your own solutions.

13

Browser Experience in HTML5

Browsers have notoriously been isolated from the rest of the operating system for security reasons. With HTML5, several APIs have come forth that allow tighter integration with the operating system of the device that the user may be on and to offer more typical user experiences of a native application. We have grouped three of these APIs into this chapter on the browser experience. The three APIs allow for the following types of user experiences:

- Drag and drop of objects outside the browser and inside the page
- Application cache storage to allow for offline web page usage
- Desktop notifications to alert users to events in the browser window

In this chapter, you will learn about these APIs even though they are more nascent than the other APIs we have covered and have room for improvement. We will start with one of the more refined and end with an API that is not yet supported by the majority of browsers but has great promise. So, let's dig in with the drag and drop API.

Drag and Drop API

The drag and drop API has been added to the HTML5 APIs to allow users to select an object, drag the object to an area on the page, and drop the object triggering some action. The basis of the drag-and-drop functionality is the combination of four pieces:

- A draggable object from within or external to the browser
- A drop zone to receive the object
- Events that allow control of the behavior of the drag and drop
- A data store to transfer contextual data on the object

To allow an object in a browser to be dragged, there is a new attribute titled `draggable`. The `draggable` attribute has three potential values: `true`, `false`, and auto. If draggable is set to true, then the object can be dragged by the user. If the attribute is set to false, then the object cannot be dragged. If the value is set to auto, then the browser will use the default draggable value for the type of object as if the draggable attribute were not provided. For example, you have probably noticed already that you can grab an image on a page and drag it around. When you drop it, of course, nothing happens since there is no drop zone defined; yet it can still be dragged. To create a draggable div, the code would look like the following:

```
<div class="divClass" id="myDiv" draggable="true">My Div</div>
```

To create an area where an object can be dropped, an attribute named dropzone has been added in HTML5. The dropzone attribute can have one of three values: copy, move, or link. The value you choose depends on the type of action you want performed when the object is dropped. A sample dropzone declaration on a div looks as follows:

```
<div id="divDropzone" dropzone="copy" …
```

The dropzone attribute also can use a filter, such as a list of formats like f:/image/png, which states that only images files of type PNG can be dropped onto the drop zone.

Next, you must handle the actual start of the dragging and dropping of the item by catching events that are triggered by the elements that you have now designated as the draggable object and the dropzone object. When the user starts to drag an object, the ondragstart attribute or dragstart event will be fired. By calling a function on this event, you will be able to then store some data about the object that is being dragged. When the object is then dropped on the dropzone, the dropzone will fire an attribute event titled ondrop or the drop event. When this event is fired, the data that has been stored on the object being dragged can then be retrieved and used to perform any functions the script chooses. To pass this information, you use a new interface titled DataTransfer.

The DataTransfer interface has various attributes and methods, but the two that will be used to pass information are setData and getData. The following are the methods available with the DataTransfer interface:

- setData(format, data): Sets the data, of type format (such as text) into the data store.
- getData(format): Retrieves the data from the data store, of type format.
- clearData([format]): Clears the data store of the optional format provided. If no format is provided, then the entire store is cleared.
- void setDragImage(image, long x, long y): Uses the image at x,y coordinates to show the user.
- void addElement(element): Adds the element provided to the data store.

Table 13.1 shows the version of each browser that supports the drag and drop API.

Table 13.1   **Drag and Drop API
Browser Availability**

Android	2.1+
Chrome	10.0+
Firefox	3.6+
Internet Explorer	6.0+
iOS Safari	-
Opera	-
Safari	3.2+

BEGINNER RECIPE:
Dragging and Dropping Across `divs`

This recipe will use the drag-and-drop functionality to allow the user to drag a note image to a corkboard `dropzone`. When the drop of the note occurs, a new copy of the note image selected will be added to the corkboard, as shown in Figure 13.1.

This recipe will show you the basics of creating a drag-and-drop use case by using the attributes of `draggable` and `dropzone` along with the key events and `DataTransfer` interface. Listing 13.1 shows the code for this example, but you can follow these steps to create the file:

1. Create a blank HTML page with the `style` and `body` sections shown in Listing 13.1. In the `body` section, make sure to add the event handler attributes to the note images and the board `div`.

2. Add the `fileAttributes` section to the HTML body where the recipe will display the file attributes.

Figure 13.1   Sample output showing basic drag-and-drop functionality
using draggable notes on the left and a drop zone on the right

3. Add the `dragStartHandler` and `dropHandler` functions, which both take the target element that the event triggered on, along with the event itself.

4. Add the `getStartPos` and `init` functions, which retrieve the drag start position in the element being dragged and initialize the style, respectively.

Listing 13.1 **A Basic Drag-and-Drop Example**

```
<!DOCTYPE html>
<html>
<head>
<meta charset="UTF-8" />
<title>13.1 Basic Drag and Drop</title>
<style>
#notes {
  float:left;
  height:220px;
  width:50px;
  text-align:center;
  border-style:solid;
  border-width:2px;
  border-color:#333;
  background-color:#666;
}
#board {
  float:left;
  width:300px;
  height:220px;
  border-style:solid;
  border-width:2px;
  border-color:#333;
  background-image:url('corkboard.png');
}
</style>
<script>

// variables to hold the offset of the click on image
var imgOffsetX = 0;
var imgOffsetY = 0;

// function to handle starting the drag
function dragStartHandler(tgt, evt) {
  evt.dataTransfer.setData("Text", tgt.id);
}

// Handler for drop action
function dropHandler(tgt, evt) {
```

```
// prevent the default browser action from occurring
// for example open a new tab with the item dragged
if(evt.preventDefault) {
  evt.preventDefault();
}


// retrieve the id of the image being dragged
var elImgId = evt.dataTransfer.getData("Text");

// create a new image instance
var oImg = new Image();

// set the src of the image
oImg.src = document.getElementById(elImgId).src;

// set the image position
oImg.style.position='absolute';
var newX = evt.x - imgOffsetX;
var newY = evt.y - imgOffsetY;

var divLeft = tgt.x;
var divTop = tgt.y;
var divWidth = parseInt(tgt.style.width);
var divHeight = parseInt(tgt.style.height);

// make sure image is fully in the div
var imgWH = 50;
if (newX<tgt.offsetLeft) {
  newX=tgt.offsetLeft
} else if (newX+imgWH>(tgt.offsetLeft + divWidth)) {
  newX = tgt.offsetLeft + divWidth-imgWH;
}
if (newY<tgt.offsetTop) {
  newY=tgt.offsetTop;
} else if (newY+imgWH>(tgt.offsetTop + divHeight)) {
  newY = tgt.offsetTop + divHeight-imgWH;
}

// position image
oImg.style.left = newX+'px';
oImg.style.top = newY+'px';

// append image to the div dropzone
tgt.appendChild(oImg);
}
```

```
// help function to set the point of click on the note image
function getStartPos(evt) {
  imgOffsetX = evt.offsetX;
  imgOffsetY = evt.offsetY;
}

// initialize the board width and height
function init() {
  document.getElementById('board').style.width = '300px';
  document.getElementById('board').style.height = '220px';
}

// call the init function on page load
window.addEventListener('load',init,false);

</script>
</head>
<body>
  <h1>Drag notes to the corkboard:</h1>
  <div id="notes">
    <img id="note_blue" src="post_blue.png" onmousedown="getStartPos(event);"
➥ondragstart="dragStartHandler(this, event);"><br>
    <img id="note_green" src="post_green.png" onmousedown="getStartPos(event);"
➥ondragstart="dragStartHandler(this, event);"><br>
    <img id="note_pink" src="post_pink.png" onmousedown="getStartPos(event);"
➥ondragstart="dragStartHandler(this, event);"><br>
    <img id="note_yellow" src="post_yellow.png" onmousedown="getStartPos(event);"
➥ondragstart="dragStartHandler(this, event);">
  </div>
  <div id="board" dropzone="copy" ondrop="dropHandler(this, event);"
➥ondragover="return false;"></div>
</body>
</html>
```

When the page loads in the browser, each image sets an ondragstart event handler to call the dragStartHandler with the respective element. Note how you do not need to add the draggable attribute since the default setting for images is draggable. In the div board line, you set the div to be a dropzone and set the ondrop and ondragover event handlers. The ondragover event handler is needed to override the standard browser functionality and simply returns false when the event is raised. If the user selects a note and starts dragging the note, then the dragStartHandler function will be called. In addition, the onmousedown event will trigger a helper function that simply stores the x and y coordinates in variables for use in calculating where to position the note on the board. In the dragStartHandler function, the script sets the ID of the element that is being dragged in the DataTransfer interface.

The user then drops the note onto the board, and the `dropHandler` function will be called. The first thing you do in the drop handler is negate the default behavior of the browser by calling `preventDefault` on the event. This will allow you to control the behavior of the drop action in the browser. The script then gets the element ID from the data store, creates a new image, sets the source, and does some calculations to set the position of the new image on the board. Note that the positioning will work in only some browsers such as Chrome based on the positioning methods available, but this is not critical to the example. Once the image is created and positioned, you then append the image to the board `div`, resulting in a copy of the note image.

This is a simple example of the drag-and-drop functionality. In the next recipe, you will incorporate these concepts with other drag-and-drop events to have much more control over the drag-and-drop experience.

ADVANCED RECIPE:
Leveraging Events and dataTransfer

In the previous recipe, you used just the essentials of the drag and drop API to catch an image being dropped onto an area and make a new image to be added to the area. The drag and drop API interface provides several other events besides the basic drag-and-drop events to allow you to control both the drag and drop behaviors. With these events, you can control behaviors such as the type of items that can be dragged along with where they can be dropped. The following are the other events that the drag and drop API produces:

- `dragstart`: The drag operation has started on a draggable object.
- `drag`: The object is being moved.
- `dragenter`: A drag operation enters into an available dropzone.
- `dragleave`: A drag operation leaves an available dropzone.
- `dragover`: An object is being dragged over an available dropzone.
- `drop`: An object is released onto an available dropzone.
- `dragend`: A drag operation on a draggable object has ended.

In this recipe, you will employ the drag and drop API to create the mathematical game commonly referred to as the Towers of Hanoi and created by mathematician Édouard Lucas in 1883 (you can find more on the history of the game on Wikipedia at http://en.wikipedia.org/wiki/Tower_of_Hanoi). The basic rules are that you have three posts, with the leftmost post containing a series of disks stacked from largest to smallest. The number of the disks can vary between different boards. The goal is to move the stack to the rightmost post, moving one disk at a time and only onto either an empty post or a post with a larger disk than the one being moved. We will use the drag and drop API events and `dataTransfer` object to create this game, making sure to enforce the rules of play.

During the play of the game, if the player attempts to place a disk onto a stack that has a smaller disk, then the code will not allow the disk to be dropped. However, if the move is valid, then the disk will be moved and added to the stack. In addition, if the user attempts to move a disk that is not on the top of a particular stack, then it will be disallowed. After each move of a disk onto the rightmost stack, you will check to the see whether the user has successfully moved the entire stack and congratulate. Let's get started and see how to use the various events to enforce the rules of the game:

1. Create the page shown in Listing 13.2 with the `style` and `body` tags for the blocks and three drop zones. Note that on the blocks you add the `draggable` attribute to make sure the browser understands that these `div`s can be dragged.

2. Add the `script` tags, add the `initTowers` function, and add the `window.addEventListener` to trigger the initialization.

3. Add the event handlers for the blocks; the `blockHandleDragStart` and `blockHandleDragEnd` functions will allow only the top block of a tower to be dragged. The functions will also change the style on the start and end of the dragging motion.

4. To go with the block handlers, you need the drop zone handlers. Add the tower drop zone handler functions, `towerHandleDragOver`, `towerHandleDragLeave`, and `towerHandleDragDrop`, to control the tower drop zone's style when moving a block over it and handle the dropping of a block on a tower.

5. Add the global variable declarations at the top of the script for the tower block game map (the two-dimensional array named `towers`), the number of blocks for the game, and the counter for the number of moves made by the player.

> **Note**
>
> You can find the images for this recipe on the book's website (see the introduction for location information).

Listing 13.2   **Employing Drag and Drop for Towers of Hanoi**

```
<!DOCTYPE html>
<html>
<head>
<meta charset="UTF-8" />
<title>13.2 Towers Game</title>
<style>
.towerDropZone {
  float: left;
  height: 200px;
  width: 200px;
  margin: 5px;
  padding: 15px;
  position:relative;
```

```
    background-color:#fff;
    background-image:url(tower.png);
    background-repeat:no-repeat;
    background-position:bottom;
}
.towerDropZone.over {
  border-radius: 15px 15px;
  background-color:#EEE;
}
.tower {
  width: 200px;
  position:absolute;
  bottom:1px;
  border:none;
}
.block {
  height: 25px;
  margin:1px auto;
  border: 1px solid #ccc;
  border-radius: 15px 15px;
  background-color:#00F;
  color:#FFF;
  text-align:center;
  font-size:19px;
  font-weight:bold;
}
</style>
<script>
// Declare the map of towers, number of blocks and step count
var towers = [[],[],[]];
var numblocks = 4;
var numMoves = 0;

// Initialize the event handlers and state
function initTowers() {

  // Set the event handlers for the tower drop zones
  var towerDropZones = document.querySelectorAll('#towers .towerDropZone');
  [].forEach.call(towerDropZones, function(tdz) {
    tdz.addEventListener('dragover', towerHandleDragOver, false);
    tdz.addEventListener('drop', towerHandleDragDrop, false);
    tdz.addEventListener('dragleave', towerHandleDragLeave, false);
  });

  // Set the event handlers for the individual blocks
  var blocks = document.querySelectorAll('.block');
  [].forEach.call(blocks, function(block) {
```

```
    block.addEventListener('dragstart', blockHandleDragStart, false);
    block.addEventListener('dragend', blockHandleDragEnd, false);
  });

  // Set up the map of initial block state on tower 0
  for (var i=numblocks-1;i>=0;i--) {

    // add the block to the tower map on first tower (3,2,1,0)
    towers[0].push(i);

    // Create the different widths for the blocks
    document.getElementById(i+"block").style.width = (90 + i * 30) + "px";
  }
}

// Handler for a block dragging over a tower drop zone
function towerHandleDragOver(e) {
  // prevent the default action from occurring so we can drop
  if (e.preventDefault) {
    e.preventDefault();
  }

  // Set the effect to the move option
  e.dataTransfer.dropEffect = 'move';

  // Set the look of the tower to show available
  this.className = "towerDropZone over";

  return false;
}

// Handler for a block drag leaving a tower drop zone
function towerHandleDragLeave(e) {
  // Set tower drop zone look back to normal
  this.className = "towerDropZone";
}

// Handler for dropping a block on a tower drop zone
function towerHandleDragDrop(e) {

  // prevent the default action
  if (e.preventDefault) {
    e.preventDefault(); // necessary; allows us to drop
  }

  // Change the tower drop zone look back to normal
  this.className = "towerDropZone";
```

```
// Get the JSON data passed through dataTransfer
var blockInfo = JSON.parse(e.dataTransfer.getData("Text"));

// Set the origin / destination towers, and block info
var blockId = blockInfo.blockId;
var blockNum = parseInt(blockInfo.blockId);
var fromTowerId = parseInt(blockInfo.fromTowerId);
var toTowerId = this.id;

// Get tower element
var tower = document.getElementById("tower"+toTowerId);

// Logic to determine if the block can be dropped on tower
var towerheight = towers[toTowerId].length;
if ( towerheight == 0) {
  // Tower empty - Insert block before <p> holder in the tower
  tower.insertBefore(document.getElementById(blockId),document.
➥getElementById("p"+toTowerId));
} else {
  // Tower has blocks - get top block value on tower
  var topBlock = towers[toTowerId][towerheight-1];

  // check if block can be put on top of block
  if ( topBlock > blockNum) {
  // insert block before top block to go on top
  tower.insertBefore(document.getElementById(blockId),document.
➥getElementById(topBlock+"block"));
  } else {
    // block can not be put on top of current top block
    // return false to kill action
    return false;
  }
}

// Update the game map locations for this block
towers[toTowerId].push(blockNum);
towers[fromTowerId].pop();

// Increment the number of moves made
numMoves++;
document.getElementById("numMoves").textContent = numMoves;

// Check to see if game is over - all blocks in order on 3rd tower
if (towers[2].length==numblocks) {

  // Game complete - make blocks not draggable
  var blocks = document.querySelectorAll('.block');
  [].forEach.call(blocks, function(block) {
```

```
      block.draggable = false;
    });

    // notify user
    alert("Congratulations - you have moved the tower.");
  }
}

// Handler for a block starting to be dragged
function blockHandleDragStart(e) {

  // Retrieve the block id and origin tower id
  var blockId = this.id;
  var fromTowerId = this.parentNode.parentNode.id;

  // Get variables to be able to check if the block grabbed
  // is the top block on the tower
  var towerheight = towers[fromTowerId].length;
  var topBlock = towers[fromTowerId][towerheight-1];
  var thisBlock = parseInt(blockId);

  // Check if this is the top block on the tower
  if (topBlock == thisBlock) {

    // block is the top block so we can move it
    this.style.opacity = '0.4';

    // create the JSON packet for passing info with dataTransfer
    var blockinfo = {
      "blockId": blockId,
      "fromTowerId": fromTowerId};

    // set the data for the dataTransfer
    e.dataTransfer.setData("Text", JSON.stringify(blockinfo));

  } else {

    // block is not the top block
    this.style.opacity = '1.0';

    // return false to prevent the block being dragged
    return false;
  }
}

// Handler for a block drag action ending
function blockHandleDragEnd(e) {
```

```
    // set the block opacity back to normal
    this.style.opacity = '1.0';
}


// Call our initilization function when page loads
window.addEventListener('load',initTowers,false);

</script>
</head>
<body>
  <h1>Towers Game</h1>
  <p>Move the pieces on the left stack to the right most tower.<br>
  A block may only be moved onto an empty tower or a tower with a larger
➥block.</p>
  <div>Number of moves made: <span id="numMoves">0</span></div>
  <section id="towers">
    <div class="towerDropZone" id="0">
      <div class="tower" id="tower0">
        <div class="block" id="0block" draggable="true">1</div>
        <div class="block" id="1block" draggable="true">2</div>
        <div class="block" id="2block" draggable="true">3</div>
        <div class="block" id="3block" draggable="true">4</div>
        <p id="p0" />
      </div>
    </div>
    <div class="towerDropZone" id="1">
        <div class="tower" id="tower1"><p id="p1" /></div>
    </div>
    <div class="towerDropZone" id="2">
        <div class="tower" id="tower2"><p id="p2" /></div>
    </div>
  </section>
</body>
</html>
```

So, now that you have built up the page and ideally played a couple rounds by dragging the blocks back and forth, you have an idea of how the events are triggered based on the actions of the player. But let's take a couple minutes and go through some of the details in how the game logic integrates with the drag-and-drop functionality.

When the page loads, the recipe declares the global variables for the game map (if you have programmed position-based games, then a game map will be second-nature for you; otherwise, a game map can be thought of simply as a representation of where the game pieces are at any specific time), the number of blocks for the game, and the counter for number of player moves. The game map in this case is a two-dimensional array that keeps track of what blocks are on each of the three towers. The drop zones, or towers, have integer-based IDs starting at zero, which map directly to the towers array. Upon running the `initTowers` function, the page registers the drop zone handlers for each drop zone tower and then the event handlers for the blocks that will be moving around. Then the script sets the current game map by adding into the array for tower zero (the first tower) the four blocks, 3, 2, 1, 0. You will notice you add this in reverse order, which references that block 3 is bigger than block 2, and so on. In addition, you use this order then to size the blocks through the style property dynamically, and this concludes the initialization of the game board.

Let's take a look at the game flow now. When the user drags a block from one tower to another tower, several things occur as events are fired. First, the drag start event is fired, and the `blockHandleDragStart` function executes. This function first verifies that the block selected is the top block of the tower that the block was on. If it is not, then the function returns `false`, which prevents the block from being able to be dragged. If it is the top block, then the recipe creates a JSON string with some key information: the block ID and the tower ID from which the block is being dragged. This data is then set into the `DataTransfer` interface so that when the block is dropped onto a new tower, you will have the block selected and the tower from which the block was moved. To show the user you are dragging the particular block, you also change the opacity of the block in the function.

As the block is then dragged into a drop zone, or tower, the drag-over event is fired, and the `towerHandleDragOver` function executes. The purpose of this function is to let the player know that they have moved over a drop zone. This is performed by changing the style of the tower `div` area that is being dragged over, as shown in Figure 13.2.

One key item, though, is the inclusion of the `preventDefault` command. As you saw in the previous recipe, to prevent the browser from performing the default action, which can cause issues with the game flow, you must use this command. If the block is just "passing through" the tower drop zone, then the drag leave event will be fired, and the `towerHandleDragLeave` function will be executed. This function changes the style of the tower drop zone being left back to the normal view.

When the block is dropped onto a tower drop zone, the bulk of the game logic is executed in the `towerHandleDragDrop` function. When this function is launched,

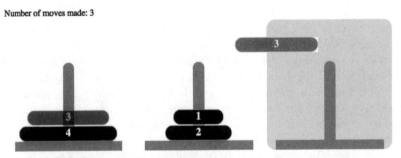

Figure 13.2   Sample output showing block 3 being dragged from the first tower to the last tower. The event drag start has fired already, and the drag-over event has just fired as you get into the drop zone.

you will first call the preventDefault method to again prevent the browser from using its default logic for a drag-and-drop event. Next, the recipe will retrieve the dataTransfer information to be able to use this data in the game logic. The key to the logic is to determine whether the block can be dropped, and this is done by checking the game map to see whether the tower the block is being dropped on is either empty or has a larger block already on the tower. If the tower has a smaller block, then the block cannot be added, and you will return false, which will prevent the drop from occurring on the tower. If the block can be added, then you "insert" the block either before the top block (to display the blocks correctly) or before a placeholder on the tower, which is the paragraph tag (<p id="px">). Once the block has been added to the HTML, the recipe then updates the game map, increments the counter for the number of moves, and lastly checks to see whether the player has completed the game.

To check whether the player has completed the game, you do a very simple check to see whether the last tower has all four blocks. Since the game logic prevents a smaller block from being lower on a tower than a larger block, you do not need to verify the order. If the game is solved, then the player should not be able to move the blocks anymore, so the code makes the blocks not draggable by programmatically setting each block's draggable attribute to false. This ends the game; to play again, the player must reload the page.

You could enhance this recipe greatly with features such as changing the color of the drop zone based on whether the block can be dropped on an area. But we will let you add those features if you want, now that you understand the flow of events with the drag and drop API and know how to add logic based on when the events fire.

In both of the examples of the drag and drop API, you have passed simple text strings with the DataTransfer interface. The DataTransfer interface, as mentioned earlier, can handle multiple types of information being transferred, including images, files, and so on. These recipes touch on just the basics of getting a drag-and-drop solution functional. There are many other features to the drag and drop API, including different behaviors, objects that can be dragged, and dragging from the desktop into a browser. In Chapter 14, Working with Local Files, you will learn how the dragging and dropping of files from outside the browser to a drop zone in the page is handled with some of the special features of the DataTransfer interface.

Tip

If you find yourself having a difficult time debugging your drag-and-drop programming because every time you drop an object onto your drop zone the browser launches a new tab or window with just the object that you are dragging, then most likely you have left out the preventDefault method call on the event being fired. The browsers will execute their default processes for handling a drop action based on the type of object being dragged without this method. For example, in Firefox, if you are dragging an image and drop it onto a drop zone that does not execute the preventDefault method, a new tab will be opened, showing just the image that you were dragging.

Application Cache and API

On smartphones and tablet devices, if you want an application to always be available, then you need a native app. If you want to use an application from a website, then you need an Internet connection—that is, until application cache came along. Application cache means you can run online applications offline, not just on smartphones or tablets but on desktop browsers as well.

Table 13.2 shows the version of each browser that supports the application cache and API.

Table 13.2 **Application Cache Browser Compatibility**

Android	2.1+
Chrome	10.0+
Firefox	3.6+
Internet Explorer	-
iOS Safari	3.2+
Opera	10.6+
Safari	4.0+

The application cache is a list of files, captured in a *manifest*, that tells the browser to download these files and store them so that when the user comes back to the page, the files are available to be used. This is incredibly useful if you don't have a connection, but even if you do have a connection, this will speed up your page's loading time because the files have already been loaded.

Any page that references the manifest will automatically be stored, but that does not mean you want to, or indeed should (consider file size and type limit restrictions), store everything offline. What you want to offer the user is a suitable offline experience. If you have an application design, then the key files for using the app should be stored offline.

Browser Cache Security

Since the application cache is storing files on the user's file system of the developer's choosing, there are security implications associated with the website or application. It is not too far-fetched that a malicious file could be cached from the web server on the client's machine. With this security issue in mind, a browser will ask the user prior to caching any files whether the user trusts the site for storing data and files on the local system. Figure 13.3 shows a sample of how a browser will ask the user for permission.

This website (www.html5developerscookbook.com) is asking to store data on your computer for offline use.   Allow   Never for This Site   Not Now   ×

Figure 13.3   Permission request for application caching

Referencing a Manifest File

It is easy for the browser to reference the manifest file; simply add the manifest attribute to the `html` element, with the name of your manifest file (.appcache), as follows:

```
<!DOCTYPE html>
<html manifest="application.appcache">
<head>
</head>
<body>
</body>
</html>
```

> **Note**
>
> Any file (.html, .php, and so on) referenced in the manifest file will be downloaded and cached.

Your web server might not know what to do with an .appcache file, so you might need to add the MIME type to your server. You can do this via IIS, or if you're using Apache, use the following code on your server:

```
AddType text/cache-manifest .appcache
```

BEGINNER RECIPE:
Creating a Manifest File

You do not need any special software to create the manifest file; you can use any basic text editor such as Notepad. Save the file as *xxx*.appcache. At the top of the file, you must include the following:

```
CACHE MANIFEST
```

> **Note**
>
> We suggest not creating the manifest file until you finish your app or website, because you don't want to store unfinished files as they may disrupt development. Clearing or refreshing the cache isn't as straightforward as refreshing the page (we'll cover this later in the chapter).

From here, you can just start listing files that want to be stored, as shown here:

```
CACHE MANIFEST
css/main.css
js/jquery.js
images/logo.png
```

That should be all you need. If you created an HTML page and included a manifest file listing files, as in the previous listing, then after visiting the page while online, the page and supporting files will be cached. If you then disconnect your Internet connection and refresh the page, the page will display normally. Files listed in the manifest can be either relative or absolute addressed.

But there is more you can do. You can split the manifest file into three sections: CACHE, FALLBACK, and NETWORK:

- *CACHE*: Files that should be cached on the client browser device for use when the Internet connection is not available
- *FALLBACK*: A list of files and their replacements when a connection is not available to the Internet
- *NETWORK*: Files that require a connection only and should not be cached

CACHE

The CACHE section is basically the same as in the previous example. Files listed like those in the previous example or with a CACHE heading are "explicit" and will be downloaded and cached on the browser. They can include files stored externally, but you cannot use wildcards when caching files, so `css/*` will not work.

> **Warning**
> Do not cache the manifest itself in the cache because it will be nearly impossible to inform the browser of a new manifest.

FALLBACK

The FALLBACK section of the manifest is incredibly useful and can act as a way of detecting whether the user is online or offline. Using FALLBACK, you can tell the browser what file to use if a specific file is unavailable because of the user being offline. For example, if you had a large CSS file that was not necessary for offline use, then you could omit the file from the CACHE section and instead use FALLBACK, as shown here:

```
CACHE MANIFEST
FALLBACK:
online.css offline.css
```

So, in this example, if the user is offline but the HTML page calls online.css, the manifest file has told the browser to switch to offline.css (note the files are separated by a space), which has been cached. Handy, isn't it? This is restricted not just to CSS files but could work for images, JavaScript files, HTML pages, and even movie clips. Just put each declaration on a new line.

With FALLBACK, you *can* use a wildcard technique. So if you wanted all files to have a fallback, you could use the following:

```
/ /offline.html
```

So, if the user is offline, all files after the slash, such as /page1.html, will be shown offline.html instead. Remember, though, once a file, such as page1.html, has been opened and it references the manifest file, then it will be downloaded and available offline.

You could go further with FALLBACK and offer certain directories or just HTML pages as a generic fallback:

```
/js/ /offline.js
*.html /offline.html
```

NETWORK

The NETWORK section tells the browser which files are available only with a connection, and it stops these files from being downloaded. Usually resources that go in this section are resources that require a database or server connection, such as a login page:

```
CACHE MANIFEST
NETWORK:
login.aspx
```

Updating the Cache via the Manifest

When the browser sees the manifest file for the first time, it downloads the files in the list, and it will not refresh the cache until you force it. You can do this via the API, which will be covered later; by clearing the browser cache (Firefox has the option of deleting a manifest on a site-by-site basis; select Firefox > Options > Advanced); or by updating the manifest file. Updating a file that is listed in the manifest will not force an update; you must make a change to the manifest itself. An easy way of doing this, rather than adding or deleting resources, is to leave or update a comment. You can make comments in the file by starting the line with a hash (#), as shown in the following example. Comments must be on their own line.

```
CACHE MANIFEST
# v1.0 - 06.28.2011

CACHE:
magic.js
style.css
```

Refreshing the cache can be as simple as just updating a comment.

BEGINNER RECIPE:
Using Web Pages Offline

You have read the logic, so now you'll see an example. In this web application, you will create a simple multiplication of two numbers provided and allow the user to use a "contact us" type of form if online. If the user is offline, then you will fall back to a static page with contact information. In this recipe, you will have the following:

- Three HTML pages
- One JavaScript file
- Two CSS files
- Two images

On the first HTML page are two input fields (the new HTML5 input type, of course), and the button will multiple the two numbers together (there is no validation in this example). When the submit button is fired, the result will display, and there will be an option to contact a fictitious company with your results via a contact form. However, the contact form will display only if there is a connection, so you will offer a FALLBACK option, which is a page that simply has a telephone number on it.

Also in the app you have a CSS file that has some layout styles and then a separate CSS file that loads a pretty font (for example, it could be coming from a web font service). You want this pretty font to display only if the user is online.

Finally, an image will simply tell you whether the user is online (a check mark graphic) or not (an X graphic).

Listing 13.3 shows the HTML for this application, and Listing 13.4 shows the manifest file. You can see it in action in Figure 13.4.

Listing 13.3   HTML to Display the Calculation Form

```
<!DOCTYPE html>
<html manifest="13_3_cookbook.appcache">
<head>
<meta charset="utf-8">
<title>Offline</title>
<script src="13_3_calculation.js"></script>
<link rel="stylesheet" href="13_3_offline_style.css" />
<link rel="stylesheet" href="13_3_offline_style2.css" />
</head>
<body>
  <h1>Submit a calculation</h1>
  <label for="first">First</label>
  <input required type="number" id="first" name="first" />
  <label for="second">Second</label>
  <input required type="number" id="second" name="second" />
  <input type="submit" onclick="calculate()" value="Calculate" />
  <div id="resultHolder">
    <h2>Your result is <span id="result"></span></h2>
    <p>Now you have your result, you can <a
➥href="13_1_offline_contact.html">contact us</a></p>
  </div>
  <img src="connection-tick.gif" width="50" height="50" alt="">
</body>
</html>
```

Submit a calculation

First

Second

[Calculate]

✔

Figure 13.4   Output for submitting a calculation while online

Listing 13.4   **Manifest for the Calculation App**

```
CACHE MANIFEST
# Version 1.0

CACHE:
13_3_calculation.js
13_3_offline_style.css

NETWORK:
13_3_offline_style2.css

FALLBACK:
connection-tick.gif connection-cross.gif
13_3_offline_contact.html 13_3_offline_offline.html
```

If you try this example while online, you will see the pretty Comic Sans font and the check mark graphic (see Figure 13.4), but if you then go offline and refresh, the app has no font assigned, and the X graphic is showing (see Figure 13.5). If you complete the calculation and attempt to access the contact form, you will instead see the "Ring us" page shown in Figure 13.6.

Submit a calculation

First

Second

[Calculate]

Figure 13.5   Output for submitting a calculation while offline

Ring us

Our contact form requires you to have an internet connection. Instead, you can ring us on 123-456-789.

Figure 13.6   The substitute page for the contact form while offline

Plenty of options are available to you with the application cache. Your app might be all on one page, or it might be spread across several pages so you need to consider which files to store and which files need Internet access.

There are some browser differences. IE9 does not support offline web applications fully; however, it appears to cache the initial page, CSS, and JavaScript fine and work offline, but this cache should not be relied upon. Chrome, Firefox, and Safari work as expected and show the fallback image and HTML page. Opera 11 shows the fallback image, but when connecting to the form, instead of showing the fallback page, it shows a connection error page.

Application Cache API

When the browser reloads a page that has a manifest, it first checks to see whether there are any changes, and then if there are changes to the file, it does the update in the background. If you open a page with a manifest in Chrome, open the Developer Console, and refresh the page, you will see it returns the following:

```
Document was loaded from Application Cache with manifest http://
website/13_3_cookbook.appcache
Application Cache Checking event
Application Cache NoUpdate event
```

If you change the manifest and refresh again, you will see more activity:

```
Document was loaded from Application Cache with manifest http://website/13_3_
cookbook.appcache
Application Cache Checking event
Application Cache Downloading event
Application Cache Progress event (0 of 5) http://website/13_3_offline_style.css
Application Cache Progress event (1 of 5) http://website/13_3_calculation.js
Application Cache Progress event (2 of 5) http://website/13_3_offline.html
Application Cache Progress event (3 of 5) http://website/13_3_offline_offline.html
Application Cache Progress event (4 of 5) http://website/connection-cross.gif
Application Cache Progress event (5 of 5)
Application Cache UpdateReady event
```

There are several events in the ApplicationCache object, as listed next. The browser provides by default the load event, but the application cache API gives you further options if you want to use them.

- checking: The browser is downloading the manifest for the first time or is looking for an update to the file.

- noupdate: The manifest has not been changed.
- downloading: If the browser is looking at the manifest for the first time, then it will download the resources; otherwise, it has found an update and is downloading that update.
- progress: The browser is downloading a resource listed.
- cached: The resources have now been downloaded and cached.
- updateready: The resources in the manifest have been downloaded, and the browser cache can be updated. The swapCache function can then be fired to make the browser use the latest manifest. Note that the swapCache function needs to be called; otherwise, the browser will still use the old cache.
- obsolete: The manifest file could not be found.
- error: The manifest file could not be found, the page referencing the manifest did not download properly, or a fatal error occurred when checking the manifest.

These events give you options, such as using an addEventListener to tell the user when an update is ready, and then calling the swapCache function:

```
applicationCache.addEventListener('updateready', function() {
    //do something
    alert("There is an update to the cache")
    applicationCache.swapCache();
})
```

Notification API

The Notification API, otherwise known as the Web Notifications API, is a newer set of APIs that allow browser pages to alert users through a desktop notification. The API is quite nascent and supported currently only through a WebKit specification and thus WebKit-based browsers. The calls via the WebKit notifications interface are similar to those defined in the W3C draft specification, so when in the future the Web Notifications API is supported by browsers, the update should be minimal.

Many times, a user will put the browser window into the background while using other applications on their system. When the browser page alerts the user that their session is about to expire, a stock has hit its mark to sell, or some other event that might be important to the user, the alert could be located behind other windows of the desktop. With the Notification API, the browser page can now ask the user's desktop to display a notification on its behalf. The notification will be displayed like other installed application notifications, usually in a corner of the user's screen.

The WebKit Notification API provides two interfaces titled NotificationCenter and Notification. The NotificationCenter interface provides the ability to request permission for notifications by the user, maintain the state of permission, and create notifications. The following are the methods available on the NotificationCenter interface:

- `Notification createNotification(in DOMString iconUrl, in DOMString title, in DOMString body)`: Creates a notification instance based on the icon, title, and body provided

- `Notification createHTMLNotification(in DOMString url)`: Creates an HTML page–based notification

- `Int checkPermission()`: Retrieves the current origin's permission level for notifications

- `void requestPermission([in Function callback])`: Requests user permission for displaying notifications

The `NotificationCenter` interface is exposed in WebKit browsers through the window object by referencing a window attribute titled `webkitNotifications`. For example, to create a notification from JavaScript, you would use the following line:

```
window.webkitNotifications.createNotification('icon.png','My Title',
➡'My Notification');
```

As you can see, the interface has two different methods for creating notifications: `createNotification` and `createHTMLNotification`. The `createNotification` method takes parameters passed to display a standard desktop notification with an icon, title, and body. Besides these values, there is no other customization that can be performed on the notification when using `createNotification`. With `createHTMLNotification`, a URL of a source page is passed to the method. This URL page can then have formatting and the like to provide additional functionality, such as hyperlinks. In either case, a `Notification` instance is returned.

Once the `Notification` instance has been created, you can then use the `Notification` interface methods to control the display of the notification. In the WebKit `Notification` interface, there are two methods, `show` and `cancel`, which are explained here:

- `show()`: Adds the notification to the desktop queue to be displayed if permission has been allowed

- `cancel()`: Removes a notification from the desktop or the queue

The `Notification` interface also has event handler functions to provide details of the notification when it is displayed, when it is closed, or when an error occurs, as listed here:

- `ondisplay`: The notification has been displayed on the desktop.

- `onclose`: The notification has been closed either manually or via the `cancel` method.

- `onerror`: An error has occurred with the notification.

You will look at working with the `Notification` interface events in the last recipe of this chapter.

Notification Permissions

Since the Notification API is able to display pop-ups of any nature on the user's screen at any time, there is a natural concern over security and unwanted advertising content. The Notification API thus includes a permission system by which a user must first be asked whether they want to allow or deny notifications for a particular origin. When permission is requested from the user, a drop-down bar or similar method will be used by the particular browser to ask the user for permission, as shown in Figure 13.7.

Note that the request for permission can be displayed only from an intentional user action, such as clicking a button or link. Requesting permission when a page loads will have no effect, and the permission request will not be displayed to the user for security purposes.

It is also important to realize that permission for notifications is set by origin, not by page. So, if a user denies notifications for one of your pages, then notifications will be denied for the entire domain. If permission has not been provided by the user and you create a notification, the notification will not fail but will also not be displayed. In the final recipe of this chapter, you will see how to check what the current "permission level" is by the user for the domain.

Browser Compatibility

Table 13.3 shows the version of each browser that supports the Notification API. Note, however, that the Notification API is implemented using WebKit because the general specification is in draft. It is expected that the release specification will have a notification method without leveraging WebKit.

Table 13.3   **Notification API Browser Availability**

Android	-
Chrome	10.0+
Firefox	-
Internet Explorer	-
iOS Safari	-
Opera	-
Safari	-

Figure 13.7   Chrome notification permission request bar

BEGINNER RECIPE:
Displaying a Simple Notification

This first notification recipe will use the WebKit notifications to request permission from the user and then create and display a notification when the user clicks the fire notification button. The user can fire as many notifications as they like, and a new notification with an incrementing unique number will be displayed. If the desktop has reached its limit for the number of notifications that can be shown, then the notifications will be queued for display.

It is a simple recipe but will show the basics of displaying desktop notifications on the desktop. Let's fire off our first notification by launching into Listing 13.5:

1. Create a blank HTML page with the HTML body tags as shown in Listing 13.5, including the Set Permission and Fire Notification buttons selection.

2. Add the `window.addEventListener` line for the page `load` event and the `init` function, which attaches the click event button handlers.

3. Add the global variable `notificationCount` to keep a unique ID for each notification.

4. Add the `setPermission` function to request permission if the `webkitNotifications` interface is supported.

5. Add the `fireNotification` function, which creates and then displays the notification.

Listing 13.5   Using `createNotification` to Display an Event

```
<!DOCTYPE html>
<html>
<head>
<meta charset="UTF-8" />
<title>13.5 Basic Notification</title>
<script>
// counter for notifications
var notificationCount = 0;

// initialize the page
function init() {

  // reference the buttons
  var btnSetPermission = document.getElementById('setPermission');
  var btnFireNotification = document.getElementById('fireNotification');

  // set our button click event handlers
  btnSetPermission.addEventListener('click',setPermission,false);
  btnFireNotification.addEventListener('click',fireNotification,false);
}
```

```
// Request the user permission for notifications
function setPermission() {
  // check if the webkitNotifications is supported
  if (webkitNotifications) {
    // request permission from the user
    window.webkitNotifications.requestPermission();
  } else {
    // Let the user know that notifications are not supported
    alert("Notifications are not supported on this browser.");
  }
}


// Function to fire the notification
function fireNotification() {
  // increment our notification counter
  notificationCount++;

  // create the notification passing in icon, title, body
  var notification = webkitNotifications.createNotification(
    'icon_notification.png',
    'Number '+notificationCount,
    'This is notification '+notificationCount);

  // now show the actual notification
  notification.show();
}


// Add our page load listener to initialize
window.addEventListener('load',init,false);

</script>
</head>
<body>
  <h1>Basic Notification Recipe</h1>
  <p>Click set permission to allow notifications, then fire a notification.</p>
  <section>
    <button id="setPermission">Set Permission</button>
    <button id="fireNotification">Fire Notification</button>
  </section>
</body>
</html>
```

When Listing 13.5 is loaded into the browser, the init function will run and add the click event handlers to the two buttons, Set Permission and Fire Notification. You will need to click the Set Permission button first to have the browser display the authorization prompt. (Remember to run this in Chrome or another WebKit-based browser.) When the permission is asked, select the Allow option, which will tell the browser it is OK for any page from the origin of the page to request the desktop to display desktop notifications. Inside the `setPermission` function, you first test to see whether `webkitNotifications` is available. If the interface is available, then the script executes the `requestPermission` method of the `webkitNotifications` interface. This will launch the request for permission to the user. If you have previously set the permission to allow notifications, then calling `requestPermission` again will do nothing. You can reset the permission for the page's origin to allow for testing, as shown in the following tip.

> **Tip**
>
> When testing notifications with these recipes or your own pages, you will notice that once you have allowed or denied notifications, you will not be able to use the `requestPermission` method to ask the user to allow or deny notifications again. To reset the preference for notifications, you must go in to the settings of the browser and reset the permission manually. In Chrome, you can find this option under Preferences > Under the Hood > Privacy – Content Settings... > Notifications > Manage Exceptions..., as shown in Figure 13.8.

To reset the notification permission for your domain, roll over your entry, and click the X to remove your entry from the Hostname Pattern list, as shown in Figure 13.9. This will reset the permission and allow the JavaScript code to ask with the `requestPermission` method.

Once the permission is set to allow desktop notifications, you can click the Fire Notification button. This will execute the `fireNotification` method, which increments the counter of notifications and then creates a notification through the `createNotification` method. Passed into the method is an icon URL that we have created, the title that includes the counter, and the text of the body of the notification with the unique counter as well. After having created the notification, you still must call the `show` method to tell the browser to ask the desktop to show the notification. If

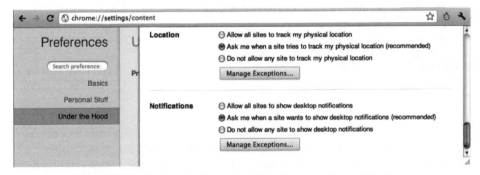

Figure 13.8   Section in Chrome settings for managing notifications

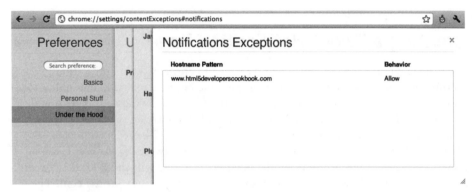

Figure 13.9   Hostname Pattern list in Chrome to reset notification
permissions

permission has not been allowed or permission has been denied, then the notification
will not display.

Each time you click the Fire Notification button, a new notification will be created
and displayed. In Figure 13.10, you can see an example of clicking the Fire Notification button several times.

> **Note**
>
> Each desktop environment will have a limit to the number of notifications that may be
> shown at one time to the user. If you create a notification and the desktop is currently
> showing the maximum number of notifications that can be shown, then the notification
> will be queued until room is available on the desktop by the user removing a notification
> or the notification being automatically removed.

This recipe showed a simple example of creating and displaying desktop notifications through the WebKit notifications. In the next recipe, you will use these methods
along with others and events to create notifications of new tweets from a Twitter user.

Figure 13.10   Sample output showing desktop notifications

ADVANCED RECIPE:
Creating a Tweet Notification Page

After the previous recipe in which you were able to create desktop notifications, you probably have some ideas of how you might use the Notification API. The ability to notify the user of an event when they are not in the browser window is quite useful.

In this recipe, you will use the Notification API to display on the desktop notifications of new tweets from a particular Twitter.com user. The recipe will use the Twitter API `statuses/user_timeline` to retrieve new tweets by the user and then display the tweets as notifications on the desktop. The page will check for new tweets by the user repeatedly with a 60-second span between requests to Twitter.com. The first time the request is made, the page will by default grab the three most recent tweets to display. For more information on the Twitter API, see the documentation for the REST API at http://dev.twitter.com/doc and the specific API method the recipe will use at http://dev.twitter.com/doc/get/statuses/user_timeline.

Figure 13.11 shows the output of the code as desktop notifications of a couple recent tweets.

> **Note**
>
> The Twitter API has the ability to perform callback functions through the Twitter REST API. This recipe leverages this callback technique to be able to make direct JavaScript calls to the Twitter API. You must use this callback method along with a JSONP format to get around cross-domain request security issues that are normal with these client-based requests. In addition, you could use a third-party library such as jQuery to perform the call or even build your own proxy in your same domain. Note that like most APIs online, the Twitter API enforces rate limits on its API for abuse, and if you use it too much, you may receive an "over rate limit" error.

In addition to the `createNotification` and `show` methods that you saw in the previous recipe, you will also use the `cancel` method to remove notifications automatically after a certain time frame. The recipe will use the event handler of `ondisplay` to trigger a timer to automatically remove the notification displayed after 15 seconds. The script will then wait a minute and ask Twitter for any new tweets.

Figure 13.11   Sample output showing desktop notifications of tweets

In the previous recipe, you may have noticed that it was difficult to know whether permission had been provided or what the current permission level for notifications was. In this recipe, you will use the checkPermission method on the webkitNotifications interface to allow the user to view the permission at any time. Typically, this is not something you would show to the user in your pages but something that can be useful in your scripting. The checkPermission method returns an integer value describing the current permission state for desktop notifications, as shown in Table 13.4.

Typically, to call an external web service with a callback function, you would inline the script source as the URL of the REST call. This recipe shows an exciting alternate method using a web worker to retrieve the results, parse them, and then send them back to the main thread. This is done by using the importScripts command in the web worker, as covered in Chapter 12, Communication and Threading. This allows the main thread to continue without being blocked when the call is made to Twitter and allows the results to be processed. You simply create a new web worker each time you want to retrieve the results, and the web worker ends after processing the results. The one caveat about this is that the notification cannot be launched from the web worker since the notification is part of the window object, which is not available in the web worker. So, you simply send the information to the main thread to show the notification. With this web worker model, there will be two files. Listing 13.6 is the main page, and Listing 13.7 is the web worker. Let's start with the main page, as shown in Listing 13.6:

1. Create a blank HTML page with the HTML body tags and buttons Set Permission, Check Permission Level, and Grab Tweets.

2. Add the script tags and the global variables tworker and lastTweetId.

3. Add the script tags and setPermission function for requesting permission for the desktop notifications.

4. Add the checkPermissionLevel function for retrieving and displaying the current permission level.

5. Add the grabTweets function, which starts the web worker, assigns listeners for messages from the web worker, and handles the creation of notifications.

Table 13.4 **Permission Levels for Desktop Notifications**

Permission	Value	Explanation
PERMISSION_ALLOWED	0	Permission has been given by the user for desktop notifications.
PERMISSION_NOT_ALLOWED	1	Permission has been allowed or denied by the user. Typically, the request for permission has not been performed.
PERMISSION_DENIED	2	The user has denied permission for desktop notifications to this origin.

Listing 13.6   **Creating Notifications in the Main Thread**

```html
<!DOCTYPE html>
<html>
<head>
<meta charset="UTF-8" />
<title>13.6 Twitter Notifications</title>
<script>

// set our web worker reference
var tworker = null;
// set the last tweet read
var lastTweetId = 0;

// function to initialize our handlers
function init() {
  //set the handlers
  var btnSetPermission = document.getElementById('btnSetPermission');
  var btnCheckPermission = document.getElementById('btnCheckPermission');
  var btnGrabTweets = document.getElementById('btnGrabTweets');

  btnSetPermission.addEventListener('click',setPermission,false);
  btnCheckPermission.addEventListener('click',checkPermissionLevel,false);
  btnGrabTweets.addEventListener('click',grabTweets,false);
}

// function to request user permission for notifications
function setPermission() {

  // check if the browser supports notifications
  if (webkitNotifications) {

    // check notification not allowed yet
    if (webkitNotifications.checkPermission() == 1) {

      // request permission and callback to this function
      webkitNotifications.requestPermission(setPermission);
    } else {
      // verify that permission has been given
      alert('Permission has been given.');
    }
  } else {
    // notification not supported
    alert('Notifications are not supported on this browser. ');
  }
}
```

```
// Check the notification
function checkPermissionLevel() {

  // verify that notifications are supported
  if (webkitNotifications) {

    // get the current permission level
    var permissionLevel = webkitNotifications.checkPermission();

    // map the permission level to the equivalent
    switch (permissionLevel) {
      case 0:
        // PERMISSION_ALLOWED
        alert('Current level: PERMISSION_ALLOWED (0)');
        break;
      case 1:
        // PERMISSION_NOT_ALLOWED
        alert('Current level: PERMISSION_NOT_ALLOWED (1)');
        break;
      case 2:
        // PERMISSION_DENIED
        alert('Current level: PERMISSION_DENIED (2)');
        break;
    }
  }
}

// function to get the Tweets and create the notifications
function grabTweets() {

  // verify in the log that we are creating the web worker
  console.log('creating worker');

  // create the web worker instance for getting the user tweets
  tworker = new Worker('13_7_tweetworker.js');

  // message event handler for messages from the web worker
  tworker.addEventListener('message', function(msg) {

    // determine type of message from the worker
    switch (msg.data.msgType) {

      // received a tweet message to display a notification
      case 'TWEET':

        console.log('creating notification');
```

```
    // grab the icon, title and body from the worker message
    nIcon = msg.data.icon;
    nTitle = msg.data.title;
    nBody = msg.data.body;

    // create the notification
    var notification = webkitNotifications.createNotification(nIcon, nTitle,
➥nBody);

    // set the ondisplay event handler
    notification.ondisplay = function(event) {

      // play notification audio
      var audio = new Audio('13_6_notify.mp3');
      audio.play();

      // set a time out to remove the notification after 15 seconds
      setTimeout(function() {event.currentTarget.cancel()}, 15000);
    }

    // set the onclose event handler
    notification.onclose = function() {
      // log that the notification was closed
      console.log('Notification closed.');
    }

    // set the onerror event handler
    notification.onerror = function() {
      // log that the notification had an error
      console.log('Notification Error.');
    }

    // Display the notification
    notification.show();

    break;

// The web worker has finished
case 'END':

  // If we have a last tweet then store for next search
  if (msg.data.lastTweetId>0) {
    lastTweetId = msg.data.lastTweetId;
  }

  // set a timeout to search again in 1 minute
  setTimeout('grabTweets()',60000);
```

```
      break;
    }
  }, false);

  // Kick off the worker search with the last tweet id
  tworker.postMessage(lastTweetId);
}

// window load event handler
window.addEventListener('load',init,false);

</script>
</head>
<body>
  <h1>Creating Notifications from new Tweets</h1>
  Click on Set Permission first to authorize notifications.<br>
  Then click Grab Tweets to start listening for new Tweets.
  <br><br>
  <button id="btnSetPermission">Set Permission</button>
  <button id="btnCheckPermissionLevel">Check Permission Level</button>
  <button id="btnGrabTweets">Grab Tweets</button>
</body>
</html>
```

Now that the main page is complete, you need to create the web worker JavaScript file that will retrieve the tweets and perform the parsing of any tweets returned, as shown in Listing 13.7:

1. Create a .js file for the web worker with the onmessage handler for receiving messages from the main page. The onmessage handler will also perform the import of the REST API script from Twitter.com.

2. Add the getResult function, which is the callback function from the importScripts REST API call. This function will handle the parsing of any tweets retrieved and send them back to the main thread for display. And that is it for the web worker.

Listing 13.7   Leveraging a Web Worker to Follow Tweets

```
// 13_7_tweetworker.js
// Web worker thread for retrieving set of tweets

// callback function to parse tweets result
function getResult(data) {

  // variable for holding max id of tweet list
  var maxId = 0;
```

```
// check if we have tweets to parse
if (data.length>0) {

  // variables for our notification
  var tIcon = '';
  var tTitle = '';
  var tBody = '';

  // loop through resultset in reverse
  for (var i=(data.length-1); i>=0; i--) {

    // grab our profile image, screen name, and tweet
    tIcon = data[i].user.profile_image_url;
    tTitle = data[i].user.screen_name;
    tBody = data[i].text;

    // return the tweet info back to the main thread to display
    postMessage({msgType:'TWEET',icon:tIcon,title:tTitle,body:tBody});

    // store the id_str as the max id so we do not show again
    maxId = data[i].id_str;
  }
}

// tell the main thread we are done this loop
postMessage({msgType:'END',lastTweetId:maxId});
}

// Catch message from main thread
onmessage = function(event) {

  // grab our starting id of the last tweet
  var lastId = event.data;
  var qString = '';

  // check if our last id is a real tweet id
  if (lastId != 0) {
    // if a real tweet id then use the since_id
    qString = '&since_id='+lastId;
  } else {
    // no prior tweets read so grab a max of three
    qString = '&count=3';
  }

  // use importScripts as a JSONP method instead of inline script tags
  // currently following screen name BreakingNews but you can change
  // to whichever twitter user you would like to follow
```

```
importScripts('http://api.twitter.com/1/statuses/user_timeline.json?
➥screen_name=BreakingNews'+qString+'&callback=getResult');

}
```

After loading the main page in your browser and before clicking Set Permission, click the Check Permission Level button. This will call the checkPermissionLevel function. The function will verify that webkitNotifications is available and then perform the checkPermission method to retrieve the current permission level as an integer value. The value is then translated into its meaning and displayed as an alert. This will allow you to quickly validate whether permission is set correctly for the domain for showing desktop notifications. You can play around with this by removing the permission in the browser settings, denying permission, and finally allowing permission to view the changes in the permission level. If you have not set the permission to allow notifications, then you will want to do so prior to moving on with the recipe.

Upon loading the code, a global reference is set to the web worker, named tworker, and a global variable named lastTweetId is set that will store the "bookmark" for the last tweet that you have read for the user. At load time, this variable is set to zero so that you know it is the first time loading the page and no prior tweets have been read. When you launch the web worker to retrieve the list of tweets, lastTweetId will be passed to the web worker to be used to determine tweets to display. You need to keep this variable in the main page because once the web worker has completed retrieving and parsing the tweets, the worker will go away. A new web worker is created each time you make the request for tweets.

To start the process of retrieving tweets for the user and displaying notifications, click the Grab Tweets button. This will execute the grabTweets method, which will first add a logging message in the console log to verify that you are starting the retrieval process. Next, the function will create a new web worker from the tweet-worker.js file. Before going into this worker, let's see what the rest of the grabTweets function does, because the web worker as designed will do nothing until you tell it to start processing with a message. The next step for the grabTweets function is to assign the onmessage event handler to the web worker so that when the web worker sends back messages, you can access them. You will use a similar style of message communication as in the recipes of Chapter 12, Communication and Threading, with web workers, where the web worker can send back different types of messages based on a JSON-formatted payload with a message type and the parameters associated with that message type.

There will be two different types of messages from the web worker to the main page: a TWEET message and an END message. If you receive a msgType of TWEET, it means that the web worker has found a tweet for display, and you will then use the rest of the payload to display a notification with the icon of the user image, the username as the title, and the tweet as the body. The code in this recipe creates the notification; adds the ondisplay, onclose, and onerror event handlers; and finally shows the notification. The `onclose` and `onerror` event handlers will simply log a console log message to show when the event is caught. You will use the `ondisplay` handler to play a sound when the notification is displayed and set a timeout to automatically remove the notification from the desktop if the user has not already closed the notification. Then the notification is shown with the `show` method.

The END message will signify to the main page that the web worker has finished its retrieval and processing of any tweets. By having the web worker tell you that the thread is finished, you can make sure you do not have multiple workers (threads) running at the same time and assure that you wait a given time between when a worker finishes and a new worker is kicked off. The END message will contain the last tweet ID or the value zero if no tweets were retrieved. The last tweet ID will update the bookmark if needed to keep track of the last message retrieved. After setting the last tweet ID, the timer is then set for kicking off the `grabTweets` function again. We have not bothered adding a stop feature for this recipe, but you could easily add one with a flag to prevent future retrievals and cancel the current web worker if needed. At the end of the `grabTweets` function, the code tells the web worker to start by sending a message passing the bookmark, `lastTweetId`, to the web worker.

Let's now jump into the web worker and briefly go through the retrieval of the user tweets. In the web worker, there are basically two sections: the request for the information through the `onmessage` event handler and the parsing of the result set in the `getResult` function. The web worker is kicked off with the message with the last tweet ID, so the web worker `onmessage` handler takes the last tweet ID and creates a URL REST request by leveraging the `importScripts` method of workers. Like doing inline `script` tags, `importScripts` simply loads an external script or set of scripts into the web worker. This will allow you to get by cross-domain security issues. On the request URL, you make sure to use the callback querystring option to name the `getResults` function to launch with the results. Also, you dynamically set some of the parameters based on whether this is the first request or a follow-on request. See the Twitter API documentation for further explanation of these search options.

Once the callback function `getResults` is called with the JSON results, the web worker checks to see whether there are any tweets by seeing whether the length of the data is greater than zero. If the length is greater than zero and thus you have tweets to parse, the script loops through each child of the results and pulls out the image URL, the username, and the tweet. Once the script has these fields, the web worker then posts a message back to the main thread with the information for the notification. After sending the message, the web worker stores the ID of the tweet in a variable to send back at the end of processing to the main page as the next bookmark of tweets to start with. You may notice that the script parses the tweet result set in reverse order. The reason for this is that the first record is the newest going to the last record, which is the oldest. Because you want to display the notifications in the order in which the tweets were written, you need to display them in reverse. This recipe has shown how notifications can be shown, automatically removed, and tied into other APIs to alert users even when they may not be viewing the browser window of events from the page.

Summary

In this chapter, you learned about some of the smaller API extensions. The drag and drop, offline storage, and notifications APIs provide the means to greatly improve the user experience with both websites and applications. The APIs provide a higher level of integration that is quickly removing the differences between the browser experience and native applications. It will be interesting to see how these API extensions are used in the future.

14

Working with Local Files

Until HTML5, working with files in the client browser has had minimal attention and support. Typically, the breadth of functionality has consisted of simple file selection for posting to a web server. With HTML5 and a supplemental API set, the File API, we now have an increased set of functionality and more importantly a standardized set of functionality to get basic attributes of files and read different file types into the client browser through JavaScript. In this chapter, you will learn about the new set of functionality with the File API through recipes that will cover the basics as well as some newer File API specifications that are on the horizon.

File API Overview

The File API provides a standardized way to interact with user-selected files in the client browser. The interfaces of the File API can be broken into three functional areas:

- Selecting a file or files in the `FileList` interface
- Retrieving attributes about the files through the `File` interface
- Reading the actual file through the `FileReader` interface

The `FileList` interface is a list of files selected by the user and may be traversed like an array. The `File` interface provides properties on the selected file. With these two interfaces, scripts can loop through selected files and retrieve key properties on the files as follows:

- `name`: The name of the file
- `type`: The type of the file in MIME format and ASCII encoded
- `size`: The size of the file in bytes
- `lastModifiedDate`: The date and time that the file was last modified

File API Security

The File API interacts with information and data outside the browser container on the client's device. This interaction with the local file system naturally sparks concerns of security. The HTML5 File API specification handles file read access security concerns by allowing the JavaScript to interact only with those files to which the user provides access. The File API is not able to navigate the directory structure or select files on its own without the user's interaction through the file selection.

Table 14.1 shows the version of each browser that supports the File API. The level of support varies between browsers, however, and will be noted where applicable in this chapter's recipes.

Table 14.1   File API Browser
Availability

Android	3.0+
Chrome	9.0+
Firefox	3.6+
Internet Explorer	10.0+
iOS Safari	-
Opera	11.1+
Safari	-

BEGINNER RECIPE:
Getting File Attributes

This recipe will use the `File` interface to get the name, type, size, and last-modified date of a file selected by the page visitor through the standard file input element. Before showing how to get this information, the recipe will show how to validate that the `FileList` interface is available in the browser. To display the attributes of a file, as shown in Listing 14.1, perform the following steps:

1. Create a blank HTML page with a file input element, and add the `onchange` event handler to be called when a file is selected.

2. Add the `fileAttributes` section to the HTML body where the recipe will display the file attributes.

3. Add the `handleFile` function, taking `fileInput` as the parameter.

Listing 14.1   Displaying the Attributes of a File

```
<!DOCTYPE html>
<html><head>
```

```
<meta charset="UTF-8" />
<title>14.1 Retrieving File Attributes</title>
<script>
// handle the file selected
function handleFile(fileInput) {

  // reference our section to display the attributes
  var fileAttributes = document.getElementById('fileAttributes');

  // verify the browser supports the files interface
  if (fileInput.files) {

    // reference the file using the files interface
    var file = fileInput.files[0];

    // create the output
    var output = 'File attributes:<br>';
    output += 'name: ' + file.name + '<br>';
    output += 'type: ' + file.type + '<br>';
    output += 'size: ' + (file.size/1024).toFixed(2) + 'KB<br>';
    output += 'last modified date: ' + file.lastModifiedDate;

    // set the output to the section
    fileAttributes.innerHTML = output;

  } else {
    // files interface not supported by browser
    fileAttributes.innerHTML = 'files interface not supported';
  }
}
</script>
</head>
<body>
  <h1>Select File Below:</h1>
  <section>
    <input type="file" id="input" onchange="handleFile(this)" />
  </section>
  <br>
  <section id="fileAttributes"></section>
</body>
</html>
```

When the visitor to the page created in Listing 14.1 selects a file from the browse button of the file input element, the onchange event handler will call the handleFile function with the file element passed as the parameter. Inside the handleFile function, you first get a reference to the display section element and then check to verify that the browser supports the FileList interface. If the browser does not support the

`FileList` interface by checking for the presence of the `Files` array, a message is displayed in the `fileAttributes` section, but you could handle this by continuing with your logic or asking the visitor for more information.

If the `FileList` interface is supported, you grab a specific instance from the array of files, a `File`, by referencing the first file in the `Files` array, `fileInput.files[0]`. You then use that `File` interface instance to get the `name`, `type`, `size`, and `lastModifiedDate` properties. A conversion is performed on the `size` attribute since the unit of measure is in bytes and it is more common to see file sizes referenced in kilobytes. The equation converts the bytes into kilobytes. You could enhance this by having a function take the bytes and show the conversion in kilobytes, megabytes, or another unit based on the total number of bytes as is done in normal directory listings.

> **Note**
>
> The `File` interface inherits from a `Blob`, so it includes the `size` and `type` attributes. With the `File` interface, the `name` and `lastModifiedDate` attributes are added. However, in several browser platforms, the `lastModifiedDate` is not available and will return an `undefined` value when asked for.

In this recipe, you took a file that the visitor selected and showed the file's attributes. This can be convenient for filtering files prior to uploading to servers or just showing a confirmation to the user. The next recipe will expand on this and provide an interface for the visitor to select multiple files to be processed.

BEGINNER RECIPE:
Processing Multiple Files with Drag and Drop

The `FileList` interface provides the capability to handle an array of `File` objects from the local file system. This recipe shows how a drag-and-drop area can be used with the `FileList` to handle multiple files selected by the user. This can have several different uses, including the filtering of files by name, size, or type, and confirmation by the user of the files they selected. Once the files are dragged and dropped onto the drop zone, the script will loop through the `FileList` sequence using the `length` property. The `length` property returns the numbers of elements, or `File` objects in the `FileList`, and can be used to "walk" through the sequence of files. For each `File` object, the page will display the file attributes in a table to confirm to the viewer what was dropped onto the page's drop zone. To create the drag-and-drop page, follow these steps and the code in Listing 14.2:

1. Create the page in Listing 14.2 with the `style` and `body` tags for the drop zone and `filesSelected` section. Make sure that the `input` element has the `multiple` attribute and the `onchange` event handler.

2. Add the drop zone event listeners in an `init` function, and add the `handleFileDrop` and `handleDragOver` functions for enabling the drop zone.

3. Add the `displayFiles` function to loop through the files selected and display the attributes in the table.

4. Add the `clearTable` function and the `addEventListener` load trigger.

Listing 14.2   Looping Through Multiple Files with `FileList`

```
<!DOCTYPE html>
<html>
<head>
<meta charset="UTF-8" />
<title>14.2 Processing Multiple Files with FileList</title>
<style>
#dropZone {
  width:300px;
  border: 2px dashed #bbb;
  -moz-border-radius: 5px;
  -webkit-border-radius: 5px;
  border-radius: 5px;
  padding: 25px;
  text-align: center;
  font: 20pt bold;
  color: #bbb;
}
#fileTable {
  border: 1px solid #000;
  -moz-border-radius: 5px;
  -webkit-border-radius: 5px;
  border-radius: 5px;
  padding: 5px;
  visibility:hidden;
}
tr:nth-child(odd)  { background-color:#eee; }
tr:nth-child(even) { background-color:#fff; }
</style>
<script>

// initialize our drop zone
function init() {

  // Setup the drop zone and listeners.
  dropZone = document.getElementById('dropZone');
  dropZone.addEventListener('dragover', handleDragOver, false);
  dropZone.addEventListener('drop', handleFileDrop, false);

}


// handle files dropped
function handleFileDrop(evt) {
```

```
  // stop our drag and drop
  evt.stopPropagation();
  evt.preventDefault();

  // retrieve the filelist
  var files = evt.dataTransfer.files;

  // display the filelist selected
  displayFiles(files);

}

// handle files dragged over
function handleDragOver(evt) {

  // turn off drop zone while over
  evt.stopPropagation();
  evt.preventDefault();
}

// display the files selected
function displayFiles(files) {

  // clear the current table
  clearTable();

  // display number of files selected
  var fileCount = document.getElementById('fileCount');
  fileCount.innerHTML = files.length + ' File(s) Selected';

  // set up fields for table generation
  var fileTable = document.getElementById('fileTable');

  if (files.length>0) {
    var row;
    var cell;
    var textNode;

    // loop through filelist and create rows
    for (var i=0; i<files.length; i++) {

      // add our row
      var row = fileTable.insertRow(i);

      // add the file name cell
      cell = row.insertCell(0);
      textNode = document.createTextNode(files[i].name);
      cell.appendChild(textNode);
```

```
      // add the type of file cell
      cell = row.insertCell(1);
      textNode = document.createTextNode(files[i].type);
      cell.appendChild(textNode);

      // add the file size cell
      cell = row.insertCell(2);
      textNode = document.createTextNode((files[i].size/1024).toFixed(2)+'KB');
      cell.appendChild(textNode);

      if (files[i].lastModifiedDate != undefined) {
        // add the file last modified date cell
        cell = row.insertCell(3);
        textNode = document.createTextNode(files[i].lastModifiedDate);
        cell.appendChild(textNode);
      }
    }
    fileTable.style.visibility = 'visible';
  } else {
    fileTable.style.visibility = 'hidden';
  }
}


// clear the table
function clearTable() {

  // get our table
  var fileTable = document.getElementById('fileTable');

  // loop through and remove the present rows
  while (fileTable.rows.length>0) {
    fileTable.deleteRow(fileTable.rows.length-1);
  }
}


// initialize our window
window.addeventlistener('load',init,false);

</script>
</head>
<body>
  <h1>Drag multiple files to the drop zone below:</h1>
  <section id="fileSelection">
    <!--
    // Multiple file section can also be done with the multiple attribute
    <input type="file" id="input" multiple="true"
➥onchange="displayFiles(this.files)">
    -->
```

```
    <div id="dropZone">Drop files here</div>
  </section>
  <section id="filesSelected">
    <br>
    <div id="fileCount"></div>
    <table id="fileTable">
    </table>
  </section>
</body>
</html>
```

After the page is loaded in the browser, the drop zone is initialized through the init function called by the window load event listener. The init sets the dropzone variable to the dropzone div and registers two event listeners for the dragover and drop events. When the dragover event is triggered, the handleDragOver function will be called, while the handleFileDrop function will be called with the drop event. When the files are dropped on the drop zone and the handleFileDrop is called, the script will retrieve the FileList and pass it to the displayFiles method.

The displayFiles function calls the helper clearTable to clear out any past results. The clearTable removes the rows from the table until all are removed. Next, the displayFiles checks the length of the FileList to verify that files were dropped onto the drop zone. The script loops through the FileList using an index to get each File interface. With each File object, the attributes are retrieved and added as a new cell in the new row to the table. Finally, the script displays the table by making it visible, as shown in the sample execution in Figure 14.1.

With the use of the drop zone and the FileList sequence, HTML5 makes it easy for visitors to submit files to the client page. Up to this point, however, you have looked at the attributes of a file and not the data in the file. In the rest of the chapter, you will learn about reading different types of files in the client JavaScript.

Drag multiple files to the drop zone below:

```
Drop files here
```

4 File(s) Selected

contacts.csv	text/csv	531.01KB	Thu Feb 26 2009 14:13:16 GMT-0500 (EST)
contacts.xls	application/vnd.ms-excel	767.50KB	Thu Feb 26 2009 14:11:38 GMT-0500 (EST)
DSC_4269.JPG	image/jpeg	3185.01KB	Fri Sep 18 2009 15:02:06 GMT-0400 (EDT)
good_code.png	image/png	38.18KB	Sun Mar 06 2011 14:53:32 GMT-0500 (EST)

Figure 14.1   Sample output showing multiple attributes from files
dragged and dropped onto the page

> **Tip**
>
> The `type` attribute of the `File` interface that is inherited from the `Blob` interface returns the Multipurpose Internet Mail Extensions (MIME) type of the file. The MIME type is a `DOMString` in all lowercase and ASCII encoded. This MIME type string can be used to filter based on file types such as `image` or the like. As shown in Figure 14.1, there are two images of different types, but the MIME starts with `image`, so you can easily validate that both files are images. The MIME type provides a simple and effective way to perform file filtering and verification, as you will see in the next section.

The `FileReader` Interface

To read files into client memory, the HTML5 File API specification provides a new interface called `FileReader`. This interface provides methods, attributes, and events that allow developers to asynchronously read files from client-side JavaScript. Through the `FileReader` events, you can display or process the data of the files. Several different types of files can be read because the `FileReader` interface has four different read methods depending on the type of file you may be reading:

- `readAsArrayBuffer(Blob)`: Returns the file contents as an `ArrayBuffer`
- `readAsBinaryString(Blob)`: Returns the file contents as a binary string
- `readAsText(Blob [,encoding])`: Returns the file contents as a text `DOMString`
- `readAsDataURL(Blob)`: Returns the file contents as a `DOMString` that is a data URL

Since the `FileReader` interface is asynchronous, this allows for the main thread of the page to continue processing, while events are used to catch key stages of the file being read. Table 14.2 shows the events that are defined as part of the `FileReader` interface.

Table 14.2   **The `FileReader` Events**

Event Name	Attribute	Purpose
loadstart	onloadstart	Triggered when the read of the file begins
progress	onprogress	Triggered during the read of the file at the will of the browser
abort	onabort	Triggered when an abort action is performed
error	onerror	Triggered when an error is encountered during the file read
load	onload	Triggered when the file has been successfully read
loadend	onloadend	Triggered when the file read has completed, either in success or in failure

By using the appropriate `FileReader` read method and listening to the `FileReader` events, you can use the `FileReader` interface to perform work in the client browser that would normally happen at the server after uploading a file. In this next recipe, you will use the `readAsDataURL` method to create thumbnails of selected images in the user's browser and show their corresponding attributes.

> **Note**
>
> File reading may be employed as a synchronous interface by leveraging the `FileReaderSync` with a web worker, since the Web Workers API allows the methods to act on a different thread than the main one. The `FileReaderSync` interface has the same methods as the `FlieReader`. See the W3C Working Draft for more information on synchronous File API usage.

INTERMEDIATE RECIPE:
Previewing Images Through `readAsDataURL`

The `readAsDataURL` method of the `FileReader` interface takes a supplied `Blob` or `File` reference and reads the data into a URL that can be loaded in an appropriate container. In this recipe, you will let the visitor select multiple files and then filter the images from the set of files, read them through the `readAsDataURL`, and load them into image containers for viewing as thumbnails. Normally, to replicate this functionality prior to the HTML5 File API, you would have needed to upload the files to a server, process them on the server, and then load them into the client browser page. This required increased overhead in sending the files back and forth and processing the files on the server. By using the HTML5 File API, you can remove the need to send the files back and forth and leverage the processing power of the client's machine to perform the handling of the files.

This recipe will use the `readAsDataURL` method along with the `onload` `FileReader` event to read the files selected. Also, the recipe will display the attributes of each file when you mouse over the thumbnail. To get started with this recipe, perform the following steps to create Listing 14.3:

1. Create a blank HTML file and add the `body` HTML from Listing 14.3, which includes the multiple file `input` element, a display section for the thumbnails, and a display section for the attributes.

2. Add the `style` section, which includes three style sets for handling the selection and deselection of the images.

3. Add the `handleFiles` function in the script as shown in Listing 14.3, which is triggered when the files have been selected.

4. Add the `showFile` function to show the attributes of the file moused over.

5. Add the `clearFile` function, which simply clears the attribute area when the focus is no longer over the image.

Listing 14.3   **Previewing Images with** readAsDataURL

```
<!DOCTYPE html>
<html>
<head>
<meta charset="UTF-8" />
<title>14.3 FileReader - imgPanel Local Images</title>
<style>
.highlight,.unhighlight {
  max-height:100px;
  max-width:100px;
  -moz-border-radius: 5px;
  -webkit-border-radius: 5px;
  border-radius: 5px;
  margin:10px;
}
.highlight {
  border: 5px solid #6f0;
}
.unhighlight {
  border: 5px solid #000;
}
</style>
<script>

// load the image files selected
function handleFiles(files) {

  // set our defaults
  var fileLimit = 10;        // maximum files at one time
  var sizeLimit = 500;       // KB file size limit
  var imageType = /image.*/;  // mime type of images - regular expression

  // reference the image panel and clear
  var imgPanel = document.getElementById('imgPanel');
  imgPanel.innerHTML = '';

  // calculate the file size limit in bytes
  var sizeLimitBytes = sizeLimit*1024;

  // check if the number of files is greater than limit
  if (files.length<fileLimit) {

    // loop through the filelist
    for (var i = 0; i < files.length; i++) {

      // reference the current file
      var file = files[i];
```

```
        // verify the file is an image
        if (file.type.match(imageType)) {

            // verify the file is not above the max size
            if (file.size<sizeLimitBytes) {

                // create an image container for the file
                var img = document.createElement("img");
                img.file = file;
                img.className = 'unhighlight';
                img.addEventListener('mouseover', showFile, false);
                img.addEventListener('mouseout', clearFile, false);
                imgPanel.appendChild(img);

                // create our reader to read the file
                var reader = new FileReader();
                // set the onload event of the reader
                reader.onload = (function(aImg) { return function(e) { aImg.src =
➥e.target.result; }; })(img);

                // read the file as a data url for the image
                reader.readAsDataURL(file);

            } else {
                // file is too big
                alert(file.name+' is larger than '+sizeLimit+'KB.');
            }
        } else {
            // file is not an image mime type
            alert(file.name+' is not an image.');
        }
    }
  } else {
    // too many files were selected
    imgPanel.innerHTML = 'Only '+fileLimit+' files can be selected at a time.';
  }
}

// display the info on the image moused over
function showFile() {

    // highlight the current image
    this.className = 'highlight';

    // get references to our attributes panel and file
    var fileAttributes = document.getElementById('fileAttributes');
    var file = this.file;
```

```
  // create our file info
  var fileinfo = 'File info:<br>';
  fileinfo += file.name + '<br>';
  fileinfo += file.type + '<br>';
  fileinfo += (file.size/1024).toFixed(2) + 'KB<br>';
  fileinfo += file.lastModifiedDate + '<br>';

  // display the file info
  fileAttributes.innerHTML = fileinfo;

}

// reset after rolling off of image
function clearFile() {

  // clear the file attributes panel
  var fileAttributes = document.getElementById('fileAttributes');
  fileAttributes.innerHTML = '';

  // set highlight on image back to normal
  this.className = 'unhighlight';
}

</script>
</head>
<body>
  <h1>Select the images to preview.</h1>
  <section>
    <input type="file" id="input" multiple="true"
➡onchange="handleFiles(this.files)">
  </section>
  <section id="imgPanel"></section>
  <section id="fileAttributes"></section>
</body>
</html>
```

When the page created in Listing 14.3 loads, the visitor is prompted to choose a file or set of files. After the files are selected, the onchange event of the input element is triggered, which launches the handleFiles function and passes the files that have been selected. The handleFiles function is the workhorse of the script and first sets key default values. These defaults include the maximum number of files allowed, the maximum size of each file, and a regular expression that will be used to match on image MIME types. The file size and number of files are limited to prevent overloading of the client browser's memory since the processing will be performed in the memory of the client machine. In this recipe, you will be looping through the files,

File info:
DSC_0880sm.jpg
image/jpeg
212.46KB
Fri Jun 05 2009 20:09:23 GMT-0400 (EDT)

Figure 14.2   Sample output showing image files selected by the user
and displayed through the `readAsDataURL` method

which will create multiple `FileReader`s acting at the same time. The script could be more intelligent about the processing and have a pool of readers, which would not take the next file until a reader frees up, but we will leave that up to you.

The script next checks that you have fewer files than the maximum and, if not, displays an appropriate message. If you have a manageable number of files, then you loop through the `FileList` and verify that each file is an image by matching on the MIME type and ensure that each is less than the file size maximum you have put into place. If each file meets these requirements, then the recipe creates an image container with properties including the `mouseover` and `mouseout` events to show the attributes. Now, the script is ready to read the file by creating a new `FileReader` for each image. The script sets the `onload` event on the `FileReader` to load the result of the `FileReader` into the source attribute of the image element, which creates the actual thumbnail, as shown in Figure 14.2.

Lastly, you tell the `FileReader` to read each file through the `readAsDataURL` method, which will return the data URL result for the image source. The rest of the function handles the failure of the various checks put in place and displays the appropriate message to the user. The `showFile` and `clearFile` methods display the attributes of the file.

This recipe shows a basic implementation of the `FileReader` interface and one of the read methods available. In addition, we hope this recipe has shown you how you must be conscious of running multiple asynchronous reads concurrently in the client's browser. To see this limitation in action, increase the limits on the file size and number of files (but do so carefully because it is easy to max the memory in your browser). In the next recipe, you will learn about some additional functionality on the `FileReader` interface that will allow you to abort processing and catch errors that may occur.

ADVANCED RECIPE:
Parsing a CSV File with `readAsText`

By now you should be excited about the prospects that the `FileReader` interface provides for processing files in the client browser. This methodology can move processing that has been problematic to the client side. One such area that is typical is the import of files such as comma-separated value (CSV) formatted data documents. Typically, the file is uploaded to the server and then parsed either immediately or on a scheduled basis, and then it is imported into a database for use in the website or application. This process can end up using precious server cycles.

In this recipe, we will show an alternative available with HTML5 by using the `readAsText` method. The recipe will allow the user to select a local CSV file. The file will then be read and parsed in the client's browser, showing the rows and fields. Note, though, that the CSV parsing logic in this recipe does not deal with the intricacies of CSV structures. There are multiple locations on the web where you can find robust parsing algorithms for CSV files. This recipe is meant more to show the flow of using the `FileReader` and the `readAsText` method. Once parsed, the fields could be put into JSON strings and sent via an Ajax web service call to a server for processing.

Besides the new method, `readAsText`, the recipe will also employ a function on the `FileReader` called `abort`. This method allows the script or user to abort the read process. When the `abort` method is called and successful, an `ABORT_ERR` is thrown by the `FileReader` to verify that the abort has occurred. The `FileReader` has five possible errors that can be thrown because of issues reading the file or `Blob` provided, as shown in Table 14.3.

Table 14.3   **Possible `FileReader` Errors**

Error Constant	Value	Explanation
`NOT_FOUND_ERR`	1	An error is thrown when the file to be read is not found.
`SECURITY_ERR`	2	An error is thrown when a file may have changed while a read occurred, a file is deemed unsafe, or too many reads are being made on the file.
`ABORT_ERR`	3	An error is thrown when the abort method is called.
`NOT_READABLE_ERR`	4	The file cannot be read. Typically, this is because of permissions on the file.
`ENCODING_ERR`	5	An error is thrown when a `readAsDataURL` result is not in the form of a data URL. This is not for encoding issues with reading files as text.

In this recipe, you will explore one of the last event handlers that the `FileReader` provides, `onprogress`. The `onprogress` event handler provides notification of progress reading the file and can be used to display status to the user. The `onprogress` event handler contains three attributes: `lengthComputable`, `loaded`, and `total`. The `lengthComputable` attribute is a boolean flag that marks whether the `loaded` and `total` attributes are available. The `loaded` attribute is the number of bytes read so far into memory, while the `total` is the total number of bytes to be read. By dividing `progress.loaded` by `progress.total`, you can provide a completion percentage that can be displayed to the user. In this recipe, as the file is read into memory, the page will show a progress bar indicating the status. Note, though, that the `progress` event is at the discretion of each browser's implementation of the `FileReader` interface, so it is not assured as to when or how often the event will be fired. The following steps will create the code in Listing 14.4:

1. Create a blank HTML page with the HTML `body` and `style` tags as shown in Listing 14.4, including the file selection, cancel button, file info section, and file output `div`.

2. Add the style tags and styling for the various classes including hiding the cancel button.

3. Add the `script` tags and global reference to a `FileReader` instance called `textReader`. This will be the `FileReader` instance for reading the CSV file selected.

4. Add the `addEventListener` `load` line and the `init` function that registers the functions for the `textReader` events.

5. Add the corresponding event functions: `onErrorHandler`, `updateProgress`, `onAbortHandler`, `onLoadStartHandler`, and `onLoadHandler`.

6. Add the `cancelFileReader` function to allow the visitor to abort the read process.

7. Add the `handleFile` function, which starts the read process on the file, selected through the `readAsText` `FileReader` method.

Listing 14.4   Displaying a CSV File's Contents

```
<!DOCTYPE html>
<html>
<head>
<meta charset="UTF-8" />
<title>14.4 Basic File API</title>
<style>
#fileInfo {
  border: 1px solid #000;
  -moz-border-radius: 5px;
  -webkit-border-radius: 5px;
  border-radius: 5px;
```

```
  padding: 5px;
  visibility:hidden;
}
#progHolder {
  float:right;
  width:200px;
  height:30px;
  border:solid;
  border-width:1px;
  background-color:#999;
  text-align:center;
}
#progMeter {
  width:0px;
  height:30px;
  background-color:#9FF;
}
#btnCancel {
  visibility:hidden;
}
</style>
<script>
// set up a filereader
var textReader = new FileReader();

function init() {
  // set up our filereader handlers
  textReader.onerror      = onErrorHandler;
  textReader.onprogress   = updateProgress;
  textReader.onabort      = onAbortHandler;
  textReader.onloadstart  = onLoadStartHandler;
  textReader.onload       = onLoadHandler;
}

// handle the selected file
function handleFile(inputFile) {

  // the csv mime type for regular expression
  var csvMimeType = /text\/csv/;

  // reference our selected file
  var file = inputFile.files[0];

  // verify that the file is a csv file
  if (file.type.match(csvMimeType)) {
```

```
    // make the file info section visible
    var fileInfo = document.getElementById("fileInfo");
    fileInfo.style.visibility = 'visible';

    // kick off the reader to read the csv file
    textReader.readAsText(file);

    // set our file info - the filereader is asynchronous
    // so this will display
    var output = 'File attributes:<br>';
    output += 'name: ' + file.name + '<br>';
    output += 'type: ' + file.type + '<br>';
    output += 'size: ' + (file.size/1024).toFixed(2) + 'KB<br>';
    output += 'last modified date: ' + file.lastModifiedDate;

    // display the file attributes
    var fileAttributes = document.getElementById('fileAttributes');
    fileAttributes.innerHTML = output;

  } else {
    // inform user that the file is not a csv
    alert(file.name + ' is not a CSV file.');
  }
}

// cancel filereader function
function cancelFileReader() {

  // tell the filereader to abort
  textReader.abort();
}

// triggered filereader onloadstart handler
function onLoadStartHandler(evt) {

  // get our local element references
  var btnCancel = document.getElementById('btnCancel');
  var progMeter = document.getElementById('progMeter');
  var fileoutput = document.getElementById('fileoutput');

  // reset our cancel button, progress meter, and file output
  btnCancel.style.visibility = 'visible';
  progMeter.style.width = '0%';
  progMeter.innerHTML = 'loading...';
  fileoutput.innerHTML = '';
}
```

```
// triggered filereader onload handler
function onLoadHandler(evt) {

  // set our progress meter to 100% and hide the cancel button
  var progMeter = document.getElementById('progMeter');
  var btnCancel = document.getElementById('btnCancel');
  progMeter.style.width = '100%';
  progMeter.innerHTML = 'loaded.';
  btnCancel.style.visibility = 'hidden';

  // split the file into an array for processing
  var fileArr = evt.target.result.split('\n');

  // process each row and set to rows in a table
  // this is a simplistic processing for csv and
  // does not handle differences in csv format
  var strDiv = '<table>';
  for (var i=0; i<fileArr.length; i++) {
    strDiv += '<tr>';
    var fileLine = fileArr[i].split(',');
    for (var j=0; j<fileLine.length; j++) {
      strDiv += '<td>'+fileLine[j].trim()+'</td>';
    }
    strDiv += '</tr>';
  }
  strDiv += '</table>';

  // set our output
  var fileoutput = document.getElementById('fileoutput');
  fileoutput.innerHTML = strDiv;

}


// progress handler for the filereader
function updateProgress(evt) {

  // reference to our progress meter
  var progMeter = document.getElementById('progMeter');

  // compute and display the progress
  if (evt.lengthComputable) {
    var loaded = Math.round((evt.loaded / evt.total)*100);
    if (loaded < 100) {
      progMeter.style.width = loaded + '%';
    } else {
      progMeter.style.width = '100%';
    }
  }
}
```

```
// handle any abort of the filereader reading
function onAbortHandler(evt) {
  alert('File read cancelled');
}

// handle any error with the filereader
function onErrorHandler(evt) {
  switch(evt.target.error.code) {
    case evt.target.error.NOT_FOUND_ERR:
      alert('File Not Found!');
      break;
    case evt.target.error.SECURITY_ERR:
      alert('File security error.');
      break;
    case evt.target.error.ABORT_ERR:
      break;
    case evt.target.error.NOT_READABLE_ERR:
      alert('File is not readable.');
      break;
    case evt.target.error.ENCODING_ERR:
      alert('File encoding error.');
      break;
    default:
      alert('An error occurred reading the file.');
  };
}

// initialize our window
window.addeventlistener('load',init,false);

</script>
</head>
  <h1>Select a csv file to process.</h1>
  <section>
    <input type="file" id="input" onchange="handleFile(this)">
    <button id="btnCancel" onclick="cancelFileReader();">Cancel
➥Processing</button>
  </section>
  <br>
  <section id="fileInfo">
    <div id="progHolder">
      <div id="progMeter"></div>
    </div>
    <div id="fileAttributes"></div>
  </section>
  <br>
```

```
<div id="fileoutput"></div>
</body>
</html>
```

When the page is loaded into the browser, the visitor can browse for a CSV file to read. When the file is selected, the `handleFile` method is called with the file passed. The `handleFile` method first checks to validate that a CSV file has been selected by matching a regular expression for the MIME type. If the file does not match the CSV MIME type, then an alert is displayed informing the user that the file is not a CSV-formatted file. If the file is a CSV-formatted file, then the code calls the `readAsText` method of the `FileReader` instance with the file passed as the parameter. This begins the read process as an asynchronous process that will trigger the appropriate events as the read progresses. To verify that the read is asynchronous, you have placed the display of the file attributes after calling the `readAsText` function. The attributes will be displayed right after calling the `readAsText` since the read is not blocking the main thread of the script.

In the `init` function of the script, you registered the `onLoadStartHandler` function to be called when the `onloadstart` event occurs. The `onloadstart` event will be triggered when the `FileReader` begins reading the file. When this event occurs, the `onLoadStartHandler` displays the cancel button, progress meter, and output div.

As the file is read, you update the progress meter by having the `updateProgress` method called when the `FileReader` triggers an `onprogress` event. The `updateProgress` method checks to validate that the `loaded` and `total` attributes are available by checking the attribute `lengthComputable`. This attribute basically states, if true, that the `loaded` and `total` attributes are available. The `updateProgress` will use `loaded` and `total` to calculate the percentage complete and display this value through a progress meter, which is built by setting the width of the `progMeter` div in the `progHolder` div.

If the file finishes being read by the `FileReader`, then the `onload` event will be triggered, and the function `onLoadHandler` will be called with the results in the event passed to the method. In the method, you turn off the cancel button and mark the progress as 100 percent so that the visitor knows the file has been read into memory. Since CSV files are line-oriented, you next split the result on line breaks to create an array of lines by executing the following line:

```
var fileArr = evt.target.result.split('\n');
```

The result reference is the text file in memory. After you have split the result into the array of lines or rows of comma-separated values, the script then loops through each array element and splits the values by the comma character. As the script loops through each row, the values are added to an output string, which is displayed in the file output div when all the rows are complete, as shown in Figure 14.3.

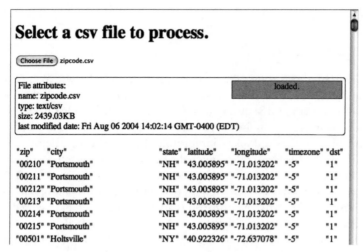

Figure 14.3   Sample output showing a selected and parsed CSV file

The method used to parse the comma–separated value file in this recipe is rather simplistic; it does not handle cases such as commas that are embedded in the values, and it does not understand the difference between quoted and unquoted values. You can find more encompassing parsing methods online, but for the purpose of showing how the `readAsText` method works, this recipe uses a simple model.

This recipe includes the abort option through a cancel button. If the visitor clicks the cancel button while the `FileReader` is reading the file, then the `cancelFileReader` method is called, which in turn calls the `abort` method on the `FileReader` instance, `TextReader`. This instructs the `FileReader` instance to cancel the read process, removes any information already read from memory, and triggers the `onabort` event. In turn, the script will catch the `onabort` event with the `onaborthandler` method and display a message to the visitor, confirming the cancelation of the reading.

You will also notice that the script includes an error handler for any errors passed with the `onerror` event. When a read process is aborted, an error event is created, called `ABORT_ERR`, and the `onErrorHandler` method will be called with this error. The script will simply ignore this error since you take care of the abort elsewhere. However, other errors that may be encountered will be handled with an appropriate message to the user.

This recipe shows the power of using the `FileReader` interface for processing a CSV file on the client browser. The results of the CSV file parsing could be filtered, displayed, and packaged up for transmittal to a web server with no work on the server. The recipe includes the functionality of reading a file, aborting the process, and handling errors that may occur. This should provide a template to start processing your files in your own web pages.

File API Extended Specifications

You are probably wondering at this point if you can navigate the system directory, create files, and write to them. Two newer specifications are being prepared based on the File API to handle these exact use cases. The first is the File API: Directories and System, and the second is the File API: Writer specification. These specifications have gone through several renditions and are still in flux, so they have not been implemented by many browsers. In fact, the only browser to support these extended File API objects and methods is Chrome at this time.

> **Note**
>
> With Chrome 12 and newer versions, the browser uses a custom version of the `requestFileSystem` call, `webkitRequestFileSystem`. The parameters for the call are the same, but you will need to conditionally use the correct call based on the Chrome version. Ideally, as the specifications solidify and more browsers support the File API specifications, the calls will again be generic and the same across the board.

There are several objects and methods in the Directories and Writer File APIs, but a couple are key to this recipe and working with the file system and files. Here are some of the more useful directories and system interfaces:

- `FileSystem`: Represents the file system being worked with
- `Entry`: Represents a generic entry in the file system
- `DirectoryEntry`: Represents a directory in the file system
- `FileEntry`: Represents a file in the file system

And here are some of the more useful file writer interfaces:

- `BlobBuilder`: Used for managing `Blob`s of data used with the file interfaces
- `FileSaver`: Used to monitor writing events and progress
- `FileWriter`: Used for writing, truncating, and appending to a file

The `DirectoryEntry` and `FileEntry` interfaces are built on the `Entry` interface, which has standard copy, move, and remove methods. The Directories and Writer API sets have corresponding events and a set of possible errors. In addition, the APIs provide for both asynchronous calls, for embedded use, and synchronous calls, for use with web workers. Each of the interfaces has methods and attributes, and we recommend you review the most up-to-date specifications for current information. However, Table 14.4 describes some of the methods you will be leveraging in this chapter.

The `FileWriter` interface also has the attributes of `length` and `position`, which can be used for positioning the location to append or write information in the file.

Multiple methods are associated with the directory and system including copying and moving, and there are file and directory attributes that you would find in a normal directory and file explorer. These methods and attributes would make it

Table 14.4   **Key File Directory and System, and Writer Methods**

Interface	Method	Purpose
FileSystem	requestFileSystem	Requests a file system in which to store application data
Entry	copyTo	Copies an Entry of either a Directory or File to a given location
Entry	getMetadata	Retrieves metadata about this Entry
Entry	getParent	Retrieves the parent DirectoryEntry of the Entry
Entry	moveTo	Moves an Entry from its current file system location to a different location
Entry	remove	Deletes the Entry, whether a file or directory
Entry	toURL	Returns a URL for the given Entry that can be used for reference
FileEntry	createWriter	Creates an instance of a file writer for writing to the file
FileEntry	file	Returns the file that the FileEntry is pointing to
FileWriter	seek	Sets the position of the location in the file for executing the next write method
FileWriter	truncate	Changes the length of the file either by shortening or by extending
FileWriter	write	Writes the data provided into the File at the current position

fairly easy to make your own file and directory explorer. Unfortunately, we do not have the room here to create a recipe such as this, but you can find all the necessary information for using these methods and attributes in the Directories and System API specification. One thing to note, though, is that these interfaces appear to deal with a file system that is "generated" by the browser in a sandbox specific to the originating domain for security purposes. In the next recipe, you will create a file in a local file system and write some data to the file.

ADVANCED RECIPE:
Creating a Local File

In this recipe, you will create a page that uses a local text file to store a list of user-added email addresses. The page will allow the user to add an email address, which will be appended to the file; display the list of email addresses from the file; and remove the file.

> **Note**
>
> Since there is no security permission interface for allowing a user to authorize the browser to access the local file storage at this time, you must instruct the Chrome browser that permission is given by launching the browser with two arguments; `--unlimited-quota-for-files` and `-allow-file-access-from-files`. To launch the Chrome browser with these arguments, you can launch Terminal in the Mac OS and use the following command:
>
> ```
> open /Applications/Google\ Chrome.app -n --args -unlimited-quota-for-files
> ➥-allow-file-access-from-files
> ```
>
> This command will launch the Chrome browser, passing in the command-line arguments that instruct the browser to allow file access and set an unlimited quota for the files. If you do not launch Chrome in this manner, you will receive security or permission errors that prevent you from accessing the file system.

This script would normally use the `requestFileSystem` method to retrieve a reference to the local file system; however, in Chrome 12 and newer, the browser uses its own version of the method, `webkitRequestFileSystem`, since the specification has been in flux. In addition, conditional logic is used in the script to create a `Blob` object through either the `BlobBuilder` or the `WebKitBlobBuilder` depending on the browser version. To create the page, perform the following steps to create Listing 14.5:

1. Create a blank HTML file and add the `body` HTML from Listing 14.5, which includes the email input element, multiple `button` elements, and display `div` for the list of email addresses to be displayed.

2. Add the `fileErrorHandler` function, which will handle any directory or file errors that are encountered by the asynchronous code.

3. Add the `fileAction` function in the script shown in Listing 14.3, which gets the file reference and acts as a dispatcher based on the action requested by the user.

4. Add the `writeToFile`, `readFromFile`, and `removeFile` functions, which handle the specific action with the passed-in file reference.

5. Add the event listener for the page load, which will kick off the `fileAction` method to show any email addresses if the storage file exists.

Listing 14.5 Storing a List of Emails in a Local File

```
<!DOCTYPE html>
<html>
<head>
<meta charset="UTF-8" />
<title>14.5 File Creating / Writing Async</title>
<script>
```

```javascript
// File API error handler
function fileErrorHandler(e) {
  var msg = '';

  // Set the appropriate error message based on code
  switch (e.code) {
    case FileError.NOT_FOUND_ERR:
      msg = 'File or directory not found.';
      break;
    case FileError.SECURITY_ERR:
      msg = 'Security issue found.';
      break;
    case FileError.NOT_READABLE_ERR:
      msg = 'File or directory cannot be read.';
      break;
    case FileError.ENCODING_ERR:
      msg = 'Address of file or directory malformed.';
      break;
    case FileError.NO_MODIFICATION_ALLOWED_ERR:
      msg = 'File or directory cannot be modified.';
      break;
    case FileError.INVALID_STATE_ERR:
      msg = 'File or directory state error.';
      break;
    case FileError.SYNTAX_ERR:
      msg = 'Syntax error with writing to file.';
      break;
    case FileError.INVALID_MODIFICATION_ERR:
      msg = 'Modification requested is invalid.';
      break;
    case FileError.QUOTA_EXCEEDED_ERR:
      msg = 'Not enough space in storage quota remains.';
      break;
    case FileError.TYPE_MISMATCH_ERR:
      msg = 'Wrong type for file or directory.';
      break;
    case FileError.PATH_EXISTS_ERR:
      msg = 'Path already exists.';
      break;
    default:
      msg = 'Unknown file API error.';
      break;
  };

  console.log('File API error: ' + msg);
}
```

```
// Function to get fileSystem and dispatch action
function fileAction(actionType) {

  var fileName = 'HTML5FileText.txt';

  // Begin the asychronous process of working with the file system
  // Retrieve the fileSystem object
  window.webkitRequestFileSystem(window.PERSISTENT, 1024 * 1024,
➥function(fileSystemObj) {

    // Retrieve a reference to the file or create the file if not present
    fileSystemObj.root.getFile(fileName, {create:true}, function(fileEntry) {

      // Dispatch to the handler function
      switch (actionType) {
        case 'write':
          writeToFile(fileEntry);
          break;
        case 'read':
          readFromFile(fileEntry);
          break;
        case 'remove':
          removeFile(fileEntry);
          break;
      }
    }, fileErrorHandler);
  }, fileErrorHandler);
}

// Async handler for appending entry to file
function writeToFile(fileEntry) {

  // Create a writer to the file
  fileEntry.createWriter(function(fileWriter) {

    // onwriteend handler for the writer
    fileWriter.onwriteend = function(e) {
      console.log('Write to file successful.');
      readFromFile(fileEntry);
    };

    // onerror handler for the writer
    fileWriter.onerror = function(e) {
      console.log('Write to file failed: ' + e.toString());
    };
```

```
    // Create a blob for use in adding to file
    var bb = new (window.BlobBuilder || window.WebKitBlobBuilder)();
    var emailToAdd = document.getElementById('emailAddress').value + "<br/>";
    bb.append(emailToAdd);

    // Seek the end of the file and then add the blob
    fileWriter.seek(fileWriter.length);
    fileWriter.write(bb.getBlob('text/plain'));

  }, fileErrorHandler);
}

// Async handler for reading file
function readFromFile(fileEntry) {

  // Retrieve the file object
  fileEntry.file(function(file) {

    // Create a file reader
    var reader = new FileReader();

    // onloadend reader handler
    reader.onloadend = function(e) {
      // Display the file results
      var emailDiv = document.getElementById('emailList');
      emailDiv.innerHTML = this.result;
    };

    // Read the file using the reader
    reader.readAsText(file);
  }, fileErrorHandler);
}

// Async handler for removing file
function removeFile(fileEntry) {

  // Remove the file
  fileEntry.remove(function() {
    console.log('File removed.');
  }, fileErrorHandler);
}

// Read from file by default
window.addEventListener('load',fileAction('read'),false);

</script>
</head>
```

```
<body>
  <input type="email" id="emailAddress" /><button onClick="fileAction('write');">
Add Email</button>
  <button onClick="fileAction('read');">Read Emails</button>
  <button onClick="fileAction('remove');">Remove File</button>
  <br/><br/>
  <div id="emailList"></div>
</body>
</html>
```

To launch the page created in Listing 14.5, make sure to launch Chrome via the command line with the arguments for providing permission to the local file system. If Chrome is not launched with these parameters, then the page will not be able to work with the local files. When the page loads, the page is told to load any emails from the file and display them in case the file exists currently. This is done by calling the fileAction function with the read value. In the fileAction function, you start a series of asynchronous function calls by first getting a reference to the file system via the webkitRequestFileSystem method. You pass to the function the duration of the file flag, size of the file, inline callback function, and error handler. The duration flag informs the browser how to handle the files, specifically, whether to allow the browser to remove the files if necessary (TEMPORARY) or to leave the files alone (PER-SISTENT). In this example, you have created one generic error handler for all the directory and file method calls even though some of the error codes may not be applicable. The set of error codes is consistent, however, across the File APIs. You could, of course, have separate error handlers for more specialized error messages and actions based on your need.

After you have a handle to the file system, the script then executes the getFile method on the file system root object, passing in the filename, an opening parameter, success callback, and error handler. In this case, when you get the file, you inform the method to create the file if the file is not present by setting the create flag to true. If the flag were set to false, the method would not create the file if not present and would act only as an opening function. After getting the file entry, the script then dispatches the flow to the readFromFile function, which continues the asynchronous flow by getting the file and reading it via a file reader object instance. When the file reader object finishes reading the file, the results are then displayed in the result div, as shown in Figure 14.4.

Now that the file is created, the user can add email addresses by entering them and clicking the Add Email button, which will kick off the fileAction. The fileAction will launch the writeToFile where you will create a fileWriter to work with writing the text to the file. The script first sets some handlers for when the fileWriter is complete, onwriteend, and, if the writing of the text fails for any reason, onerror. The script uses the BlobBuilder to create a Blob object of the email address that was entered. In this case, you conditionally select the interface since it differs between

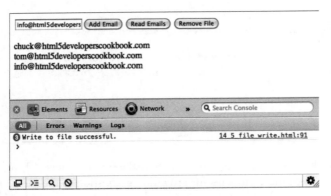

Figure 14.4   Sample output showing email addresses read from the file
after being added

versions of Chrome. Then the script uses the seek method of the file writer to move
the location to the end of the file based on the length property, and you then call the
write command to add the `Blob` in a text format. Note that you add an HTML break,
`<br/>`, at the end of each email address when you append the address to the file. This
is purely for ease of use in displaying multiple email addresses in the `div` when the file
is read. You could format the data of the file in a layout that best fits your information.
Upon completing the write out to the file of the new email address, the script triggers
a read to update the list displayed on the page.

Lastly, the script provides a removal option for the file, which calls `remove` on the
`FileEntry`. This will remove the file from the file system. If you leave the page and
return without removing the file, the file will persist since you asked the file system
for the file to be persisted with the `webkitRequestFileSystem` call. The months
ahead should see quite a bit of forward progress with these specifications, and it is
expected that the various browser manufacturers will begin to incorporate the File
API: Directories and System API and the File API: Writer API more.

Summary

In this chapter, the recipes demonstrated how to view file attributes and read files
through the new File API in the client browser. In addition, you learned about some
of the newer file specifications, which will add functionality beyond just reading
files. By shifting the workload that would normally have to be performed through
server-side processing to the client browser, you can distribute the processing to client
machines and improve the overall experience of the visitor.

15

Integrating Device Data

Over the past 20 years, the Hypertext Markup Language has come a long way and is constantly evolving through the work of browser creators and various groups such as the W3C working groups. HTML5 as we know it is a collection of HTML tags and attributes, JavaScript APIs, and CSS styles. In this book, we have covered many of the extension APIs created as part of HTML5. However, the work effort to further the browser experience for users, especially as users use more and more mobile devices, has not stopped and in fact is stronger than ever. In the past couple years, there has been an explosion of new mobile devices with a fundamental difference from the mobile phones of the past. No longer is the device a mobile phone with numerous other features but instead is a mobile device with the phone as just one feature.

In this chapter, you will learn about one of the most exciting and new areas of the browser experience: integration with device features such as cameras, microphones, gyroscopes, accelerometers, and device applications such as contact databases, calendaring apps, and picture galleries. With these device APIs, it is expected that web pages will be able to perform a wide range of functions including video conference calls, appointment scheduling in a user's calendar, insertion of pictures from a user's gallery, battery level checks, or other tasks that have typically been limited to native device applications or specialized plug-ins. Very shortly web developers will also have the benefit of tying into this functionality.

Brief Device APIs History

The W3C Device APIs and Policy Working Group was formed in May 2009 to create a set of client-side APIs and events to interact with device hardware and applications. The group defined in its original charter several different APIs that were quite broad and overlapped several other groups. The expected end date of the group's charter was set for July 2011. However, the group for various reasons re-chartered in November 2010 with a more focused set of APIs. The group is now labeled the Device APIs

Working Group and is expected to create several APIs focused on device integration between November 2010 and the new end date of June 2013.

As you can imagine, the breadth of API coverage for a topic such as device APIs is quite broad. The working group is making great headway in creating API and event specifications for use by browser manufacturers. Even though it is early, some browsers have already begun including these APIs. The API set and events of the Device APIs Working Group include the following:

- *Application Registration API*: Provides the ability for web applications to register as an application in the system and allow the application to handle calls with a registered data string identifier

- *Battery Status event**: Provides an event for battery status changes, including the battery level and plugged in status

- *Beep API*: Provides control of the device system beeps

- *Calendar API**: Provides read access to the calendar events on the device

- *Contacts API**: Provides read access to contacts and their information from the device's contact storage application

- *Gallery API**: Provides access to the gallery of the device, which could include audio, video, and image files

- *Generic Sensor API*: Provides integration and support for various sensors on the device

- *HTML Media Capture**: Provides attributes and HTML abilities to capture media live on the device such as audio, video, and images

- *Media Capture API**: Provides a programmatic interface for capturing media via the camera and microphone of a device

- *Menu API*: Provides control of the application device menus

- *Messaging API**: Allows a client page to send an `mms`, `sms`, or `mailto` URI scheme-based message

- *Network Information API**: Retrieves the current network connection type for the device

- *Tasks API*: Provides access to the personal tasks managed on the device

- *Vibration API*: Provides control of the vibration of the device

At this point, the APIs listed are very young and any that have been implemented in a browser are the exceptions. In fact, at the time of writing this book, only the Contacts API has made it to the state of a last call on the specification draft. The specifications marked with an asterisk (*) have some form of draft published on the www.w3.org site. By the end of 2011, many of these APIs are expected to have working draft versions of their specifications. In this chapter, we will go through a portion of these APIs, showing some of the more evolved ones, along with some recipes with

API implementations that are available now. Note that given the nascence of these APIs, it is too early to say which browser platforms will support what features.

Contacts API

The Contacts API is designed to allow the user interacting with a browser page to share information about a contact (or contacts) from their local contact application with the page. The user may choose to share only particular fields with the page. In addition, the user can select to only provide contacts that match the criteria requested by the page, such as those that have an address state value of "CA." The API is a read-only API, so new entries cannot be added at this time. The Contacts API specification recommends the use of current industry formats such as a vCard to add or update contacts in a user's contact repository. Because the API provides access to personal and confidential information, the browser agent is required to ask permission of the user prior to providing access to the Contact APIs.

If permission is given, then the JavaScript on the page can use a Contacts interface to begin finding contacts. The Contacts interface has one method, find, which allows the script to find one or more contacts, as shown here, in the find method signature:

```
void find (DOMString[] fields, ContactFindCB successCB, optional ContactErrorCB
errorCB, optional ContactFindOptions options);
```

The parameters to the find function are explained here:

- DOMString[] Fields: An array of DOMStrings representing the contact record fields to be returned
- successCB: The success callback function to launch on success
- errorCB: An optional callback function to be launched on failure
- Options: Search options to match contact records on, such as first name

To prevent blocking the page while searching contacts, the find method uses callback functions on success or failure. If there are matching contacts and fields to be returned, then the success callback function will be launched with a results variable containing an array of the results. If the find method executed without error but no results are returned, then a null value will be passed into the success callback function, representing that no matching contact records were found.

The contact record returned is an instance of the Contacts interface, which contains several attributes and other contact interface subtypes such as ContactName, ContactAddress, and so on, since a contact could realistically have multiple subcomponents such as multiple addresses. Table 15.1 shows the attributes for the Contacts interface. We will not describe all the subinterfaces here, but they can easily be referenced in the W3C draft of the Contacts API at www.w3.org/TR/contacts-api.

Table 15.1   **The** `Contacts` **Interface Attributes**

Attribute Type	Attribute	Description
`DOMString`	`id`	Unique identifier for the contact
`DOMString`	`displayName`	The name of the contact
`ContactName`	`name`	Full name of the contact
`DOMString`	`nickname`	Nickname of the contact
`ContactField`	`phoneNumbers`	One or more phone numbers for the contact in a `ContactField`
`ContactField`	`emails`	One or more email addresses for the contact in a `ContactField`
`ContactAddress`	`addresses`	One or more addresses for the contact in a `ContactAddress` object
`ContactField`	`ims`	One or more instant message identifiers in a `ContactField`
`ContactOrganization`	`organizations`	One or more addresses for the contact in a `ContactOrganization` object
`Date`	`birthday`	The contacts birth date in `Date` object
`DOMString`	`note`	The note field on the contact record
`ContactField`	`photos`	One or more photo URL for the contact
`[DOMString]`	`categories`	Array of `DOMStrings` representing the categories for this contact
`ContactField`	`urls`	One or more URLs for this contact in a `ContactField`

Note

At this time, the Contacts API is not known to be supported by any browser agent. However, it is expected that browser agents will support this API shortly and possibly prior to the publication of this book. We are providing the following recipe as an example; it may contain errors or differences to actual implementations that may take form.

BEGINNER RECIPE:
Retrieving All Contacts and Mobile Numbers

Even though it would probably not be recommended to retrieve all contacts of a user, sometimes this may be applicable. This recipe will use the find method of the Contacts interface with the success and error callback functions to retrieve all contacts, check whether the contact has a mobile number, and display the contact's name and mobile number in a div on the page. To create this recipe, perform the following steps, resulting in Listing 15.1:

1. Create a blank HTML page with a button element and the result div. Add the click handler to the button to launch the findAllContacts method.

2. Add the script tags to the page and the findAllContacts method, which launches the contacts request.

3. Add the contactsFindSuccess callback function and the contactsError callback function to handle success and failure events from the contacts request, respectively.

Listing 15.1   **Retrieving and Displaying all Contact Mobile Numbers**

```
<!DOCTYPE html>
<html>
<head>
<meta charset="UTF-8" />
<title>15.1 Retrieve All Contacts</title>
<script>
// Initialize the page function
function init() {
  // set the button handler
  var btnFindAll = document.getElementById('findAll');
  btnFindAll.addEventListener('click',findAllContacts,false);
}


// Success callback function for finding contacts
function contactsFindSuccess(contacts) {

  // Get reference to our div for displaying the results
  var divResults = document.getElementById('divResults');

  // Loop through the contacts results
  for (var i in contacts) {

    // For each contact loop through any phone numbers
    for (var j in contacts[i].phoneNumbers) {
```

```
      // Check if the phone number is a mobile number
      if (contacts[i].phoneNumbers[j].type === 'mobile') {

         // Display the contact name and phone number
         divResults.innerHTML += contacts[i].displayName + '(' +
➥contacts[i].phoneNumbers[j].value + ')';
      }
    }
  }
}

// Error callback function for finding contacts
function contactsError(error) {
  // Handle the error appropriately, in this case just display
  alert(error.code);
}

// Function to find the contacts
function findAllContacts() {

  // Check if the Contacts API is available
  if (navigator.contacts) {

    // set the array of fields to retrieve
    var arrFields = ['displayName', 'phoneNumbers'];

    // perform the find method on the contacts
    navigator.contacts.find(arrFields, contactsFindSuccess, contactsError);

  } else {

    // let the user know that the Contacts API is not supported
    alert('The Contacts API is not supported in this browser... yet');
  }
}

// Initialize the page on load
window.addEventListener('load',init,false);

</script>
</head>
<body>
  <h1>Retrieve all contacts with mobile phone numbers</h1>
  <button id="findAll">Find All Contacts</button>
  <div id="divResults"></div>
</body>
</html>
```

In this example, when the user clicks the Find All Contacts button, the findAllContacts function will be called to make a request on the Contacts interface. In the findAllContacts function, the code first checks to see whether the Contacts interface is available. If the interface is not available, then an alert will be shown, but you could replace this with alternative logic as required by your solution. If the Contacts interface is available, then the code creates the array of fields that you want to have returned by the Contacts find method. The code then calls the find method and provides the array of fields, a success callback function, and an error callback function.

The phoneNumbers field that is retrieved via the Contacts interface is structured as a ContactField interface. The ContactField interface is comprised of type, value, and pref attributes, as shown in Table 15.2.

The type attribute is a DOMString, and with a type of phoneNumbers, the type attribute can be either home or mobile. The value attribute is the actual number, and the pref attribute is a boolean value that lets you know whether the value is the preferred value or primary value for this contact. When the success callback function, contactsFindSuccess, is called, a result set is passed to the function. This result set is an array of contact interface instances that you can then loop through. In this case, we have named the results variable contacts.

In the success callback, the recipe first creates a reference to the result div on the page so that you can display any matching results. Next, the function loops through the contacts array. For each contact, the recipe loops through the phoneNumbers for that contact. For each phone number, the code checks the type to see whether the phone number is a mobile number. If the phone number is a mobile, then the code displays the name and the phone number in the result div.

The Contacts find method used in this recipe asks for all contacts with success and error callback functions. The find method can take a fourth parameter that is optional, of type ContactFindOptions. Based on the Contacts API specification, this interface implementation is up to the specific browser agent. However, the basics of this interface is the creation of a filter that is matched on the contact fields requested. This is a simple filtering method and will match any of the fields requested and in any position in the values. For example, if the filter value "son" is provided and the fields displayName and emails are retrieved, then any contact that has the string "son"

Table 15.2   **The ContactField Interface Attributes**

Attribute Type	Attribute	Description
DOMString	type	The classification of this value
DOMString	value	The actual value of the field
Boolean	pref	A flag to signify that this field is the primary or preferred value

in either set of fields will match, such as "**son**ny@....com" or "Chuck Hud**son**." The expected statement of this example would be as follows:

```
{filter: 'son'}
```

Until a browser agent actually implements the Contacts API with filtering, we can only guess at the extent of control we will have over the filtering, but it appears that the filter will provide at least some basic screening of the contacts on the device.

> **Note**
>
> The Contacts API is designed purely as a read-only service of the contacts data on the device. To perform addition and update of contacts in the data store on the device, you would put the contact information into a standard format for the contact application such as a text-based vCard and then reference this card text through an `href` element so that a user can download the card into their contact application.

Messaging API

The Messaging API is designed to allow a page to use the `sms`, `mms`, and `mailto` URI schemes to send messages to a particular address. The API is quite simple because it has one interface and one method: `device` and `sendMessage`. The device interface is expected to be part of the navigator interface, so to check for the support of the Messaging API, you can use this:

```
if (navigator.device.sendMessage) {
  … your sendMessage code here …
}
```

If the browser agent supports the Messaging API, then you can use the `sendMessage` method to send a message to a given recipient. The structure of the `sendMessage` method is shown here:

```
void sendMessage (DOMString to [,Blob attachments] [, messagingErrorCB]);
```

The `to` parameter takes a URI scheme that matches either the `sms`, `mms`, or `mailto` scheme and can accept querystrings that include `body` elements and the like. The `attachments` field can be for pictures or videos, and the final parameter is an optional error handler. So, to send a basic message via SMS, you might call `sendMessage` as follows:

```
navigator.device.sendMessage('sms:+17705551212?body=Hi%20Tom');
```

If an error callback function is added, which would be recommended because otherwise you would not know that a `sendMessage` failed, then an error object will be passed to the handler with an error code. Table 15.3 provides the list of possible error codes.

Even though the Messaging API is a short specification, the implications are extraordinary. Now client pages will be able to send text messages, videos, and pictures through MMS messages and email straight from the device's browser.

Table 15.3   **The Messaging API Error Code Values**

Value	Constant Term	Description
0	`UNKNOWN_ERROR`	An unknown error occurred.
1	`INVALID_ARGUMENT_ERROR`	An invalid parameter was passed with the `sendMessage` method.
3	`TIMEOUT_ERROR`	The request to send a message timed out.
4	`PENDING_OPERATION_ERROR`	The browser is already waiting on a callback.
5	`IO_ERROR`	An error with the communication occurred.
6	`NOT_SUPPORTED_ERROR`	The `sendMessage` method is not supported.
20	`PERMISSION_DENIED_ERROR`	The user or browser did not authorize the method call.
30	`MESSAGE_SIZE_EXCEEDED`	The message scheme limit was exceeded for this message type.

Tip

It is expected that the `sendMessage` method will be implemented in browser agents to support the URI functionalities so that features such as multiple recipients will be enabled. If this is the case, then it would be easy to send a message to multiple SMS recipients by just separating the numbers with commas, as in "sms:+17705551212,+18025551212...."

Network Information API

Determining the connection speed of a browser is important to be able to throttle data and functionality for better user experiences. The Network Information API aims to expose a simple `type` attribute that will signify the type of connection that the device currently has. Based on this value, a page could change its behavior to fit the size and speed of the data pipe that is available. The value of the type of connection can be one of the following: `unknown`, `ethernet`, `wifi`, 2g, 3g, 4g, and `none`. A new interface is provided called `Connection`, which has one attribute associated with it: `type`. So, to retrieve the current connection type, you would use the following:

```
var connectionType = navigator.connection.type;
```

Knowing the type of connection, you can dynamically change style sheets between full and light versions or change the logic on the page to retrieve only partial results when on a slower connection.

In addition to the `Connection` interface, there are two new events: `online` and `offline`. These events are tied to the `window` object and can be used to check a change in the connection type if `online` is fired or handle the device if it goes offline.

> **Tip**
>
> An `online` event could be sent multiple times as a user changes connection types. Your code should be streamlined to minimize the functionality that is run on this event since the event could be repeatedly sent based on rapid connection type switching.

Battery Status Events

The Battery Status events allow you to capture events associated with the device's battery state. In the Battery Status Event Specification, there are two status changes possible that will trigger an event. The first status change is triggered when the device is either plugged into a power source or unplugged from the power source. The second event signifies a change in the battery charge level by 1 percent or more. In either case, a battery status event will be dispatched. The event will then have attributes available: `isPlugged`, which is a boolean value, and `level`, which is a float and ranges from 0 to 100, with 100 meaning that the battery is fully charged. If the level is null, then the browser was not able to report the battery level.

To sign up for handling a battery status event, an `onbatterystatus` property and an event `batterystatus` are available. Either of the following examples is valid:

```
window.addEventListener('batterystatus', function (event) {
  alert(event.level);
}
```

```
window.onbatterystatus = function (event) {
  alert(event.level);
}
```

In either case, the level of the current battery will be alerted to the user. If you wanted to alert the user if the plugged-in status changed, then you could use `event.isPlugged` to retrieve the boolean value if the device is plugged in.

> **Note**
>
> If the browser is not able to determine the current battery level, between 0 and 100 inclusive, then a `null` value will be assigned to the level property.

HTML Media Capture

HTML Media Capture is designed to instruct browser agents to launch media capture tools based on new parameters and attributes to the file input element. By providing information on what types of information to accept for the file input and a recommendation of what to use to "capture" the input, the browser agent can launch the appropriate device capture mechanism. The capture could take the form of a video, audio, or picture because they are all forms of media that are typically available on devices with cameras and microphones such as smartphones, tablets, and laptops.

Normally, the file input element opens the file-browsing window to select an appropriate file to be submitted. HTML Media Capture uses the accept attribute of the file input to recommend a file picker that is appropriate, such as the camera for accepting an image. The following are the three different accept attribute values available:

- image/*: For accepting images from the camera or user's gallery of images
- audio/*: For accepting audio input through recording via the device microphone
- video/*: For accepting video files recorded through the device camera and microphone

An additional attribute can be added to suggest what method the browser should use to capture the input. The capture attribute can take one of four values: camera, camcorder, microphone, or filesystem. The default value, if a capture attribute is not provided, is filesystem. So, a sample file input element for capturing audio from a microphone would be as follows:

```
<input type="file" accept="audio/*" capture="microphone">
```

Between the accept and capture attributes, you will be able to use the device microphone and camera in some interesting ways. Already there are groups working to implement streaming of full duplex audio/video calls between devices using HTML Media Capture and other HTML5 technologies such as WebSocket.

INTERMEDIATE RECIPE:
Capturing Pictures with File Input

In this recipe, you will use the accept and capture attributes on the file input element to have the browser launch the device's built-in camera picture capture screen, have the user take the picture, and then return the picture to the page. With the picture file returned to the page, HTML Media Capture will take the file and load it into a new image element that is scaled as a thumbnail and added to the page. To create the code in Listing 15.2, follow these steps:

1. Create a blank HTML page with the file input element and thumbnails div.
2. Add the script tags to the page and the handleCapture function, which handles the file that is delivered via the onChange method of the file input.

> **Note**
>
> At the time of writing, this example runs on devices with Android 3.0 and newer, which support HTML Media Capture. Thus, the screenshots for this recipe are from an Android tablet.

Listing 15.2   **Capturing a Camera Image**

```
<!DOCTYPE html>
<html>
<head>
<meta charset="UTF-8" />
<title>15.2 HTML Media Capture</title>
<script>
// Function to handle the HTML media capture of a file
function handleCapture(files) {

  // Set the image matching pattern
  var imageType = /image.*/;

  // We expect only one picture at a time but loop through any files provided
  for (var i = 0; i < files.length; i++) {

    // Retrieve the file from those passed in
    var file = files[i];

    // Check if the file is an image type
    if (file.type.match(imageType)) {

      // Create our new image element
      var newImg = document.createElement("img");
      newImg.classList.add("obj");
      newImg.file = file;
      newImg.style.maxHeight = "100px";
      newImg.style.maxWidth = "100px";

      // Append the new image element to the thumbnails area
      var thumbnails = document.getElementById('thumbnails');
      preview.appendChild(newImg);

      // Load the image element with the contents of the file
      var reader = new FileReader();
      reader.onload = (function(aImg) {
        return function(e) { aImg.src = e.target.result; };
      })(newImg);
      reader.readAsDataURL(file);
    }
  }
}
```

```
</script>
</head>
<body>
  <h2>Media Capture - Camera</h2>
  <input type="file" accept="image/*;capture=camera"
    capture="camera"
    onChange="handleCapture(this.files)"></input>
  <div id="thumbnails"></div>
</body>
</html>
```

When the page is loaded in the browser, the normal "Choose file" prompt is provided, as shown in Figure 15.1.

When the user clicks "Choose file," the browser is told through the `accept` and `capture` attributes to launch the camera selector, which in this case launches the Android picture-taking screen, as shown in Figure 15.2.

Once the picture is taken, a picture file is sent to the page, and the `handleCapture` function is called with the file passed as an argument. In the `handleCapture` function, you first check the file to verify that it is an image type and then create a new image element that you add to the page and load with the file. In Figure 15.3, the "Choose file" button has been clicked a couple times, and the resulting pictures that were taken have been added as thumbnails to the `div` for viewing.

Media Capture - Camera

Choose file   No file chosen

Figure 15.1   Sample output from Listing 15.2 showing the page ready to capture an image

Figure 15.2   The default camera screen is brought up by the device for capturing the image.

Media Capture - Camera

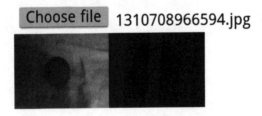

Figure 15.3   After the image has been taken, the user is automatically returned to the web app, and the thumbnail is displayed.

Device Orientation and Motion Events

Device Orientation and Motion Events originally started as a specification in the
Device API Working Group but was later moved into the Geolocation working group,
so you will not see it in the current list of the Device API Working Group. We have
left it as part of this chapter since it is specifically focused on integrating with the
internal gyroscope of the device that the user may be using at the moment. Many
phones, tablets, and even computers have this internal gyroscope built into the hardware, and browser agents such as Chrome have already implemented the events into
their JavaScript engines.

The Device Orientation specification from the W3C organization specifies three
new events, as listed here:

- `deviceorientation`: Provides orientation in an alpha, beta, gamma format
  showing the spatial positioning of the device

- `compassneedscalibration`: An event fired by the browser agent that states
  that the compass of the device is in need of calibration

- `devicemotion`: Provides acceleration, acceleration including gravity, rotation
  rate, and interval used for device movement

All three of the events in the device orientation are fired on the `window` object and
are registered for as any normal event on the `window` object. The `deviceorientation`
event provides through event data passed into your handler four attributes that can be
read: `alpha`, `beta`, `gamma`, and `absolute`. The `alpha`, `beta`, and `gamma` properties
correspond to orientation of the device such as the tilt or rotation of the device. The
`alpha` property represents the rotation, while the `beta` and `gamma` correspond to the
tilt left/right and front/back. For example, a laptop sitting on the desk would have
a `beta` of 0 and a `gamma` of 0, while the `alpha` would have a value representing its
orientation. For a laptop, the orientation is based on the keyboard, not on the screen,
while the orientation of a mobile phone would be the phone itself. The `absolute`
property signifies whether the browser is able to provide absolute values for the orientation angles. If the device is not able to set the value absolutely, then this value will
be false. In most of our testing, this value was indeed false, although the `beta` and
`gamma` angles were absolute, and the alpha was set to an arbitrary 0 when the page was
executed.

The `compassneedscalibration` event is a straightforward event that notifies the
window that the internal compass of the device is in need of calibration. The event,
according to the specification, may be canceled by the website or application, and
the default device calibration user interface could be replaced by a custom calibration provided by the web application. However, the details on this event are still to be
determined.

The `devicemotion` event is a more complicated event because it contains attributes
for the acceleration, rotation, and interval. The `acceleration` attribute is an instance

Table 15.4   **The** `devicemotion` **Event Attribute Values**

Attribute	Type	Description
`acceleration`	`DeviceAcceleration`	The acceleration of the device represented as X, Y, Z values.
`accelerationIncludingGravity`	`DeviceAcceleration`	The acceleration of the device including the effect of gravity represented in X,Y,Z values.
`rotationRate`	`DeviceRotationRate`	The rotation of the devices shown via alpha, beta, and gamma angles.
`interval`	`double`	The interval, in milliseconds, at which the acceleration and rotation data is collected. This is expected to be a constant.

of a new interface, `DeviceAcceleration`, which provides the acceleration attributes x, y, z in a double data type format to show the X, Y, Z directional acceleration. The rotation rate is also an interface instance, but of `DeviceRotationRate`, which provides the rotation in the format of alpha, beta, gamma. All attributes of the `devicemotion` event appear as optional attributes in the specification. Table 15.4 shows the attributes of the `devicemotion` event in more detail.

INTERMEDIATE RECIPE:
Creating a Bubble Level

If you have had the opportunity to play in the mobile device programming area, you will most likely have seen a bubble level sample native app that is available on most mobile platforms to show the orientation of the device. The `deviceorientation` event can be used to provide the same type of functionality in client-side JavaScript by looking at the `beta` and `gamma` event fields. (You do not need the `alpha` field since the bubble level does not use the rotation of a device.) In this recipe, you will create a rudimentary bubble level using layered `canvas` elements to build up a composite bubble level and display the `beta` and `gamma` values, as shown in Figure 15.4.

You could improve the algorithms for positioning to add features such as bounding the bubble to the circle, but this recipe will show the basics of handling device orientation data. To create this bubble level, use Listing 15.3 and perform the following steps:

1. Create a blank HTML page with the three `canvas` elements that comprise the bubble level and add the `spans` for displaying the `beta` and `gamma` values.

2. Add the `style` section for styling the `canvas` elements.

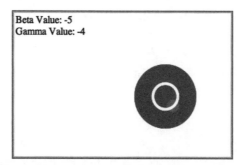

Figure 15.4   Sample output showing the bubble level canvas layers and
beta/gamma values on a laptop while being tilted

3. Add the `init` function, which includes the definition of the
   `deviceorientation` event handler in the `script` tags.

4. Add the launching of the `init` function when the page loads with the
   `window.addEventListener`.

Note

This recipe requires that your browser support the `canvas` element and that the device
you launch this page on has an internal gyroscope for providing the `beta` and `gamma`
values.

Listing 15.3   Creating a Bubble Level with Beta and Gamma Values

```
<!DOCTYPE html>
<html>
<head>
<meta charset="UTF-8" />
<title>15.3 Bubble Level</title>
<style>
#canvas {
  height:100px;
  width:100px;
}
</style>
<script>

// canvas and context reference variables for drawing
var cvsBackground;
var ctxBackground;
var cvsBubble;
var ctxBubble;
var cvsCircle;
var ctxCircle;
```

```
// Variable holders for the beta and gamma values
var tempBeta = 0;
var tempGamma = 0;

// The canvas location and center variables
var canvasX;
var canvasY;
var canvasXCenter;
var canvasYCenter;

// Initialize the canvas object references and orientation event handler
function init() {

  // Grab references to the canvas objects and their contexts
  cvsBackground = document.getElementById('background');
  ctxBackground = cvsBackground.getContext('2d');
  cvsBubble = document.getElementById('bubble');
  ctxBubble = cvsBubble.getContext('2d');
  cvsCircle = document.getElementById('circle');
  ctxCircle = cvsCircle.getContext('2d');

  // Set the canvas coordinates and center coordinates
  canvasX = parseInt(cvsBackground.offsetLeft);
  canvasY = parseInt(cvsBackground.offsetTop);
  canvasXCenter = parseInt(cvsBackground.width/2);
  canvasYCenter = parseInt(cvsBackground.height/2);

  // Draw the bubble level background
  ctxBackground.fillStyle='#0c0';
  ctxBackground.beginPath();
  ctxBackground.arc(canvasXCenter,canvasYCenter,50,0,Math.PI*2,true);
  ctxBackground.closePath();
  ctxBackground.fill();

  // Draw the bubble
  ctxBubble.fillStyle='#0FF';
  ctxBubble.beginPath();
  ctxBubble.arc(canvasXCenter,canvasYCenter,10,0,Math.PI*2,true);
  ctxBubble.closePath();
  ctxBubble.fill();

  // Draw the center circle to designate level
  ctxCircle.strokeStyle='#fff';
  ctxCircle.lineWidth='5';
  ctxCircle.beginPath();
  ctxCircle.arc(canvasXCenter,canvasYCenter,20,0,Math.PI*2,true);
  ctxCircle.closePath();
  ctxCircle.stroke();
```

```
// Add the listener for deviceorientation events
window.addEventListener('deviceorientation', function(event) {

  // Check if the beta or gamma have changed
  if (parseInt(event.beta)!=tempBeta||parseInt(event.gamma)!=tempGamma) {

    // Set our beta and gamma variables
    tempBeta = parseInt(event.beta);
    tempGamma = parseInt(event.gamma);

    // Set the adjustment variables
    var adjX = 0;
    var adjY = 0;
    var adjFactor = 3;   // Scaling factor for bubble movement
    var adjMax = 40;      // Maximum adjustment for bubble

    // Determine the new position of the bubble
    if (tempBeta*adjFactor > adjMax) {
      adjY = -adjMax;
    } else if (tempBeta*adjFactor < -adjMax) {
      adjY = adjMax;
    } else {
      adjY = tempBeta*adjFactor * -1;
    }
    if (tempGamma*adjFactor > adjMax) {
      adjX = -adjMax;
    } else if (tempGamma*adjFactor < -adjMax) {
      adjX = adjMax;
    } else {
      adjX = tempGamma*adjFactor * -1;
    }

    // Move the bubble to the new position
    cvsBubble.style.left = canvasX+adjX+'px';
    cvsBubble.style.top = canvasY+adjY+'px';

    // Set our span values for displaying the beta and gamma
    var spanBeta = document.getElementById('betaValue');
    var spanGamma = document.getElementById('gammaValue');
    spanBeta.innerHTML = tempBeta;
    spanGamma.innerHTML = tempGamma;

  }
}, true);
}


// call the init function on page load
window.addEventListener('load',init,false);
```

```
</script>
</head>
<body>
  <h1>Chapter 15 Bubble Level</h1>
  <!-- The canvas elements are layered as defined below -->
  <canvas id="background" style="position:absolute; left:100px; top:150px;">
    The bubble level background.
  </canvas>
  <canvas id="bubble" style="position:absolute; left:100px; top:150px;">
    The bubble which moves to show the level.
  </canvas>
  <canvas id="circle" style="position:absolute; left:100px; top:150px;">
    The overlaid circles to show the center of the level.
  </canvas>
  <br>
  Beta Value: <span id="betaValue"></span><br>
  Gamma Value: <span id="gammaValue"></span>
</body>
</html>
```

When the page loads in your browser and the `init` function is called, the script will first create the various components of the bubble level. The bubble level is comprised of three `canvas` elements: the background, the bubble, and the foreground center ring. The purpose of having the bubble level split into these three components is twofold. First, this allows for a layering to take place with the bubble above the background but below the center ring to look like a real bubble level. Second, this allows you to programmatically move the bubble without having to redraw the elements with each movement.

After drawing the bubble level components, the script sets the event handler for the `deviceorientation` event. The function for the event handler is designed to first check whether there has been any change in the beta and gamma values and then set the temporary holding variables to the new values if there is a change. Next, the function sets some position adjustment variables, which are used in the calculations for positioning the bubble canvas. The `adjFactor` variable is used to "accelerate" the movement away from the center the farther the bubble gets, while the `adjMax` variable is the maximum distance the bubble can be moved. After calculating the new top and left coordinates of the bubble canvas, you move the canvas and display the updated beta and gamma angles. Notice that when dealing with the `beta` and `gamma` angles, you use just the integer portion of the double value provided with the event. In our testing, the angles provided are extremely granular, so to prevent moving the canvas on the minutest change of the angle; we opt to move the canvas only when a whole degree of change has occurred.

Summary

In this chapter, you learned about some of the new and upcoming APIs and event specifications that are being created to provide access to all types of device information and features. It is only a matter of time before these specifications are complete, published, and available for use in the various browser platforms. web applications in the end will have many of the integrations that native device applications provide. There are still several specifications to be completed around the device APIs, but the efforts show how HTML5 continues to grow in its functionality.

Recipes

Beginner Recipes

Intermediate Recipes

Advanced Recipes

Index

H

X